FROM COLONY TO NATION

Engendering Latin America

EDITORS:

Donna J. Guy
Ohio State University

Mary Karasch
Oakland University

Asunción Lavrin
Arizona State University

FROM COLONY
TO NATION

Women Activists and the Gendering
of Politics in Belize, 1912–1982

ANNE S. MACPHERSON

University of Nebraska Press | Lincoln and London

Library of Congress Cataloging-in-Publication Data
Macpherson, Anne S.
From colony to nation: women activists and the gendering of politics in Belize, 1912–1982 / Anne S. Macpherson.
p. cm. — (Engendering Latin America)
Includes bibliographical references and index.
ISBN-13: 978-0-8032-3242-6 (cloth : alk. paper)
ISBN-10: 0-8032-3242-x (cloth : alk. paper)
ISBN-13: 978-0-8032-2492-6 (paper : alk. paper)
1. Women political activists—Belize—History.
2. Women social reformers—Belize—History.
3. Women in the labor movement—Belize—History.
4. Belize—History. I Title.
HQ1236.5.B42.M33 2007
322.4'4082092782—dc22
2006024961

Set in Minion.

Contents

ILLUSTRATIONS

MAPS

TABLES

Acknowledgments

In 1988, when I was still an undergraduate, I broke out of the classroom and experienced Belize for the first time through Canadian Crossroads International, a nongovernment organization dedicated to development education in Canada and in the Third World. Miss Sadie Vernon at the Belize Christian Council, who was then the Crossroads country liaison in Belize, laughed merrily when I asked for a placement at SPEAR, the Society for the Promotion of Education and Research. If I wanted to go and hang around with those intellectuals, she said, good luck and God bless. I did go and ended up working on SPEAR's newspaper and participating in its program of popular education workshops in places as different as the Garifuna village of Hopkins, the mainly mestizo sugar town of Orange Walk, and Cayo District's Mayan communities, through which I gained a critical perspective on an exceedingly complex national reality. The most important outcome of that formative six months in Central America, part of which I spent in Nicaragua, was an unexpected surge of interest on my part in the nonrevolutionary isthmus, particularly Belize and the Caribbean coast of Central America. Without Canadian Crossroads, Miss Sadie's open mind, and SPEAR's new brand of Belizean development work, this book would never even have been conceived.

The dissertation on which this book is based was nurtured along through all phases by communities of teachers and friends in Belize, Canada, and Madison, Wisconsin. In Madison I benefited immeasurably from the scholarly example, theoretical vigor, and creative engagement of my advisors, Francisco A. Scarano, Florencia E. Mallon, and Steve J. Stern, who accepted my passion for the history of a small and marginalized country and consistently pressed me to make my work speak broadly to Latin American, Caribbean, postcolonial, and women's history. Francisco had a great sympathy for my project owing to his devotion to developing the historiography of his Puerto Rican patria and his deep comparative knowledge of Caribbean historiography and his insights consistently led to provocative conversation about my arguments. Florencia's belief in imperfection in process has helped me to become a better and more productive writer, and her analysis of the state has sharpened my own. Steve's incisive untangling of interpretive muddles was repeatedly enlightening, particularly on the questions of gender norms and conflict with which he has engaged himself.

Steve, Florencia, and Francisco did not exaggerate when they told me that my graduate school peers would make the process not only bearable but positively good. My heartfelt thanks go to those who showed me the ropes in seminars, research, and writing—Patricia Alvarenga, Sarah Chambers, Greg Crider, Eileen Findlay, Roger Kittleson, and Karin Rosemblatt; to my own "cohort"—Nancy Appelbaum, Patrick McNamara, and René Reeves; and to those in the community I happily landed in upon returning from my research year in Belize—Lillian Guerra, Leo Garofalo, Jean Weiss, Danny Holt, Ileana Rodriguez Silva, Erika Sanders, Cynthia Milton, and Solsirée del Moral. To Nancy, who started with me and has been a friend, sounding board, and example ever since, thank you for the excellent company through grad school, for the experience of coediting with Karin Rosemblatt *Race and Nation in Modern Latin America*, and most lately for interlibrary loan aid. It was also fortifying to be part of the Women's History Community and the Teaching Assistants' Association at UW-Madison as well as the "Third World View" collective at WORT-FM.

In Belize I was immensely fortunate to live with friends and their friends and relatives, which provided me with a model of family life and generosity that I hope to emulate always. In 1991, when I was conducting research for my master's thesis, I lived with Adele Catzim and with Shilpa and Shipra Hakre. Adele's parents, Francisco and Maria Catzim, and her sisters always made me feel welcome in their home as well. In 1992 and 1993

Ana Salazar and her daughters Ximena and Mayita in Belmopan offered me a home. In Belize City, Sandra Jones and her son Devin Lovell took me in with a warm embrace in 1993, as did Liz Miller in 1994. In Orange Walk, Yolanda Gongora and her daughter Madeleine were my hosts, as were Don and Bets Neal and their son Dwayne in Dangriga. In Cayo, Lilia Zaiden and her son Luis opened their home to me in 1988. Assad Shoman graciously hosted me for short periods in 1994 and 1996 and talked history and politics with me over drafts of his own book, *13 Chapters of a History of Belize*. My thanks to all of you for your warmth, company, and lessons on living—in Belize and elsewhere.

Other friends who contributed to my social and intellectual life in Belize over the years are Dylan Vernon, Diane Haylock, Dean Roches, Dennis Jones, Judy Williams, Lucy Castillo, Maria Castellanos, Natalia Moguel, Arnoldo Melendez, Regina Neal, Debra Lewis, Phil Westman, Campbell Smith, Godfrey Smith, Tony Villanueva, and Simone Waight. My oldest Belizean friend is Cheryl Gabourel, whom I met at the Council of Voluntary Social Services, the organization I was first placed with by Crossroads. Cheryl and her daughters have been a loving supportive presence not only during my stays in Belize but though letters in between visits. In 1993–94 I had the pleasure of getting to know the women of the Belize Organization for Women and Development (BOWAND) in Belize City—in particular Sandra Carr, Joyce Flowers, and the late Catherine Pelayo—which at the time was blossoming as never before owing to the dedication of its members. I am especially appreciative to BOWAND for granting me access to its organizational files, which have been crucial to my analysis of early Belizean feminism in the 1979–82 period.

All of these hosts and friends helped me to find the mainly elderly women and men whom I interviewed about their political lives. To the roughly one hundred Belizeans who spoke with me about their sense of the nation's history and their roles in shaping it, thank you for your open doors and willingness to teach me about the devotion it takes to act politically for the long haul and to talk to me about the joys of seeing change happen in large and small ways. You pressed glasses of cool water and soft drinks into my hands and were equally generous with the memories and opinions you supplied to my thirsty ears. Many of you disagree with each other, and most of you will disagree with at least parts of what I argue in this book. But in your willingness to converse with me, you have helped to document the history of issues you hold dear: popular participation in politics, leaders' accountability to the people, and women's crucial activism in the social movements of the twentieth century that created the Belizean nation, with all its fault lines and internal hostilities. I would like to single out the late Elfreda Reyes, one of the first women I spoke with when researching my master's thesis, who was politically active from the 1930s to the 1970s, and retired schoolteacher Adolfa Garcia, a pioneer of independent Mayan women's activism. Not only did Mrs. Garcia take me to the Lamanai and mission ruins on the New River in Orange Walk District, but in her interview she spoke the words, in the Creole lingua franca, that I have chosen for the title of this book's introduction.

The overwhelming majority of you, my informants, readily agreed with my hypothesis—based on Zee Edgell's novel *Beka Lamb* and a reading of the newspapers of the 1950s—that women had been politically important in the creation of the nation; none of you were surprised that the history books on Belize did not mention this fact. This book not only includes women, which virtually all of you would approve of, but also analyzes the costs, benefits, and nature of different groups of Belizean women's engagements with colonial and national politics. I have striven to make clear and respect the differences between my analysis and yours as well as the differences among the many interpretations I heard in homes from Orange Walk in the north to Benque Viejo in the west to Dangriga in the south.

During the archival phases of my research, in 1991, 1992, 1993–94, and 1996, the staff of the Belize Archives Department in Belmopan and the National Library in Belize City were extremely helpful. My thanks go to Mr. Hulse at the old National Collection in the Bliss Institute and to Mrs. Joy Ysaguirre and her staff at the Leo H. Bradley National Library. I am constantly impressed by Mr. Charles Gibson's leadership of the Archives, where I have benefited from his assistance as well as that of Margaret Ventura, Anita Lisby, Marvin Puc, Luis Avila, Paul Banner, William Jones, and Rebecca Chan. My thanks especially to Marvin, Luis, and Paul who located and photocopied so many documents for me, week after week, and to Charles for making room for me in October 1996 during the turmoil of building construction and renovation. My thanks also to Lizet Thompson at the Archives, who answered my last minute footnote questions by email. The Archives truly is an exemplary institution, vital to the preservation and ongoing rediscovery of the Belizean past and deserving of both governmental and popular support. I also want to thank my father, Alan G. Macpherson, and Michael Barkham for looking up specific documents for me in the British Colonial Office archives.

Catherine Legrand, now of McGill University, was my first professor of Latin American history, at Queen's University in Kingston, Ontario. Catherine first suggested that I think about becoming a historian of Latin America when I was a sophomore and later pushed me toward graduate school in Madison. She has always been an inspiration in her natural collegiality, her excellence in research and teaching, and her sense of awe and delight in the work of making and remaking history. After my first trip to Belize, I returned to Kingston and wrote an undergraduate thesis on the social history of the Caribbean coasts of Nicaragua and Costa Rica under her direction. I thank also my other superb professors at Queen's: George Lovell, David Eltis, and Abigail Bakan. Jeanne Wolfe at McGill University's School of Urban Planning enabled me to return to Belize in 1990 as her research assistant. Jeanne was engaged in a project, funded by the Canadian International Development Agency, to formulate an urban plan for Belize City and her perspective on Belizean life and politics has been of lasting value to my understanding of the country and has significantly contributed to this book. I also thank her for introducing me to Philip Goldson, one of the founders of the nationalist movement. O. Nigel Bolland, undoubtedly the finest social historian of modern Belize, encouraged my project in 1992, when we first discussed it on a beach in Grenada, and since then through email.

Since coming to SUNY College at Brockport in 1998 I have been blessed to be part of a truly collegial, dedicated, and productive history department. I am particularly grateful to the late Robert D. Marcus, my former chair, who protected me from (most!) service obligations in my first two years on the job, to student Eric Sterling, who helped me analyze voter lists, and to our departmental secretary, Teri Rombaut, who has helped me in innumerable ways. During my years at Brockport I have also been sustained by three Caribbean feminist scholars, who have taken an active interest in my work: Belizean Zee Edgell of Kent State and Alissa Trotz and Melanie Newton, both of the University of Toronto, from Guyana and Barbados respectively. It was a wonderful education in scholarly collaboration and the details of getting a book published to work with Karin Rosemblatt and Nancy Appelbaum, and all our contributors, on *Race and Nation in Modern Latin America*. I am particularly thankful to Karin for initiating the project and bringing me on board.

The Mellon Fellowship in the Humanities funded my graduate studies in 1990–92 and in 1995. The Wisconsin Alumni Research Foundation funded my graduate work in 1992–93. My research trip in the summer of 1992 was made possible by a grant from the Latin American and Iberian Studies program at the University of Wisconsin-Madison. Canada's Social Sciences and Humanities Research Council funded me from mid-1993 to the end of 1994, the main period of research. Dennis Jones, as SPEAR's director, very kindly sponsored my researcher's visa for that period. I received a pretenure leave from teaching during 2002 thanks to a Nuala McGann Drescher Award from United University Professionals, an award aimed at increasing diversity within the tenured professoriate at SUNY.

My parents, Joyce and Alan Macpherson, very generously kept me going during several semesters of graduate school, and for their material and emotional support over the long haul I am deeply grateful. Their own passion for research and teaching, their unwavering belief in my abilities, and genuine interest in Belize have sustained me through long periods without seeing them. Their visit to Belize in December 1993 and January 1994, during which they met many Belizean friends, brought together two significant parts of my life. My brother Ewan Macpherson, also my inimitable Madison roommate in 1995–96, spurred me on to finish by earning his own doctorate in May 1998. My husband, Jamie Spiller—first fellow graduate student and now Brockport colleague—has lived with this project for a decade, providing sympathy and constructive criticism, especially during the grueling process of writing the dissertation. When I finally brought him to Belize in January 2000, he met several of my friends, climbed Xunantunich with me, and enjoyed the relaxed pace of Tom's Cabins on Caye Caulker. Jamie knows better than anyone how challenging it was for me to finish this book through my pregnancy with our daughter Aelis, and then as we nurtured her through colic, and—more easily—watched her become a delightful preschooler. I thank Aelis for understanding about night classes and for making lots of drawings to decorate my office.

I would like to thank the members of my doctoral committee—Professors Francisco Scarano, Florencia Mallon, Steve J. Stern, Gay Seidman, and Richard Ralston—for the final official conversation about the dissertation and for their care in suggesting ways of improving it. Finally, I thank the anonymous readers for the University of Nebraska Press, copy editor MJ Devaney as well as Elizabeth Demers, Joeth Zucco, Heather Lundine, and all the other UNP staff who have helped guide this project to publication.

Abbreviations

BCNS	Black Cross Nurses
BCWAD	Belize Committee for Women and Development
BEC	Belize Estate and Produce Company
BHCS	British Honduras Contingent Society
BHERA	British Honduras Elected Representation Association
BHFW	British Honduras Federation of Women
BHTA	British Honduras Taxpayers Association
BHTU	British Honduras Trade Union
BHFW	British Honduras Federation of Women
BHFWPA	British Honduras Federation of Workers' Protection Association
BHSSC	British Honduras Social Services Council
BHWTU	British Honduras Workers' and Tradesmen's Union
BLDC	Belize Literary and Debating Club
BOWAND	Belize Organization for Women and Development
CARICOM	Caribbean Community
CDS	Carib Development and Sick-Aid Society
CSAG	Catholic Social Action Group
CDW Act	Colonial Development and Welfare Act
DWA	Department of Women's Affairs
DWO	Development and Welfare Organization
DWD	Domestic Workers' Department
ESPC	Empire Starch Products Company
GWU	General Workers' Union

IWL	Infant Welfare League
LPOB	Loyal and Patriotic Order of the Baymen
LUA	Labourers' and Unemployed Association
MC	Miscellaneous Collection of Belize National Archives
MP	Minute Paper held at Belize National Archives
NIP	National Independence Party
NP	National Party
PAC	People's Action Committee
PC	People's Committee
PDM	People's Democratic Movement
PP	Progressive Party
PUP	People's United Party
POU	Public Officers' Union
ORC	Outdoor Relief Committee
RAM	Revolitical Action Movement
RHN	Rural Health Nurses
SDD	Social Development Department
SPEAR	Society for the Promotion of Education and Research
PNM	Trinidad and Tobago's People's National Movement
UBAD	United Black Association for Development
UDP	United Democratic Party
UFCO	United Fruit Company
UNIA	United Negro Improvement Association
UWGS	United Women's Groups
WIRC	West India Royal Commission
WAM	Women's Action Movement
WAV	Belize Women Against Violence
WPS	Women Pioneers
WWU	Women Workers' Union

FROM COLONY TO NATION

Introduction

"Never a Coward Woman"

Elfreda Reyes was born in 1900, a colonial subject in the Crown Colony of British Honduras, and died in 1992, a citizen of the sovereign nation of Belize. Six years before her birth, the Creole working class—male mahogany laborers and urban working women descended from African slaves and in some cases also British settlers—demonstrated and rioted in Belize Town. Their actions announced a new form of popular class presence in colonial politics, a class- and race-conscious force capable of organizing to claim rights and to violently confront the colonial elite.[1] In response to the 1894 protests, the Creole middle class—a small but pivotal strata of shopkeepers, artisans, and junior state employees—settled on an strategy—one they would employ long-term—of seeking legislative power within the colonial framework rather than pursuing a nationalist alliance with the popular classes. Central to this strategy was its ritual show of allegiance to crown and empire, taking place each September 10 to mark the anniversary of the 1798 Battle of St. George's Caye that drove off a Spanish fleet. During the 1910 "Tenth" ceremonies, Elfreda's teachers chose her to deliver the schoolchildren's address of loyalty to the governor.[2] As an activist in the 1930s and 1950s, however, Elfreda joined the fight against British rule. She died bedridden and largely unknown, but when I met her in 1991, ten years after Belizean independence, her sense of her importance in the political dramas that produced this improbable nation-state did not seem to have faded nor had her enthusiasm soured. Her identity as a player was intact despite her absence from the history books.[3]

Though she had no children of her own, Elfreda spent her last years surrounded by extended family in Belize City's Mesopotamia neighborhood. The area was named for the Belizean veterans who settled there after they came back from serving in the Middle East during World War One—some rioted against merchant power and white privilege upon their return in 1919. By then, Elfreda had joined the unskilled urban labor force and was earning less than two dollars a week as a domestic servant to British and local white families. Labor and nationalist movements expanded elsewhere in the Caribbean, Latin America, and the British Empire during the 1920s.[4] But in British Honduras embryonic labor organizing and black nationalism were aborted first by a state crackdown after the 1919 riot and then by a reform project organized jointly by the colonial state and the Creole middle class. Part of the middle class formed a notably conservative branch of Marcus Garvey's Universal Negro Improvement Association that included a key group of women reformers but suppressed black nationalist politics. Because these women accommodated colonial rule, they did not—unlike their contemporaries in many independent Latin American and Caribbean nations—launch a suffrage movement, but they did share the drive to improve maternal and infant health and in so doing gave legitimacy to women's public voices.[5]

When the reform project collapsed at the beginning of the Depression, Elfreda, now widowed, emerged as a leader in the first sustained popular mobilization for labor rights and against colonial rule. Within that movement, working women from the Belize Town Creole community and from largely Garifuna Stann Creek Town to the south collectively imagined and claimed a gender-inclusive citizenship that also embraced mestizos and Mayans. They confronted the state-middle class alliance and provoked an expansion of its reform project.[6] Elfreda was thus part of the historic wave of unrest that swept Britain's colonies in the 1930s, prompting unprecedented imperial funding for reform and planning for controlled conditional political evolution. Parallel unrest across Latin America produced similarly reformist but often more successfully populist state projects. Elfreda insisted on women's prominence in the anticolonial movement, in terms of both numbers and commitment: "Those men were so coward," she claimed, "the women were more steadfast." Working-class women

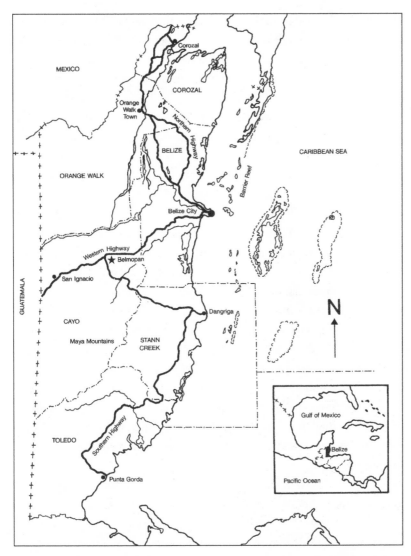

MAP 1. Belize. (Dangriga was formerly known as Stann Creek Town.) Source: Richard Wilk and Mac Chapin, *Ethnic Minorities in Belize: Mopan, Kekchi, and Garifuna* (Belize: SPEAR, 1990), 8.

were firmly excluded from the franchise for the colonial legislature, whose restoration in 1936 marked the end of eight decades of crown colony rule and forty-four years of the Unofficial Majority of merchant-employer-landowners on the Legislative Council. But it was an illusory victory for the middle class.

Elfreda got married a second time in 1940, to a man who disapproved of and blocked her political activism. But the 1940s were something of a lull in Belizean popular mobilization in any case, a decade dominated by the rise of legal "responsible" trade unionism for men and colonial social welfare programs aimed at domesticating and depoliticizing poor women. The main effect of the latter was to professionalize middle-class women reformers. Widowed again at the end of the decade, Elfreda was poised to reprise her militant role within the mass labor-nationalist movement of the early 1950s. The movement represented a populist alliance between the lower classes—now organizationally inclusive of rural mestizos and Mayans—and a young middle-class leadership imbued with Catholic doctrines of social justice.[7] Elfreda became a prominent speaker and organizer and was a founder of the nationalist campaign to secure a minimum wage for domestics. "At that time you couldn't call union to no mistress or nobody at all," she recalled, claiming to have won her own five dollars a week by refusing to be treated "like a slave" by her female employer. Though the campaign failed, the nationalists did secure universal adult suffrage in 1953; most Belizean women and men thus gained the vote simultaneously.

Disgusted with what she perceived as nationalist leader George Price's use of women militants for his own empowerment and his flirtations with Guatemala, Elfreda split with the majority of her female comrades in the late 1950s, joining the largely middle-class opposition party that carried on the politics of reform. But she ploughed as much energy into a daycare for poor working mothers as into mostly fruitless electoral campaigns against the nationalists, who gained significant control of the state when Britain granted internal self-government in 1964. She hardly merited the epithet of party hack leveled at her by young Black Power radicals in the late 1960s, as she had declined, for example, to run for Belize City Council because "you agitated outside better." Though she did not share the rising generation's condemnation of party politics as neocolonial, she did acknowledge that the system had limitations.

Elfreda's activism had waned by the late 1970s, during the final push for independence. She was not hailed as a political foremother by Belize's first self-proclaimed feminist group—which sought political ground beyond party politics and an independence that would change women's relationship to the state—as it had limited knowledge of the history that Elfreda had lived and made. Indeed, she played a significant part in the transformation of the political arena that the popular and middle classes brought about during the twentieth century, in the struggle between colonial-middle class reform and labor-nationalist militance, and in the growth of women's political organization—even as her own trajectory suggests the partial containment of popular and female politics by the colonial and then, more effectively, by the national state.[8]

This book restores to the historical record Elfreda Reyes and the countless other women who authored and joined in these political dramas, but it also uses this new knowledge to transform historical interpretation, thus combining for the Belizean case what have been distinct phases in more developed feminist historiographies.[9] Leading Caribbean feminist historians have urged precisely the move from recuperating knowledge to deploying it in reinterpretations of everything from plantation society to postcolonial authority. Similarly, Indian scholars Kumkum Sangari and Sudesh Vaid argue that: "A feminist historiography rethinks historiography as a whole and discards the idea of women as something to be *framed* by a context, in order to be able to think of gender difference as both structuring and structured by the wide set of social relations." Critical theorist Anne McClintock presents this feminist move as necessary to any credible analysis of imperialism, race, class, or nationalism—key aspects of the "social relations" discussed in this book—and theories of all these as indispensable to feminist scholarship. Her observation underscores how, ever since Joan Wallach Scott identified political history as a bastion of resistance to "material or even questions about women and gender" in 1988, feminist historians have breached the walls, thus contributing to a retheorization of modern politics.[10]

In this book, gender analysis transforms current understandings of Belize's reformist and nationalist traditions, the organizations and movements that constituted them, and indeed the entire process of political struggle and alliance that produced Belizean independence in 1981. I present women as political actors who, often in conflict with one another, shaped that process. But I also show how gender—as a power relationship between men and women as well as a field constitutive of race and class hierarchies and political, particularly state, power—was always at stake.[11] In so doing I recapture the dynamism that Belizean historiography possessed in the 1970s and 1980s, when evidence of indigenous, slave, worker, and peasant resistance was first systematically gathered and seriously analyzed.[12]

Belize is somewhat more familiar to anthropologists than to historians because of the attention its remarkable human diversity—variously described as cultural, ethnic, or racial—has attracted.[13] Much of the anthropological literature has focused on the Maya (Yucatec, Mopan, and Kekchi) and on the Garifuna, labeled "Black Caribs" in the colonial lexicon for their mixed African and indigenous Windward Islands ancestry. The more culturally westernized Creoles, with their African and/or European ancestry, have garnered less anthropological notice, but they are central to this book. All of these groups identified themselves as more or less distinct throughout the twentieth century—because of their social interactions with each other and to the extent that they were affected by elite discourses of racialization—although narrower geographic and broader ethnic and/or political identities (such as Afro-Belizean) were also salient. Like Nigel Bolland, I reject analyses of Belizean politics that rely on simplistic static understandings of ethnic "complexes," especially when they sideline class factors, as well as the idea that "Belizean people are now fixed in unchanging ethnic groups and social identities as if they lived under glass cases in a museum."[14] Later in this introduction I analyze the shifting but mutual construction of race and nation in the political struggles that this book focuses on. Culturally, both colony and nation have bridged the Afro-Caribbean and Mesoamerican regions, but given the earlier and stronger political activity of Creoles and the Garifuna—a pattern particularly marked among women—and the colony's political similarities to the rest of the British Caribbean, this book dialogues more strongly with scholarship on the former region and the wider African diaspora. Nonetheless, Mayan and mestizo women do appear in the pages to come; indeed, the book helps to dispel notions of female political invisibility in these cultures.[15] Throughout the book, I will use colonial terminology such as "Black Carib" and "Indian" only in quoting contemporary sources. On a related note, although the colony of British Honduras officially became the colony of Belize only in 1973, nationalists had begun to use the latter term much earlier. For simplicity, then, and with no implication that national independence was inevitable, I refer throughout the book to Belize. The main urban center, Belize Town, became Belize City in 1943, while the new capital of Belmopan was constructed from 1967–70.

The book's primary contribution to Belize's political historiography is to show that the contested, contingent making of the nation was a gendered process. The existing literature pays virtually no attention to women as historical actors or to gender as central to political power and struggle. When it does acknowledge women's activism, it blames them for the decline of the movements in which they were involved. In beginning to rectify this situation, this book also clarifies a number of other problems in the political historiography. First, the presence of popular actors has not always been acknowledged or analyzed; when it has, they have sometimes been cast as virile rebels, sometimes as dupes of self-interested elites. I avoid such extremes, exploring instead how subaltern actors negotiated, adapted, manipulated, and resisted, without ever achieving total unity or gaining complete autonomy. Second, middle-class reformers have tended to be misunderstood either as far more radical and anticolonial than they ever were or as merely mimic men, willing tools of colonial power. Again, this book restores to them, and the organizations they built, a more complex and nuanced subjectivity and agency. Third, the book complicates the standard narrative that portrays the 1930s labor rebellion as leading to 1940s trade unionism and so to the nationalist movement of the 1950s. Instead it shows that trade unionism in the 1940s grew out of the colonial reform tradition and was only belatedly appropriated to the nationalist cause. It was rather the race- and gender-inclusive popular culture of anticolonialism that was the most significant creation of the struggles of the 1930s.

This study also transforms the existing literature on Belizean women.[16] It overturns the assumption that Belizean women were not politically active beyond church and charity work until the advent of party auxiliaries in the 1960s or before the development of women's nongovernment organizations in the 1980s, thus providing a fuller and clearer analysis of the origins of present-day women's politics. Women's studies on Belize, like the broader scholarship on contemporary British Caribbean women that has emerged in recent years, has lacked an accurate historical grounding, particularly for the century between emancipation and mass nationalist struggle. In covering the second half of that lacuna, this book demonstrates women's vital and variegated political presence from the 1910s onward as well as the relevance of politics to the history of Belizean women. In connecting political history and gender studies, this book clearly shows that the making of modern Belize was a gendered process in which women of all ethnic groups were actors.

My reinterpretations of Belizean history connect to debates in the historiographies of the Caribbean and Latin America, comparative women's and African diaspora politics, British and comparative imperialism, and nationalism and postcolonial nations. In the next section I situate myself within and highlight my contributions to five such debates: 1) the capacity of subaltern and female subjects for historical agency, 2) the possibilities for and the character of colonial and national hegemony 3) the relationship of gender to colonial racism and its reworking by nationalist and postcolonial forces 4) the contingent and contested nature of the nation, and 5) the relationship of gender to labor mobilization and labor's relation to state projects.

Subaltern and Female Subjectivity

The political life story of Elfreda Reyes shows that subaltern and female subjects need not be autonomous, unified, purely resistant, or transparent to themselves (or to historians) to challenge narratives that dismiss their presence altogether—their "traces of independent initiative" are enough.[17]

Scholars seeking to restore the histories of women, workers, and colonial "others," among them white U.S. feminists and members of the Subaltern Studies school in South Asia, have succumbed at times to "the siren attractions of the idea of the self-constituting subject" in recent decades.[18] In seeking to avoid the ahistorical pitfalls of the strongly postmodernist subject as an all-too-fluid effect of powerful discourses, lacking any agency, these scholars risk establishing an equally ahistorical standard for resistant agency from below.[19] Mrinalini Sinha, for example, frankly admits that she had to wean herself from a belief that Indian feminists would "naturally" critique both "male nationalist patriarchy and imperialist feminism." Her assumption, she recognized, created an ideal of feminist praxis that failed to account for the historical contexts that made certain subjectivities and strategies possible.[20]

Others have long understood subjectivity as formed on fields of difference and in the fray of social and political struggle that has produced the present. Their subjects, in Nancy Fraser's words, built "collective identities [that were] at once discursively constructed *and* . . . enabling of collective action." These middle-ground theorists share an optimism about the possibilities for subaltern and female agency but are wary of constructing new heroic or teleological narratives of emancipation. Florencia Mallon, one historian who takes this approach, argues against heroization by emphasizing the contingency and vulnerability of hard-won subaltern political unities and their typical reproduction of gender oppression. Intellectuals of the African diaspora have long grappled with the fluid, fractured yet historically constituted and potentially integrated nature of subjectivity in a world where racialized difference has made the inclusion of black peoples in the Enlightenment project at best conditional. Frantz Fanon, for example, is frequently cited by postcolonial and feminist theorists precisely because of his eloquence on this subject. Black feminists, particularly in the United States, have played a critical role in deconstructing the category of "woman" as itself repressive of class, race, and other differences, differences that make feminist unity neither automatic nor impossible.[21]

Evelyn O'Callaghan, a literary scholar at the University of the West

Indies, situates Caribbean women's particular dilemmas of subjectivity within the region's history of indigenous demographic collapse, African slavery, and intense, enduring colonial rule—historical conditions that render impossible any utopian search for a pure or essential Caribbean subject. She insists that Caribbean women have negotiated among several racist discourses of black womanhood—sexless mother, beast of burden, libidinous degenerate—rejecting them all for an integrated self-respecting female subjectivity and agency.[22] For her, this tradition of female selfhood manifests itself in the resistant lower-class Caribbean woman, the "jamette" who subverts colonial and national hegemonies through very public wit, sexual prowess, and defiance. The Belizean version of this resistant female subject is the Creole "*bembe*" or bully woman, Elfreda Reyes being a primary example. Indeed, *bembe* subjectivity and practice were prominent in the history of labor-nationalist mobilization in Belize, from the 1894 and 1919 riots to the more sustained efforts of the 1930s and early 1950s. They also have deeper roots, in the Caribbean's history of slavery and emancipation.[23]

O'Callaghan, however, recognizes only one kind of effective Caribbean female subject. She explicitly excludes the middle-strata West Indian woman who, in her view, extinguished her subjectivity and agency in accepting racist Victorian gender norms and colonial rule. Yet the conventionally respectable middle-class West Indian woman has been a potent social and political force in the region's history for the past century or more.[24] In twentieth-century Belize, such women embraced and promoted a conservative Caribbean womanhood and a maternalist, class-conscious political practice. While they shared or at least willingly accommodated themselves to the racism and paternalism of colonial rule, their agency was not snuffed out—indeed it shaped a reform tradition that placed real limits on masculine authority. More fruitful than judging these women as failing to meet a modern ideal of resistance is the approach of Caribbean historian Patricia Mohammed, who makes the concept of "bargaining with patriarchy" central to her analysis of *all* Caribbean women's identities and politics.[25] This stance recognizes both the constructed nature and agency of Caribbean female subjects in their historical contexts without positing an impossibly autonomous or pure resistance. The early Belizean feminists who appear at the end of this book were no exception: they could not have constructed a new space for women's mobilization without having first developed a network of relationships with the state, political parties, and nongovernmental organizations.

In this book, the first to historicize or theorize the political subjectivities of Belizean women, I have strived to neither heroize *bembe* politics nor deprecate reformist politics or the lateness of explicitly feminist politics' emergence. Elfreda Reyes's blanket dismissal of men as "so coward," for example, simply does not hold up under scrutiny, and unnecessarily embellishes subaltern women's political record. Rather, I explain the historical conditions, initiatives, and limitations out of which *both* broad forms of Belizean female political subjectivity emerged. These forms of political subjectivity gave rise to traditions and identities that shaped both of the major currents in twentieth-century Belizean politics and the historic struggles between them. In so doing, I have avoided tendencies in the existing Belizean historiography to cast popular actors as either passively uninvolved in politics or as resistant heroes and to either misconstrue middle-class reformers as radicals or to caricature them as toadying anglophiles.

Hegemony and Gender

The dynamic Gramscian theory of hegemony defines it as rule achieved through alliance, negotiation, and struggle rather than through total consent or accession to the dominant ideology. It is sustained by a constant testing and relegitimation of an always contingent and partial moral-political authority that is vulnerable to subversion from within and attack from without. It is a hegemony theorized as process as much as outcome, an approach that clarifies the way that political subjects are formed in the often conflictual articulation of hegemonic alliances and projects, whether or not such projects achieve cultural revolution and/or state power.[26] But not all politics can be subsumed under the rubric of attempted or achieved hegemonic articulation, and it is vital to recognize historical contexts in which political subjects have formed in relations of outright hostility and competition.

This book's history of Belize demonstrates the importance of gender analysis in explaining the character of hegemonic projects, both colonial and national, as well as their success or failure. Specifically, I show that no hegemonic project achieved cultural or political authority in Belize without winning the allegiance of subaltern women, particularly activist Creole and Garifuna women. Although the state is certainly not the sole arena in which hegemonic articulation occurs, it is a key institution in the promotion of hegemonic projects and the maintenance of hegemonic outcomes. While the modern state, colonial or national, has developed as an institution of hegemonic masculine authority, it has maintained that authority not only by forging vertical alliances with men, alliances that have reproduced female exclusion and/or subordination but also, and sometimes simultaneously, by incorporating politically active women's demands and expectations into its rhetoric and practice.[27] Instances of hegemonic negotiation and alliance between women and modern states are in fact common, perhaps normative. Yet women's political presence has been more marked in some societies than others, the Caribbean being a region where particularly women of African descent have been prominent in slave, peasant, and wage labor and in a "rich tradition of organization and struggle . . . since the post-emancipation period" that has included church-, race-, class-, and party-based activism. If Indian women, in British imperial thinking, were overly subordinated by native patriarchal practices, African and Afro-Caribbean women were insufficiently domesticated within male-controlled institutions. In a similar pairing, McClintock notes that "Arab women were to be civilized by being undressed (unveiled), while sub-Saharan women were to be civilized by being dressed (in clean, white, British cotton)." Indeed, Indian nationalists' stereotyping of lower-class Indian women as "coarse, vulgar, loud, quarrelsome, devoid of superior moral sense, sexually promiscuous" matches if not echoes an established and pervasive imperial discourse about black women.[28]

Belize's nationalist leadership of the 1950s did bargain with *bembe* politics in successfully forging a hegemonic alliance with the popular classes. They approached poor black women without making the moral judgments typical of the colonial reformers and made the nationalist campaign centrally about women's key demands. Given the close connection between concepts of hegemonic alliance and populist articulation, it becomes useful to include the Belizean nationalist project, and indeed British Caribbean nationalism as a whole, in the category of mid-century populist projects that achieved some degree of hegemony. Research on the gendered dimensions of rule in Peron's Argentina, Vargas's Brazil, Popular Front Chile, Cardenas's Mexico, Muñoz Marin's Puerto Rico, and for that matter the U.S. New Deal, is expanding.[29] My analysis of Belize shares this scholarship's sensitivity to the terms of engagement between subaltern and elite, between male and female, between civil society and state actors involved in populist hegemonic projects, as well as its emphasis on these projects' contingency. But it also illustrates that such projects did not depend on formal national independence or industrialization, and, most importantly, that in contexts where women were highly mobilized, state alliance with the popular classes included direct articulation with them, unmediated through the usually male-dominated institutions of family, union, or party.

By contrast, the failure of *colonial* hegemony in Belize and the wider British Caribbean must be explained—in part—by reference to the racialized, moralistic, paternalistic approach officials and middle-class reformers took not just to the popular classes as a whole but black women in particular.[30] To achieve colonial hegemony, the reform alliance would have had to bargain with *bembe* politics in a way it was simply not willing to do. Nonetheless, this book treats the reform projects of the 1920s to the 1950s as hegemonic in intent and finds that the colonial state's close alliance with the Creole middle class depended on a negotiated relationship with women reformers. But the state-middle class alliance could not by itself achieve hegemony. Clearly then, this books explains rather than assumes the failure of colonial hegemony, breaking with the approach of existing Belizean historiography as well as with that of leading Subaltern Studies scholars.[31] These scholars' proposition, based on their interpretation of nineteenth- and twentieth-century Indian history, that the colonial state is alien must be radically qualified in thinking about the Caribbean. Because the region's indigenous peoples were destroyed or severely marginalized in the three centuries after 1492, the replacement population of Africans, poor whites, and later Asians was no more native than its white colonial masters. Deep conflicts within Caribbean slave and postemancipation societies, as well as the gradual creolization of the nonwhite majority, created the basis for political and cultural work that produced popular claims to authentic native belonging, but still the colonial state and white people (many of whom were themselves creolized) could never be as profoundly "other" in the Caribbean as in Asia or Africa. The gendered moralism of the colonial state in Belize and other modern colonies, then, and not its intrinsic colonial character, is most salient to explaining the failure of its hegemonic project. Notably, the colonial state in India made its "civilizing mission" centrally about regulating gender relations and practices it deemed degrading to women, provoking an equally gendered nationalist response that was respectful of domesticated middle-class women if not their "vulgar" and "quarrelsome" subaltern sisters.[32] The latter was a mistake not repeated by Belizean and other British Caribbean nationalists.

Gender, Racism, and Racial Politics

The attitude of British officials and their middle-class allies toward working class Creole and Garifuna women in twentieth-century Belize had its roots in a long history of gendered, sexualized European racism. While evidence exists that Europeans had cast Africa as an eroticized region, and black women in particular as sexually lascivious, since well before the 1400s, it was in the age of exploration and particularly from the late eighteenth century onward that an ideology linking sexuality, race, and empire became dominant among the emerging bourgeois and intellectual elites of Europe. Within that ideology, black women were cast as the embodiment of sexual immorality and as agents of civilizational degeneracy. The latter stereotype stemmed in particular from a rising obsession in the second half of the nineteenth century with interracial desire, sex, and reproduction, which confirmed biologized racism's assessment of Africans, new world blacks, and hybrid mulattos as permanently inferior.[33]

Critics of Enlightenment universals have argued that race was an invention of the modern period, dating from the 1500s, and that racism was constitutive of liberalism beginning in the late 1700s. Thomas Holt has argued that "'racism' was embedded in the very premises of a presumably nonracist liberalism," and that "virulently racist ideology was not merely some aberrant anachronism." Holt's conclusion is particularly relevant here, for it stems from his research on emancipation and its aftermath in nineteenth-century Jamaica and on British colonial policy in the Caribbean, a region too often glossed over in histories of empire in this period. With others he has traced a hardening of British racial ideology in the aftermath of slave emancipation in the 1830s, a process linked to the exslaves' refusal to accept that freedom meant seasonal wage labor, landlessness, political disenfranchisement, and a bourgeois Christian morality. In particular, the Morant Bay rebellion of 1865, following the 1857 Indian Mutiny—and both reviving the specter of the Haitian Revolution—legitimized racist "truths" that non-European peoples were unfit to govern themselves.[34]

Feminist scholars' contributions to this critique range from Ann Laura Stoler's argument that racist assessments of non-Europeans were centrally about contrasting their lack of sexual self-control with the Victorian middle-class ideal of sexual self-discipline to Antoinette Burton's conclusion that nineteenth-century British feminists identified with the racist imperial cause, assuming the role of enlightened civilizer in their relations with colonized women. Most importantly, a slim historiography has emerged that demonstrates how specifically Caribbean exslave *women's* resistance in the postemancipation period fueled harsher gendered imperial racism in Britain. Their refusal to acquiesce to the ideal of domesticity promoted by British middle-class moral authorities invigorated racist stereotypes of them as women of the public sphere, whose sexual morality was thus thoroughly impugned and linked to their peoples' "unfitness" for political rights.[35]

This gendered imperial racism was reworked in nationalist projects in the Americas, first in Latin America and the Spanish Caribbean, later in the British Caribbean. Latin American liberals in the decades around 1900 often bought into the dominant ideology by encouraging white immigration and excluding peoples of African and indigenous ancestry from full citizenship. But simultaneously populist reformers began to articulate both raceless nationalisms and nationalisms that constructed the mulatto and mestizo not as degenerates but as hybrid agents of a long-term project of national whitening.[36] Still, dominant transatlantic definitions of degenerate black femininity were influential. For example, black women were excluded from elite Cuban and Puerto Rican nationalisms based on shifting notions of racial brotherhood, transcendence, or whitening or were symbolically whitened for subordinate inclusion.[37]

As I have argued previously, ideas of whitening miscegenation seem to have had less currency in the postemancipation British Caribbean, where mixed-race middle groups sought clear separation between themselves and the black masses and where a post-Morant imperial policy prevailed of limiting social mixing between British administrators and locals.[38] In Belize, the Creole middle class witnessed the 1892 advent of the Unofficial Majority on the Legislative Council, which empowered the white merchant-landowner elite, and then the 1894 urban riot, and so it chose to court the colonial state as its only viable ally. Angered by its political exclusion but fearful of popular black unrest, middle-class leaders opted for colonial accommodation, founding their claims to legislative—not executive—rights by articulating an origin myth that emphasized their white male ancestors' participation in the 1798 Battle of St. George's Caye (in which local and British forces defeated a Spanish fleet), their command of loyal male slaves during the battle, and thus their securing of the colony for Britain. The Battle of St. George's Caye myth denied the middle class's black maternal origins, suppressed public recognition of its own racial hybridity, posited an unequal cross-race fraternity, denied Mayan claims to native authenticity, and demonized all things "Latin." It was the annual September 10 celebration of the myth that Elfreda Reyes (then Stanford) participated in at age 10. By the 1910s middle-class Creole women who accepted the limits—both gendered and racialized—of the myth, were forging a respectable female public activism that, even within the Garveyite movement, depended on a partial suppression of black identity and its morally negative connotations. This reformist politics of racial uplift, despite invoking local patriotism and native belonging, "remained locked within hegemonic articulations of gender, class and sexuality" by accepting "white middle-class models of gender roles and sexuality" as ideal and as necessary for political rights.[39] I have found no evidence that the myth captured the Creole popular imagination until the advent of combative party politics in the 1950s, though middle-class attachment to it dates from its construction in the 1890s.

As in Cuba, the strong popular element of British Caribbean nationalisms provokes the question of how popular Afro-Caribbean ideas of black manhood and womanhood were incorporated, from above or below, into nationalist popular alliances. Clearly, a proud subaltern black womanhood was central to nationalist politics in Belize, but it was black women themselves who in the 1930s began to articulate a *multiracial* nationalist coalition exclusive of whites. In 1949, Antonio Soberanis and Luke Kemp (key labor leaders of the 1930s) published a pamphlet that directly challenged the Battle of St. George's Caye myth by positing Belize as a historically black and Indian nation.[40] With the emergence of the middle-class nationalist leadership, three racialized constructions of Belizean nationalism were promoted starting in the 1950s. First was a Cuban-style discourse of racelessness that insisted on the primacy of a Belizean political identity—as a result the 1961 census did not ask people to describe themselves ethnically or racially. Second was a construction of Belize as an historically Mayan nation oriented toward Central America rather than the emerging Commonwealth Caribbean, a construction that the pyramid-like design of the late-1960s parliament building in the new capital of Belmopan made literally concrete, even if it did not address any of the problems of the contemporary Maya. Third was a discourse of folkloric multiculturalism that still insisted on the nonpolitical nature of ethnic identities but that celebrated cultural diversity as a national characteristic.[41]

Unlike Soberanis and Kemp's pamphlet, none of these elite nationalist constructions directly criticized the middle-class Battle of St. George's Caye origin myth and its suppression of black identities. Indeed, blackness was more clearly linked to ideas of the Belizean nation in 1919 and the 1930s than in the 1950s and 1960s because the nationalist leadership was reluctant to recognize its own origins in the colony's history of slave rebellions, Creole and Garifuna workers' strikes and riots, and subaltern black women's militance. The Black Power movement of 1968–74 in Belize certainly contested the marginalization of black identity in the nationalist project, but it was unable to reconstruct the history of Creole and Garifuna people's central roles in creating the potential for nation-state formation or to connect with the mestizo and Mayan population as the 1930s movement had done. Moreover, Black Power gender politics precluded any serious recognition of women's political significance and legitimacy. With the influx of Guatemalans and Salvadorans since independence, a clearly chauvinist linking of black and Belizean identities has unfortunately emerged, which is entirely contrary to the spirit of the 1930s female imagining of the future nation.[42]

Because middle-class reformist, nationalist, and Black Power constructions of the Belizean nation suffer themselves from racialized and gendered limitations, the legacy of gendered imperial racism has never been openly discussed, problematized, or deconstructed. As a result, no positive link has ever been made in Belize between black women's resistance and the emergence of the nation, in contrast to other places in the Caribbean such as Jamaica, where the maroon leader Nanny was made a national heroine in the 1960s, Trinidad and Tobago, where labor activist Elma François became an official national heroine in 1987, and Cuba, where the Afro-Cuban mambisas of the late nineteenth century have garnered the popular admiration of many. Still, the nationalist project's refusal to fully reproduce gendered colonial racism—whether on principle or as a strategic move to cement its alliance with militant Creole and Garifuna women—makes such a link possible. Certainly the evidence that this book provides, for the first time, of subaltern black women's importance in nation building could be deployed in future political attempts within Belize to create alternatives to the legacy of gendered imperial racism.

The Contingent and Contested Nation

Despite Belizean historians' disinterest in hegemony as an analytical tool, they have, in line with the Gramscian theory of hegemony, treated the Belizean nation as a contingent and contested creation. Political science scholarship has focused on contestation from without, i.e., the Guatemalan state's claims to sovereignty over Belizean territory, which did delay Belizean independence for over a decade.[43] But historians have been more interested in nationalism's conflicts with the forces of reform—conflicts that defined the emergence of party politics in the 1950s—and the nationalist leadership's "betrayal" of its mass popular base. Fortunately, Belizean historiography since the 1970s has assumed a critical stance toward the nationalist movement and party, avoiding the production of heroic emancipatory narratives and unintentionally enabling the feminist critique presented in the second half of this book. This happy situation is the result of most scholars' autonomy from the postcolonial state and the sobering corruption of party politics in the 1960s and 1970s, a period when the still officially colonial state was nationalist-dominated and sovereign in many respects. Thus, the optimism and exuberance of Jamaican independence in 1962, for example, was not replicable in Belize in 1981, a moment that few experienced simply as triumphant fruition. Indeed, the slogan of the moment, "independence is just the beginning," was an implicit challenge to triumphalism.

Belizean historiography, then, has already "rescued history from the nation," to paraphrase Prasenjit Duara, by problematizing the concept of a "cohesive, collective [national] subject."[44] This book reinforces Duara's argument that national identities have frequently repressed other, equally valid and modern identities by analyzing both the symbolic incorporation of gender into nationalist and postcolonial politics and women's negotiation and/or rejection of such symbolism. A key example of this is nationalist women's manipulation of an increasingly domestic definition of proper nationalist womanhood during the transition in the late 1950s from street protests and labor mobilization to elite negotiations with the British. From within the nationalist party, they used the doctrine of domesticity that was gaining force to launch a mass mobilization for female home ownership, a major economic resource, even as the labor movement was losing momentum and autonomy.

Despite gendered conflicts within the nationalist hegemonic alliance, I do not treat the shift to national rule as either insignificant or a "failure." Even in its ambivalences, contradictions, and backsliding, decolonization

was experienced by Belizeans as a meaningful change in their relationship to the state and in their relationship to both neighboring countries
and to Britain and the United States and it established their status and
their rights as citizens. I thus part with the more pessimistic conclusions
of some scholars about the postcolonial nation-state. These include Paul
Gilroy, whose analysis in *The Black Atlantic* privileges diaspora identities
and politics, sidelining the challenging aspects of black and Third World
nationalisms. Subaltern Studies scholars have offered a mix of pessimism
and apology for the character of the Indian state, at times condemning
it as an elitist and dominating force that has failed to achieve hegemony,
at others contextualizing its limits in terms of the elite's westernization
through colonial education and the false expectations created by ideologies of modernization. Partha Chatterjee in particular locates the creative
difference between the Indian state and European nationalism in its gender ideology, even though he recognizes that this posited not women's
liberation but a new patriarchy.[45]

Overly pessimistic or dismissive interpretations of decolonization and
postcolonial rule risk preserving the subaltern subject as somehow separate from and untainted by the compromises of independence. Rather,
as historiographies of the Mexican Revolution, Southern Cone populist
projects, and Cuban and British Caribbean nationalisms have shown,
workers, peasants, indigenous peoples, and women have all actively participated in the making and remaking of postcolonial nation-states and
have shaped and been shaped by their accomplishments as well as compromises.[46] Indeed, as Mallon notes, in colonial contexts where "nationalist elites had often benefited from the social arrangements reproduced
under colonialism, subaltern movements and political vision had to attain
an even larger and more militant presence in nationalist coalitions if the
nation was ever to come into its own."[47] This is certainly true of Belize.
The nationalist leadership's early reliance on a popular mass movement in
which organized labor and women were vital forces made the establishment of a Belizean nation more likely, but it also paved the way for later
conflicts as the popular base became vulnerable to deliberate demobiliza-
tion in the negotiated transition to self-government.

Gender, Labor Mobilization and Politics

Historians of labor in Latin America and the Caribbean have begun to recognize the importance of gender in processes of class formation, labor organization, and labor's conflicts and negotiations with a variety of state projects. Yet many of those on the cutting edge of this literature acknowledge that much remains to be discovered and analyzed in order to fully historicize the "gender ideologies and practices of the popular classes" or to understand how gender shapes "working class culture and politics" as well as the "projects of national-popular states."[48] Latin American scholarship is now the most dynamic in the twentieth–century field. Recent British Caribbean labor history, on the other hand, has been most insightful about connections among labor, gender, race, and politics during the aftermath of abolition in the nineteenth century.[49] This book brings the two literatures together, illuminating the gendered connections between labor politics and Belize's two broad political traditions, thus furthering the new labor history's growing appreciation of gender as constitutive of processes of class formation, working-class identity formation, labor organizing, and both conflict and negotiation with a variety of state projects.

First, I link the early and strong political activism of Creole and Garifuna working women to the historically-produced predominance in their communities of consensual unions, single motherhood, female household headship, and women's farming and/or wage earning. By contrast, mestizo and Mayan women were more securely contained within patriarchal households and communities, a factor that compounded their disconnection from wage labor in rural Belize. Thus, popular political consciousness was gendered differently in different working-class and semiproletarianized communities in the colony, and the politics of organized labor followed suit.

While 1894 and 1919 represent moments of at least temporary Creole working-class unity, the history of organized labor in Belize dates only from the 1930s. Three key moments demonstrate the variety of relations between labor and state projects, and how gender plays differently into each. First, in the illegal labor movement of the 1930s women were not only numerous but probably the best organized force. Further no male

breadwinner or family-wage ideology emerged and the masculine authority of the leadership was muted. At the same time, relations between
labor and the colonial state were extremely conflictual, a situation influenced not only by the ire of capital and by middle-class fears, but also by
British views of the labor movement as representing a racialized gender
disorder.

By contrast, the colonial state's reform project gave its official blessing
in the early 1940s to the first "responsible" trade union, which met British
expectations by organizing itself around regularly employed male workers. Concomitantly, it had a very small female membership, bolstered the
state's domestic female ideal, and steered clear of politics in its early years.
Yet it had not forfeited all autonomy or capacity for confrontation with
capital or the state, and in the late 1940s its leadership invoked British
Labor Party socialism as it demanded higher wages and stronger labor
rights for the men flooding home from wartime work programs overseas.
Not until the nationalist takeover of the union in 1950, however, did it
break with its original colonial loyalty and commitment to a male breadwinner ideology.

In the third moment of the early 1950s, the labor movement became a
critical partner in the formation of a popular-national state project. But
in contrast to the parallel project in Chile, for example, organized male
workers were not the state's dominant allies, for militant women were
equally important to populist alliance, both within the labor movement
and beyond it. The labor movement and nationalist leadership granted
legitimacy to women's wage labor but stopped short of recognizing that
they were family breadwinners and household heads. This ambivalence
reflected the larger paternalism of the nationalist state project, a paternalism that working women continued to negotiate and contest, even when
the labor movement split and collapsed later in the decade.

The Belizean case, then, deepens the new gendered labor history's
appreciation of both the importance and range of gendered cultures of
labor organization and politics. Perhaps most importantly, it suggests the
existence of an Afro-Caribbean pattern of gender as constitutive of labor-
nationalist state projects that seems to contrast with Latin American

populisms. Working-class women's less male-mediated relationship with nationalist leaders in the former region—a relationship rooted in their autonomy within families and communities—may well have weakened hegemonic constructions of the male breadwinner and made the post-colonial state more vulnerable to working women's claims to citizenship and labor rights.

Transforming Belizean Historiography

This book is based on a wide variety of previously unmined archival documents, including colonial government minute papers, court records, and the files of Belize's first feminist organization, as well as on new readings of newspapers and government reports. In addition, I interviewed nearly one hundred women and men, including national and local politicians and political brokers and people whose rank-and-file political activism peaked somewhere between the 1930s and the 1970s. These interviews took place in four ethnically distinct regions of Belize: heavily Creole Belize City, predominantly Garifuna Dangriga, the mixed mestizo-Mayan Cayo District, and Orange Walk District, with its mestizo-Mayan-Creole profile. Corozal and Toledo Districts, where I did not conduct interviews, are mentioned in the book but feature less prominently. A variety of Belizeans, including friends, hosts, and other informants, suggested people I might approach. I also got ideas from lists of names collected from newspaper reports and previously published material and sometimes through local party offices. Given that my objective was to gather the widest possible sample of testimonies to test my hypothesis that women were central to political struggles in twentieth-century Belize, I categorize the material generated as interviews rather than as full-fledged oral histories (which typically cover a wider variety of topics, are undertaken over a longer period of time, and involve a deeper, more reciprocal relationship between researcher and informant). Even though I spoke with most people only once—although usually for a fairly lengthy period—they were uniformly willing, even excited, to talk about women's political contributions in the past, and several commented on the decline of family story-telling in the cable-television age in Belize. Only two women asked for payment (both in Dangriga where anthropologists have been a frequent presence and where there is a high level of ethnic organization), and only one asked after our meeting that I not use my notes from our interview, a request I have respected. Notably, the male political leaders I spoke with all acknowledged that women's political participation was in some way important, a fact that may help to explain women's readiness to go on record, although it is also possible that my position as a foreigner and/or Canadian outside of party politics soothed any anxieties women may have felt. I have tried to act as their collaborator in sharing their proud memories with a wider audience at the same time that I test their memories against each other and the documentary record and maintain my own critique of the movements that they did so much to shape. There is a huge amount to be done, and done quickly, to preserve the memories of older Belizeans, and I hope that my efforts help to further interest in this work, particularly among Belizeans themselves.

The book falls into three pairs of chapters: the first covers 1912–1930 (a period of fledgling popular mobilization and a fragile reform project), the second 1931–54 (a period marked by two sustained popular anticolonial movements bracketing a more robust reform project), and the third 1949–82 (the period of transition from nationalist movement to postcolonial rule).

Chapter 1 is about the rising popular challenge to colonial power of the 1910s, a process that led toward the riot of 1919 in which the Belize Town working class attacked *en masse* the elite and their property. It establishes the previously neglected local causes of the riot and thus reveals that poor women of the Creole and Garifuna communities were particularly active in protests through the decade. It thus challenges the long-held idea of "the exservicemen's riot" as reproduced in the existing historiography.[50] The chapter also establishes the social world of the colony's working women from which their politics developed. It shows that the poor but feisty Creole woman—a kind of tamed *bembe*—was a key figure in the hegemonic fantasies of the local elite, which centered on gaining popular approval for a restored colonial legislature from which the masses would be excluded.

Chapter 2 is about the alliance and reform project of the colonial state and the middle class that coalesced in reaction to the unrest of the 1910s and particularly the 1919 riot. It demonstrates that the Creole middle class adapted Marcus Garvey's internationally popular doctrine of black separatism to the cause of respectable reform, founding a local branch of Garvey's United Negro Improvement Association and a linked Black Cross Nurses group in 1920. The chapter thus moves beyond an existing celebratory interpretation of the Nurses as apolitical community volunteers.[51] Garveyism provided an ideal political space for reformist women, and indeed the Nurses became the most formidable reform group of the 1920s, particularly through their strong alliance with the colonial state. Yet the reform project had limited hegemonic potential, for it firmly excluded labor issues from legitimate discussion, approached the women and men of the popular classes as morally disordered, and idealized a culturally whitened respectability.

Chapter 3 is about the popular labor and anticolonial mobilizations of the 1930s that posed an unprecedented challenge to the colonial order. It shows that renewed colony-wide protests in the early years of the Depression, particularly in the wake of the ruinous 1931 hurricane, formed the basis for the rapid growth and militance of the new worker-led Labourers and Unemployed Association (LUA) in the mid-1930s. Creole and Garifuna women in particular forged a strong alliance with the LUA's male leadership, sustaining its democratic and inclusive vision and practice. This interpretation turns on its head an existing argument that casts the LUA as a failure and attributes its weakness to its reliance on women.[52] These women directly confronted female reformers' class exclusivity and established a racially and gender inclusive anticolonial political culture, which survived the LUA's decline. The chapter explains that decline in terms of colonial state repression and reform and of the long-awaited restoration of an elected legislature in 1936. The association's male working-class founders backed the middle-class progressives elected, facilitating a largely state-enforced shift of political action from the streets to the colonial legislature. League women, though voteless, did begin to link their tradition of public activism to electoral campaigns.

Chapter 4 is about the major colonial-middle class reform project of

1935–54 that sought to suppress popular nationalism. Now part of imperially mandated policy provoked by unrest ranging from the West Indies
to Africa and India, Belizean reform finally embraced the labor question
and gained the resources to expand social welfare. I show that the plan to
modernize colonialism was deeply gendered and racialized, that its goal
was to morally rehabilitate the racially and sexually degenerate masses,
remaking their sexual, familial, economic, and political desires and behavior. By documenting the founding of the General Workers' Union under
the rubric of "responsible" trade unionism, I challenge the current view
of the union as a direct link between the LUA of the 1930s and the later
nationalist movement.[53] As a disciplinary project, reform had little populist appeal. Rather, women welcomed new state services without ceasing
to identify as workers, heads of households, or with the simmering culture
of anticolonialism. Rising unmet expectations of the state in fact fueled
renewed popular nationalism at the close of the 1940s, a movement that
reformers utterly failed to contain.

Chapter 5 is about the mass labor-nationalist movement of the early
1950s, the forging of a multiethnic, cross-class, gender-inclusive populist
alliance within that movement, and the ultimate domination of the alliance by the increasingly elitist People's United Party (PUP). Its young Jesuit-
educated nationalist leadership forged an enduring tie with women by
appealing to them as workers, voters, and activists and by promising them
jobs, state services, and family security. But the leadership never addressed
issues of women's economic subordination or domestic violence, and as
the PUP turned from mass to machine politics, neutralizing the popular
nationalism that had created it, it recast women as patriotic anticommunist mothers and party loyalists. The majority of women maintained their
alliance with it and negotiated enough leverage to remain a potent force
within it. This chapter broadens existing accounts of the nationalists' popular base both within and beyond the labor movement and complicates
the leadership's betrayal of that base.[54]

Chapter 6 is about three distinct challenges to the PUP after 1961, each of
which posited a different gender politics and all of which gave nationalist
women negotiating power with the party leadership and made gender an

ongoing issue in political struggle. Thus, the chapter paints a more vigorous and meaningful picture of party politics than previous interpretations
have allowed for but also challenges existing party-focused accounts of this
period.[55] In the first challenge, the *anti*national National Independence
Party drew on the decades-long tradition of middle-class women's activism in developing a much stronger female leadership than in the PUP. In
the second, the youth-based Black Power movement of 1968–74 denounced
both parties as neocolonial and unmanly, politicized black masculinity as
naturally dominant over women, and broke taboos on public discussion
of sexuality, abortion, and domestic violence. Black Power thus enabled
the birth of Belizean feminism—the third challenge—in the late 1970s.
Although early feminists adopted a more subdued stance in promoting
the transcendent importance of selected women's issues in the bitterly
partisan run-up to independence in 1981, by resisting the alliances that
empowered but also compromised their political foremothers and rejecting the politics of respectability, these women opened a small vulnerable
space for a new relationship between gender and politics in a Belize finally
freed of the struggle between colonial reform and nationalism, though
not of its divisive legacies.

1 The Making of a Riot

Women, Wages, and War on
the Home Front, 1912–1919

In the relative early morning cool of Saturday 26 July 1919, Annie Flowers left the Belize Town market with a heavy basket of provisions for the kitchen of Mrs. Hofius, the merchant's wife who employed her as a cook. Annie crossed Haulover Creek bridge and walked up Queen Street past the northside police station to where a group of women stood talking by the Baptist church fence. Here she set down the basket and joined in the conversation about the explosive politics of the week just ended. The night before, Friday, agitator Claude Smith had called a public meeting to channel popular unrest into labor demands, but it broke up violently when police and visiting British marines from the HMS *Constance* came to arrest him. The night of Tuesday 22 July, war veterans of the British Honduras Contingent, recently returned from the Middle East, had marched through downtown, methodically smashing the plate glass of the ten largest merchant stores. When they cut the town's electric generator, thousands of civilians began a long night of looting and violence. Nine-year-old Kathleen Soberanis (sister of future labor leader Antonio Soberanis) slipped out of her parents' house and returned with biscuits and cloth from Brodie's Ltd., and Winifred Flowers, 20, a domestic servant, followed the crowd and saw women "hauling this, hauling that." The largely Creole working class of Belize Town effectively paralyzed the police and Territorial Force militia, beating and insulting middle-class Creole men as well as British officials, who telegraphed the *Constance* for assistance.[1] The crisis of July 1919 and the immediate prewar and war years leading up to it were formative in the development of both Belize's popular-nationalist and colonial-reformist political currents.

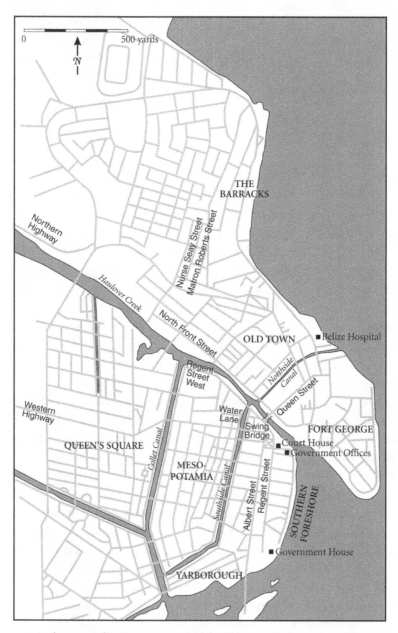

MAP 2. In the 1910s Belize Town consisted of the Old Town, Yarborough, and Barracks areas on the south and north sides of Haulover Creek. In the 1920s Mesopotamia and Fort George were developed. Belize Town became Belize City in 1943, and further expansion occurred mostly after World War Two.

FIG. 1. *(top)* Regent Street in 1910. The Hofius household where Annie Flowers worked would have been on or near Regent Street in the affluent Southern Foreshore area. Source: *Belizean Studies* 5:1 (January 1977): 7.

FIG. 2. Swing Bridge over Haulover Creek in 1928. Annie Flowers would have crossed a simpler fixed wooden bridge but amid a similar crowd. Source: *Belizean Studies* 8:1 (January 1980): 10.

FIG. 3. Queen Street Baptist Church in 1939. The original church and fence, where Annie Flowers stopped in 1919, were destroyed in the 1931 hurricane but rebuilt on the same spot. Source: Robert Cleghorn, *A Short History of Baptist Missionary Work in British Honduras, 1822–1939* (London: The Kingsgate Press, 1939), frontispiece.

Annie Flowers expressed the prevailing subaltern anger and hope for change in a deeply subversive statement, spoken to the women by the church fence but loudly enough for William Hoar, a white colonial official, to hear from the steps of the police station.[2] Claiming that she was "quite sober, but in a terrible passion," he reported her words to the Riot Commission in September. "The black man have no pluck. The women have to be behind them all the time or else they do nothing; but if they were all like me I would take their [the white men's] wives and daughters and bloody well live with them: that would teach them that this country belongs to the blacks. The next night there is a row my strong arms will shove hat pins in the eyes of the bloody white men, for they have to get out of this town now, and there's one of them standing there." Annie picked up her basket and, as she passed him, muttered to Hoar: "When the ship goes we will know what to do with the white bastards."

If black men would not free the black nation from its colonial shackles, by driving out the white foreigners, then black women, borrowing a sexual aggression constructed as masculine, surely would. Annie Flowers captured the masculine, patriarchal character of colonial authority and imagined black women, rather than the black men who she deemed politically lacking, as its violators. She thus publicly dropped the veil of subaltern unity against the racist colonial order. Outside of the courts, where the authorities adjudicated numerous domestic disputes, such revelations were unusual. Annie, however, had been sorely provoked, in part perhaps by the fiasco of Claude Smith's labor meeting, more likely by the actions of Samuel Haynes.

Haynes, a young Creole officer in the returned contingent, organized a band of fifty loyal veterans on the night of the riot and managed to clear several stores and streets before dawn. He established a surly peace a full day before the marines landed, held a meeting to elect a Contingent Committee, and then led it into a meeting with Governor Sir Eyre Hutson, who agreed to investigate problems with veterans' land grants, separation allowances, and other relief.[3] Although Haynes raised the issue of merchants' price inflation, which was of most intense public interest, particularly to women, he did so not as a black radical and champion of the colony's laboring masses, as the existing historiography would have it.[4] Rather, he expressed the more ambivalent spirit of the established middle-class campaign to end crown colony rule and the Unofficial Majority on the appointed Legislative Council (a majority composed of merchants, landowners, and forestry employers), to revive the elected colonial legislature that had dissolved itself in the face of Mayan rebellion in 1871, and to negotiate with rather than overthrow British authority. In 1930, a decade after he founded Belize Town's United Negro Improvement Association (UNIA) branch and departed for Philadelphia to work for Marcus Garvey, Haynes proudly claimed his role in rescuing white colonial authority in July 1919. "If the truth were told, it was I whose appeal to sobriety and reason saved the handful of Europeans in Belize from a savage massacre when the returned soldiers rioted in an orgy of rum in the summer of 1919 . . . I rose to the occasion and silenced the radicals."[5]

Samuel Haynes and Annie Flowers imagined two different nations in 1919 and two different ways of achieving them. Hers was the angry black protonationalism of the rioters, hazily defined but clearly popular, while his was the hedged patriotism of the Creole middle class. Hers was the most ideologically developed expression of an uncoordinated but wide-spread wave of popular frustration with the hierarchies and exclusions of the colonial order during the 1910s. It was this fragile oppositional consciousness—not just the presence of the war veterans—that made her radical voice, and the riot, possible by 1919. His was a political strategy dating from the 1890s, when the shock of the 1894 Creole laborers' riot first provoked the middle class to position itself as the colonial state's reformist junior partner. Hers was a nationalism carried by strong women at once proud of their strength and resentful that men's lack of "pluck" necessitated it. He declared the "emancipation of native women imperative," by which he meant that women should volunteer to reinvigorate the campaign for an elected legislature in which men of his class would wield power.[6] As during the riot itself, Haynes prevailed. Annie Flowers's more radical and inclusive politics were silenced and would lurk in the shadows of popular political culture until their resurgence in the deeper crisis of the mid-1930s.

This chapter examines the processes of the 1910s that laid the ground for both the 1919 riot and for the joint state-middle-class reform project of the 1920s that followed. It shows, first, that existing explanations of the riot as caused by male war veterans' overseas radicalization are inadequate. Once we take seriously male and female civilians' presence in the riot, we must seek explanations on the home front that are attentive to questions of gender. That search leads to a second main argument—that during the 1910s, especially during the war, there was continuous but fractured colony-wide popular unrest in which poor Creole women were active. Third, unrest reinvigorated racialized and gendered middle-class anxieties about its political and cultural authority, which were articulated as fantasies of antigovernment "native unity" before the war but as empire loyalty during the war. No hegemonic project of nation formation existed in the 1910s; even those middle-class individuals who publicly embraced a black identity shied away from alliance with the laboring majority. Fourth, the chapter shows that both popular demands and middle-class pressures yielded embryonic state reform prior to the riot, though that shock vastly accelerated the reform process. Finally, middle-class women's participation in war work and early reform expanded their public activism, legitimizing their central role in postriot reform.

The leading historian of Belize in the 1910s, Peter Ashdown, argues that the riot was the product of returning war veterans' radicalized political consciousness of British autocracy and racism, an analysis that ignores political tensions on the home front. In constructing political agency as exceptional and male and in positing that it originated outside the colony, Ashdown reproduces the idea of "the exservicemen's riot," dismissing the civilian mob of men, women, and children as mere looters with no political agenda.[7] He agrees with Governor Hutson's view that "the only serious grievance of the local population was profiteering" but ignores his further comment that "many of the looters were women intent on getting a bit of their own back."[8] The possibility that these women may have shared something of Annie Flowers's radical critique is not considered. In Ashdown's interpretation of the riot, neither women as agents nor gender as an operative social and political dynamic, defining—and defined by—race and class, receive any serious mention. Instead, he regrets that the riot ringleaders did not include Samuel Haynes in their group, assuming that only he could have steered subaltern momentum away from "pointless" looting and toward a black "coup d'etat".[9] Haynes's intent, however, was not to bring down the colonial order but rather to negotiate a transition to responsible government within the colonial framework.

Evidence of the potential for popular movements is more abundant than the existing historiography would suggest, although Annie's explicit anticolonialism was rare. The demands of Mayan *milperos*, Garifuna farmerhousewives, and the Belize Town working class had no organizational connection, but they did focus on a common issue—the abusive economic and political power of the landlord, employer, and merchant class that had dominated the appointed Legislative and Executive Councils since the 1870s and had won an unofficial majority on the Legislative Council

FIG. 4. Garifuna women at Dangriga (then Stann Creek Town), 1911. Source: Walter J. Gadsby, *On the Shores of the Caribbean Sea: Stories of far-off British Honduras* (London: J. W. Butcher, 1911), opposite page 36.

in 1892. In repeatedly calling on British officials to intervene defensively or even effect systemic change, protestors sustained a popular definition of good government and subject-citizens' rights. The gender politics of the communities that produced these demands varied considerably; Creole and Garifuna women were more directly involved in engaging the colonial authorities than were Mayan and mestizo women, whose voices were more strictly mediated by household and community patriarchy. As in the late nineteenth century, poor black women's political assertiveness fueled the imperial assumption that Caribbean and African people were morally, even biologically, disordered and unfit for self-rule.[10]

Rising subaltern protest—particularly its gender and race character—thus jeopardized the middle class's goal of achieving legislative authority through a politics of respectability, as it did for similar groups in other British Caribbean colonies.[11] The prewar years formed a temporary break in Belize's middle-class strategy of alliance with the colonial state, during which time the middle-class press attacked governors Eric Swayne (1907–13) and William Collet (1913–17) as autocratic and, following the achievement of a hard-won municipal franchise for Belize Town, asserted a mythical native unity in swaggeringly masculine terms. But middle-class confidence in popular support for its political leadership melted away as real conflict increased from 1914 on, and the fiction of native unanimity gave way to a renewed emphasis on loyalty to empire and to calls for the colonial state to stem social and political conflict. Collet became a welcome force against the unruly masses, which, at least in Belize Town, were demonstrating an antiwhite political identity. Governor William Hart-Bennett's five-month tenure in 1918 seemed to offer more constructive reform possibilities, but these were not realized until after the 1919 riot.[12]

Wartime state reform mainly consisted in the introduction of compulsory elementary education, an innovation paralleled elsewhere in the British Caribbean in the early twentieth century but that also was a response to local perceptions of youth unrest.[13] Beginning under Hart-Bennett—and coinciding with an accelerating wave of subaltern protest—reform in 1918–19 came to include some price controls and wage increases, a significant effort to deal with the global influenza epidemic, and proposals to diversify the economy away from forestry, making it possible for rural people to produce food by protecting them from rent-gouging and eviction. The belated and insufficient nature of these actions, however, as well as the state's banning of the Garveyite *Negro World*, fueled popular perceptions of state hard-heartedness, and hopes for a middle ground dwindled.

Respectable middle-class women's key role in initiating and cementing the postriot reform alliance had roots in their voluntary war work and service during the influenza epidemic. Propertied women entered the municipal franchise in 1912 without struggle and showed little interest in exercising their voting rights. Middle-class female activism, however, did not depend on the vote and may indeed have gained respectability because of women's distance from municipal elections. Their community-service work—acceptable in gendered terms—yielded political influence after the riot. During the 1910s, then, both middle-class and subaltern women acted politically in concert with men, growing more hostile to each other as class and race tensions heightened.

Belizean political dynamics of the 1910s contrast sharply with those of neighboring Mexico and nearby Cuba but bear strong resemblance to those in other British Caribbean colonies, particularly Trinidad and Tobago. Mexico lost population and prosperity during the revolution of the 1910s, but popular and racially inclusive discourses and projects of nation-state building were created, and women claimed new roles both as *soldaderas* and feminists. Similar processes in Cuba in the late nineteenth century had lost considerable momentum by the 1910s, but the real possibility of "a nation for all" lived on in the popular imagination, and Cuban feminists actively protested women's exclusion from the franchise.[14] Compared to Mexico and Cuba, which were exceptional even within independent Latin America, the British Caribbean was relatively quiet in the 1910s. The first wave of labor organizing, begun in the 1890s, was petering out in most colonies, and even in those with some elected representation the franchise excluded the mass of working people. Demands for political reforms came largely from the status- and race-conscious middle class and seemed calculated to deflect popular interest. Neither universal suffrage nor nationalism were on the table, and not even an elitist form of feminism emerged. While Barbados retained its elected legislature, and Jamaica began to rebuild its elected element in the 1880s, Belize, like Trinidad and Tobago, remained a crown colony. Both colonies spawned middle-class reform groups in the first decade of the twentieth century, and in both cases political struggle focused on gaining municipal elections. These were also the only two colonies in which veterans and civilians erupted into violence in 1919, but postriot repression produced different results: Trinidad's labor movement grew less radical but survived, while the possibilities for organizing labor in Belize withered.[15] And unlike the Mexican Revolution and Cuban War of Independence, which legitimized lower-class Indian and black women as patriotic activists (at least temporarily), the July 1919 riot only stigmatized them more strongly in the minds of officials and native Belizean reformers.

Women's Lives in Wartime

Even if Annie Flowers's exceptionally clear postriot expression of political consciousness was unusual, the wider body of evidence concerning working-class and peasant women points consistently to the fact that they had politicized their roles as household managers, family heads, and often sole breadwinners. By 1919 an antiwhite, anti-imperialist interpretation of wartime hardships was circulating among the working women of Belize Town, giving a newly potent meaning to their customary struggles and frustrations with merchants, landlords, and officials. This section analyzes urban and rural women's initiatives in the colonial economy and courts, showing how these were arenas in which they honed the skills of negotiation and confrontation they would increasingly deploy as political actors as the war dragged on.

Estella and Gertrude Bradley, for example, became the family providers when their father abandoned their mother and four younger siblings, probably in 1914. Perhaps unemployment led Joseph Bradley to surrender this role to his young adult daughters, for by 1915 the number of men hired in the Belize District for forestry work had dropped almost 60 percent from the last prewar hiring period, and wages were down almost 50 percent. The meager prewar income of the mahogany cutter and *chiclero*, habitually reduced through debt to employers, shrank still further. Or perhaps Bradley could only pay rent on his small riverbank farm by withdrawing his monthly ten to twelve dollars from the family. With food prices soaring due to war in Europe and local price gouging, the cost of living rose 300–400 percent during the war. Whatever the reason, Joseph Bradley disappeared, after twenty-three years of common-law marriage to Estella and Gertrude's mother.[16]

The now female-headed family rapidly built up rent arrears to their landlord Dr. Karl Heusner, a white Creole municipal councilor, and the first native physician in the colony's history.[17] The women sought to escape his demands for payment by moving to cheaper lodgings, but Heusner and his clerk Charles Stanley Johnston tracked them down and seized the women's "household furniture [and] stock-in-trade" in lieu of rent, thus preventing them from "carrying out [their] business and depriving them of the profits." Estella and Gertrude engaged the law firm Woods, Slack, and Franco—all three partners of which were Heusner's colleagues in the colony's white elite—and filed suit for damages.

FIG. 5. Estella and Gertrude Bradley's rented lodgings were probably in a more cramped and crowded neighborhood than the one depicted here from 1906. Source: Rupert Boyce, *Report to the Government of British Honduras upon the Outbreak of Yellow Fever in that Colony in 1905* (London: Waterlow and Sons, 1906), plate 7, fig. 13.

Albert Johnston, Charles Stanley's brother, murdered William J. Slack, one of the sisters' solicitors, in January 1916, because Slack had filed suit against him for debt. Heusner was the only prominent man to sign Charles Stanley's huge clemency petition for Albert, a petition with an unusually low proportion of female signatories.[18] Connections between the Bradley case and the petition, the largest of the 1910s, remain unclear, but it is possible that many women refused to help Charles Johnston in his brother's hour of need because he had so recently collaborated with Heusner's persecution of the Bradley sisters. There is no evidence to suggest that women were more sympathetic than men to Slack or to what he represented as the colonel of the Volunteer Force militia: the war and white authority. Estella's and Gertrude's own litigation underscores subaltern women's willingness to confront white masculine power when it endangered family well-being.

Both sisters had owned sewing machines and laundry equipment, suggesting that they worked as seamstresses and laundresses. In addition, Gertrude lost her books and baking pans to Heusner and Johnston. She explained that she was buying barrels of flour on credit, grossing two dollars and netting eighty-five cents a day selling home-baked bread, buns, and sweets. She was also making three dollars a month as a laundress for one Miss Robateau. Even if Gertrude only baked twenty days a month, she would still earn twenty dollars a month, twice the pay of a wartime mahogany cutter, making her a lucrative target for Heusner.

The outcome of Estella's and Gertrude's suit is lost, but their case usefully illuminates the social and economic fabric of working women's lives during the 1910s, particularly as wartime conditions aggravated endemic poverty and unemployment. Even the establishment Creole paper, the *Clarion*, noted in a parody of the Creole vernacular that "De war meck mose a we peachliss wid de hungry and nuttn fe nuttn and bery little fe ten cents." [The war makes most of us speechless with hunger and nothing for nothing and very little for ten cents.] Wartime hardship exposed, particularly among the urban Creole working class, women's customary responsibility for family and social welfare. Census-takers in 1911 had reported women's identities as workers and family heads. One told the enumerator that "my occupation is none. Go and let de Guvna know how I living so dat he can sen' some occupation fo' me." Another insisted that "I is de head of de family," dismissing her husband as a "figurehead" who refused to work. [19] During the war, these roles took on added social and political importance in subaltern female consciousness. Table 1 illustrates the range of female occupations in 1911, the concentration of wage earning in the Belize District, and the importance of farming for Garifuna women in the Stann Creek District. "Domestic duties" meant non-wage-earning women.

Rural people of all ethnic groups struggled to survive in the 1910s, squeezed by diminishing opportunities for male seasonal wage labor in chicle and mahogany or with United Fruit (UFCO) at Puerto Barrios in Guatemala as well as by private landlords' increasing demands for up-front rent payments, which men's wages had normally covered. The powerful Belize Estate and Produce Company (BEC—founded in the mid-nine-

TABLE 1: Female occupations by district, 1911.

OCCUPATION	BELIZE	COROZAL	ORANGE WALK	STANN CREEK	TOLEDO	CAYO
Sugar cane planters				1		
Sugar cane workers		1	1		47	
Banana planters				88		
Banana workers	3			7		
Coconut planters				1		
Corn planters		2				
Corn workers		8	1			
Farm workers	5			3		
Small cultivators	39			295		
Small cultivation workers	8	1	3	37		
Other Agricultural Workers	2				136	
Clerks	51					
Hawkers & peddlers	1					
Hotel & boardinghouse keepers	6			1		1
Shopkeepers	26	3	1	3	1	2
Commercial laborers	1					
Cooks	197	32	60	46	16	3
General domestics	951	78	289	108	27	4
Housekeepers*	241	472	284	76	14	
Maids	147	1		13		
Nurses	37	4		6	1	1
Other servants	92	7		4	2	2
Domestic duties	1560	1026	734	654	946	1289
Music Teachers	6					
School mistresses	5					
Bakers & cake makers	28	7	15	12	6	4
Cigar makers	3	4	10			
Milliners & dressmakers	262	18	32	31	19	17
Other industries	3	6		1	8	1
Chicle laborers	2					
Tailors	2					
Washerwomen	419	84	126	31	26	63
Civil service & government workers	9	2	3			
Organists		2				
Variously employed	11					
Total	4117	1758	1559	1418	1249	1387
Total less domestic duties	2557	732	825	764	303	98

* The category of housekeepers was not broken down by sex, but the vast majority was undoubtedly women. In some cases "housekeeper" may have been a euphemism for "common-law wife."

SOURCE: *British Honduras Census of the Population 1911*, 30–34 (Table 5).

teenth century and owning huge tracts of land—was particularly harsh with its tenants.[20] Farm families managed to increase production of corn, beans, and "ground food"—mainly vegetables and cassava—through men and women devoting more energy to self-provisioning. There was little domestic agriculture to offset the soaring prices of imported food.[21] The urban working class, which had to buy its bread, often from low-profit vendors like Gertrude Bradley, probably suffered the most of any social sector during the war. The price of flour, a staple of the Creole diet, was officially and disingenuously listed at four cents per pound in 1917, at a time when colonial officials were themselves paying nine cents to supply the prison bakery. By May 1918, flour had gone up again, to ten cents per pound. Price inflation encouraged theft: in September 1918 a big shipment simply disappeared, allegedly into the Petén and Mexico, leaving Belize without any flour at all. The *Clarion* worried that the rising price of fish in Belize Town and of food in general in Corozal would drive poor women in particular to immorality and larceny. Innovation was perhaps more prevalent. Although urban women had little opportunity to substitute plantains and corn tortillas for flour, as did mahogany contractors, who used them to feed their workers, they did create such a strong demand for cheap prison-produced coconut oil, as a replacement for expensive imported lard, that the prison authorities received funding to continue processing four thousand coconuts each month.[22] Women's degree of autonomy from domestic patriarchy both necessitated and facilitated their strategies for protecting family welfare.[23]

They could not extend the strategies they had developed to the recently opened arena of electoral politics, for although approximately 20 percent of adult women qualified to vote in the municipal elections of 1912, 1915, and 1918, very few of Belize Town's working women were among them.[24] The voteless majority consisted of domestic servants, laundresses, shop clerks, midwives, government staff including nurses, shopkeepers, teachers, and seamstresses, as well as the numerous household managers—married and single—who baked at home and sent their children out to sell, who provided child care, or who depended on men for survival. Neither Annie Flowers nor most of the women who signed Johnston's 1916 clemency petition ever appeared on a voter list. Women in the district towns and villages had no local elections in the 1910s, but their cash incomes and job opportunities were even more limited than they were in Belize Town.

About seventy years after slave emancipation, domestic service was still the most common job for urban Creole women, especially those with only a few years of primary school.[25] Winifred Flowers, born in 1898, would sell her mother's johnny cakes to hungry shop clerks before beginning her school day. Her schooling ended, and she became "one of the working girls in Belize," minding children, cooking food, and cleaning floors for white people.[26] In 1930, when she was old enough to vote, she did not qualify. The government claimed that domestics made $3–$10 a month as early as 1912, but a large protest petition in 1918 gave a figure of $2.50–$5 a month.[27] Women laboring as private domestics during the war, like Annie Flowers, would have been among the most deprived and the most likely to want "a bit of their own back" from the merchant stores in July 1919. Laundresses probably made little more than domestics, especially in Belize where competition cheapened labor. It took Mrs. Margaret Williams long years of hard labor as a laundress to build the modest home that stood between her and the Poor House in 1916. That same year laundress Florence Bacab of Orange Walk, one of the few female Mayan wage earners of the town and colony, took a Creole laborer to court for the $1 he owed her. In 1920 Mrs. Georgiana Smith was hired at $6.25 a week, less the cost of water, firewood, and soap, to do *all* the Belize Hospital's laundry.[28]

Midwives were equally hard pressed to earn a living and secure payment from clients whose own incomes were shrinking. Three Orange Walk midwives went to court in 1916 to recover $5–$6, the standard fee for delivery and eight days of postnatal care. In Belize Town, 17 percent of legally registered midwives in 1916 qualified to vote the year before, but in all cases this was because of property ownership, not income. The same was true of women shopkeepers. In 1919 just 26 of 137 general merchandise, grocery, and saloon operators were women—7 of them (27 percent) voted in the last municipal elections before the riot, but of these, only Paula Sabido qualified by income in 1915 and 1918. Charlotte Rock and Henrietta Munnings, 2 of 13 female green grocers (15.4 percent) in the

Belize market in 1924, were the only of their group to qualify in the 1910s, both by property rather than income. [29]

None of the above occupations could earn working women enough money to gain the vote unless they already owned property. More importantly, none, as the Bradley sisters' case shows, afforded women without access to male wages security of shelter or food supply. Even seamstresses, some of whom did have incomes high enough to qualify as voters, would have been sorely affected by the tripling and quadrupling of the cost of living. There are known no lists from the 1910s, but the 1925 *Handbook*, written by two civil servants, gives us an idea of seamstresses' economic position. Sixteen of thirty-seven (43.2 percent) seamstresses listed were voters in 1924, twelve as property owners and four by income. The most notable of the latter was Ella Lord, who qualified as early as 1915, the year she was paying $7 a month rent on a house in Albert Street, which she shared with her mother, midwife Diana Gladden. Lord was the common-law wife of barber William Meighan and the mother of his five children, aged 5 to 11, in 1917, when she was in receipt of an army separation allowance because he had sailed in 1916 with the Second Contingent. As a self-made businesswoman, Lord was very different from propertied lady seamstresses. Most of the latter belonged to the circle of established Creole families; three were also piano teachers.[30]

Women, particularly poor women, practiced the arts of confrontation and negotiation in the colonial courts as well as in the struggle for daily survival. Mayan midwives, as we have seen, treated the magistrate as a kind of state patriarch who they hoped would discipline wayward clients. So notorious were subaltern women's verbal conflicts with each other that in 1913 one *Clarion* columnist, intending to amuse middle-class readers, created a story of two women suing and countersuing for abusive language.[31] Indeed, court records for the colony, as elsewhere in Latin America, reveal that subaltern women's solidarity with each other was as contingent a phenomenon as subaltern unity in general.[32]

Court records of the 1910s illuminate two aspects of Annie Flowers's sexualized critique of colonial rule and Creole manhood in 1919. First, highly sexualized discourse was commonplace in subaltern disputes. In a typical police court case, the Belize district commissioner was so appalled by both Sarah Myvett's and Tilla Dawson's language that he threw the case out after reprimanding the women, each of whom brought three female witnesses. In the Supreme Court, Carlotta McLiverty sued her neighbor Nina Hulse for $1000 for defamation of character. Hulse had publicly accused Carlotta of performing an abortion on herself and of sharing a sexual partner with her mother (midwife and voter Ethel McLiverty). Carlotta may have been defending a respectable Victorian sensibility as well as her mother's livelihood. A less European-derived sense of pride and dignity was perhaps at stake in comparable cases among poor folk in northern Belize. In Orange Walk Town, Catalina Chan accused Marciala Ongay of insulting her in the street, calling Teodoro and Maximiliana Uk as witnesses. Ongay countersued. At Bound-to-Shine Bank in rural Orange Walk, Estella Hamilton accused Gertrude Pollard of insulting her, calling Basilia Requena as her witness.[33] The culture of verbal and physical violence among poor women, itself conditioned by gender, race, class, and colonial oppression, played some role, though not necessarily a decisive one, in the development of their political critiques and practices.

Second, Annie Flowers's contestation of native manhood was unusual only for taking the form of an explicit political metaphor. Women of all ethnic groups used the courts to pursue men for child maintenance and to seek justice for insults and assault.[34] The tension embedded in Annie's political insult, between pride in female strength and resentment of men's weakness, is particularly evident in records of maintenance disputes. Even the most independent women risked male violence—rape, assault, murder—when they defied male authority, no matter how that authority was defined ethnically and individually.[35] In Orange Walk, for example, José Guzman hanged in 1913 for stabbing his wife to death in front of their children. When arrested, he said: "What man would allow a woman to get the better of him [?]" Court documents as such inevitably paint an overly strife-ridden picture of any society, but the Belizean records do make clear that gendered conflict and violence were endemic in this society at all levels and in all regions.[36] Annie Flowers's hostility to the colonial authorities and to black men, like the Bradley sisters' refusal to defer to Heusner's white male power, emerged from the context of deep-rooted personal gender conflicts between Belizean women and men of all ethnic groups.

Women's ability to claim middle-class status depended on a combination of occupation, personal wealth and that of their male kin, and education. Only the privileged few attended the colony's two girls' high schools: the Catholic St. Catherine's Academy, founded in 1883, and the Anglican St. Hilda's College, founded in 1897. There they were "finished" as socially accomplished and marriageable daughters of officials, merchants, and landowners through a curriculum emphasizing the liberal arts and languages.[37] No elite feminism brewed among the schools' alumnae, though young graduates may have been the "suffragettes" who in 1913 briefly lobbied for a lowering of women's voting age. Some middle-class women were enfranchised property-owners, like the six private-school owners who qualified to vote in 1921 and the two boarding-house owners who qualified in 1924. Ida Staine's boarding house, where several white officials were staying, was the scene of ugly violence during the riot. Similar was Wilhelmina Temple, who built up her bakery business during the war to such an extent that by 1921 she qualified to vote. But nurses and particularly teachers were also members of the middle class, though their incomes were not much higher than those of some seamstresses and midwives. Many female teachers had only elementary education themselves and had risen through the pupil-teacher apprenticeship system to become qualified teachers. For the lower rungs of the middle-class, respectability and education mattered intensely in distinguishing themselves from the working-class women among whom they lived, shopped, and worked, and with whom they shared exclusion from the municipal franchise.

Until the late 1910s, elite as well as middle-class women confined their public service to church work and friendly societies. Propertied women did not take up the vote with any enthusiasm; after all, they had not campaigned for it. Indeed, of 907 men and 466 women registered in 1912, only 698 (51 percent) bothered to vote. The number of registered women voters in the 1910s peaked in 1915 at 577, but so few candidates ran that year that all were acclaimed.[38] Elite and especially middle-class Creole identities were not constructed as purely "public and male," however, and women were not excluded from "friendly societies, newspaper editorials" or municipal politics.[39] Broadly middle-class and more specifically propertied women may have bought into the politics of masculine political authority during the 1910s, but respectable Creole gender norms had some flexibility even before the war, influenza epidemic, and riot forever politicized women's community service and legitimized their greater public activism. In 1912–13, however, the male Creole establishment was distinctly alarmed by the prospect of increased rights for even middle-class women, let alone their more vocal subaltern counterparts.

On the Home Front, 1912–19

"Native Unity" and Creole Masculine Authority, 1912–13

From 1907 through the end of Sir Eric Swayne's governorship in early 1913, the Creole establishment—both its tiny white minority and its mixed-race majority—articulated through the Legislative Council and the *Clarion* a disingenuous "populist indignation" against the colonial administration.[40] These leading men's anger was incited further by the promotion of Swayne's colonial secretary, William Collet, to the governorship (1913–17). Their hostility echoed the anti-British rhetoric of the early 1890s, when leading Creoles joined forces with the white expatriate elite to protest the dominance of officials on the Legislative Council and won an unofficial majority in 1892. By the late 1890s "brown" middle-class Creoles realized that only the white elite was benefiting from the change. This, combined with their alarm at the 1894 laborers' riot, inspired them to begin courting British officials as allies in hopes of reviving an elected colonial legislature. The strategy of empire loyalty centered on the Battle of St. George's Caye myth that posited unequal but harmonious cross-race fraternity as the colony's central tradition. That myth was neither accepted nor appropriated by the popular classes as a basis for real political inclusion. Middle-class empire loyalty lasted until 1907 when Swayne and Collet attempted to regulate the system of seasonal wage advances. The principal forestry employers and their professional allies reacted by forming the People's Committee (PC) of 1907. At first it was proposed that seven white men—all merchants and professionals—should make it up, but when several prominent "brown" Creoles objected to its nonrepresentational character, publican H. H. Vernon and grocer Wilfred A. Haylock were included.[41] Haylock then spearheaded the committee's campaign to achieve a restricted municipal franchise for Belize Town, a battle won in 1911. Middle-class Creoles greeted the change as the first step toward true legislative empowerment. In the immediate prewar years, then, the Creole establishment was again allied with the white expatriate elite, an alliance fueled by Swayne's and Collet's bias toward the UFCO and the growth of trade with the United States in chicle as well as bananas.[42]

Mixed-race middle-class Creoles did not dominate the Belize Town Board; rather, they again saw their wealthier and whiter colleagues take control. In 1911, when only men could vote, and again in 1912 when propertied women entered the franchise, Archibald R. Usher was elected Belize Town Board chair. Usher was a PC member, an unofficial member of the Legislative Council, leading forestry employer, and recently retired manager of the powerful BEC. Also topping the polls in 1912 were Philip Stanley Woods and William J. Slack. Woods, whose son was married to Usher's daughter, was the owner-editor of the *Clarion* newspaper, which catered to British and elite interests.[43] Slack, a lawyer from Guernsey who had arrived in the colony in 1897, was colonel of the Volunteer Force militia from 1905–16 and would become a leading recruiter for the British Honduras Contingent in 1915.[44] In 1912 these men ran against the less prestigious Independent Association slate, led by Guyanese lawyer Frans Dragten, who in the 1920s would press for legislative elections and represent the UNIA. An equally ineffective working-class opponent of the PC clique was elderly stevedore Simon Lamb, whose Rising Race Committee protested Usher's takeover of the September 10 celebrations in 1912 and his cooptation of the name Baymen's Association. Usher may well have been trying to court the working class through cultural leadership, but he gained no lasting influence; in 1919 he, like Woods, was attacked during the riot.[45]

Leading Creoles' prewar "populist indignation" consisted of a rhetoric of native unity and masculine authority; they never engaged in an actual process of building political alliance across the lines of class, race, and culture. They expressed their heightened sense of masculine dignity and wounded male pride through the *Clarion*, where Woods asserted the press's "aggressive virility" in confronting the administration. For example, his columnist J. V. Thompson, an Antiguan living and teaching in the northern district of Corozal and a resident in the colony since 1890, denounced UFCO's power as "humiliating to our manhood".[46] "Men who are an honour to Manhood" would respect the *Clarion*'s campaign against state neglect and bungling. Thompson even called for his journalistic brothers-in-arms to teach "the all-embracing nobility of Manliness" and thereby "purify and elevate the manhood of the country."[47] But native masculine authority was thrown into question in 1912–13 by factors other than UFCO's power. First was the ushering of propertied women into the municipal franchise. Second was the colonial administration's effort to legalize divorce. Third, and most dramatically, was the abduction by "Indian rebels" of five young Mayan women from the western Cayo district across the border into Guatemala.

Thompson processed each of these crises for the paper's middle-class readership through letters written between two characters he created in mid-1912, Keziah Mimms of the Overpond neighborhood of Belize Town and her cousin Jane Biggs of Cayo. They were poor married Creole housewives with a little Baptist schooling who he endowed with Annie Flowers's political interest and wit but tempered with respect for local authorities. In these letters, Thompson cloaked editorial opinion in the Creole lingua franca of the laboring masses, at the same time mocking them as unworldly and picturesque. Thompson's choice of poor black women as the vehicles for "popularizing" elite native opinion was not accidental. He lived and worked among Mayan and mestizo laborers but knew that Creole characters would be required to amuse and soothe the Belize Town readership. Through Keziah and Jane, Thompson was at once able to capture a real aspect of popular culture—subaltern women's interest in politics—and to domesticate popular political consciousness. Keziah and Jane were nonsexualized creations, unlike early twentieth-century constructions of the Puerto Rican *jíbara*, or white peasant woman, by that colony's literary elite.[48] As the supporters, but never the lovers of leading middle-class men, the cousins reinforced the denial of interracial sex at the heart of the Battle of St. George's Caye myth and certainly did not symbolically reverse historically potent stereotypes of white virginity and black lasciviousness.

Propertied women's municipal franchise was the easiest of the three gendered crises for Thompson to dispose of, for there had been no campaign for suffrage, nor did women register or vote in large numbers. Throughout 1912, the *Clarion*'s editorials and features defended masculine authority through negative coverage of the English suffragettes, mocking them as spoiled rich women without honor or husbands, whose use of violent methods was illogical and scandalous.[49] Just before the formal granting of municipal suffrage, Thompson had Keziah reassure the paper's readers that native women, regardless of class, rejected suffragism as a risky behavior, almost a malignant disease. "De backra hooman da Hinglan da play de juice. Dem go bout de treet da smash glass sash winda and dem husban benk account fe pay lawyer. . . . Dem call crazy backra hooman dem So-flea-git. . . . pray Massa de So-flea-git jome neba come to we poo country." [The white women of England are playing the deuce. They go about the streets smashing glass sash windows and their husbands' bank accounts to pay lawyers. . . . They call those crazy white women suffragettes. . . . pray Master the suffragette germ never comes to our poor country.] [50] Thompson then contrasted the smooth, germ-free entry of women into Belize Town's franchise with British men's inability to control their own women. Turning gendered imperial racism on its head, he cast nonwhite colonial women as the civilized teachers of Christobel Pankhurst and her "crazy backra hooman" in England. "It would not be a bad thing to send a deputation of selected ladies from Darkest British Honduras to teach good behaviour to those enlightened women, who belong to the England that sends us officials that tell us we are not ripe for self-government."[51] Thompson clearly felt that the peaceful inclusion of "selected" ladies in the franchise strengthened the cause of native rights, and he lamented their low turnout for the December 1912 elections.

Approval was contingent, however, on native women simply accepting—rather than claiming—political rights. When a small number of educated young women began suffrage agitation in 1913, Thompson condemned them as silly for demanding what they already had. The brief suffragist stir was otherwise confined to the paper's gossip column, where an unnamed "young lady" was alleged to be discussing suffragism at her tea parties, and the "Belize suffragettes" were mocked and then complimented as "good housewives."[52] If these suffragettes had any serious agenda, it was probably to have their voting age lowered to that of their brothers and beaux, but their playing at politics lasted only long enough to expose the *Clarion*'s conflicted attitude to female political power.[53]

Proposals to legalize divorce apparently threatened Creole masculine authority more seriously, for the *Clarion* took a strong antidivorce editorial line, reprinting a London article that attributed divorce to men's atrophied virility and their women's assumption of domestic power. But there was some popular support for divorce. In the summer of 1912 J. O. Byron Menzies, something of a middle-class eccentric, attracted large crowds to three prodivorce public meetings in Belize Town, the second of which unanimously approved of his position. Thompson countered with the argument that divorce was irrelevant to poor Creole women, perhaps an indirect reference to their low marriage rates and high rates of single motherhood. The scale of popular interest, however, may indicate a politicization of domestic gender conflict by subaltern women, even a plebeian relish at the prospect of respectable men and women airing their domestic troubles in court. Thompson deployed Keziah again, this time to defuse middle-class tension by deflecting domestic disharmony onto the popular classes. "Belize hooman doan gwine wate fe hax backra leef fe lef dem husban and go look fe tarra bass. Fe me part, ah wooden devose Johnny, bekasn who fe say me is gwine fe swap black dawg fe black munkey; de man dem is dat lie-ad when dem come cot'n you." [Belizean women aren't going to wait to ask white men permission to leave their husbands and look for another boss. For my part, I wouldn't divorce Johnny, because who could say I wouldn't swap a black dog for a black monkey; men are such liars when they come courting you.][54]

Thompson indulged in a similar fictional airing of the working class's domestic negotiations at election time in December 1912. By now the divorce debate had fizzled out, although Menzies campaigned independent of any political grouping, claiming "I have the ladies on my side."[55] Thompson, however, portrayed women of the popular classes as more interested in domestic than political power by setting Keziah up to misunderstand the Irish home rule crisis. "When man marrid him mus subjick heself to home rool, and behave heself when he in de house. All day dem hab dem own way too mutch when we watchful eye no pon dem fe kip dem trate; but de minnit dem come in de house dem mus top all dem fool fool manumas ways. . . . De hooman dat caan mek she husban bow he hed to she Home Rool betta she hax mudda fe come lib wid she an laan am how fe rule she husband." [When a man is married he must subject himself to home rule and behave himself when he's in the house. All day they have their own way too much when our watchful eyes are not upon them to keep them straight; but the minute they come in the house they must stop all their foolish ways. . . . The woman who cannot make her husband bow his head to her Home Rule better ask her mother to come live with her and teach her how to rule her husband.][56] Clearly, then, establishment Creoles wanted to prevent women from gaining legal or political rights, except in the form of a symbolic gift that would have no effect on actual power relations.

The Creole establishment used the third crisis as an opportunity to assert a protective masculine authority over the colony's women and to deride the British as weak patriarchs. It was a critique that soon boomeranged on them. In February 1912, five young women from the Mayan village of Bullet Tree Falls in the Cayo district were abducted into the Petén by the Tzul "bandits," led by the notorious Eluterio Hernandez. Thompson had Keziah mock Governor Swayne's and Colonial Secretary Collet's inability to secure the border in a letter to Jane in Cayo: "Wha' de matta wid Guv'na ah' Missa Kallic tall tall! Two-tree Injin da kick up an' prance up ah Cayo; dem go da man house, dribe way him nyoung pickney gal . . . an Guv'na an' Missa Kallic tan da Belize yah da worry pipple wid dem pallytix." [What is the matter with the Governor and Mister Collet at all, at all! Two or three Indians kick up and prance up in Cayo; they go to a man's house, drive away his young daughters . . . and the Governor and Mister Collet stand in Belize worrying people with their politics.] Woods too pinned blame squarely on Swayne: the abducted women and their menfolk became non-racialized citizens, equal in worth to any government officer, their plight the result of "the people" having no voice in government.[57]

Thompson's questioning British masculine competence, strength, and paternal benevolence, was an attempt to displace the memory of the middle class's failure when it had been confronted with a similar scenario in 1907. When the Tzuls "terrorized" Cayo that year, Colonel Slack's Volunteer Force rode out from Belize Town to restore order but got lost in the bush. The Tzuls escaped over the border. Thompson's tactic, however, did not work, since in 1912 and 1913 leading Creole men risked, and got, a repeat of 1907. One of the *Clarion*'s own correspondents mocked the so-called British protection of *both* the "gaily bedecked Police Force and a brilliant city volunteer army [i.e., the Volunteer Force]." In 1913 when Hernandez again returned to Cayo the *Clarion* heralded a renewed Volunteer Force effort as the deed of manly patriots and smeared Swayne as "effeminate." The operation again failed; it was the police who ultimately hunted Hernandez down. The Volunteers then sought to reestablish their military prowess by holding a nine-day camp at the Barracks on the north side of Belize Town.[58]

Leading native men could practice as soldiers, but they could not independently resolve the Cayo crisis, and their masculine authority was tainted by subaltern women's public assertiveness and propertied women's enfranchisement as well as military failure. Indeed, the specific crises of 1912–13 simply underscored the Creole establishment's unmanly political subordination. For all its bellicose rhetoric, leading Creoles were too fearful of both British disapproval and the potential for popular unrest to really go beyond a "stir up in the papers" against Swayne and Collet.[59] Protesting too much, the *Clarion* insisted that the elite *did* have popular support for its honorable struggle for native rights, a struggle in which it *did* shape the political desires of its own womenfolk as well as those of subaltern women and their silent men. But it was no longer amusing or politic to trot out Keziah Mimms; real men and women were beginning to speak their own minds and in their own voices and to act independently of the men who had claimed native leadership without ever building it in civil society.

Rising Popular Frustration and "Empire Loyalty," 1914–17

In November 1915 H. H. Vernon, a member of the People's Committee of 1907 and a respectable middle-class Belize Town Board member, joined the huge crowd thronging the Belize Town waterfront to see off the first British Honduras Contingent. He did not mingle with the masses but headed for the Court House balcony where Governor Collet and other notables were presiding. Two policemen barred his way, but they allowed through several white men whom Vernon deemed to be of lesser standing. Although reluctant to speak about "the colour question," Vernon was angry enough to write to the *Clarion* to protest his humiliation.[60] The "special invitation" required to ascend to the verandah was evidently "a white face." In his protest, Vernon uneasily appealed to both the idea of native unity and the idea that his status was superior to that of the crowd, a tension-ridden discourse that the laboring majority was already beginning to expose.

Vernon was outraged that he, "a native of some standing," sober, financially independent, and "filling positions of honour and responsibility," should be spurned by the white elite with whom he felt entitled to stand above the crowd. Drawing a parallel of racial injustice between his own repudiation and the crowd's rough handling by the police, he conjured up a cross-class sympathy that did not animate his stroll to the Court House steps. His rhetoric of native rights and solidarity included reference to those cultural icons, the Baymen. "[W]e as natives," Vernon exhorted, must make the officials understand "that our ancestors . . . fought for this place, and that it is ours." His hints of racial solidarity and black nationalism were perhaps geared to appeal to brewing popular opinion, but when protest turned violent Vernon and the entire Creole middle class cooled toward the masses and called for imperial loyalty and discipline. They no longer were interested in native unity, let alone black solidarity or anticolonialism.

The *Clarion* became "conspicuously more respectful" to the colonial

administration over the course of Collet's governorship owing to the outbreak of war, the inception of Garveyite politics, and an unorganized but
widespread rise in popular unrest.[61] The last factor in particular, hitherto
unexplored in scholarship on Belize, opens up questions about subaltern
women's political agendas and methods, the gender politics of different
ethnically-defined communities, and that of the Creole middle class. The
data are not abundant but what there is does demonstrate that those with
a stake in the colonial order felt increasingly threatened from below during the war years and suggests that poor urban Creole women were active
participants in and creators of an emerging popular political culture.[62]

Ashdown has characterized the popular challenge of the 1910s as rising black consciousness fostered by local Garveyites, who apparently
knew of Marcus and Amy Ashwood Garvey's founding of the UNIA in
Jamaica in 1914. That year, black reformer Hubert Hill Cain began publishing and editing the *Belize Independent*, always described as Garveyite,
which condemned white oppression and was "exchanged and borrowed
in stores and rum shops."[63] That same year the short-lived Young Belize
Party (YBP) threatened several prominent white citizens, prompting
Collet to push through a law criminalizing antiwhite agitation. The party
soon disappeared. Ashdown's next cluster of conflicts comprises Vernon's
1915 humiliation and Slack's murder in early 1916. The popular antipathy for white men and their war that emerged at that time was again in
evidence in August 1918, when arsonists torched the public buildings and
the people of Belize Town either stood back to watch or actually cut the
Fire Brigade's hoses.[64] Ashdown, however, misses the larger processes of
subaltern unrest and state reform that were at work during these crises,
processes that extended beyond Belize Town and the politically dominant
Creoles and beyond the male and Garveyite political consciousness that
Ashdown privileges. He also oversimplifies the trajectory of elite-popular
relations—elite anxieties did indeed rise in 1914–15, but they were soothed
in late 1915 during the formation of the contingent, only to sharply rise
again over fear of popular unrest with the 1916 murder of Colonel Slack,
after which prewar hegemonic fantasies could no longer be maintained.

Elite fears, fueled by the YBP and *Independent*, erupted in reaction to an early 1915 petition from skilled workmen, asking the government for relief work at their usual wages. The *Clarion* immediately condemned them as selfish and claimed they had been inflamed by "professional agitators," possibly meaning Cain and the *Independent* or even the remnants of the YBP. Luke D. Kemp, who was Cain's "Garvey Eye" columnist in the 1910s, recalled years later that in 1915 the government seized pamphlets promoting self-government and "dealt with" the authors.[65] Whatever the accuracy of his memory, the *Clarion* viewed the workers as pawns of political subversives and admonished them to join in the empire-wide defense effort. "We are all suffering," Woods editorialized, and skilled men should be content with "a living wage and rations."[66] Gone was native unity, replaced by a moral scolding of easily misled and greedy workers.

Elite fears seem to have subsided with labor migration to the districts and by the formation of the British Honduras Contingent beginning in August 1915.[67] Collet envisioned two racially differentiated forces, the first comprising fifty men from the Volunteer Force, which would represent the Creole establishment, and the other fifty woodcutters. "These are a very different class of men," he wrote the Colonial Office, "for the most part they are of a lower grade of life, but they would be exceedingly useful wherever a knowledge of bushwork is required," such as East or West Africa. But the order was to form one contingent, causing Collet to complain that "it is not an easy matter to maintain discipline in an unpaid force consisting of men of different colours, ranging from pure white to almost pure black."[68] When he presented himself to potential recruits not as the King's appointee but as "the representative of the Colony," with a commission from its people, his racism was only temporarily and tactically submerged, as H. H. Vernon's experience at the contingent's departure makes clear.[69]

The Creole establishment, once so critical of Collet, now exhorted support for the war effort through enlistment, grateful belt-tightening, border protection, and food production. Woods rhapsodized about the contingent bringing honor to the colony and then return home, minds opened, as better citizens ready to plant the seeds of progress in their native land.[70] Slack, during his endless series of recruitment meetings, specifically called on the colony's mothers to let their sons go: "I am firmly of the conviction that war does sometimes prove itself to be the cleansing power of humanity. . . . I know some of the mothers who did not want their boys to go. I have had some of you to see me. . . . But that body of that son that you brought into this world, what is the good of it, if it has not got a man's spirit inside it. Will you be satisfied to have a son who shirks his duty? . . . I say it is an honour to these boys to be able to serve their King and their Country. Don't let them hide behind your petticoats. . . . There is still the necessity for men to enlist. . . . [P]rove yourselves at this time that you are worthy sons of those worthy baymen of one hundred years ago."[71] Thompson pitched in by giving Keziah Mimms one last appearance to express her pride as a mother that her son had voluntarily joined the contingent. "Ah . . . tenk de Lawd dat me son is a man an not ah slacka," she wrote to Jane in Cayo, parroting the Creole elite's exhortations to all young men, Creole, Indian, and "Carib," to prove their manhood by fighting for homeland and empire.[72]

The politics of empire loyalty opened up new possibilities for middle-class and elite women's public participation, particularly through voluntary war work. In 1915 Mrs. Violet Slack, wife of William, had as many as ninety "ladies" sewing and knitting for the soldiers and was sending regular parcels of their work to former Governor Swayne's daughter in London. Ladies held musical evenings and cricket benefits to raise money for the war effort. Their work was formalized late in 1915 when Archibald R. Usher, chair of the British Honduras Contingent Society, launched a ladies' auxiliary dedicated to fund-raising, which was still busy a year later. This auxiliary brought together elite wives, like Usher's own, and women who would become leading Garveyites, including Methodist teachers Miss Ann McField and Miss Eva Cain. The women of Stann Creek's merchant elite, Mrs. Bowman, Mrs. Genico, and Miss Josephine Kuylen, put on a war fund-raiser, while in Corozal Misses Eledora and Carmita Romero, Angela Rosado, and Maria Aragon, all from merchant families, knitted socks under the supervision of the local nuns. Even in Benque Viejo on the Guatemalan border, the daughters of the town's tiny nonlaboring class did war work through the Red Cross branch run by Pallotine sisters. The

FIG. 6. The Benque Viejo Red Cross group in 1915. Source: *Belizean Studies* 5:1 (January 1977): 13.

señoritas, in white boots and embroidered white dresses, included Vicenta and Agripina Castellanos, Florita Mendez, and Euphemia Coleman.[73]

Fears of subaltern unrest were renewed and exacerbated with the January 1916 murder of Colonel Slack and the popular support for Slack's murderer, Albert Johnston, which was articulated in antiwhite terms. "Some, it was said, believed this 'foul murder' a 'brave act' while others were insisting that [World War One] was a 'white man's war' . . . "[74] The *Clarion* perceptively warned that such sentiments were widespread and gaining ground through subtle changes in subaltern behavior: "We could give many instances of the same spirit manifested in threats, in curses and averted looks directed against those who for some reason or indeed for no reason have incurred displeasure. We fear that a very considerable portion of this community entertains such feelings, are not slow in giving expression to them, and are, we very much fear, gaining adherents."[75] Elite fears intensified when the head of the colonial medical service was stabbed to death in April by a psychiatric patient.[76]

As related above, Charles Stanley Johnston, Albert's brother and Karl Heusner's clerk, gathered 650 signatures in a clemency petition after Albert was sentenced to death.[77] The petition itself was of course pitched to the authorities in the most respectful terms, but its very scale speaks to the potential for opposition to the politics of empire loyalty. Notable among the men who signed were William Henry Arnold, organizer of a large 1918 proreform petition, and Claude Smith, who sought to organize labor in the aftermath of the 1919 riot. That only thirty-five women signed may have been due to Charles's involvement in persecuting the Bradley sisters or simply because the organizers had opted for a strategy of seeking only male petitioners. Of the thirty-five women, six were voters, one of them market vendor Henrietta Munnings, another baker Wilhelmina Temple. The majority had Creole names—Craig, Gabb, Pattico—but there were also a Rosita Romero and three women who were probably Garifuna: Mary Avilez and Daisy and Marie Lopez. Though Collet rejected the petition's argument of insanity, and Albert Johnston hanged, the authorities may well have noted with worry the increasingly panethnic character of unrest.

Antiwar sentiment seems to have continued into the summer of 1916. Weeks after the rejection of the clemency petition, Superintendent of Police Robert Wyatt feared "the biggest riots that Belize has ever seen," owing to conflicts between the townsfolk of Belize and the men gathering to sail as the Second Contingent.[78] Civilians, Wyatt reported, were "thoroughly incensed" by several soldiers' attacks on them. Dr. James Cran, Slack's replacement as commanding officer of the Volunteers—renamed the Territorial Force—retorted that the source of the problem was police and civilian insults to and interference with soldiers. Wyatt was no alarmist, so his apprehension suggests that the conflict was indeed serious.[79] It seems plausible that antiwar antiwhite sentiment had led to popular anger toward the men volunteering to serve the empire.

The Johnston controversy and the clashes between recruits and civilians in Belize Town erupted during a period of renewed border trouble in Cayo.[80] Rebels opposed to Guatemala's President Estrada Cabrera seized the Guatemalan border post, Plancha de Piedra, at the end of April, but were soon driven back into the Petén by Estrada's troops. The latter then received an arms shipment purchased by Cayo merchant and Guatemalan consul J. A. Massiah and brought to Benque Viejo, on the Belizean side of the border, by a Territorial Force guard. British officials were alarmed enough to patrol the Benque-Cayo road, where they rounded up a few men, and in May the colonial secretary asked the district commissioner to assess local support in Cayo for the rebels. That loyalties were in doubt is not surprising. Pablo Guerra, the *comandante* of Plancha, was the leading resident and merchant of Benque Viejo, while British and Creole merchants in Cayo suspected ethnically Lebanese merchants Habet and Sabala of supplying the anti-Estrada rebels. Fighting went on in the Petén all summer and flared up again in October and November, when the district commissioner feared an attack on Benque's stores. As in 1912–13, the *Clarion* celebrated the manhood of the Creole volunteers but now in the idiom of empire loyalty. Specifically, the militia's success in delivering the arms shipment inspired several egregiously bad poems. One had a "Britisher" entering an Indian village dance and throwing a rowdy Mexican who challenged British sovereignty across the border. Another dwelt on the volunteers' strict orders to stay inside the colony and their willingness to fight "any old side of the frontier line." It also constructed Cayo as the home front of World War One: "We watched the Mopan like the watch on the Rhine."[81]

In September 1916, after the Second Contingent had left and during a lull in the Cayo troubles, Garifuna men loading UFCO bananas onto trains in the Stann Creek Valley went on strike for higher wages.[82] It was a brief stoppage, and not taken seriously by management, but it was one more indication that popular unrest extended beyond Belize Town. Northern Belize District and southern Orange Walk District, an ethnically mixed area of small farms and mahogany works, was another site of subaltern contestation of class, race, and colonial power in 1916 and 1917, one where women took a direct role in defending family welfare. Claude Smith's advocacy on behalf of poor farmers evicted for squatting had resulted, he said, in his framing for the theft of five tons of logwood from Sarah Faber, the landowner in question.[83] Faber's nephew, William Cadle Price (father of future nationalist leader and prime minister, George Price), and lawyer J. J. Franco were persecuting Smith in order to derail his advocating for the over one hundred people evicted. His imprisonment, he claimed, was entirely due to his having "befriend[ed] the oppressed" and having opposed "the trampling of the poor" and the squashing of "the liberties and rights of Citizens."

Smith's antielite and nativist discourse parallels that of one of his clients, Mary Hormbay, who petitioned Collet herself for aid after her family's fields were destroyed in the eviction process. Hormbay described herself as "a poor and needy helpless woman," the mother of four "poor distressful unfortunate little children," and the wife of a man whose family had been farming a piece of Faber's land since 1848.[84] Her pleas of poverty and invocation of motherhood were classic petitioning strategies; more interesting is her self-description as "born and bred in this Colony," a phrase that echoes Smith's talk of citizen rights. Hormbay was beginning to articulate a politicized native identity and claiming a right to government aid on that basis, not simply as a victim.

By mid-1917, the *Clarion* was reacting to popular unrest in two distinct ways. First, Woods began to publish the police court proceedings, thus painting the culture of the urban working class in unflattering terms by exposing its petty disputes. This reaction corresponded with Collet's introduction of compulsory education in 1915 in Belize Town and his formation in late 1917 of a committee to plan for a reform school, both prompted by a perception of juvenile delinquency in popular Creole culture.[85] But the *Clarion*'s second innovation was to begin to incorporate rural people's demands for secure land tenure and food production into its discourse of empire loyalty. In an editorial titled "Let us be Men," Woods constructed import substitution as part of the war effort: "We also in British Honduras are at war. . . . [L]et us bear our trials like potential heroes."[86] He even published a letter from Corozal advocating rent-free land tenure for the war's duration.[87] Inside the colonial administration, too, voices in favor of policy change were beginning to be raised. The Medical Department's 1917 report implicitly criticized BEC's insistence on up-front cash payments of annual rent by noting the severe food shortages in Orange Walk Town that year.[88] In 1918–19, however, conditions and conflicts would worsen, first drowning out but ultimately legitimizing such reformist voices.

Acceleration, 1918–19

Parallel with the global wave of popular rebellion linked to the Bolshevik victory in Russia and frustration with World War One but most immediately inspired by local cost of living issues, a wave of protest petitions flooded into the governor's office in 1918. Rural petitions came from every district. First was a collective one from the largely Mayan villages of Yo Creek, Guinea Grass, San Lazaro, Trinidad, Chan Pine Ridge, and San Miguel, all in the north.[89] Fully 142 *milperos*, all men, signed on to protest BEC's rent demands, gaining support from the district commissioner, who feared that harsh conditions would drive the peasantry across the border into Mexico. Quickly informed by officials, BEC's manager characterized the Mayan farmers as lazy, destructive, and willfully refusing to pay rent, a representation that persuaded the government not to intervene. Although the superintendent of the Botanical Station, who read the petition, regretted "that this misunderstanding should have occurred at this time when all the corn for food is urgently needed," his idea of teaching this "common ignorant class of men" the rudiments of crop rotation was rejected. Indeed, the farmers who petitioned in the name of British justice in 1918 were by 1920 selling their corn across the border to Mexican chicle gangs, leaving Orange Walk Town starved for tortillas.[90] In this case, typically, Mayan men acted as community and family representatives, and their womenfolk's influence over the timing and content of the petition remains buried in the archives. Women who were, as we have seen, willing and able to take each other, their husbands, and their debtors to court, did not engage directly with the state on matters of community interest. Family and community patriarchal authority was surely negotiated among the Maya of northern Belize, but men's role as official community representatives was intact.

With Governor Hart-Bennett's arrival in April 1918, small farmers' hopes of government aid were raised.[91] The Northern River Planters' Association, from the Belize District, applied to purchase 330 acres for family farms, to grow rice, beans, and plantains. At the same time, two small planters wrote protests that were couched in class terms. Alexander Bailey had lost all his plantains to a wealthy mahogany contractor, who ordered his foremen to strip the trees to feed his workers, while Daniel Brewster had had his bananas rejected by the UFCO. Bailey petitioned so that the authorities "may see what the rich does with the poor," while Brewster pointed out that "we are suffering very bad. . . . Sir, I enclose contract and beg for justice for I think you is the one . . . who . . . will give justice to the poor."[92] Evidently Hart-Bennett's reputation as a benevolent patriarch was well earned. Just after his death, the Sibun River Union of farmers wrote the government to mourn his passing, reminding the acting governor of Hart-Bennett's promise to connect them to the Belize consumer market by road or canal.[93]

Many urban petitions in 1918 demanded wage increases. One of the earliest was all-female, from six pupil nurses, whom Dr. Thomas Gann, the principal medical officer, supported, observing that they were overworked and underfed. The government's ultimately positive response to their petition came under Hart-Bennett and after months of bureaucratic delays.[94] Next came the first groups of war veterans, who returned home to high unemployment and official reluctance to grant them farmland owing to the spurious belief that Creole men could not do agricultural work.[95] On the heels of their protest, the leading clergy of all denominations petitioned for increases in teachers' salaries to compensate for price inflation.[96] Late in the year, just as the mahogany gangs were returning to town, the police demanded a pay hike. Just as Gann had supported his pupil nurses, so Superintendent Wyatt backed the constables, arguing that their pay of $20–$30 a month was insufficient to keep a family fed, clothed, housed, and out of debt. He recommended a minimum of $40 a month.[97] This family wage did not apply to female government workers. Poor House attendant Catherine Savery petitioned for a pay hike from $8 a month, which Unofficial Archibald Usher decried as "hardly a living wage. . . . I have often wondered how she manages to subsist." Usher and his fellow appointed legislators granted her a raise to $12 a month, which presumably put their minds at rest.[98]

Other petitions called on the government to regulate merchants' inflated pricing of staple foods, particularly after the establishment of the Food Control Commission (FCC) in January 1918, which had an obvious bias in favor of merchants.[99] Residents of Corozal Town, sixty-seven men and twenty-four women, complained that local merchants were charging "unjust and unfair" prices, and asked the FCC to fix prices.[100] In Cayo the district board decided on its own to do just this.[101] In Punta Gorda a delegation of Garifuna men met with the district commissioner to protest prices; he lectured them about merchants' hardships and their own laziness.[102] In Stann Creek, Garifuna and Creole carpenters dealt with the cost of living crisis by demanding employment on local public works. They based "the justice of our claim" on their status as ratepayers to the district board.[103] While their claim to this identity fell short of a citizen consciousness, it did imply a right to expect government responsibility and fairness.

These two demands—for agricultural development and cost of living controls—informed the political analysis of the large petition that landed on Governor Hart-Bennett's desk in May 1918, signed by 365 men and 82 women of Belize Town. "No man or woman knows his or her master when they are hungry," the petitioners cautioned, "it is no use talking about vital rights and do nothing. . . . The more the matter is delayed the more serious and dangerous the situation grows."[104] Led by handyman William Henry Arnold, the petitioners—among whom the authorities could find no influential people—seem to have come from the largely Creole lower middle class and "upper echelons" of the working class. Significantly, they identified themselves as "natives and citizens" as well as "your labouring people." To prevent impending chaos, the petitioners demanded that existing "unofficials"—merchants and employers like Usher—be removed from the Legislative Council and replaced with "men that . . . [would] look after the rights of the people of this community," employed and unemployed. They accused the elite unofficials of wielding their legislative majority to keep wages low and prices high and to retard agricultural development, particularly food production. Arnold and his petitioners urged Hart-Bennett to preempt the horrifying but all too likely possibility of popular rebellion by curbing the "more than equal rights" of the men who ruled as merchants, urban and rural landlords, forestry employers, and appointed legislators.

A more cogent critique of the Unofficial Majority and its self-interested economic policy could hardly be imagined. Yet the petitioners, evidently fearful of the popular classes, did not question the fundamental legitimacy of colonial rule. They articulated no cross-class native let alone nationalist identity and called for electoral reform, not universal suffrage or self-government. Caught between an increasingly restless majority and the traditional politics of the colonial elite, the middle class welcomed the reformist, even populist Hart-Bennett as their salvation. Just as predictably, Arnold and his colleagues had no organized response when ameliorative policies fell short.

The arsonists who torched the public buildings on the evening of Saturday, 18 August, were certainly aware that the entire elite of the colony—officials and natives alike—was attending a charity auction and sale for the Red Cross at Government House, hosted by Miss Hart-Bennett, the governor's sister. When the alarm sounded, the governor and other leading men rushed to help the fire brigade; Hart-Bennett was fatally injured in the process. The crowd and even the police were indifferent to the fire. Some cut the fire hoses while "a number of women" looted a store with impunity. The *Clarion* labeled these actions "Hunnish"—i.e., anti-British—and called on the government to repress the "dangerous and ugly spirit abroad. . . . How many more lessons does this Government want before it takes steps to bring about reform?"[105] Systematic reform foundered with Hart-Bennet's death, though the arrival of influenza soon after prompted an ad hoc reform effort that proved historic for middle-class women.

When the global influenza epidemic hit the colony in late October, the government swiftly appointed a committee, composed of conservatives J. J. Franco, Archibald Usher, and Dr. Gann, wealthy Garveyite coconut planter Isaiah Morter, and the clergy, and called on both elite "ladies" and middle class "women" to volunteer.[106] Clearly women's war work had legitimized an expansion of their traditional church-based charity. The death toll was very heavy in the north, particularly in Mayan villages, where a Mrs. Parsons was nursing the sick, and in Corozal Town, where Gann was seeing one hundred patients a day.[107] The acting district commissioner of Corozal accused merchant Manuel Romero of hoarding arrowroot, used to feed patients, and then selling it at "extortionate" prices. Other merchants were doing the same with tinned milk.[108] The official pleaded for the FCC to immediately fix the price of arrowroot. In Belize Town, the first indication of the epidemic was the closure of the prison workshops on 2 November, for both inmates and warders were infected.[109]

Headed by Usher, the Influenza Committee quickly chose two middle-class Creole "ladies" to hire a brigade of "women" to pay house calls. These were Miss Eva Cain (Mrs. Usher's associate in the BHCS's auxiliary and future UNIA leader) and Mrs. Wallace, probably the seamstress and voter Sarah Wallace. They recruited sixteen women, who were paid the handsome sum of one dollar per day to locate the sick, do their housework and laundry, bathe them, and empty their slop buckets. Three of the women were voters, two by property and one by income. Another, listed as Ann Flowers, might have been the same Annie Flowers who less than a year later would demonstrate such a sharp analysis of gender, race, and power in colonial society.[110] If Cain and Wallace operated as these women's class superiors, they in turn were distinguished from the elite "lady workers" who volunteered at the two relief depots, handing out food to the healthy relatives of the sick who had been provided with certificates by the clergy.[111] The physical intimacy of the paid recruits with the sick could not contrast more sharply with the distance maintained by the volunteers; Cain and Wallace mediated between the two racially-defined extremes of the colonial class hierarchy.

The epidemic had barely died out in early 1919 when a renewed cycle of labor demands, political tensions, and mix of state reform and repression began. Most importantly, Acting Governor Walter banned the importation of Garvey's *Negro World* in January, and two thousand copies were seized at the post office. This prompted Hubert Hill Cain to lead a protest deputation, which Walter met with but did not yield to. Copies continued to be smuggled in through Mexico and Guatemala, however, so that Annie Flowers may well have read the February issue, which attacked colonialism and referred to all colonies as "the property of the Blacks."[112] Indeed, her desire for a completion of the riot's assault on the colonial order is suggestive of an ephemeral but popular Garveyite consciousness.

Sir Eyre Hutson took over the governorship in March and soon rein-
stated the process of ameliorative reform, raising the Medical Department
staff's salaries, hiking the chicle tax to generate revenue, and proposing
extensive public works and agricultural development, including road-
building.[113] Perhaps seeing in him another Hart-Bennett, laborers on the
Stann Creek railway and the Sibun road works appealed to Hutson for
increased wages.[114] The Manatee Planters Association was explicit about
this: Hart-Bennett had encouraged the farmers to join together, and now
they hoped Hutson would "take our Association under your fostering
care."[115] Both groups of laborers received pay hikes, while officials prepared a plan and budget for granting land to the association.

The government's efforts to meet returning veterans' demands after 8
July were far less successful. Veterans were greeted as heroes, welcomed by
the people and fêted by the establishment Contingent Welfare Committee.
But their expectations of land and cash grants, wage levels, and even back
pay were disappointed, although the government issued emergency wages
to them on 10 July. That same day the middle-class Creole men of the
British Honduras Elective Representative Association (BHERA), launched
in April by Frans Dragten, held a meeting to discuss the expansion of political rights.[116] Although the BHERA excluded expatriate whites, most veterans distrusted it. On 12 July a Sergeant Vernon led a deputation of veterans
to see Hutson, protesting the recent hiring of British clerks in several big
merchant stores. During the next ten days Cain's *Independent* reported on
antiblack attacks in Britain and condemned the Hutson administration's
tolerance of racism in Belize, while veterans displayed increasing dissatis-
faction at military parades and expressed open anger when offered $1.25
per day relief wages at a meeting on 21 July.

Charles Sutherland was one of the veterans whose anger at British racism within the army and colony reached a boiling point between 8 and
22 July.[117] Sutherland left with the Second Contingent in 1916, a respectable artisan, Anglican, and married father of two. According to testimony
given in 1920 by his then estranged wife Susan Sutherland, he brought
home gonorrhea and radical antiwhite politics from the Middle East. He
hosted meetings in their rented home where the riot plot was hatched, at

the same time insulting and threatening her for refusing sexual relations. Expressing his rage as an oppressed black man and colonial subject, "he said he had not come to stay. He was going to Africa—I said I was not going with him. He said he was going to Africa because he was going to get even with the white sons of bitches for all they had done to him at the Front. We had a quarrel over that." Charles planned to write a book about his treatment in the Middle East but more immediately cooperated with others in planning the attack on elite property and persons.

It was contingent men who began smashing merchants' plate glass windows on the night of 22 July, but they "soon became intermingled [with] and dispersed among the throng of their adherents."[118] As Sergeant Vernon himself exhorted the crowd, "the civilians are with us and we are with the civilians."[119] It is clear that the working women of Belize Town were among those civilians, as they had been in the 1894 riot. The riot commissioners themselves repeatedly referred to the crowd as "men, women, and children," and when Archibald Usher ventured out to read the Riot Act, he addressed it likewise to "men, women, and children."[120] Police Sergeant Major Blades, who had collared Albert Johnston in 1916, testified that the crowds were "composed of men, women, and boys, and a few Contingent men."[121] At Brodie's store there was a crowd of four hundred, which "seemed to be against the merchants. . . . I heard the remark several times, 'white son of a _____.' Most of the time it was coming from boys and women."[122] Women who had gone penniless and hungry since 1915 were indeed "getting a bit of their own back," as Governor Hutson testified.[123]

Significantly, Claude Smith's 25 July laborers' meeting was advertised on 22 July, on posters put up all over town, to men, women, and children of "the labouring classes."[124] A gender-inclusive community rebellion had suddenly created the possibility of not only a labor movement, but one that might recognize women as workers and family heads and see the connections between wages, prices, and consumption. No wonder that Annie Flowers was bitter the next morning about Samuel Haynes's invigoration of reformist middle-class politics. Instead of postriot labor organizing, the people of Belize got a state-run Labour Bureau, catering only to war veterans and paying only twenty-five cents per day. Poor women, instead of taking their place in an anticolonial labor movement, were reduced to petitioning for outdoor relief at $1.00 per week.[125] Nigel Bolland's conclusion that the postwar British Caribbean had strong labor consciousness but weak labor organization rings especially true of Belize.[126] Charles Sutherland, jailed with his fellow ringleaders through much of 1920, also lost political momentum. From jail he accused a prison guard of having seduced Susan, causing her to live "in bigamous adultery." Emphasizing his financial support for his children, Charles constructed himself as a good father not in the rebellious language of the riot or popular mobilization but in terms of the conventional morality of the colonial order.

Neither black men nor black women freed the nation from its colonial shackles in July 1919. Indeed, the very idea of a Belizean nation was ill-defined, for the elite and middle class had continued to blend patriotism with empire loyalty, and popular protest was primarily geared toward eliciting paternal care from the colonial state. Yet as individuals and communities demanded state action, they developed a popular articulation of native and citizen rights, particularly rights to make a living and sustain their families. Working-class women, particularly of the urban Creole community, were central to this process. The subaltern protests and violence of the 1910s prompted the middle class, too, to look to the state for reform. Prewar middle-class fantasies did not develop into a real hegemonic project in the 1910s, but state-led reform breathed its first shallow breaths. The outburst of enraged black womanhood and manhood was very far from bringing colonial rule to an end; instead it shocked the colonial order to its foundations, making expanded and accelerated reform imperative. The riot burned, flaming with the anger of women and men who were beginning to imagine their own nation, but burned out, damped down by the respectable class and colonial authorities that dared not let that vision live.

Annie Flowers came very close, on that distant Saturday morning, to imagining *herself* as the sexual/political violator of white women, a "virago" compensating for the allegedly weak masculinity of her male allies. In the 1910s, no elite women, white or Creole, had evinced any interest in questioning their own class interests or indeed the culture of respectability that continued to frame their public activities. For elite and especially middle-class women, their quiescence may have been due to their men's willingness to expand that frame. Enfranchised in 1912 without struggle, then praised for their war work and service during the influenza epidemic, they did not have to fight their way out of a strictly defined domestic arena. The riot, unlike Annie's vision, did not see the bodies or authority of such women violated. On the contrary, it brought respectable women, particularly of the new Garveyite movement, into the streets and homes of poor neighborhoods as key agents of the postriot hegemonic project. Annie—a real Keziah Mimms and thus much harder to manipulate—would have to wait fifteen years for another crack at the colonial order and color-class hierarchy that underpinned those female reformers' public authority.

2 A Fragile Peace

*Colonial Reform, Garveyism, and
the Black Cross Nurses, 1920–1930*

In late 1919 and early 1920, the colonial administration disbursed close to
$1,000 to the Belize Town Board to pay a bounty on each mouse or rat
brought in by the public. The Rat Destruction Campaign was hugely successful, with about thirteen thousand animals bagged between November
1919 and February 1920. Despite grumbling from the political elite, the
bounty was raised from five to ten cents per animal in January, and not
until early May did Governor Hutson order the campaign over.[1] It had
been a strategy for promoting urban sanitation, but it was also a cleverly
disguised form of public assistance to the urban poor during the postriot
period of martial law. Assuming many rat catchers were young, it also
addressed the Riot Commission's perception of "increasing lawlessness"
among the colony's rising generation. This was the period during which
the authorities jailed the riot ringleaders, including Charles Sutherland,
and repressed their supporters. These were also the months during which
"prominent middle-class black Creoles" organized the Belize Town local
of the UNIA, and the associated Black Cross Nurses BCN branch.[2] Hutson,
though initially wary of renewed rebellion, soon allied with Garveyite and
other middle-class reformers in confronting the political and economic
elite's opposition to structural change. The Nurses in particular became
key state allies. The twin innovations of the 1920s—the activist alliance
between a reformist state and middle class and the acceptance of women
reformers as legitimate public actors—strengthened and defined each
other. Garveyism contributed to both but otherwise remained wedded to
the paradigm of lobbying for an elected colonial legislature.

Reformers had a genuine zeal for the project of improving living standards, indeed had hegemonic intent, but proved unable to build any strong or transformative connections with the colony's popular classes in the 1920s. Hutson's purpose was to answer some of the popular classes' grievances through economic modernization—specifically agricultural development—and a more interventionist social policy that would position the state as benevolently paternal. With no funds available from Britain, he pressed for increases in land, property, and income taxes, as well as export duties, but of course faced the powerful opposition of the merchant-employer-landowning class, especially in the Unofficial Majority on the Legislative Council.[3] By working with middle-class reformers as well as progressive colonial officials, he tried to bring a measure of public pressure to bear on this elite. Hutson's successor, Sir John A. Burdon (1925–31), aligned with the existing oligarchy on economic policy but approved ongoing efforts in public health and juvenile reform. Throughout the decade, middle-class groups allied with state reformers to prevent any recurrence of the 1919 riot and to break the elite's monopoly on political power. They sought enough connection with the popular classes to give them legitimate claim as native representatives but not so much as to foster popular organizing that might turn autonomous, discrediting middle-class claims to social leadership and political rights. Women reformers specifically positioned themselves as maternalist uplifters of poor mothers—a role geared to confirming middle-class cultural and political fitness—but developed no cross-class discourse or practice of black female solidarity or sisterhood.

The weakness of 1920s reform as a hegemonic process, then, stemmed from its proponents' *conscious* refusal to deal with the popular classes as rights-bearing political subjects or to address basic economic inequalities as well as their inclination toward moral judgment. This chapter illustrates this weakness by analyzing the decade's three main reform thrusts: constitutional (to make the Legislative Council partly and narrowly elected), cultural (to reinvigorate the September 10 celebrations of the Battle of St. George's Caye myth), and social. It also explores Garveyite men's and women's politics in each. Indeed, the prominence of the Black Cross

Nurses, and of the social reform arena in which they were so active, is suggestive of the maternalist, paternalist, and in some respects eugenic character of the state-middle-class alliance as a whole. Social reform took off, yielding sanitation, maternal and infant health promotion, compulsory education, and juvenile rehabilitation, but a parallel effort in labor reform was critically absent. Unions remained illegal, and middle-class reformers including Garveyites did not press for labor rights, hoping instead to forge legitimate leadership over the laboring majority in the three arenas outlined above. Hutson, whose tenure coincided with the postwar trade depression, opened a Labour Bureau and provided relief work but only for war veterans; other than that all he did was assign the superintendent of police to give him a weekly report on unemployment levels in Belize Town.[4] Burdon, who presided over an export boom with record male employment levels through 1929, could afford to ignore labor issues.

The cost of ignoring "the labor question," as Frederick Cooper and others have argued, was an inability to contain the wave of labor unrest that swept the empire in the 1930s. Only in its wake did British colonial policy embrace trade unionism as a controlling measure and only then did native Belizean reformers follow suit. By contrast, in other British Caribbean colonies some middle-class progressives sought to organize labor much earlier. A. A. Cipriani in Trinidad and Tobago and Charles Duncan O'Neale in Barbados are important examples, not least because each enjoyed some Garveyite cooperation. Belize not only produced no popular or middle-class led union in the 1920s, but it also fell behind as other colonies, notably Trinidad and Grenada, gained elected legislative representation. In Guyana the late imposition of crown colony rule in the 1920s was balanced by the relative strength of the labor movement. These labor movements were not free of paternalism, but they created possibilities for popular claims to equal rights that the Belizean reform project consistently denied. Cipriani's Trinidad Workingmen's Association, for example, maintained popular support and a progressive legislative agenda, even as it grew more moderate and less representative of the working class.[5]

The Belize UNIA's disinterest in labor confirms the view that its conservatism earned it "a respectability unmatched in any other colonized country during the 1920s."[6] Much of the existing scholarship on the early Garveyite movement gives the strong but erroneous impression that the founders of the colony's UNIA in early 1920 were the same people who led the July 1919 riot, thus painting the UNIA as a radical and popular movement. Its leaders had signed up 832 members by the time of its inauguration in April 1920, and by January 1922 had built a Liberty Hall, which opened that month with an industrial and craft exhibition, an event repeated in 1923. But the leadership emphasized racial uplift through education, the pursuit of a limited legislative franchise, and the celebration of the 10th. It eschewed labor organizing and explicitly disavowed political sedition. As a result of these politics as well as financial disputes, the UNIA soon went into decline and was little more than a small fractured friendly society by 1930. The leadership invited Hutson to the 1920 inauguration, but he declined, viewing Haynes as "a troublesome agitator and very intimate with the editor of the 'Independent' [H. H. Cain]." Nonetheless, when Marcus Garvey visited the colony in July 1921, Hutson was willing to meet with him. He stated his support for the UNIA's efforts to "promote the material, social and educational advancement of the people of the Negro Race so long as such movement proceeds by proper and loyal methods." Garvey in return proclaimed himself a loyal British subject. He also took Haynes back with him to the United States; at his send-off both British and Ethiopian anthems were played.[7]

Hutson singled out the Black Cross Nurses as an example of acceptably loyal Garveyite practice, thus portending their close alliance with the state in the 1920s and beyond. Launched about a month before the UNIA local, the Nurses were the most successful element of middle-class Garveyism, gaining expertise and influence with the state as a small, cohesive, well-trained group of maternal and infant health educators. Led by former teacher Mrs. Vivian Seay, the Nurses moved well beyond traditional female charity work and beyond the role of educated wife/community volunteer that Garvey himself promoted, for their public leadership soon overshadowed their domesticity. They expanded middle-class women's public activism and leadership within the colonial reform tradition, even advocating legal divorce and limited women's suffrage. Yet these accom-

plishments did not threaten colonial, middle-class, or Garveyite masculine authority. Not only were the Nurses loyal colonial subjects, but they
also promoted the male-headed nuclear family and aimed to individually
uplift poor women, not to collectively organize them. Any trace of cross-
class black sisterhood in the Nurses' politics was heavily overshadowed by
their didactic, disciplinarian stance. In addition, their activism jibed with
the officially gender egalitarian structure of the UNIA, with its parallel male
and female executives. Barbara Bair has shown that U.S. Garveyism was
in fact "separate but hierarchical" in practice, fostering female resistance
within the organization, but in Belize the success of the Nurses became
male Garveyites' raison d'être.[8] The Nurses thus faced neither colonial nor
male opposition as they developed their distinctly class-bound maternalist practice in relation to urban working-class mothers.

My analysis of postriot Garveyism leads to the conclusion that no movements involving the popular classes emerged in Belize during the 1920s,
nor were there any mass protests. The peace of the 1920s was nonetheless
fragile. Subaltern actors peppered the state with demands to fulfill expectations of benevolence but withheld support from proposals for narrow
constitutional reform and from state and middle-class efforts to monitor
hygiene and parenting. That surveillance was hardly seamless—reformers'
capacity to respond to commonplace demands was expanding, but it was
far from adequate to the goal of social and labor control. With the onset
of the Depression, the fragile postriot peace shattered. But the patterns of
female reform activism and state-middle-class alliance established in the
1920s endured, defining the rapidly developing contest between colonial
reform and popular nationalism.

Shadow and Substance

The Campaign for an Elected Legislature, 1921–1925

In April 1925 Archibald R. Usher, speaking for his fellow unofficials on the
Legislative Council, explained their vote against constitutional reforms
offered by Britain, reforms that would have maintained the Unofficial
Majority and made it partially elected if in return the Legislative Council

would grant veto rights to the governor. "We are asked to grab at a shadow and give away the substance," he argued, implying that the substance was the voice the "native community" had supposedly enjoyed through the appointed Unofficial Majority since 1892. The shadow was an elective principle rendered meaningless by increased executive powers. Middle-class groups anxious to recover the voting rights lost in 1870 vociferously contested Usher's position and the vote of the Legislative Council, arguing that "half a loaf" was better than none. These groups, however, had little popular support behind them, for during the four years of constitutional discussions leading up to April 1925, they had not tried to organize a mass movement, nor had their proposals for a limited franchise attracted popular interest. Thus, scholars' claims that the unofficials closed the door on reform for fear of "an uncontrolled flood of democracy" conjure an illusory subaltern menace from one phrase in a colonial office document and one Garveyite meeting. While the colony's elite had not forgotten the potential for another riot, in the mid-1920s it viewed the greatest immediate threat to its dominance to be an empowered governor intent on raising taxes to fund social programs and agricultural development. In this section, I demonstrate the middle-class limits of "popular" agitation for representative government, thus illuminating the weakness of state-middle-class reform as a hegemonic project in the 1920s.[9]

Constitutional discussions began in early November 1921 when Governor Hutson's recent appointee to the Legislative Council, progressive lawyer Frans Dragten, revived the idea of the elective principle at a meeting of the newly organized Belize Literary and Debating Club (BLDC). Two Creole civil servants presciently argued against Dragten that without universal manhood suffrage change was pointless. He had an easier time convincing his fellow unofficials, who promptly and unanimously requested the restoration of legislative elections. Simultaneously, the Colonial Office appointed Honorable E. F. L. Wood, parliamentary under-secretary of state to the colonies, to visit the West Indies in order to investigate postwar unrest. His report, published in 1922, opposed all unofficial majorities in the region, elected or appointed, but the Colonial Office was prepared to make an exception in the case of British Honduras, if the governor was given veto powers. This was more than the unofficials had bargained for; their own plan was simply to legitimize their dominance through a carefully controlled electoral process. [10]

In June 1923 the local Franchise Commission held public hearings on the proposed changes. The commission included two executive councilors and two legislative councilors (including Usher)—all four from the merchant-employer class—and, nominally representing the "public," P. S. Woods, H. H. Vernon, and Dragten. A dozen groups and individuals addressed the commission, including the British Honduras Taxpayers Association (BHTA) and H. H. Cain of the *Independent*, though not the UNIA or its political arm, the Progressive Party (PP). The PP first formed to contest the December 1918 Belize Town Board elections, gaining two or three of ten seats, but seems to have then dissolved, cohering again only three years later for the next elections. In late November 1921 it squared off against the new BHTA, headed by Usher and Vernon but also including the Garveyite H. H. Cain on its executive. Despite his presence, the BHTA was hostile to the PP, dismissing its candidates as more ambitious than competent. Notably, at its founding in October 1921, the BHTA leadership seemed to anticipate Dragten's imminent proposal for legislative elections, declaring its goal to be to "educat[e] the people politically so that they may more highly appreciate the small political rights they at present enjoy, and make fuller and better use of them, in preparation for the time when, with some form of Representative Government established, for this must come someday, they will be able to select and support the men best fitted to represent them in the Councils of the Colony." Until then, the BHTA declared itself "empowered by the people to speak on their behalf." The PP took just two seats in 1921, one going to tailor and UNIA leader Calvert M. Staine, who did not participate in the June 1923 public hearing on the franchise.[11]

The BHTA clearly felt that a restrictive franchise was necessary to the process of political education, for it proposed to the Franchise Commission voter qualifications of $360 per year income, $800 in real property or $96 per year in rent payments, and candidate qualifications of $1500 per year income or $2500 real property. Several other presentations to the commission made similar recommendations, though the Chamber of Commerce—represented by George Grabham, manager of BEC—and others proposed much higher voter qualifications. H. H. Cain was the most democratic of those supporting a wider franchise—he recommended $200 per year in income, $500 in real property or $72 per year in rental payments for voters, and $500, $750, and $120 respectively for candidates. He testified that the mahogany cutters were intelligent enough to vote and claimed that the $200 restriction would include them in the electorate, a doubtful proposition. Although all who addressed the commission supported the enfranchisement of women, at twenty-one or thirty years of age, what is most notable is that at this critical juncture the UNIA and PP did not participate, and that although the most democratic voice was that of a Garveyite leader, even he did not support universal suffrage.[12]

The Franchise Commission submitted its recommendations to Hutson in August 1923, opting for high qualifications: $720 in income, $1200 in real property or $120 in rent, for voters, $2000 in income or $3500 in real property for candidates. It also excluded women entirely. Hutson, presumably not wishing to stir up fruitless debate, did not make public the commission's position until June 1924, simultaneously with a draft constitutional bill expressing the Colonial Office's reaction. Following Wood's position, the bill accepted the Unofficial Majority and the commission's high qualifications but included the infamous "clause six" that granted gubernatorial veto powers. The BHTA held a small protest meeting that focused on clause six, but the BLDC and the PP meetings accepted clause six and contested the restrictive franchise. Both groups proposed identical voter qualifications of $360, $600, and $72, and the PP also called for the same qualifications to apply to candidates. Both also included women in the franchise, the BLDC at age twenty-five, the PP at age twenty-one. Critical to Peter Ashdown's argument for popular interest in the entire process is a report of the PP's public meeting on 13 July 1924 where its resolutions were voted on. Attending the meeting were "the labour element in the town, *and* the ones" who could expect to vote under the PP's guidelines. PP leaders Morrel Staine and Henry G. Longsworth described the meeting as "well attended by all classes of the community," but their proposed franchise *excluded* "the labour element," for most working men and women earned well under the $360 bar. There is no evidence that the PP ever held another public meeting.[13]

The BLDC's and PP's counterproposals had no effect on property restrictions in the draft bill, but they did bolster Hutson's efforts to have the Legislative Council amend the bill to include propertied women. Women's participation in politics, he argued at the opening of formal discussions, would be of benefit to the entire colony. The councilors were divided: the attorney general and Archibald Usher moved to include women over thirty but were upstaged by two white expatriates' proposal to enfranchise them at twenty-one. This was too much for P. S. Woods, an acting councilor, who opposed any amendment on the grounds that "a woman's proper place was at home minding the babies and making puddings." But the original motion carried, and wealthy women were included in the revised bill. Clause six was amended to exclude all financial matters from the governor's new authority.[14]

The Colonial Office sent a final bill to Hutson in March 1925, accepting the amendment to include women but rejecting the amendment to clause six. On 5 March, PP leaders Calvert and Morrel Staine spoke at a BHTA meeting, arguing that the restrictive franchise would exclude men of their own tailoring trade as well as carpenters. They did not mention the obvious exclusion of forestry workers. The BHTA endorsed the PP's proposals of the previous year, including the idea of setting women's voting age at twenty-one, and the two groups sent a joint resolution to Hutson, accepting clause six but again requesting broader voting rights. But the next day, when the Staine brothers wrote to Usher to tell him about the resolution, they arbitrarily raised women's voting age to thirty. The BHTA also held meetings in Stann Creek Town, Corozal, and Cayo, all of which voted to accept London's offer. This was an unusual expansion of political action beyond Belize Town—and one not carried out by the Garveyites—but as the meetings were small and unrepresentative, they further illustrate the middle-class limits of constitutional activism. The unofficials, in rejecting the bill, explicitly noted that only one hundred people attended the BHTA's Belize Town meeting.[15]

As president of the BHTA, Archibald Usher knew firsthand the paucity of popular support for or even knowledge about the "half a loaf" option being pushed by his own organization, the PP, and the BLDC. These middle-class groups made gestures toward an inclusive movement for political rights, but their rejection of universal suffrage bled those gestures of any hegemonic potential. Because middle-class reformers had never mobilized the mass of the colony's working people around the issue of constitutional change, Usher and his fellow unofficials were free to claim popular support for their own posturing on the bogus grounds that they were true representatives of the native community, thereby defending that community from British executive autocracy. They closed the door on constitutional reform in April 1925, securing elite privilege not against "an uncontrolled flood of democracy" from below but against Britain's efforts to check them from above.

The Garveyites in particular do not emerge from my reinterpretation of the constitutional debates as politically well-organized or effective, even in the pursuit of their limited democratic vision. The UNIA itself never held a public meeting, did not address the Franchise Commission in 1923, and did not react to the draft bill in 1924 or the final bill in 1925. The PP was also silent in 1923 and held only one public meeting in 1924. It did develop the most inclusive franchise proposals of any organization but was much more the voice of the artisan class than of the mass of forestry laborers, let alone domestic servants. Although in late 1924 it elected three men to the Belize Town Board and was able to nominate two others, including Calvert Staine, its only action in March 1925 was to send the Staine brothers to the BHTA's meeting. The fact that overnight they could change the recommendation on women's voting age suggests that there was little more to the PP than its male artisan leadership.

By 1925 the decline of the male UNIA leadership and the growing strength of the BCNs was becoming evident, but neither they nor any other women took a direct part in the constitutional negotiations. It seems likely that the laborers and artisans who approved the PP's gender-inclusive and low-income voter qualifications in July 1924 were both male and female. But again, the Staine brothers' decision in March 1925 to change women's age of political majority suggests that women's equal rights were not part of the PP's core agenda, and that women were not in a position to contest their decision. A gender analysis, then, tends to confirm my argument that Ashdown has exaggerated the PP's record of popular mobilization, and thus the democratic character of the middle-class-led project.[16]

In a very indirect sense the PP's intervention in July 1924, as mediated through Hutson's pressure on the Legislative Council to enfranchise propertied women, provided working-class women with a claim to voting rights. In the mid-1930s, when the restoration of legislative elections was again on the agenda, the final draft bill of 1925 provided the basis of constitutional discussions. At last middle-class women, led by the Black Cross Nurses, spoke out for propertied women's inclusion at age 21, a suggestion that was at once vociferously contested by organized working-class women who articulated a popular definition of citizens' rights as universal womanhood and manhood suffrage.[17] That was the substance lacking in the period 1921–25, and it seems reasonable to conclude that because of its absence, neither the urban working class nor popular sectors in the rural districts cared that the merchant-employer elite on the Legislative Council had crushed middle-class political aspirations.

Blood of our Sires

The Battle of St. George's Caye Myth and Cultural Reform

The second reform effort through which the colonial authorities, native elite, and middle class sought to connect with the popular classes was the revival of September 10 celebrations, and thus of the political myth that grew up around the 1798 Battle of St. George's Caye. As with constitutional reform, the UNIA did not play a leading role in this arena, though Garveyites were eager participants in the celebrations, and Cain promoted them in the *Independent*. For them, and the non-Garveyite middle class, the rituals of the 10th provided a cultural counterpart to constitutional reform, for each was an arena in which they sought to lull race and class animosities. Indeed, the men of the BHTA proposed the revival of the 10th at their inaugural meeting in October 1921, at the same time that they

assumed the position of political educators and representatives in antici-
pation of representative government. They announced their intention to
encourage historical research on 1798, to educate the public "in the facts of
the glorious history of their forebears" and in the "fitting and proper obser-
vance of Public Holidays . . . connected with the history of the Colony,"
specifically the 10th celebrations.[18] British officials supported this cultural
project through annual funding for holiday events but also by symbolically
accepting middle-class loyalty on behalf of the Crown and empire.

The 10th went largely unmarked during the 1910s. Certainly the moment
was overshadowed in 1918 by Hart-Bennett's death, in 1919 by martial law
and the Riot Commission hearings, and in 1920 by a yellow fever outbreak.
In October 1920 Hutson and the Executive Council determined to celebrate Empire Day in May 1921 in proper style, but by March of that year
they had come to a consensus that the 10th should be the premier holiday
in the colony. Yet money was lacking, perhaps due the trade depression's
effect on government revenues, and the September 1921 celebrations were
apparently canceled. It seems likely that this disappointment fueled the
formation of the BHTA the following month, for from 1922 to at least 1925
it organized the festivities and led the march of loyalty.[19]

The 10th celebrations of the 1920s had four elements—a children's
essay competition, the parade of friendly societies (including the UNIA
and Black Cross Nurses) to Government House on the morning of the
10th, the delivery there of the address of loyalty that typically rehearsed
the events of 1798, and the afternoon march of as many as four thousand
schoolchildren. Working-class adults were by and large spectators, as their
membership in friendly societies was limited. Evidently they made their
own 10th revelry, for the *Clarion* repeatedly sought to counter what it saw
as a spirit of mindless self-indulgence by the urban working class with editorials on the deeper meaning of the 10th: British justice, liberty, and stability stemming from "our forefathers'" loyalty and devotion to country
and empire. Workers' children, while probably thrilled by an afternoon of
marching, sports, and free food and drink, participated under the orders
of middle-class teachers and clergy, whatever their parents' attitudes to
the event. Notably, there is no evidence of an engagement between Creole

popular culture and the revival of the Battle of St. George's Caye myth in the 1920s. None of the surviving petitions of the decade, from individuals or groups of the working class, make any mention of the battle. Poor people's appeals to and demands on government were simply not couched in terms of native rights won in 1798. Nor was there widespread financial support for the 10th. The BHTA organized the Belize Town events, as did British and Creole merchants in the district towns, but all funding came from the colonial authorities; the BHTA received $1000 in 1924 for example. In Orange Walk as late as 1928, the Spanish-speaking population was still not involved in local 10th rituals.[20]

Governor Hutson, in his 1923 reply to the address of loyalty, connected with both mainstream and Garveyite interpretations of the 1798 battle by referring to its protagonists as Europeans, slaves, and "the Creole people." Garveyites in particular emphasized the myth as a story of Creole self-creation, but they also adhered to the doctrine of compatibility between local patriotism and empire loyalty. In 1930, for example, Cain advocated building a memorial to the Baymen, whose victory forever established "British rule in the land we inherit." The ambiguity of whether Creoles inherited *because* of the British or were to inherit *from* the British nicely illustrates the character of Garveyite reformism. The UNIA did not attempt in the 1920s to develop the anniversary of slave emancipation, 1 August, as an alternative or even complementary holiday, one with more potential to incorporate popular sectors.[21]

Indeed, the patriotic 10th song *Land of the Gods* that Samuel Haynes composed in 1925 suppressed memories of 1 August; the song, renamed *Land of the Free*, has since become Belize's national anthem. "The blood of our sires which hallows the sod/ Brought freedom from slavery's oppression's rod," he wrote, eliding the slaveholders' victory in 1798 with slave emancipation in 1838.[22] *Land of the Gods* was a deeply ironic song, characterizing Belize as "a tranquil haven of democracy" in the same year that the unofficials rejected constitutional reform. But if Haynes intended it to muster middle-class and particularly Garveyite energies for a longer struggle against the merchant-employer elite and unofficials, his veiled reference to slave emancipation was not designed to undermine the cultural ritual of the 10th. Rather, Haynes's lyrics exemplified Belizean Garveyism's accommodation to Britain's interwar policy of evolutionary, earned movement toward stable capitalist self-government. Not least, Haynes extended the Battle of St. George's Caye myth's linkage of male nation-making and native political rights by urging men to leave exploitative mahogany labor to do battle as pioneer farmers: "Arise, ye sons of the Baymen's clan/ Put on your armour, clear the land." Just as the 1898 myth had erased black women from official history, so the 1920s elaboration of it excluded women from public imaginings of a transformed future.

The already shallow hegemonic roots of cultural reform centered on the 10th shrank further under Governor Burdon, who personally promoted an imperialist version of the tradition that was less open to interpretation. His main ally was Monrad S. Metzgen, a white Creole civil servant and leader of the BLDC. Following the BHTA's 1921 call for historical research on 1798, Metzgen and Burdon authored several key texts in the elaboration of the myth. First came the historical introduction of *The Handbook of British Honduras*, a commercial directory that Metzgen coauthored with fellow civil servant H. E. C. Cain. They emphasized the slaves' loyal rejection of freedom in 1798, referred to crown colony rule as "political suicide," and paid tribute to those who had begun the tradition of September 10 celebrations in 1898. Metzgen planned to follow up with a school history text, arguing to the Board of Education that few children knew anything of 1798. Burdon's first contribution to the myth was his 1927 *A Brief Sketch of British Honduras*, in which he defined 10 September 1798 as "the birthday of the colony, in as much as it freed itself that day from foreign domination and interference." To be British Honduran *was* to be British, seamlessly and proudly. Not only did Burdon erase colonialism but also local race and class autocracy, claiming that the Unofficial Majority was "the natural historical outcome of the pure democratic form of Government which the settlement evolved for itself." Gone was slaveholding, gone were contemporary middle-class claims to representative government. Burdon arrived after the unofficials' trouncing of constitutional reform, which he then expunged from his official history. Burdon's position differed from Metzgen and Cain's in that he defended the status quo absolutely whereas they were critical of crown colony rule, but the idea of the 10th as a colonial independence day nevertheless soon found its way onto the *Clarion*'s editorial page.[23]

Burdon and Metzgen then began to collaborate. The governor wrote the introduction to Metzgen's 1928 edited collection—sponsored by the BLDC—of early nineteenth-century documents written by slaveholders, which repudiated British critiques of slaves' living and working conditions by way of reference to slaves' loyalty in 1798. Metzgen in turn worked on the team of civil servants that supported the production of Burdon's three-volume *Archives of British Honduras*, published in the early 1930s. As Peter Ashdown has cogently pointed out, the flaws and biases of the *Archives*, uncritically replicated by a large number of scholars through the 1960s, "promulgated and popularized Burdon's interpretations and created historical myths which have lasted to this day and which are of more than just historiographical importance." In particular, Burdon spun a heroic Rule Britannia interpretation of 1798 that reinforced the myths of benign slavery and racial deference embedded in the middle-class version of 1898. But the chilling effects of his cultural politics on the attempt to turn the 10th celebrations into a hegemonic project were felt during his own tenure as governor, not least in his renewed hostility to the UNIA and the Nurses. Burdon ordered police surveillance of Garveyite leaders, prevented a return visit from Garvey, and refused to aid the Nurses in their effort to travel to Jamaica for a UNIA health conference. Cain's 1930 call to memorialize the Baymen can be seen as a moderate protest against Burdon for ignoring Creole participation in the 1798 battle.[24]

On 10 September 1930 an unusual celebration filled the streets of Benque Viejo, on the colony's western border with Guatemala, one that would have disturbed the Battle of St. George's Caye myth's revivalists. Escorted by a marimba band, a decorated car paraded around the tiny town carrying two boys dressed as Baymen holding up a picture of King George V, "encircled by the colours of Spain," and three girls carrying the flags of Britain, Mexico, and Guatemala. The town continued the celebrations with a playing of the Moro (a Mayan adaptation of the clash between Christians and pagans) and concluded with a night of marimba music and dancing. Five

days later the district commissioner led the town's multiracial and international population in a celebration of Mexican Independence Day. A
marimba band played God Save the King while the Union Jack was raised
and then the Mexican and Guatemalan anthems, followed by a requiem
mass for the Virgin of Guadalupe and speeches in commemoration of
Hidalgo.[25] A distinctly local need to incorporate the restless Mexican and
Guatemalan *chiclero* population, already facing unemployment as the
depression began, may explain this extraordinarily integrated week of festivities, but it also speaks to the impossibility of controlling the meaning
of the September 10 tradition from above. Notably, the popular character
of the Benque Viejo 10th in 1930 was more strongly connected to Mexican
popular nationalism than to any embrace of the revived St. George's Caye
tradition by Belizean workers. Indeed, local British authorities may have
piggybacked the 10th celebration onto the Mexican and Guatemalan festivities in order to promote its popularity.

Social Reform and Racial Uplift

Social reform, the third prong of the 1920s reform project, was the only
one that focused on the popular classes; it thus had more potential to
engage them than did constitutional or cultural reform. Still, even though
channels by which subaltern women and men could negotiate with the
authorities multiplied, allowing them to engage in the dynamics of social
reform in various ways, the didactic, objectifying character of reform had
little potential to establish a populist connection with the colony's majority. There is no completely satisfying way to label colonial social reform,
including the practice of the Black Cross Nurses. It was a somewhat loose
set of initiatives, always underfunded, that, in contrast to Latin America,
the United States, and Europe, generated no literature. But it bore resemblance to phenomena dubbed *"higienismo"* or "social hygiene" by Asunción
Lavrin, "preventive eugenics" by Nancy Leys Stepan, "cultural hygiene" by
Ann Laura Stoler, and maternalism by a wide variety of scholars. Social
hygiene, according to Lavrin, "aimed at surrounding people with a clean
environment, teaching them basic rules of personal care, and changing
their habits to prevent diseases and ensure the health of future genera-

FIG. 7. Mestiza and Mayan women of Benque Viejo may have dressed similarly to this woman from neighboring San José Succotz for the 10 and 15 September 1930 celebrations. Source: J. Eric Thompson, *Ethnology of the Mayas of Southern and Central British Honduras*, anthropological series 17: 2 (Chicago: Field Museum of Natural History, 1930), plate 27.

tions." Preventive, or neo-Lamarckian, eugenics similarly "linked a sanitary environment to racial health," applying modern science to "the social
environment"—particularly reproduction and motherhood—to improve
the human stock and combat racial degeneracy. This dominant thinking among post–World War One Latin American scientific, medical, and
liberal political elites, as well as among elite feminists, thus legitimized a
host of public health and social welfare measures. Stoler, in analyzing the
Dutch colonial empire, finds a similarly "positive" eugenics embedded in
colonial medicine's linkage of "physical, moral, and cultural degeneracy."
Stepan notes that by the 1920s all areas in the field of health reform had
been "eugenicized"; this included maternalism, as both Stoler and Molly
Ladd-Taylor, writing on the United States, have concluded. Maternalists,
who based their claims to political rights and influence on the importance
of mothering, promoted a "scientific motherhood" that emphasized modern medical authority in combating the threat of racial degeneracy. For
the elite proponents of social hygiene, preventive eugenics, and maternalism, racial health was linked to white identity and thus to the control of
black, indigenous, and mixed-race subalterns.[26]

It is not clear how the British Honduran medical staff, trained in England,
Scotland, and Canada, negotiated the connections and fault lines among
the British public health tradition, eugenics, and maternalism, though its
practices were very similar to those in Latin America. More important is
to analyze the complex relationship of Creole reformers to these powerful ideas, particularly as they existed in juxtaposition with scientific racism, negative eugenics, and the permanent condemnation of nonwhites
as biologically inferior. In India, nationalists embraced a version of social
hygiene—for example, promoting "home science" to modernize motherhood and thus improve racial health. Some African-American intellectuals conceptualized a "reform" eugenics that, like Latin America's neo-
Lamarckian version, "took into account the effects of environment and
culture in the progress of the races." Black clubwomen in the United States
implemented this ideology in their efforts to uplift poor black mothers.
As Evelyn Brooks Higginbotham has argued, their reformist politics of
racial uplift "remained locked within hegemonic articulations of gender,

class, and sexuality" by accepting "white middle-class models of gender roles and sexuality"—and, I would add, scientific authority—as ideal and necessary for political rights.[27] The dominant strategy of movements for independence and equality led by middle-class or elite nonwhites seems to have been to "deracialize" eugenics, thus contesting scientific racism while simultaneously defining the popular classes' illness, ignorance, culture, and even poverty as problems to be solved by social reform.

Garveyites were no exception to this pattern, as revisionist feminist historiography on the movement has demonstrated. Barbara Bair and others have effectively argued that the UNIA's theoretical structure of gender equality, with parallel male and female executives, masked ongoing male dominance within the movement. While Garveyite gender politics countered racist ideas of the black woman as sexually immoral and a threat to civilization, those politics idealized her as the educated but domestic mother/housewife and respectable community volunteer. The UNIA leadership's gender ideals thus represented a desire to overcome black men's and women's exclusion from "the Victorian ideology of true women and real men" that was embedded in transatlantic imperial culture rather than an effort to deconstruct that ideology. Within these conventional gender politics, respectable black women were to nurture the black community by reaching out to poor women as mothers "in charge of the health and well-being of their families." Garvey himself was critical of birth control, single motherhood and illegitimacy, female headed-households, racial mixing, and black folk culture.[28]

Some Garveyite women contested the confines of their roles and the reality of male power in the movement, but the Belize Black Cross Nurses simply turned the work of community health promotion into a vocation that violated the ideal of female domesticity in practice. The Nurses—and Belize Garveyites as a whole—pursued the social hygiene strategy outlined above, aiming to disprove racist denials of their social worth, and thereby counter the grounds on which they were refused political rights, through a preventive or cultural eugenics of racial uplift aimed primarily at poor Creoles in Belize Town. The culture and habits of the popular classes had to be changed; thus the Nurses set out to improve mothering within the urban working class. Their activism was vitally important to both Garveyite and state reformers, gained them public authority, and—crucially—established a tradition of outspoken female leadership within the colonial reform current. But because of its class-bound maternalist character, its judgmental zeal, it had little hegemonic potential.

Previous accounts of the Nurses have painted them as heroines working selflessly for the good of the Creole community, an interpretation that sidesteps the realities of class division and political conflict that shaped their practice and their reception by the public. The problem is embodied in the public image of Mrs. Vivian Wilhelmina Seay (née Myvett), who founded the Black Cross Nurses in 1920 (when she also joined the UNIA's female executive) and led them until her death in 1971. She has become in public discourse the "matriarch of maternal mothers," an icon of selfless womanhood worthy of having a middle-class Belize City street named after her. Behind the symbolism is the story of an ambitious, creative woman with a "strict code of ethics," who dedicated her considerable energies to improving those whom she deemed lacking in personal and political self-discipline. She was born a lower middle-class Anglican Creole in 1881 and married in 1905. Rather than attend the Anglican girls' high school, St. Hilda's College, which opened when Seay was 16, she entered the pupil-teacher system with a small salary. Eventually she rose to the rank of qualified teacher and taught for nine years in Xcalak, a Mayan village in Mexico, north of Ambergris Caye. She definitely returned to live in Belize Town by 1918, when she signed the Arnold reform petition, but appeared on no voters list until 1954, when the nationalist movement that she vehemently opposed secured universal suffrage. In 1935, the year that she opposed calls for womanhood suffrage made by organized working women, she was made a Member of the British Empire.[29] Like Seay, the Nurses were respectable women, not wealthy but able to devote many unpaid hours to the cause of racial uplift. They were sympathetic to the hardships caused by poverty, but Seay and her nurses never accepted it as an excuse for disrespect or disorder. This attitude exemplified the Garveyite and wider Creole middle-class commitment to native self-discipline and self-improvement.

Four interlocking areas of social hygiene reform can be distinguished within the colonial reform project: hospital and community health care (emphasizing reproductive health and infant welfare), environmental sanitation, compulsory elementary education, and rehabilitation for males in the penal system (including the opening of a boys' reformatory). The overall costs to the state were considerable, and Hutson grew weary of battling the elite over taxation, writing in 1924 that so long as the "leading European residents" could pay elderly indigent women one dollar per month to empty their slop buckets into the canals, they would never tax themselves to install a proper sewage system in Belize Town.[30] The free labor of the Nurses was most welcome in this context. For state and middle-class reformers alike, improvements in all four areas would combine to create a more eugenic social environment, thus producing subaltern subjects incapable of renewed rebellion.

In the area of hospital and community health care, a key step was the hiring of Lois M. Roberts, from England, as the new matron of the Belize Public Hospital. She signed on in September 1919, arriving by first-class passage at the end of January 1920, and within two weeks had catalogued a series of needed changes. Roberts called for better sanitation in the nurses' quarters ("badly kept"), on the wards ("dirty and ill-kept"), and in the bathrooms ("all in bad condition"). She recommended that a servant clean for the Nurses and that less "helpless" male asylum inmates clean the wards. She was critical of the hospital food, the "very badly washed[,] . . . deplorable" state of the hospital linens, which she had been counting, and the lack of storage space for linens and patients' belongings. Initially she proposed sending soiled linens to be laundered at the prison daily rather than weekly, but then she ended the practice altogether, hiring Mrs. Georgina Smith to do the job for $25 per month. Roberts was also concerned to improve the sanitation of the hospital grounds, to get a hot water supply, and to limit visiting to specific hours. She clearly injected energy into the Medical Department, for her priorities were immediately attended to, and plans for more major changes made. Most importantly, a children's ward was opened in 1920, named in honor of Governor Hart-Bennett. Not everyone was pleased with Roberts's spring-cleaning. Her demand that the ward maids be obedient to her and maintain good personal hygiene as well as "seemly" behavior with male patients and visitors evidently resulted in mass turnover—seven ward maids resigned in 1920.[31]

Roberts was also dissatisfied with the nursing staff—their uniforms ("not very tidy") and their insufficient numbers. To remedy the latter, she proposed a probationer program to train six "young girls from 20–25 years of age," of "superior status and education," who would each pay $10 per month to participate. This failed, as the class of young women she wanted did not typically choose nursing as a career, and those that did opted for the existing student nurse program through which they received a salary. At the same time, the medical staff was concerned with the extent to which the poor state of public health and dismal sanitation conditions were contributing to hospitalization and mortality, particularly infant mortality. In 1919 for example, Dr. K. Simon, medical officer for the Cayo District, attributed a high infant mortality rate (15.7 percent) to "lack of ordinary cleanliness as no trained midwives are usually available." Orange Walk's medical officer calculated that 26 percent of infants under one year old died in 1920 in his district and called for the appointment of district nurses to educate mothers through prenatal clinics and dispense free milk: "If the children get a good start in the first five years of life . . . it might even . . . raise the standard of living which is lamentably low in the outdistricts." Principal Medical Officer Thomas Gann added other factors besides ignorance and insanitary midwifery to the list of causes, also blaming illegitimacy "with the want of natural affection for, and proper care of the children which so frequently follow in its train," a pattern of men leaving families destitute during seasonal bushwork, and the fact that "a great and increasing number of mothers prefer not to suckle their children." The Black Cross Nurses came to broadly similar conclusions in their early 1920 survey of housing conditions in Belize Town's poor neighborhoods, blaming horrendous overcrowding and "maternal neglect" for infant mortality.[32]

It was Simon who began the process that would lead to the Nurses filling the gap left by the failure of Roberts's probationer program. Gann reported in late May 1921 that Simon, now posted in Belize Town, was giving "lectures on midwifery to young women of the Universal Negro Improvement Association" for twenty cents per week and had ordered them books and uniforms. Gann also backed Simon's recommendation that the Nurses begin training under Matron Roberts in "general hospital work, with special reference to cleanliness and asepsis, with a view to their ultimate employment as midwives or public nurses." Together with Simon and UNIA leader W. A. Campbell, Gann pressed the issue in June, arguing that the women "would prove simply invaluable in child welfare work . . . and in teaching the people the rudiments of domestic sanitation." Roberts, unable to get a younger, better class of nursing student, took the Nurses into her wards in July. By November they were approaching their examinations, and Gann again suggested that they be posted as "midwives and monthly nurses in Belize and even in the districts" to meet the long-standing need for "efficient service to mothers of the poorer class in their confinements." Initially, it seems that colonial officials did contemplate paid government work for the Nurses, though this prospect did not materialize.[33]

The Nurses did not begin their organized work in child welfare and education to poor mothers until 1923, when Hutson personally requested them to focus on maternity care after infant mortality spiked to 21.5 percent colony-wide in 1922. In the meantime, after seventeen of the first class of twenty passed their exams, they began to give public demonstrations of their skills, first at the UNIA's exhibition held to inaugurate the organization's Liberty Hall in early 1922. An enormous variety of mechanical inventions, needlework, fresh and tinned produce, and crafts were displayed, and the Nurses showed off their new skills in a competition to prepare an invalid meal within a budget of twenty-five cents. A few months later they staged their own Health Crusade Exhibition, at which they demonstrated bandaging and screened a film on tuberculosis and Huston awarded them their certificates.[34]

When colonial and Garveyite reformers finally joined forces in 1923, Seay assigned each Black Cross Nurse—there were now twenty-four—to a specific area of Belize Town, where she was to bring her (unpaid) knowledge and expertise to bear in visiting the homes of the poor, in which "domestic sanitation" was sorely deficient. Their practice was presumably shaped by Simon's and Roberts's teaching as well as by Gann's 1921 health pamphlet titled "Don'ts for Mothers," with its emphasis on nutritious food, breastfeeding to nine months, asepsis, the purchase of mosquito nets for babies, and the daily bathing of infants. Whether the nurses were received with universal gratitude is doubtful, for they brought no access to state benefits to poor women who had little means to purchase a balanced diet or netting and who were dependent on buckets and the canals as a latrine system. Few had adequate water supplies in their yards, as land-lords routinely ignored orders to provide and maintain vats. In the dry season drought of May 1922 a band of women marched onto Government House grounds "in a very vexatious mood over the hardships they are under-going" and declared that they would take water from Hutson's own vats if necessary. The middle class's controlling response to this rare act of collective contestation will be examined below; Hutson made sure to open his vats voluntarily in 1923.[35]

The Nurses began two other practices in 1923: their annual participation in the 10th parade of friendly societies to pledge loyalty at Government House, and the Baby Exhibition. This was a didactic competition designed to rank the infants and young children of the middle class and elite, to reward the "best" in various age groups, and thus to establish a standard of proper parenting for the popular classes. While the Nurses weeded out those entries too ill to participate, they enjoyed the cooperation of the colonial medical staff as inspector-judges and of top officials and their wives as patrons and prize-givers. The Baby Exhibition thus strength-ened the state-middle-class alliance, particularly with the Garveyites, even though it tended to reward the same children and families year after year and to stigmatize the urban poor, explicitly for their "bad" parenting, implicitly for their rates of illegitimacy. The ritual thus had little potential to build positive connections with the popular classes, particularly poor Creole mothers, or to improve their families' health. In 1924 the Nurses tried to raise funds to build a maternity clinic, where they would have had more impact on but also more control over poor women's childbirth and their infants' first days of life. The effort failed, but may have prompted the state to plan for the twelve-bed maternity ward that opened in 1927 and was constantly full thereafter. In late 1927 five nurses, including Seay, entered a six-month midwifery course on the ward, which they passed in March 1928. Their new skills enabled them to bring poor mothers more than advice, though their practical aid was itself a form of surveillance.[36]

That same year the state began to pay more attention to men's role in reproductive health, opening a twelve-bed male venereal disease ward, largely catering to the mahogany workers among whom gonorrhea was virtually endemic. The ward was constantly full in both 1929 and 1930, although medical officers had difficulty in getting the men to follow a full course of treatment. In 1929 the officer for Orange Walk District estimated that 80 percent of the seasonal mahogany cutters working for BEC in the district were infected and described the village women as a "great [untouched] reservoir of gonorrheal infection." Men's genitals, like women's pregnancies, were coming under intensified state scrutiny, though motherhood was of far more concern than fatherhood.[37]

An extreme example of female-focused social hygiene was the 1927 bill to ban the sale of liquor to women in order to prevent them drinking in public. Alcohol was one of the "racial toxins" that Latin American eugenic reformers identified as injurious to reproductive health, but that link was not explicitly made in this case. The bill originated with a Methodist minister's objection to "drinking and immorality among our girls and young women," especially those congregated in Water Lane, Duck Lane, and Regent Street West.[38] He suggested separate bar and grocery entrances, but the Executive Council, itself concerned with "the increase of drunkenness and vice among girls and women in Belize," added the ban on consumption. A group of publicans quickly responded that it was unfair to penalize respectable women "for the few disgraceful women who live in barrooms." The prohibition did not become law, but the interventions of clergy and councilors are suggestive of a political climate in which popular female morality, reproduction, and parenting were under expanded state and middle-class surveillance.

The Black Cross Nurses were the only reformist women to organize for improved motherhood until 1928, when the more elite Infant Welfare

League (IWL) formed. Its close links to the colonial administration were obvious—Governor Burdon's wife was the league's honorary secretary and Monrad Metzgen its treasurer. When Lady Burdon requested that Roberts's second-in-command at the hospital be assigned to supervise the weekly league clinic, permission was granted. Roberts also organized a fund-raising concert for the league, attended by the colonial elite. Unlike the BCNs, the IWL's lady volunteers did not need formal training, for they could count on the state to actively support their activities. Seay's work in cultivating cooperative relations with Hutson and his staff had paid off in the early 1920s, but Burdon was markedly less enthusiastic. Rather than object and lose further influence, however, Seay and her nurses cultivated a cooperative relationship with the league, even donating $50 to the new group.[39]

The league had a growing band of lady volunteers who did home visiting, but their effectiveness may well have been due to their weekly free well-baby clinic, staffed by a trained British nurse and volunteers. The clinic became very popular with poor mothers during the summer of 1928; in 1929, the principal medical officer attributed the 50 percent drop in Belize Town's infant mortality to the league. No data exits that would allow an accurate comparison of the BCN's and IWL's impact on maternal and infant health, but it is notable that the Nurses never received such official praise, even from their ally Hutson. If the league was more effective, perhaps it was because significant numbers of poor mothers were willing, indeed eager, to bring their children to the clinic. It may have been a less charged experience than a home visit from one of the Black Cross Nurses, Creole women only moderately better off than their clients, or the didactic theater of the Baby Exhibition. Or perhaps the league simply commanded greater resources and thus invited demands for aid. Indeed, both volunteers and staff were drawn into a social work role, placing children in foster homes, helping women to pursue men who owed maintenance, and giving out packages of food and medicine. That popular demands for aid persisted is indicated by Lady Burdon's 1930 admonition to poor mothers to stop bringing their sick infants to the clinic and take them straight to the hospital instead. If they needed money to pay, she instructed, they should apply to the district commissioner.[40]

Lady Burdon's speech came during the league's first "Baby Week" in early 1930, a program of events designed, like the Baby Exhibition, to teach both mothers and fathers the doctrine of modern pregnancy, parturition, and parenting. Vivian Seay spent the week preaching the virtues of powdered milk in the town's elementary schools, while Matron Roberts organized fund-raising and Lady Burdon gave a speech at Liberty Hall. Scarcely acknowledging the Nurses, she advised prenatal hospital care, regular feeding and bathing of infants, and the provision of cribs to separate babies from their parents at night. Although league rhetoric dwelt on poverty as well as parental neglect and ignorance as the causes of infant illness, here Burdon emphasized the latter factors.[41]

Poor mothers' pressure on the league to provide useful services, like the action of the female water protestors of 1922, suggests that those in the colony without adequate access to modern health care rarely accepted their "ignorance" or "immorality" as the causes of illness and mortality. Instead, they blamed poverty and the inadequacy of state services—the latter point was of course confirmed by the state's own admission that services needed dramatic improvement. Mrs. R. McField's 1930 petition to Governor Burdon clearly defined poverty as the root of her family's problems.[42] Mrs. McField, a Spanish-speaking mestiza from Cayo, had one of her six daughters draft her explanation for taking the extraordinary step of writing without her husband James's knowledge or permission. She requested that he be given a salary increase from the $60 per month he was currently receiving in his post as a compositor in the government printing office. With over half that amount going toward a government house loan, things were so hard with the family that often she could not send the children to school—their clothes were so ragged—nor could she afford even "five cents fish" at the market. Mrs. McField emphasized her own efforts to contribute, describing how her work as a laundress had made her ill. Indeed, a month after sending the letter she was hospitalized with malaria. In a second letter pressing the urgency of her need, she expressed gratitude for the doctor's and Matron Roberts's care. This time the authorities paid attention. On the recommendation of his boss, who described James as "virtually unfed," he received an extra $10 per month starting in April 1931. The much poorer women targeted by the BCNs and IWL often had no man or his employer to appeal to. They extracted what practical aid they could from the didactic reform alliance; when conditions became unbearable they were capable of marching on Government House to claim their rights.

The female water protestors' condemnation of those responsible for their living conditions found a less angry parallel in petitions from Cayo demanding improved hospital services. Written in 1921 when Cayo was the only district still without a government hospital, these petitions were organized by leading merchants and employers who had personal interest in public health care but who may also have been pressured by the mass of chicle and mahogany laborers. The first was signed by 227 residents of Cayo, Benque Viejo, and Succotz, headed by chicle contractor and merchant Alvaro J. Habet and two Jesuit priests. They asked for a hospital to be built and for road repairs between Cayo and Benque, ostensibly so that the medical officer could travel more quickly from one place to the other. Benque Viejo mounted an independent petition some months later when Hutson was visiting the district, asking that the town have its own hospital and government doctor, an idea that Gann supported. A hospital was in operation in Cayo by 1923, although as late as 1929 it was still unscreened, which undermined efforts to get the townspeople to screen their own vats and homes against mosquitoes and their larvae.[43]

The second arena of social hygiene reform was precisely that of environmental sanitation, conceived of not simply as a means of preventing disease but also, in a eugenic sense, as a way of improving the human stock. A 1913 *Clarion* editorial blaming juvenile delinquency on the poor condition of Belize Town's physical environment had claimed that the squalor of poor neighborhoods was "inimical, disastrous, and destructive to soundness of mind and body."[44] This echoed a century of sporadic efforts to sanitize the town.[45] In the 1920s education became part of improving environmental sanitation—a set of hygiene lessons that had been designed in 1919 by one of the medical officers was introduced into the curriculum in the elementary schools.[46] These lessons recruited the children to educate their parents—the lesson on hookworm, for example, instructed children to "tell my parents to keep the yard clean." But education was not enough—new laws and penalties as well as infrastructure projects, and staffing were required to make a dent in chronic problems of water supply and drainage, sewage and garbage disposal, and endemic malaria, hookworm, and tuberculosis. The 1920s witnessed a number of such initiatives, like the rat catching campaign, but for most residents of the colony, they amounted to tools by which the state might increase its surveillance and pressure them to change their habits without providing much improvement in state services in return. Really significant advances would not come until Britain began to provide imperial funding through the 1929 Colonial Development Fund and the Colonial Development and Welfare Acts of the 1940s. The initiatives of the 1920s depended on increased local tax collection. Hutson managed to get the land tax raised from a half cent per acre to one and a half cents, and to establish an income tax of five cents per $10 of income over $1000. He also pressured the district boards and Belize Town Board to collect property tax arrears, and in 1923 he ordered the revaluation of Belize Town's property rolls.[47]

One key initiative was Hutson's revamping of the Central Board of Health in 1923, a move toward centralized technocratic authority as the board now had authority over district and municipal governments. The board brought together the principal medical officer, director of public works, superintendent of police, and chairman of the Belize Town Board to coordinate the work of environmental sanitation. The board began with a staff of eight—the chief sanitary inspector and four other sanitary inspectors in Belize Town and three other sanitary inspectors at ports of entry in the districts (Corozal, Punta Gorda, and Stann Creek). By 1930 the staff had expanded modestly to twelve, with six in Belize, two in Corozal, and one in each of the other four districts, all of whom cooperated with the local governments' inspector of nuisances. The budget had grown more substantially, from under $2000 in the 1910s to $11,152 in 1923–24 to $16,227 in 1929–30. Hutson, in informing the Colonial Office of this new system, expressed only a very guarded optimism: "A beginning, has, I hope, been made, and however depressing existing conditions may be to a

FIG. 8. Twenty years after this photo was taken in 1906, Belizean reformers were still concerned to get urban children off the streets and into school and other organized activities. Source: Rupert Boyce, *Report to the Government of British Honduras upon the Outbreak of Yellow Fever in that Colony in 1905* (London: Waterlow and Sons, 1906), plate 9, fig. 17.

Medical Officer of Health with ordinary ambitions to improve conditions on modern lines, I fear that progress must be slow, owing to conservative local customs and traditions, and owing to the absence of means, at present, of raising funds." Hutson was frustrated by the elite's unwillingness to tax itself, but he also harbored racially inflected ideas about the majority: "Knowing the race that forms the main inhabitants of Belize, I am confident that if the government established a proper tuberculosis hospital, it would not be used." He did not generally act on the sense of hopelessness this statement conveys, as the creation of the Central Board of Health demonstrates.[48]

That hopelessness, though, must be understood in the context of the frustrated efforts of the 1919–22 period, efforts that focused on hookworm prevention and education. Medical and sanitary staff fanned out across the colony to test infection rates and to build latrines and encourage their use. New requirements were issued requiring residents to keep domestic livestock penned up rather than allowing them to roam the villages and requiring householders to build latrines. Public resistance to such intervention was swift: in Cayo in 1920 Gann found that half the house lots had no latrines, and that some women had developed the "filthy habit" of throwing their slop buckets' contents down onto the roofs of the public latrines, Cayo being a very hilly town. By 1923 things had improved markedly, perhaps in response to the government building a hospital. In 1921, the Creole, Mayan, and mestizo men of the village of Guinea Grass in the Orange Walk District protested the law on livestock, explaining that their pigs, on which they depended for cash to pay land rent, were dying in their pens. If forced to labor for cash, the men would neglect their crops and have to buy expensive food for their families. Villagers from Corozal were not so patient—they decamped to the Mexican side of the border as soon as the regulation was passed.[49] Such resistance and evasion—to the use of latrines, to vaccination, to building and maintaining vats—persisted through the 1920s, even as the Central Board of Health expanded its abilities to monitor and enforce sanitary regulations.

The sanitary inspectors' routine work was indeed to inspect: water storage receptacles and wells for mosquito larvae, yards for standing water, brush, and refuse, streets and drains for flooding and debris, and bakeries, markets, slaughterhouses, and both public and private latrines for cleanliness. There were, for example, twenty-one municipal latrines in Belize Town by the end of the decade, all reportedly in good condition. In addition, the inspectors organized an annual mass gassing of crab holes, disinfected homes where tuberculosis sufferers were found, and provided larvivorous fish for water barrels. This last endeavor was undoubtedly the most popular of the decade, for the public readily accepted the fish as a practical, effective, and free service from the state. Otherwise, the inspectors acted as enforcers, issuing notices to householders, landlords, and the town and district boards for sanitary offenses. It is not possible to establish whether public attitudes to inspection changed across the decade, though it seems that compliance increased in the late 1920s when provisions for prosecution increased and fining was enforced more energetically.[50] Again, people responded most positively when the authorities provided practical aid, like free fill for waterlogged house lots, or disciplined themselves by clearing overgrown crown lots.

An incident in Stann Creek Town provides a window onto the public's feelings about the inspectors and the potential for their new powers to be abused or misunderstood. In this case the inspector was a Creole from outside the largely Garifuna town, and in 1924 65 female and 204 male petitioners accused him of trying to trade leniency on sanitary infractions for sexual favors from Garifuna women and of threatening them when they refused. Several leading men of the newly-founded Carib Sick-Aid and Development Society (CDS)—formed by the small middle strata of Garifuna shopkeepers, planters, and civil servants—signed the petition for the sanitary inspector's removal. He denounced it as a "tribe conspiracy" and asked to be transferred. The respectable CDS was certainly not hostile to improved sanitation, however; in 1928 the Stann Creek Town Board, with two CDS officers on it, resigned en masse to protest the administration's refusal to enlarge the sanitation budget.[51]

That same town board had already provoked a clearly female subaltern protest concerning housing materials in 1919–20. When one of the town's principal merchant stores burned down in 1919, the town board banned thatch roofing. Garifuna farmer-housewives banded together and deployed local schoolteacher Benigno Sampson to bring Hutson's greater authority to bear in overturning the ban. The first of three petitions, dated October 1919, was written by Sampson but listed the names of fifty women and twenty-seven men. Galvanized iron roofing was too expensive, they argued, and reduced the ventilation required for cooking cassava, a staple of the Garifuna diet. By March 1920 the women were harassing Sampson daily, for no answer had been received. In April he wrote again, conveying the women's detailed description of the cassava-making process, their concern that the intense heat under an iron roof would make them ill, and their anger that one Gregoria Lambey had been given permission to put up a thatched kitchen. Finally the women dismissed Sampson as their intermediary, replacing him with Panteleon Hernandez, later an officer of the CDS. This time the government responded by setting aside the newly cleared southern portion of the town for thatched homes and kitchens, much to the town board's disgust.[52]

Such flexibility was not unusual, particularly when women protested, for state authorities understood that environmental conditions and poverty placed limits on the pace of change. The Orange Walk District Board, for example, voted to build a latrine for Apolonia Camal, "a very poor woman living in a dilapidated house" in Orange Walk Town, rather than fine her for not having one. In another case, the superintendent of police granted the petition two Belize Town women who made their living with their mule carts had made to Hutson to stop the Belize Town Board from impounding their mules. Hannah Ramsey and Catherine Latchman had traditionally put their mules to graze on Yarborough Green, but with the passage of a law against roaming livestock, the town board's dogcatcher had removed them. The superintendent of police reestablished their customary rights, except during late afternoon cricket games on the green. The Cayo Town Board struck homeowners Dominga Cocom and Benita Loj from the property tax rolls, describing them as "aged, poor and indigent," and noting that they both received "outdoor relief," the only form of welfare in the colony. The authorities may also have been more lenient with poor female homeowners struggling to fill their waterlogged house lots.[53]

More dramatic than the work of the Central Board of Health was the reclamation of land to form two new neighborhoods in Belize Town, a development that helped to accommodate the 34 percent increase in population between 1921 and 1931.[54] Fort George, with seashore on two sides and ample breezes, was created on the north side from 1923–26 and became a wealthy residential area. Its growth undoubtedly helps to explain the rising number of private septic tanks, of which there were one hundred by 1930.[55] Away from the sea on the south side, the new Collet Canal was completed in 1919, making possible the development of the working-class area named Mesopotamia. Its name came from the Middle Eastern service of the colony's World War I veterans, many of whom had priority for receiving house lots here. This process began in 1925 and may illuminate Hutson's appointment of five elite women to a Housing Advisory

Committee in late 1924.[56] By 1928 Mesopotamia was a lively community but one plagued, like older poor neighborhoods, by problems of drainage, water supply, sanitation, and overcrowding. Dozens of homeowners were unable to properly fill their lots until the government acquired a dredger in 1929 and provided free fill. A disproportionate number of the poorest homeowners were women.[57] Yet the struggle to meet government regulations did not consume all of the residents' energies. By 1928 the settlement had its own newspaper correspondent, who commented wryly on Euphrates Avenue being flooded and suggested that the government hire swimming teachers for the children. St. Ignatius School was an important center of neighborhood life, fielding sports teams and staging a wildly popular play in Creole about practitioners of obeah, the Afro-Caribbean belief system developed during slavery, being sent to the new government reform school.[58] Tragically, Mesopotamia was destroyed in the 1931 hurricane, with severe loss of life.

The final major initiative of the 1920s was the effort to establish a modern water supply for Belize Town. In the early 1920s all drinking water had to be collected during the rainy season (June–December) in private and public vats. Householders and landlords were required to install vats for their properties at the rate of 1.5 gallons per square foot of inhabited floor space, but a 1923 survey found many leaky vats, many properties without vats, and much faulty supply guttering. The Belize Town Board's public vats sold four gallons for three cents during periods of drought, usually in April and May, but in the severe dry seasons of the early 1920s could not meet demand.[59] The May 1922 march of angry women to take water from Hutson's vats at Government House is suggestive of the level of popular suffering and frustration. Immediately the BHTA held a large public meeting at which Archibald Usher bemoaned the moral and physical deprivation suffered by young girls who were sent out in search of water, and H. H. Cain blamed the shortage on the authorities. By the end of the month a petition with sixteen hundred names on it was presented to Hutson, asking for a solution to dry season droughts. Hutson willingly forwarded it to London but warned that property taxes would have to be raised to pay for improvement.[60] He moved to revalue Belize Town's prop-

FIG. 9. The completed Fort George neighborhood in 1928. Source: *Belizean Studies* 5:1 (January 1977): 3.

erty rolls in 1923 once the Colonial Office had approved the project, and a Water Commission held hearings in July.[61] Both elite and middle-class men agreed that the solution was to build several large concrete tanks, charging users by the gallon in order to pay off the cost of construction, and to enforce the law requiring landlords to build storage vats for their tenants. They were uniformly opposed to the introduction of a water rate on property to pay for the tanks. Hutson evidently did not take their views as the final word, for in March 1924 he asked the Colonial Office to send an engineer to prepare a plan for a piped water and sewer system. The expert visited in December that year but evidently plans stalled there, for Belize Town did not get a piped water supply until the late 1940s. In 1927 the town board was still selling water during the dry season and still did not have enough for the growing town's needs.[62] This, and the enduring prevalence of malaria, likely diminished popular appreciation for the authorities' efforts in the field of environmental sanitation.

The third prong of social hygiene reform was elementary education, an arena in which middle-class reformers played a significant role, as

they dominated the colony's teaching profession. The focus of education reform in the 1920s was not primarily curricular, although in 1924
the Board of Education did ask all school managers (i.e., the churches)
to make hygiene lessons mandatory, and the board also approved of
Metzgen's proposed school history text.[63] Rather, the main goal was to
increase the percentage of school-age children attending classes through
the Compulsory Education Ordinance of 1915. Originally the law applied
only to certain villages where attendance was very low, and only up to
the age of twelve, but by 1919 the law was being applied to parts of all
six districts, including the towns of Orange Walk, Cayo, Benque Viejo,
and Punta Gorda.[64] Belize Town finally required compulsory education
at the beginning of 1920, acting on the Riot Commission's recommendation to curb youth delinquency through stricter schooling.[65] In 1921 pressure from priests in San Estevan in the Orange Walk District resulted in
the local school-leaving age being raised to fourteen. By 1924 this was the
school-leaving age in Orange Walk Town and Belize Town as well, a measure that forced more than a few bright working-class teenagers to repeat
the final elementary year two or three times, for they could neither afford
high school nor legally leave school.[66]

   Middle-class cooperation with compulsory education was strong. The
UNIA for one heartily approved. At its inaugural meeting, the president
linked the interests of the race to education, "the spiritual and intellectual upliftment of our race," and added: "It is our desire to assist the boys
and girls in this community who, night after night, are walking about the
streets doing no more or less than getting into trouble. We want to see
the youngsters of Belize at our meetings. . . . Gentlemen, this is a new era
I give unto you. What are other races doing? They are trying to improve
themselves. They are trying to educate their children."[67] The Black Cross
Nurses—led by exteacher Seay—exemplified the Garveyite pursuit of self-
improvement and racial uplift through education and were held up as role
models for young girls. The Nurses also constantly gave public lectures
on health, and during Baby Week in 1930 Seay instructed schoolchildren
on the importance of drinking milk. The Teachers' Association, formed
in 1922, supported the compulsory education policy but also aimed to

increase teachers' wages.[68] One of the association's backers, a lay Catholic schoolmaster, had already argued for a teachers' union that might work with the authorities to combat delinquency: "In these days of reconstruction, active measures are being pushed in every department of civic life, and what is true of other walks of life applies equally and more necessarily I think to the teaching profession. It is generally conceded and less often been complained of in the press that our youths in the Colony are going from bad to worse. Would it not be time to consider some united action on the part of those entrusted with the training of our youths?"[69] Eventually teachers demanded that the government establish a teacher-training center.[70]

The state, teachers, and Garveyites all doubted the ability of working-class parents to properly discipline and cultivate the minds of their children. As the Industrial School Committee urged in 1918, Belize Town needed compulsory education to get idle children off the streets and to save them from themselves and their evil surroundings."[71] The chairman of the Belize Town Board took a position against representative government in the aftermath of the riot, because "parental influence" kept the educational level too low for any extension of political rights.[72] The Belize Polo Club members, bothered by "unruly boys" and their "noise, antics, and foul language" while playing cricket on the polo grounds, did not even consider parental discipline as an option and instead had the club steward commissioned as a police constable.[73] The issue of juvenile delinquency is discussed further below in the context of the courts and penal reform. The Compulsory Education Act certainly took on a law-and-order character, providing for the appointment of police constables and both Mayan and Garifuna *alcaldes* as truant officers, the former receiving an extra $24 to $30 per year for their services. The two officers appointed in December 1919 for Belize Town earned $360 per year each and thus would have been excluded from the proposed franchise of the early 1920s. These costs, and the construction of eleven new elementary schools between 1919 and 1931, increased the Education Department budget substantially.[74]

By the summer of 1921 neither the inspector of schools nor the four principal school managers (Anglican, Baptist, Catholic, and Methodist) were satisfied with the enforcement of compulsory attendance in Belize Town. The police responded by compiling lists of habitual absentees and their parents in September 1921 and the summer of 1922.[75] The typical absentee was a boy with a single mother. Only one of the thirty-three truants identified was a girl and only six fathers were named, one twice. Five of the seven father-son pairs shared a last name (71.4 percent), while only five of twenty-five mother-son pairs did (20 percent); the one girl truant also had different last name from her mother. One compilation listed either truancy or negligence as the problem—four of eleven mothers were deemed negligent (36.4 percent), one of six fathers (16.7 percent). This data suggests that most truants were being raised in households headed by single women, many of whom were likely laboring long hours for chronically low wages, making it difficult for them to monitor their growing children and to purchase the clothing and supplies needed for school. None of the mothers named appeared on municipal voter lists.

Frances Moray was one of the single mothers under state surveillance during 1921.[76] Her seven-year-old son's chronic absences from school had resulted in truancy fines that Moray could not pay. In October she was jailed as a public debtor but wrote a hasty letter of protest and appeal to Hutson just before entering the prison. Surely her "dear master" would not punish "a poor distressful woman" who was willing to pay but could not, as a result of long illness and thus inability to earn a living? Her son had also been sick for months, resulting in his absences. Before Hutson could intervene—if indeed he would have—Moray paid her debt and was released. Her angry defense of her own morality combined with a plea for paternal state aid was probably a typical subaltern strategy for engaging with the reform project. As such it underscores the project's fragility, for it raised popular expectations of benevolence that could not be met, while also impugning the popular classes as the authors of their own fates. But Moray's strategy was only one option; Eliza Martin, by contrast, asked for more disciplinary intervention with her son than the state was able to provide.[77] Martin described herself to the authorities as "a poor woman and working for barely enough to sustain me." She was a restaurant cook who was paid $1.75 per week, and though her thirteen-year-old son's father was paying two dollars a week in maintenance, he apparently took no active role in raising the boy. Martin's son, a pupil at Anglican St. Mary's School, had begun to associate with bad company, so she had found him work as a messenger, but he had done poorly and been dismissed. She wrote to the government asking that he be sent to the Free School in her native Jamaica. The response was sympathetic but limited: the police could whip him for her, as they had done at her request before, but without a reform school, little else could be done.

Neither Eliza Martin nor Frances Moray contested the importance of education as articulated by the state and middle class, indeed many parents greeted the authorities' new interest with approval, and some demanded that their children be included in expanding elementary education. In the west, the Mayan villages of Succotz and Arenal both petitioned for schools, but the district commissioner was skeptical, arguing that parents cared less about their children's attendance in the Benque Viejo schools than about the truancy fines then being meted out.[78] The Creole and mestizo parents of Isabella Bank, a village on the Belize River in the Belize District, actually started a school and hired a teacher themselves, only applying for government funding once community resources dried up.[79] To them, education was their children's only escape from lifetimes of hardship like their own. Like many petitioners, these men and women emphasized their poverty and need, referring to Hutson as their one hope. They were invited to apply for a school grant through the Education Department—one more way in which popular expectations of the state rose in the 1920s.

The fourth arena of social hygiene was penal reform, specifically for boys and men. While the 1918 Industrial School Committee backed compulsory education, it also recommended an industrial school for boys already in the court system or at risk of criminal activity, which would inculcate discipline through a program of agricultural and trades training. P. S. Woods concurred, for unless boys and girls who were "suffered to grow up in ignorance without any attempt at restraint" were checked, "a large criminal class" would become a burden on the taxpayers. Hutson took up the cause soon after his arrival. The issue of juvenile delinquency became far more urgent after the riot, as the authorities perceived a tide of black juvenile criminality threatening to swamp them. One angry man referred to poor young Creoles as "hooligans[,] . . . the majority of the rising generation of negroes in this place."[80] The newly appointed and zealously reformist superintendent of prisons, an Englishman, was equally condemning of parents' and boys' behavior, after having observed juvenile convicts: "Possibly when we have an Industrial School, the period of detention will be sufficiently long to enable those in charge to discover the inherent characteristics of a boy. . . . The circumstances of individual cases often reveal a state of parental irresponsibility, where the boy is regarded as an encumbrance, and of no moral value. Training never enters their ideas, if indeed they have any ideas at all, and their boys and girls gather their education from the streets."[81]

These fears seem to have been grossly exaggerated in the aftermath of the riot. From June through November 1920 just thirty-eight juveniles, all boys, were punished for offences by the police, usually with six to twelve strokes of the whip.[82] Only two of them also appeared on the police's list of school truants. The most common offences were theft and disorderly conduct, although some boys and girls were involved in the "hairyman" conflict of August 1920. At that time the soldiers of the West India Regiment, posted in Belize Town as part of the postriot repression, began to receive the catcall "hairyman" from civilians. They were in effect accusing the soldiers of being the thieves then active in town, who were rumored to wear hairy garments when they burgled. The worst incident erupted on a Saturday night in Water Lane, when a dispute between a soldier and a woman over money escalated into a group of townspeople hurling bottles and insults, including the "hairyman" epithet, at a number of the regiment men. The superintendent of police noted that Carl Shaw, the young son of Claude Smith "who was connected with the riots last year," had on one occasion called out the popular insult from the balcony of a saloon. No charges were laid, as Smith promised to take him to Punta Gorda where he was working as a bookkeeper, having "given up politics."[83]

Such private arrangements became less necessary after the opening of the Pomona Industrial School in early 1927, funded by the government but run by the Salvation Army. By June there were thirty-two boys there, most of them sent by their parents; by December the number of inmates had risen to forty-four, and in 1928 there were sixty-four boys.[84] So well known was the school by then that it appeared in the St. Ignatius school play mentioned above, causing much mirth. In addition to following a firm, even harsh, regimen of cleanliness, inspection, and obedience, the boys learned agricultural skills by running the school's farm, which soon became one of the principal suppliers of grapefruit seedlings in the Stann Creek Valley. The medical officer for Stann Creek visited Pomona weekly in 1930 and reported in a cliché of colonial social-hygiene thinking that "one is impressed with what good food, clothing, housing, sanitation and discipline will do for native boys."[85]

Hutson had originally insisted that a girls' reformatory was also necessary, but girls were excluded from the vocational training that Pomona offered. The new superintendent of prisons in fact believed that female juveniles were morally and intellectually hopeless, "more prone to evil" than boys and impervious to kindness. Their brothers might respond to discipline and training, but such efforts with girls were deemed a waste of time. Adult women convicts were also excluded from the training in trades and leadership available in the Belize Prison. While they did the prison laundry, male inmates learned skills that could launch them successfully into the labor market after release. The superintendent believed that men's "virile intellects" would convert them into "useful and law-abiding citizen[s]." To encourage and reward such conversion, he instituted a "red collar" system, whereby well-behaved male inmates would be granted more freedom and responsibility within the prison. He took great pride in relating the cases of felons transformed into productive, hard-working family men, a discourse echoed by the *Clarion*, which expressed astonishment that the "mere bush laborer" could become a tinsmith or tailor, as the UNIA's industrial exhibition had demonstrated was possible.[86] One of the few sites of reform—aside from the VD ward—that targeted men, the prison aimed to return them to society as morally and physically fit workers and family providers.

It was precisely because of their responsibilities as family providers that Samuel Haynes sought to secure the release of riot convicts in May

1920—their dependents, he argued, were suffering.[87] Susan Sutherland's worsening housing situation certainly confirms Haynes's point. But, despite Haynes's appeal to imperial beneficence in asking that they be released on Empire Day, Hutson preferred to pay relief to the families rather than free the guilty men so soon. A decade later, another rare reference to fatherhood was made by Dr. James Cran during the IWL's Baby Week, when he very bitterly remarked on the scarcity of men in the audience and argued that "fathers . . . were equally responsible for the bringing up of babies as good citizens."[88] Cran, who had treated Charles Sutherland for gonorrhea in 1919, was arguing that men should do more than make babies; they should also protect pregnant women and infants and participate in their children's education—paternal roles that during the 1920s middle-class and state reformers took upon themselves.

In all four arenas, social reform elicited a variety of popular reactions, none of which furthered colonial or middle-class hegemonic control. Although there was real enthusiasm for practical aid, such as larvivorous fish and IWL clinics, irritation with inadequate services, such as the small maternity ward at the Belize Public Hospital or chronic water shortages, was more common. The benevolent face of social reform in effect opened a Pandora's box of popular expectations and demands. The opposite face—that of the inspector, judge, and disciplinarian—did not win many hearts, either through the Baby Exhibition or sanitary inspections or nor school truancy prosecutions. The ward maids who resigned in 1920 to avoid Matron Roberts's strict new regime portended wider disillusionment with the eugenic tendencies of social reform, tendencies that ultimately blamed the poor for their poverty, illness, and unhealthy living conditions.

Conclusion

The 1919 riot, as the culmination of rising subaltern frustration in the 1910s, provoked a controlling but ameliorative response from the unprecedented state-middle-class alliance, in which middle-class women took on an enlarged public role as health activists. While men dominated in the arenas of political reform and cultural renewal, middle-class women focused on social reform, which had more potential for meeting critical subaltern needs. Those needs were expressed in terms both desperate and dignified by men and women of the popular classes colony-wide but were constructed in distinctly moralistic ways by agents of the reform alliance, within and outside the state. The Garveyites' participation in social hygiene reform underscores the conservatism of their politics of racial uplift. Belizean Garveyism was not a popular or mass movement in the 1920s, for it did not embrace a black nationalism or even labor organizing but rather stayed well within class lines in pursuing a colonial legislature with a limited franchise. The state-middle-class alliance's hegemonic project could only appear to be making progress so long as the export economy held steady and popular expectations of the state were at least partially fulfilled. When, in the early 1930s, the export economy declined and the state was no longer able to satisfy the demands of popular classes, it became startlingly clear just how shallow the roots were of both state and middle-class popular legitimacy. The popular classes' negotiations with the alliance during the 1920s had breathed constant life into a subaltern conception of citizen-subject rights manifested during the riot. In the 1930s that conception would result in the birth of the colony's first sustained popular movement, which turned from uncoordinated negotiation to direct and well organized confrontation, bringing women like Annie Flowers back to the streets with a definition of duty and community service sharply at odds with that of the Black Cross Nurses and their reformist allies. Reformers had developed a much clearer ideology and practice than ever before in response to the 1919 riot, and women had firmly established female leadership and public activism within key arenas of the reform project. In confronting those reformers in the 1930s, the popular classes would make equally huge strides in defining their politics, a process in which working-class women would be front and center.

3 Hurricane from Below

Popular Protest, the Labourers and Unemployed Association, and the Women's League, 1931–1941

On the afternoon of 10 September 1931, with hundreds of schoolchildren gathered outdoors to march in celebration of the Battle of St. George's Caye, the worst hurricane in living memory came down on Belize Town like "the wrath of God." With winds of 130 miles per hour and a fifteen-foot tidal wave, the hurricane cut a stunning swath through the forests northwest of Belize Town, destroyed three quarters of the town's housing and killed one thousand of its sixteen thousand inhabitants (6.25 percent). Many of the dead were the children assembled for the holiday and residents of the Mesopotamia neighborhood. The loss of Mesopotamia was a particularly harsh blow. Built up since 1925 into a "healthy and habitable" area, it was reduced to a blighted acreage of tangled timbers and mud where hundreds were crushed and drowned under their own homes and schools. The authorities carried out mass cremations and burials, while survivors, "some injured, others hungry and naked, many homeless," gathered in front of the Police Station in hope of aid. Luckier than many was twelve-year-old George Price, future nationalist leader and prime minister, who saw Wesley Church come crashing down as he walked and swam through the streets from the Jesuit-run St. John's College, then on the south side, across the swing bridge to Queen Street.[1]

Lady Katharine Burdon took eighty-three people into Government House to weather the hurricane, twenty-one whites and sixty-two "natives," countering the chaos without by reproducing within the class, gender, and racial hierarchies of the colonial order.[2] During the storm, whites sheltered near the grand piano in the drawing room, while native Belizeans

FIG. 10. Part of the Mesopotamia neighborhood after the 10 September 1931 hurricane.
Source: *Belizean Studies* 6:1 (January 1978): 28.

crowded into the hall and pantry. When night fell, Lady Katharine kept
the ailing Sir John in a dry bed in his dressing room, settled white women
and children onto sofas and large linen shelves in the linen room, and
assigned male British officials to camp beds and sofas in the drawing room.
"Native" women and children went to the dining room, where chairs had
been lashed together to form makeshift beds, and to the governor's office,
where they squeezed into overturned bookshelves. Apparently unschooled
in the history of the middle passage, Lady Katharine was amused to see
"the official bookcases packed tight with human beings." Virtue and
privilege seemed secure. Lady Katharine did not, however, take order
for granted. Her storeroom door had to be broken open after the storm
passed; to leave it so was "asking for trouble," so she quickly moved her
food supplies to "a safer place." She and the colonial secretary's wife "took
charge," assigning work to each adult and busying the servants, whom she
always referred to as black, with making a large stew of tinned food. Thus
deploying her elite white female authority, Lady Katharine avoided any
disruptions of her colonial microcosm.

Her success in maintaining order could not contrast more sharply with
the open social and political conflict of the next decade. When the Burdons

sailed for England shortly after the disaster, the fragile peace of the 1920s was visibly on the brink of collapse. The hurricane of course compounded the economic disaster of the Depression. In 1930 forest products represented 85 percent of the colony's export earnings; over the next two years the volume of chicle exports dropped 75 percent, that of mahogany 90 percent. The familiar dominoes of export dependency and open trade fell: government revenues plummeted, merchant imports contracted, and mass unemployment ensued, driving down wages, making scarce imports unaffordable, and creating widespread hardship.[3] By 1932 medical officers were seeing a rising incidence of malnutrition in the general population and severe anemia mainly in "women of child-bearing age, many of them pregnant. . . . It seemed impossible that women could conceive and carry children with so small a percentage of haemoglobin. The history of these cases was bitter and brief—they died."[4] Not surprisingly, popular protest mushroomed, yielding organized popular rebellion by mid-decade with the founding of the Labourers' and Unemployed Association (LUA). Yet the combination of hurricane and economic collapse did not by itself set into motion the LUA's "hurricane from below." Equally important were the state's own bungled, grudging attempts at relief and amelioration, and the middle class's withdrawal from direct conflict with the state and merchant-employer elite, despite its extensive critique of prevailing conditions and policies. In contrast to several other Caribbean colonies, no middle class-labor alliance emerged in Belize during the 1930s.[5]

This middle-class balking at assuming political leadership was recalled years later by the LUA's leader, Antonio Soberanis Gomez: "After the devastating hurricane of 1931 . . . a few native intellectuals rallied the masses to protest against certain official impositions. The intellectuals withdrew at the height of 'loyalty and devotion' to them, because they said they could not accomplish what the masses desired."[6] A typical middle-class reaction to the shocks of the early 1930s was that of E. E. Cain, a Creole civil servant and brother of leading Garveyite H. H. Cain. In his 1932 account, he cast the hurricane as the work of a vengeful, purifying divinity, arguing that "God visited His people" on "the Colony's birthday" to signal that "Belize must be resurrected—the people must seek a better foundation."

But for Cain the hurricane went beyond symbolism, actually purging the country of elite oppression as well as popular immorality and thus making possible "the dawning of a new era for the people." He defined this better foundation of the new era as cooperation between government and people and between capital and labor with the state mediating.[7] H. H. Cain's *Belize Independent* likewise turned to the state for leadership, attacking its negligence and cruelty, warning officials that Belizeans' culture of stoic pride had limits, that chaos and anarchy would erupt if reforms were not immediately undertaken.[8] The middle-class strongly desired to lead the masses, but its fear of mass action was stronger.

In the renewed constitutional discussions of the 1930s, for example, the middle class again opposed universal suffrage. Those discussions were initiated by the Colonial Office making its hurricane reconstruction loan contingent on the governor receiving the veto powers first proposed in the early 1920s and on the colony coming under Treasury control. Half of the unofficials assented to this change, which sharply reined in the power of the merchant-employer elite in the Unofficial Majority. The strengthened executive then moved to reintroduce a partially elected legislature, which was ultimately achieved under the constitution of 1935.[9] The middle class's long campaign for representative government was over, though its victory was undercut by steep voter and candidate qualifications and by the rapid development of mass politics through the LUA.

Soberanis, a thirty-seven year old bilingual mestizo living in Belize Town with his Creole wife—but who had family roots in Yucatan and northern Belize—worked as a self-employed barber and sometime laborer. He launched the LUA with an outdoor public meeting on 16 March 1934, two days after the Garveyite Progressive Party had ended a disappointing month-long campaign seeking government aid for the unemployed.[10] By his own account he felt "unsuited for the position of leadership"—he had not finished elementary school—but performed brilliantly, denouncing with passion middle-class cowardice and state indifference in the face of starvation. Years afterward, Soberanis attributed his success in part to the middle class's hostility to him: "The arguments advanced by intellectuals to prevent 'loyalty and devotion' to "Tony" had the effect of turning the masses of Belize into *thinkers*."[11] For the next two years, the LUA would mount mass actions that would rock the colonial order. The LUA was a far larger and broader movement than existed in 1919, with more staying power, yet it was still a contingent, vulnerable collaboration of the colony's working peoples, never a seamless unity. It had organizational presence in both Creole and Garifuna communities and panethnic colonywide support. Part illegal labor union and part anticolonial movement, it strongly advocated labor and popular political rights, developing a significant autonomy from the middle class and shredding the tattered legitimacy of the state. The LUA "initiated a national movement" but not an unambiguous struggle for national liberation, sometimes berating the authorities for their failure to provide paternal care, sometimes rejecting colonial paternalism in favor of a transition to some form of self-government based on social and economic justice.[12] It did not seek violent revolution and had no known connection to socialist or communist currents in the Caribbean or Central America, but its struggle constituted a markedly democratic process that nurtured popular political identities and a culture that would endure.[13]

Working women, particularly Creoles in Belize Town and Garifuna in Stann Creek Town, constituted at least half the LUA's membership and were among the its sharpest thinkers and most militant activists. Noting only their numbers, and perhaps assuming that women lacked the capacity for political analysis or action, Peter Ashdown has argued that women's prominence in the movement fundamentally weakened it, thus giving a gendered twist to his conclusion that LUA's struggle was "stillborn" because it did not yield a nationalist movement.[14] Nigel Bolland has contested Ashdown's view by tracing a connection between the LUA of the 1930s and the General Workers' Union GWU of the 1940s, which in turn became the mass base of the nationalist movement in the early 1950s.[15] But the GWU in fact sprang from the tradition of reform politics, not from the LUA, whose true offspring was a democratic, race- and gender-inclusive anticolonial political culture. LUA women's militance, and their organization within the movement of a Women's League, embedded within that culture a strong legitimacy for women's rights as workers and citizens and not simply as

FIG. 11. Antonio Soberanis Gomez later in life. Source: *Belizean Studies* 7:1 (January 1979): 3.

mothers and wives. Their strength protected Soberanis's more democratic leadership from male rivals, and their growing autonomy took form in the league and its demands for womanhood suffrage. It was a tenuous autonomy, however, for LUA women imagined—and struggled for—a society in which male leaders held themselves accountable to an organized and enfranchised female electorate, not one in which women shared ultimate political authority with men. Their distinctly female political consciousness grew relatively unimpeded within a popular anticolonial project that neither nurtured nor provoked an autonomous feminist politics. When the movement as a whole succumbed after 1936 to state repression and reform, female militance, lacking alternative bases of organization, faded.

The LUA was of course only one of many popular mobilizations sweeping the capitalist world in the 1930s, a period during which, according to Eric Hobsbawm, a "crisis of imperialism" occurred that spawned new forms of political alliance and rule.[16] Many such movements were larger, better organized, and more ideologically radical than the LUA, yet the Belizean rebellion of 1934–36 is significant in several ways. As Nigel Bolland has clearly established, it marked the *beginning* of the historic wave of unrest that crested across the British Empire in the 1930s, a wave historians still usually understand to have started rolling in 1935 with events in St. Kitts and the African Copperbelt.[17] Belize was thus a formative site in the invention of reformist responses to unrest by the colonial authorities, responses that culminated in the Colonial Development and Welfare Acts of 1940 and 1945. In addition, because the LUA did not immediately yield a nationalist party, its history clearly illustrates Bolland's recent argument that the chief achievement of the 1930s rebellions was the articulation of a militant, democratic working-class culture.[18]

Yet the LUA also confounds existing categorizations of West Indian popular movements of the 1930s. Soberanis does not fit into Franklin Knight's British-identified reformer category—which includes such leaders as Cipriani and Marryshow—or his populist independent category—in which Garvey and Padmore figure. Soberanis was more critical of the British than the former and far less a part of international Pan-Africanist or socialist thinking than the latter. Knight lists the much better known George Price, the nationalist leader of the 1950s, with Norman Manley, Eric Gairy, Eric Williams, and Cheddi Jagan. Bolland too seems to be thinking ahead to the 1950s when he groups Belize with Barbados and Jamaica as a place where "middle-class politicians used the trade unions as vehicles for their own advancement" and with Grenada and Guyana as a site of late-blooming labor-nationalist connections.[19] Most importantly, Soberanis and the LUA fit neither Bolland's "charismatic authoritarian" nor his bureaucratic categories. Unlike Alexander Bustamante and Uriah "Buzz" Butler, Soberanis's contemporaries of the 1930s, he did not cultivate hero-worship or dependence among the LUA membership and did not have an outsize ego. Yet he certainly possessed charisma, and terms applied to Busta and Butler such as "warrior knight," Anancy, and Moses can help to explain his power and appeal.[20] Soberanis was in essence a "charismatic democrat," a working man whose burning passion to get other workers, female and male, thinking and acting helped him over-

come his self-doubt. A central argument of this chapter is that his charismatic democratic style first encouraged female participation in the LUA
and was then reinforced by the strength of women in the movement.

Soberanis was born in 1897 in northern Belize to Canuto Soberanis
of Tzitas in Yucatan, who had migrated to San Antonio in Orange Walk
in 1894, and to Dominga Gomez de Soberanis of Corozal. He left school
in the fifth standard at age fifteen, by which time he had begun his lifelong barbering trade. He also seems to have worked at times as a forestry
laborer. In 1919, for example, he was jailed for nine months for wounding
a man in Cayo, an act consistent with the rough lumber camp culture of
the district. He married Violet Garbutt in 1922 and together they had a
family of ten living children.[21] It is likely that he settled in Belize Town in the
1920s, for in 1931 the family was living on Bishop Street in Mesopotamia. In
August 1931 Soberanis wrote to the Colonial Secretary asking that his son
Joseph, age twelve, be released from the Pomona Industrial School, where
the boy had been sent by his grandmother in May 1928 while Soberanis
was working outside the colony. Joseph had complained to his father
of conditions at the reform school during a May 1931 visit. In his letter,
Soberanis addressed the colonial secretary as "a father and a gentleman of
integrity" and explained that he felt "confident" he would "understand my
paternal love and be sympathetic to my cause."[22] That confidence in being
treated as a fellow father with protective authority over his children was
shattered when Pomona's Board of Management refused to release Joseph.
The *Independent* published Soberanis's story and correspondence on 9
September as a further example of government cruelty and disrespect; a
day later the hurricane destroyed the Soberanis family's neighborhood.

These early struggles with education, work, and family integrity are
important in understanding Soberanis's sense of broadly shared grievance, but equally notable is his post-LUA history. He founded a second
labor union in 1939 but turned over the leadership in 1942 when he left for
what would be six years of labor in the Panama Canal Zone. On his return
he sought to revive mass anticolonialism, participating in the nationalist
struggle of the 1950s and 1960s as a fairly ordinary member of the movement. He served for a time on the PUP's Central Party Council but never

became one of George Price's political brokers. He was virtually forgotten at the time of his death in 1975, when young nationalist Said Musa
(elected prime minister of Belize in 1998 and 2003) revived lost memories
of Soberanis's lifelong activism.[23] Two years before his death, Soberanis
recalled his role in the 1930s: "After seeing the sufferings and hardship of
my fellow men, I made up my mind to try and help them. It was then I
started the CRY FOR INDEPENDENCE and to free my country from COLO-
NIALISM . . . I went to almost every District and village to awake the
people and I am glad I was able to do so up to this day."[24] In short, Antonio
Soberanis did not have delusions of being exempt from the rules of colonial society; rather he found the courage to risk persecution in the cause
of creating a mass movement.

Women participated actively in labor unrest across the Caribbean in the
1930s; their militance in Trinidad and Tobago, where several different types
of labor movements emerged, has been particularly well documented by
Rhoda Reddock.[25] The gender politics of the LUA fell somewhere between
those of the leftist and black nationalist Negro Welfare Cultural and Social
Association (NWCSA) and those of the empire-loyal Butlerite movement.
The NWCSA, which formed in late 1934 out of the National Unemployed
Movement, encouraged female membership and leadership and opposed
male dominance in the family. One of its principal organizers and ideological leaders was Elma François, a factory worker and laundress arrested
for sedition in 1937 and made a national heroine of Trinidad and Tobago
fifty years later. Women in the NWCSA were expected to think and act
independently. By contrast, Butler cultivated a massive female following in 1937–38 by "articulat[ing] the desires and despair of working-class
women and [giving] importance to those issues which concerned them"
and by doing so in the cultural idiom of Spiritual Baptism, which allows
for a measure of female authority. Reddock argues that these women were
more clearly followers than NWCSA women, and that Butler conceived of
them as a kind of auxiliary to male strikers, but casts doubt on the "hero-
worship" explanation of their militance, noting that in Trinidad's 1937 disturbances women exceeded their prescribed roles. While LUA women never
aspired to or achieved the kind of executive authority that François held,

they were never merely followers or members of a crowd either. Rather they went from being Soberanis's chief supporters to being his chief collaborators. Their own trajectory of democratic self-organization may well have preserved Soberanis's charismatic democratic style and done much to build the LUA as a mass movement. It seems that the LUA's distinctiveness among the labor rebellions of the 1930s in the Caribbean and beyond is inherently connected to its gender politics, a link that suggests a new, gendered, categorization of those popular movements is needed.

Popular Politics 1931–34

Popular resentment of and disillusionment with the colonial order in the early 1930s was uneven and unorganized, but it was widespread and growing: popular stoicism was as much a middle-class fantasy as Keziah Mimms's quaint loyalty had been in the 1910s. Soberanis did not conjure the LUA's rebellion out of thin air by force of charisma but rather connected with a smoldering resentment against a state failing in its popularly defined duties and a disappointment with weak middle-class leadership. As in the late 1910s, a multitude of petitions from individuals and communities flooded the offices of the district commissioners and the colonial secretary, and, as a result of the reform efforts of the 1920s, the petitioners' expectations of the state were higher.[26] Desperate people sought emergency relief, leniency from the state's tax collectors, or the state's intervention with hard-hearted landlords. They also evinced strong interest in constitutional discussions and elite-middle-class politics in general. In Belize Town, "idle men" crowded "barber shops, billiard parlours, the liquor clubs, saloons," and parks, arenas where collective discussion led to actions like the April 1931 occupation of the town board offices and a March 1932 job demonstration. "Women politicians," it was noted, engaged in "heated debates on questions pertaining to their welfare" not only in the water lines and at the market and not only on questions of relief jobs, housing problems, food prices, and water shortages.[27] By early 1934 many laboring people—urban and rural, female and male, from all ethnic groups and districts—were eager for a new kind of political action.

The colonial authorities fueled popular resentment through their haphazard, noncommittal and tardy responses to petitions and their insulting offers of sporadic, poorly paid relief work.[28] The medical staff, still the strongest reformist block within the state, was keenly aware of worsening conditions and so "laboured under a sense of futility"—a "bottle of medicine" was prescribed, but it was known that three meals per day for a month . . . was the medicine needed."[29] Their ongoing concern to curb venereal disease among both sexes was perhaps of less popular interest in the depths of the Depression but was further hampered by the clergy's power to censor public health literature. Fliers posted in public latrines in early 1932 thus emphasized abstinence even as they attacked folk myths about syphilis and gonorrhea.[30] In May 1932 the town board clerk, a Creole, was bold enough to criticize his British superiors: "Persons who are capable of clamouring are getting relief, and more deserving cases are being overlooked, owing we feel to the want of knowledge of the community generally."[31] While the new governor, Sir Harold Kittermaster (1932–34), bore significant responsibility through his refusal to believe that starvation conditions loomed, the unofficials contributed by refusing to pass minimum wage laws in 1931 and 1932, by rejecting the legalization of trade unions, and by benefiting the merchant-employer class with lower export taxes on chicle and sawn lumber. They also gave reconstruction loan money to BEC to build a sawmill and raised the land tax, a measure that effectively hurt only smallholders, as large landowners simply refused to pay.[32] Middle-class criticism of these blatantly biased actions translated into belated and weak action that did nothing to secure mass support.

Women participated actively in the popular politics of the early 1930s, not least because they bore "the brunt of the poverty," suffering, for example, from the malnutrition-related miscarriage and puerperal death described above. Some pregnant women were among those paid twenty-five cents per day, half a man's wage, to clear lots in the Mesopotamia and Freetown areas of Belize Town after the hurricane. In San Ignacio, Aurelia Humes was a young girl doing domestic work for fifty cents a week, which she gave to her mother, who had several other children: "I knew she was suffering with food."[33] Female political activism was strongest in Creole and Garifuna communities where women had higher rates of labor force

TABLE 2. Percent of females in gainful employment, 1931 and 1946*

	1931 (AGE 15+)	1946 (AGE 10+)
Colony	15.3	16.6
Belize District	21.9	22.2
Stann Creek District	24.0	23.8

*In 1931 this category included all females fifteen and over except those who were students, retired, "unoccupied," or engaged in "home duties." In 1946 this category included all females ten and over who were wage-earners, apprentices, employers, own account workers (farmers, dressmakers, laundresses, peddlers), unpaid helpers, *and* the unemployed. Females engaged in "home duties" represented 52.8 percent of the total female population in 1931 and 64.53 percent of females over 10 in 1946. These statistics undoubtedly failed to capture the full extent of women's income-earning activities.

SOURCES: *Census of British Honduras, 1931* (Belize, 1933), 7, 13–17, and tables 6 and 12 (the percentages are based on my recalculations of the raw numbers and are higher than those listed in the census) and *West India Census 1946, Part E: Census of Population of British Honduras* (Kingston: Department of Statistics, 1948), xxxi, 24, and table 36.

participation and single motherhood and were thus more vulnerable to unemployment and its consequences. This pattern portended the marked strength and organization in the LUA of women from Belize Town and Stann Creek Town. Table 2 shows that the Belize and Stann Creek Districts had the highest rate of female "gainful employment" in the colony, table 3 shows the concentration of Creole and Garifuna women in those two districts and their principal towns, and table 4 shows that those two districts had the highest rates of "illegitimate" births in the colony. Table 5 shows that the Belize and Stann Creek Districts, where Creole and Garifuna women were concentrated, had the highest rates of adult single women and the lowest rates of both common-law and formally married women in the colony. This likely means that more of the "illegitimate" births in those districts were to single women with sole responsibility for the household rather than to common-law wives.

Only one fledgling social movement appeared prior to 1934, but its political analysis suggests how quickly popular politics had developed in the aftermath of economic and natural disaster. The Jobless Workers, a small band of Creole working men who advocated for labor rights and economic development, originated in a deputation of the unemployed to Kittermaster in December 1932. With two hundred supporters waiting

TABLE 3. Percentage of female population by census racial classifications, 1946*

	COLONY	BELIZE DISTRICT	BELIZE TOWN	STANN CREEK DISTRICT	STANN CREEK TOWN
Black	38.09	56.27	56.91	21.83	16.26
Mixed	31.69	35.60	34.96	17.41	12.30
Maya	16.18	1.23	0.84	0.11	0.20
Garifuna	7.54	0.65	0.43	57.30	69.56
White	3.91	4.92	5.30	1.47	0.74
Asiatic	2.30	0.87	0.85	1.76	0.94
Not stated	0.26	0.44	0.45	0.12	0.00

*The 1946 census was the first to calculate racial classifications by district. I have changed "Carib" to Garifuna and "American Indian" to Maya (the original category may have included a very few non-Maya indigenous people). "Asiatic" includes East Indians, Syrians, and Chinese. The "mixed" category included both mulattos and mestizos. "They were widely distributed. In the Cayo and Northern Districts it is believed that these persons were chiefly of mixed Indian and Spanish descent, while in Belize and Stann Creek they were chiefly of mixed European and African descent" (*West India Census 1946, Part E,* xv).

SOURCE: *West India Census 1946, Part E: Census of Population of British Honduras,* xiv (table A), 6 (table 14).

outside, five men told the governor that "there is poverty in many homes" and asked for good wages, labor protection, land settlement, and import substitution based on local investment. When Kittermaster replied only with long-term promises of jobs in industrial and agricultural development, the leadership put their political critique into writing. Casting the government as the pilot of the ship of state, responsible to the people, they argued for an active popular role in government: "We understand that Democracy teaches us that the free gift of God [intellect] should be utilized by the masses and not by the financial few." In January 1933, with a five-hundred-name petition supporting their efforts, they began to solicit state and private aid to start a soap factory. Among those who donated to the cause was Antonio Soberanis. Kittermaster, too, eventually kicked in some government aid including ten thousand pounds of coconuts. The Commoners' Soap Factory opened in Corozal and produced Creole Soap—names suggestive of a patriotic class and ethnic consciousness. In April the Jobless Workers provided testimonials from sixteen women and two men who had used the soap and announced that it would soon be for sale at "Mrs. Alice Lamb's shop at No. 5, Tigris St., at Mesopotamia,

TABLE 4. Percentage of illegitimate births, 1915, 1916, 1938

DISTRICT	1915	1916	1938
Belize	45.84	47.17	50.67
Corozal	37.78	34.54	
Orange Walk	31.58	32.57	
Northern*			34.07
Stann Creek	49.58	50.23	50.80
Toledo	37.82	38.58	43.19
Cayo	38.51	37.03	44.23
Colony	41.35	41.56	44.78

*Corozal and Orange Walk Districts were united as the Northern District at this time.

SOURCES: *Annual Report on the Vital Statistics of British Honduras for 1915* (Blize, 1916), paras. 13 and 14, *Annual Report on the Vital Statistics of British Honduras for 1916*, paras. 13 and 14 (Belize, 1917), and *Report on the Vital Statistics of British Honduras for the Year 1938* (Belize, 1939), 12 (table V).

Belize." They also pled for the public to buy shares in the enterprise. But three months later the factory closed when it was denied a government loan. The Jobless Workers' final words foreshadowed the intensification of popular anger at the state: "If the . . . District Commissioner [of Corozal] expects to shoulder the responsibility of hampering the living of so many needy people then he should be given timely warning that he is putting himself into a very serious position." Soon, they concluded, they would be forced to march on the Colonial Secretary's office, demanding the dole.[34]

Most protests from the colony's predominantly mestizo and Mayan regions, including Corozal District, were rural and took the form of petitions focused on tax and rent relief, secure access to land, and relief road work. Large community petitions poured into the colonial authorities from San Ignacio and Benque Viejo in the west, Ambergris Caye, the villages of Orange Walk District, and from the Mayan villages of Patchakan and Yo Chen near Corozal. Overwhelmingly, these petitions were signed only by men, who evinced a keen awareness of the Depression worldwide and sometimes appealed to the colonial state as a father who would surely meet his responsibilities, so that they, as fathers, could care for their families. In Patchakan and Yo Chen, however, a less conciliatory politics was brewing. Petitioners were planning to form an agricultural society, "that we may have where to express ourselfs [sic]." These villages helped to

TABLE 5. Women's (age 15 and over) conjugal condition by district, 1946

DISTRICT	SINGLE	COMMON-LAW	MARRIED	WIDOWED	DIVORCED
Belize	46.3	10.7	35.1	7.8	0.1
Northern	23.6	22.0	45.1	9.3	-
Cayo	28.4	20.9	41.9	8.7	0.1
Stann Creek	35.0	16.4	37.5	11.1	-
Toledo	28.5	17.4	40.7	13.2	0.2
Colony	37.21	15.16	38.50	9.08	0.05

SOURCE: *West India Census 1946, Part E: Census of Population of British Honduras*, xxi (Table C).

raise $200 for Soberanis's legal defense in 1935 when he was charged with sedition. Other petitions from these regions included a mid-1930 protest from Cayo's chicleros against wage cuts and two large ones in 1933 against education cuts, one from Corozal Town, the other from Benque Viejo. Unusually, 25 percent of the latter's signatories were female.[35]

Women in mestizo and Mayan ethnic regions experienced the crisis less as single mothers, household heads, or wage workers than as wives of unemployed *chicleros* and cash-strapped *milperos*, mothers of children who were fed with corn from rented land. Adolfa Garcia was a young girl in her village of Yo Creek during the depression, and her weekly sales of homegrown tomatoes in Orange Walk Town were part of the revival of family farming during the crisis.[36] There is no record of mestizo or Mayan women doing relief work, as Garifuna and Creole women did, likely because relief work often correlated with tax liability and thus property ownership. Although older women in particular would likely have influenced the petitions' tone and demands, the men signed and delivered the petitions as family and community heads.

The gender politics of protest were quite different in Stann Creek, where Garifuna women were the farmers "without whom there would be starvation." Henry T. Bowman, then a young citrus planter, saw hundreds of women early every morning, walking beside the railway to their provision grounds. Citrus brought wage labor for Garifuna women, particularly with the opening of a packing shed in 1933. Defining themselves as farmers, wage workers, and property owners, these women signed petitions, did relief work, and confronted the governor directly. They constituted one third of the 513 people who petitioned against the increased land tax. When Kittermaster held constitutional hearings in the Stann Creek Town courtroom, a "[d]elegation of Carib women Petitioners . . . submitted various grievances to the Chief." As a result of this meeting, Garifuna women were later able to work off back taxes by performing relief work at fifty cents per day, chopping grass and filling swamps around the cemetery and slaughterhouse.[37]

These poor Garifuna women's demands on and frustrations with the state seem also to have been directed at the nascent Garifuna middle class that had been organizing itself since 1924 in the Carib Sick-Aid and Development Society (CDS). By 1931 the CDS had parallel male and female executives, perhaps in imitation of the UNIA, and two hundred members in three branches—Stann Creek Town, Punta Gorda, and Barranco—led by L. A. Blanco, son of merchant B. C. O. Blanco. The lady president and vice president (Nicanora Ignacio and Emilia Ciego) headed a seventeen-woman team to care for hurricane refugees sent from Belize Town. In 1932 eighty CDS members, thirty-seven of them women, petitioned to have four CDS women trained as midwives. The district commissioner recommended that two of the four should come from "the remainder of the carib population," which he said openly resented the CDS.[38] It is unlikely that many of the thirty-seven female signatories were citrus workers or tax-owing farmers.

Creole women's relatively vocal and independent approach to the state was similar to Garifuna women's. One of the most powerful and poignant cases of rural female protest came from the Creole riverbank village of Flower's Lime Walk, northwest of Belize Town, an area devastated by the hurricane and unemployment. Mrs. Emily Hendy led twenty-six women, who presented themselves as "women and mothers of this village," in petitioning the state for provisions and clothing and—as in the case of rural Orange Walk where men petitioned—to ask the BEC to stop pressuring them to "pay our plantation rents in advance."[39] They referred to "our husbands' and male relatives'" unemployment but had organized and spoken as family and community representatives independently. They warned that "unless some help is forthcoming, famine, desolation, and even death will be the result." The state took three months to send Mrs. Hendy a letter instructing her to apply for relief provisions from an official stationed on the Belize River. Such delays were all too frequent, as were replies that simply declined to intervene, contributing to a growing perception of the state as callous and arbitrary.

This feeling was most explicitly articulated in Belize Town itself, where broadly similar scenarios were played out but in a context of greater desperation and tension. Urban working-class women were highly involved in the wage labor and informal economies, especially as male unemployment skyrocketed, and they did do relief work.[40] Yet women's primary demand was for shelter, not work. Whether this was due to a shift in the labor market toward cheaper female labor, as the earlier example of pregnant women chopping grass would suggest, or due to women's choice to present themselves as mothers in need rather than as unemployed workers is hard to determine. Most likely both factors shaped the documented pattern.

The Belize Town Board erected barrack-like "hutments" after the hurricane to shelter homeless renters, but at a cost of fifty to seventy-five cents a week. By 1933 many hutment tenants were in debt to the town board and began to complain about harassment from municipal officials to higher authorities. Men's petitions usually lamented the lack of relief work, which would have allowed them to pay, while most women simply asked for lenience. Representative was Hepzibah Hill, thirty-nine, with two young daughters and an unemployed "sweetheart," who owed four weeks' rent in February 1933. Private landlords were just as demanding. Mrs. Olive Moses, a mother of seven with a husband earning $3.75 per week, was five months in arrears and facing eviction when she petitioned for her son, just released from the Pomona Industrial School, to be given a set of work clothes. Other women got work directly, like the hundred on the Magazine Road rock-breaking gang in April and May 1932. Three such women rented a room in Mesopotamia from a "well-known gentleman" for $1 per week and asked him for leniency when they were laid off from the gang. His response was to remove their roof, an action so far beyond the normal range of landlord callousness that the *Independent* chastised him in its pages, though not by name.[41]

The paper also publicized the plight of women who lacked the resources to recover quickly from the hurricane. An East Indian woman was found living in a dirt-floored shack with her daughter and three grandchildren. Illiterate, she felt unable to approach the state for aid. Caroline Hewitt, an elderly homeless woman, was referred to the Poor House by colonial officials, but she "walked away without another word," perhaps preferring the street or market, where many homeless people slept, to the indignity of the Poor House. Longtime market vendor Ellen Ocean slept in her stall at the market after the hurricane and petitioned the government twice—first to ask that the town board give her son a job, then to request lenience on stall rent she had been unable to pay. She was denied both times.[42]

Somewhat different were the property-owning women who lost real estate in the hurricane. Some filed compensation claims against the government for having damaged their homes during the clearing of debris. Others received reconstruction loans, like Henrietta Diamond of Far West Street, who was threatened with eviction in late 1933 for arrears. Kittermaster himself signed the warning, and Diamond appealed to him directly, outraged that the governor who had given loans to needy people would now take their homes. Her request for leniency denied, she wrote to him again, infuriated like many by his negligent abuse of power: "Sir, if the Chief Executive of the Land, and also Chairman of the Loan Board . . . cannot 'intervene' in the matter: Then I say to whom shall we go. Oh yes, it is mighty inconvenient to be poor." Diamond was finally evicted in 1935. By then she was living with labor leader John Lahoodie, who in 1932 had himself protested the burdensome and insulting process of applying for such loans on behalf of his then wife.[43]

Although the experiences of applying for relief work, reconstruction loans, rent lenience, or shelter and of being treated harshly and arbitrarily by the colonial and municipal authorities were shared by the men and women of Belize Town, they acted individually for the most part. Evidence of three incidents of collective male action survives: the April 1931 occupation of town board offices and March 1932 job demonstration mentioned above and the Jobless Workers' movement from December 1932 to July 1933. The one episode of urban female collective action that we know of in this period originated, as in the 1920s, in the chronic problem of urban water shortages. The dry seasons of the early 1930s were all very long, and drought conditions prevailed by April each year. The water supply in the public vats was inadequate, especially with an expanding urban population, and repeatedly women would purchase tickets from the town board, line up at length for water, and receive none. A letter to the *Independent* observed that "those in authority are trying to test the pulse of the people." On Easter Monday of 1933, "a band of women and grown ups ["nearly all female"] with cans and pails" marched to Government House demanding to speak with Kittermaster. Finding him absent, they went to the colonial secretary in his office, who took them to the town clerk, who agreed to leave the vats open all day. Several days later, "a crowd of women and young folks . . . becoming harassed and angered," broke open the public vats, which the town board had closed early, leaving people with no water for the weekend.[44] Although water protests never gained momentum, there was a clear shift even in that week from demanding that the colonial and municipal authorities act in the public interest to bypassing them altogether. Urban female subalterns had given fair warning of their ability to act decisively and independently.

The urban popular classes did come together around the issue of constitutional change, though largely in the role of spectators. In January 1932 when the acting governor convened a meeting of one hundred "representative" citizens—all middle- and upper-class men—to discuss Britain's reconstruction loan offer, a "great multitude" of uninvited men and women filled the verandahs and streets around the meeting hall. Contrary to Cedric Grant's argument that "the people [were] indifferent" to politics, those gathered were clearly interested in both the loan coming through and in Britain's stipulations that made the loan conditional on breaking the power of the unofficials.[45] Once the latter grudgingly conceded, Kittermaster toured the colony testing public opinion on the proposal to allow for a partially elected legislature in the new constitution. In Orange Walk and Stann Creek organized groups of men and women presented petitions on local economic problems, but Kittermaster was unimpressed with rural peoples' understanding of colonial government or what the historic change would mean.[46] He underestimated them. True, there were only a few instances of rural self-organization, as in Patchakan, Yo Chen, and Flowers' Lime Walk, but the far more common practice of community petitioning for state aid certainly implied a political ideal and analysis. If that analysis did not engage constitutional fine points, that was because middle-class groups based in Belize Town, including the UNIA, had failed to promote popular political education through a campaign for representative government after the debacle of 1925. Indeed, when Kittermaster's constitutional roadshow ended in Belize Town, the Garveyite Progressive Party, virtually dormant for years, had to hastily organize a delegation and public meeting. The popular response was astounding. Five thousand people came out to the Battlefield—a small park area named for the Salvation Army missionaries who preached there beginning in the 1910s—indicating a massive unorganized popular desire for political change. But the PP, as in 1924–25, advised Kittermaster that a broad franchise, not universal suffrage, was appropriate.[47]

At this juncture, a significant new political voice disrupted the class and gender assumptions of the constitutional hearings. Mrs. Elfreda Trapp, a Creole woman then in her early thirties, was the wife of Solomon Trapp, one of the founders two months later of the Jobless Workers. Elfreda "received a great ovation as she rose to speak"—suggesting that she had working-class supporters at the hearings—and reminded the assembled officials and pundits of the interest of "the working women of the community," and working men, in the vote.[48] Like the PP, Trapp did not advocate immediate universal suffrage, but she specified low educational levels rather than income as the impediment. While she may in this moment have spoken out as a Garveyite, PP-identified working woman, spurred to action by the size of the PP's public meeting, by 1935 she advocated womanhood suffrage, apparently radicalized by the state's abandonment of the Jobless Workers' factory and by her participation in the LUA.

Neither mass popular interest in the franchise nor Elfreda's intervention had any effect on the draft constitutional bill produced in 1933, which retained the steep property qualifications and higher female voting age of the final bill of 1925.[49] When Kittermaster agreed with the PP's request that women qualify as candidates, the PP's own Calvert Staine doubted that "any woman could be found to stand" for election.[50] The constitutional process abated until early 1935, but in the meantime Kittermaster found a woman to serve on the Belize Town Board: Vivian Seay, head of the Black Cross Nurses. Seay and the Black Cross Nurses had been occupied since 1931 looking after hurricane refugees, expanding the Baby Exhibition to Stann Creek Town, and helping to organize a feeding program for school-children.[51] She took the unusual step of publicly campaigning in the November 1933 municipal elections for independent candidate Ricardo T. Meighan, whose victory put him on a PP-dominated town board.[52] Seay's own appointment to the board yielded middle-class hopes that her lobbying for "amelioration" would be effective. She proceeded along precisely these lines, paying particular attention to women. She first proposed a municipal Employment Bureau for women—one of only two exceptions to her career of constructing poor women as mothers—where they could register as cooks, maids, laundresses, or nannies and thus end their shameful begging for work door to door. When that idea stalled, she convinced the Palace Theatre management to form the Palace Unemployed Women's Fund with the Nurses. The fund gave weekly grocery bundles to deserving women, but it only provided two hundred families with $1's worth of groceries each up to April 1934.[53] While Seay's increasingly political activism in 1933–34 signaled the middle class's awareness of growing popular frustration, her actions also came late and essentially remained within the paradigm of charity. As such, they had little potential to lead and contain popular unrest.

Seay undertook her third endeavor, lobbying for legal divorce, just a few weeks before Soberanis launched the LUA, but it came too late and was too narrowly conceived to have any impact on popular opinion. Seay and the Nurses, like Garveyite men, backed the colonial administration's bill to confirm the legality of divorce in the colony, a bill prompted by the British Privy Council's decision that British divorce law applied to the colony. They did not contest their Roman Catholic opponents' focus on morality but argued that divorce was necessary to prevent the moral evils of adultery and illegitimacy. Seay, who spoke at the UNIA's and nurses' public meetings, a town board meeting, and an outdoor rally, argued repeatedly that divorce would improve community morality. When a town board member opposed divorce, she retorted: "I rise being much disappointed in the remarks of the last speaker. . . . He spoke as if women were the only ones to commit fornication. We are the ones who need divorce. . . . Divorce would mean a better moral community."[54] Here she verged on making a feminist argument that women's right to divorce was grounded in their right to happiness and self-respect, even on making a critique of male behavior, but ended by legitimizing divorce in the name of marital stability and morality, not women's rights. At the nurses' prodivorce public meeting, attended by a quite meager crowd of 120, one invited speaker was Mrs. E. Trapp—the same Elfreda Trapp who had spoken at the 1932 constitutional hearings. Trapp represented a potential for cross-class alliance between the Nurses and working women, one lost with the emergence of the LUA and the Nurses' hostility to its labor militance.[55]

As in Trinidad and Tobago, where a divorce bill was debated in 1931–32, that potential was already limited not only by the Catholic clergy's ability to mobilize large numbers of women but also by the irrelevance of legal marriage and divorce to many women of the popular classes.[56] Had Seay expanded her critique of male behavior to include domestic violence, she might have garnered greater interest, for church-married or not, male violence was still a primary reason that women tried to leave relationships. Just months before Seay began her lobbying, for example, the gruesome murder of Cleopha Perdomo by Candido Perez, and his guilty but insane verdict, riveted Belize Town. Cleopha had earlier fled rural Corozal District and again tried to break off her two-year relationship with Perez when he followed her to town. Similarly, Sofia Tessecum of Bullet Tree Falls in Cayo and Agatha Brown of Bomba in the Belize District were common-law wives whose partners attacked them when they attempted to leave. William Johnson of Belize Town was convicted of maiming his legal wife, who did not want him back, fearing deadlier violence in the future.[57] Not only did Seay remain silent on domestic violence, but the *Independent* published a column in April 1934 blaming a young wife for leaving her unemployed husband and thus provoking him into dragging her through the streets of Belize Town into a house where he beat her. Women, the columnist concluded, should be more sympathetic to the effects of the Depression on men. Divorce was legalized in early 1935, but there is little evidence that it reduced domestic violence—or affected the community morality Seay sought to defend.[58]

The divorce debate subsided during February 1934, the same month that the PP sponsored a silent march under the new rubric of the Unemployed Brigade, in which hundreds of men and women participated, carrying banners reading: "We want work not promises," "Our children are starving," and "We cannot meet our rents and taxes because we have no work." The *Independent* was relieved by the marchers' restraint and peaceful order, and Kittermaster responded by registering the unemployed in order to distribute relief rations. Over a thousand men and three hundred women quickly signed on, but they were offered spoiled rice and relief work at the absurdly low rate of five cents per day.[59] One month after the march, the PP dissolved the Unemployed Brigade, ending its one attempt to organize labor in order to demand change from the authorities. The middle class had indeed admitted that it "could not accomplish what the masses desired." Two days later, on 16 March 1934, Antonio Soberanis held his first public meeting on the Battlefield, labeling as cowards the leaders of the Unemployed Brigade and declaring that he would rather die than give in to injustice.[60] Fed up with middle-class ambivalence and constitutional tinkering, and with the state's insults and indifference, he broke with silent orderliness, dispensed with middle-class mediation, and sparked a period of sustained popular protest and organization. As we have seen, the fires were already smoldering. Tenants who had received no help in their lopsided struggles with landlords, poor taxpayers who had done hard labor to protect their land and homes, men and women who had seen themselves again deemed unfit to vote, rallied to Soberanis's clarion call for justice. Elfreda Trapp's 1932 demand that the authorities heed the interests of working women was in no way satisfied by Vivian Seay's ascension to the town board or the passing of the divorce bill. The working women of particularly Belize Town and Stann Creek Town embraced direct confrontation with the colonial authorities, becoming Soberanis's most important allies.

The Gender Politics of the LUA and Women's League, 1934–1936

The Labourers and Unemployed Association marked its first anniversary in March 1935 with internal elections. LUA women emerged from the electoral process without full equality in the organization, but they did win clear recognition and acceptance of their strong and cohesive presence within it. They did not contest executive posts, which were all declared open, but were elected to half the seats on the committee.[61] Every one of the six women so elected was an officer of the LUA Women's League, organized in early 1935, which had obviously held its own elections already. The Women's League was the most important expression of a trajectory of increasing female collective self-definition and power within the LUA, a trajectory rooted in their constant, enthusiastic, and mass participation in the movement since its inception. In February 1935 the league mounted a historic call for womanhood suffrage, contesting both the constitutional bill and middle-class women's limited critiques of it. By then LUA women were the most organized and articulate part of the movement and a relatively autonomous force within it, fighting for their own specific rights as female natives and citizens. Evidence indicates that Soberanis always ran the LUA as a markedly inclusive and relatively democratic organization, and that he never sought to subdue or domesticate LUA women. The league's subordinate electoral inclusion, then, did not necessarily signal a strategy of control and containment designed to reassert male authority. Women's power as Soberanis's strongest supporters *and* an authentic acceptance of women's right to political voice and leadership most likely combined to confirm women as official movement leaders.

The six women elected were Miss Sarah Johnson, Miss Pearl Tennyson, and Miss Amybell Pratt, respectively league chairlady, secretary and treasurer, the league's nursing matron, Mrs. Christobel Usher, and two league committee members, Mrs. Rosannah Branche and none other than Mrs. Elfreda Trapp, now widowed. Pratt, Trapp and her sisters Virginia and Ianthe Stanford, and other women — "all the women with Tony" — reportedly met regularly Pratt's home. Four of the six elected women gave speeches, as did Virginia Stanford, Eliza Brooks, and Susan Cacho, one of five women attending in a delegation from the LUA's Stann Creek Town branch. Their

FIG. 12. Carib International Society meeting in Barranco, 1931. The CIS was organized in 1924 by Garifuna men in Guatemala who were hoping to obtain land for small farming. Some of the Garifuna women pictured here may have attended the LUA's Barranco recruitment meeting in 1935. Source: E. E. Cain, *Cyclone!* (London: Arthur H. Stockwell, 1933), opposite page 128.

presence was indicative both of Garifuna women's political activism and the movement's initial success in building a popular coalition across the colony.[62] In May, Soberanis and Virginia Stanford traveled to the Toledo District, where they established LUA branches, and galvanized women in the Garifuna communities of Punta Gorda and Barranco and tried unsuccessfully to reach the Mayan villages in the interior. The LUA also had popular support in Mayan-mestizo districts in the north and west, but Stann Creek was clearly the second stronghold of the LUA, in no small measure because of female activism.

That LUA women organized the Women's League indicates that they possessed a specific female political subjectivity and a desire to promote women's rights. What they understood as their identity and rights, however, is less straightforward. There is no record of them mobilizing around issues of low female wages or high female unemployment or around the particular problems of single mothers or even the cost of living or housing crisis. Nor did they ever publicly address the prevalence of domestic violence. It seems highly likely that many of these problems motivated them in their establishment of working women's leadership within pro-tonationalist culture, thus linking the hardships that motivated women's protests of the early 1930s to the broad critique of colonial and employer power. But the issue that they most clearly spoke out on was that of political rights. The birth of the Women's League coincided with LUA women's defense of Soberanis's more democratic leadership within the movement; the league then quickly held its own elections, possibly prompting the LUA as a whole to follow suit, and called for womanhood suffrage in legislative elections. League activists thus seem to have identified as democrats and to have defined women's rights to democratic process and participation as the key to solving women's long list of problems. The Women's League did not define ultimate masculine authority as one of those problems, but neither were they simply an unthinking crowd mesmerized by Soberanis's heroic charisma. He undoubtedly projected strong political virility—part-responsible family man, part-angry renegade—but this seems to have combined with his humility and antielitism to encourage women's forceful participation in a movement that they felt was and should remain collectively "owned." In sum, LUA women had little occasion to politicize male authority within the movement beyond the organization of the league itself.

Women's potential to take an independent role in the struggle was noted from its inception by both the police and the press. Police Superintendent P. E. Matthews reported that from the beginning, "quite 50% of Soberanis's followers were women and they were always more truculent than the men." The *Independent*'s women's columnist described urban women's prominence in the Battlefield meetings of six hundred to eight hundred people that took place several times a week after the success of Soberanis's first meeting, often lasting from 8:00 pm to midnight. "[T]he women of Belize are politically minded even more so than men. I notice that at the Battlefield meetings women occupy the foremost places near the rostrum. . . . Yes the Battlefield is really historic so far as our women folk are concerned. They are really interested, for night after night they are the first to assemble on the Battlefield. The distance cannot be too far for them to carry boxes, chairs or benches, so they may be more comfortable in any position they occupy."[63] Such public enthusiasm translated into the necessary organizational work of building a movement, making women the backbone of the growing LUA.

During the first months of popular agitation, March through September 1934, Soberanis elaborated the LUA's critique of colonial injustice as the cause of labor exploitation and family hardship. He did so in an unpredictable process of conflict and celebration. At his inaugural meeting, for example, he first denounced the leaders of the Unemployed Brigade for giving up so easily, then expressed his "compassion and sympathy for his people," referring to the domestic suffering of the working class in explicitly anticolonial terms. "You have suffered long—5 cents a day can't keep you—your children are starving and so are you. Are you British subjects or objects? [Voices: "Objects"]." By bringing his young son forward and saying, "I wish to place him under your care, for when I am dead and gone, I want you to give him a good education," Soberanis opened channels of trust and responsibility between himself and the crowd. Including both women and men as fellow parents, Soberanis founded the LUA as a shared community, not as a vehicle for his patriarchal wisdom.[64] His fundamental attitude toward poor Belizeans thus contrasted strikingly with middle-class critiques of working-class parenting, ritualized through the 1930s in the Baby Exhibition. In the subsequent weeks and months, in speeches on the Battlefield and in Stann Creek Town and in writing, Soberanis attacked Britain and the monarchy, Governor Kittermaster and other officials, local professional elites, and the BEC, for its treatment of its employees and tenants and for its undue influence with the governor. In April he threatened Superintendent Matthews with a repeat performance of "the licking he got in 1919," a statement that landed Soberanis in court.[65] When he was cautioned rather than jailed, the largest Battlefield meeting yet celebrated his victory.

Soberanis also developed a discourse of what the LUA was fighting for, beyond the general goal of justice. In Stann Creek he presented himself as a patriot fighting for a "better administration" and soon elaborated on this in the LUA's first petition to government, in May. The movement—now better defined through the distribution of membership cards—presented it in person, five hundred people marching with Soberanis to Kittermaster's office. It demanded an eight-hour day, a $1.50 per day minimum wage, government relief work, and 90 percent native labor on all government projects.[66] There was no specific mention of women's wages or unemployment, but neither did LUA discourse explicitly embrace the male breadwinner model. Framing the petition demands in nationalist terms, Soberanis now claimed authority on the grounds that he was "under instructions from . . . thousands of People" to "raise the cry of British Honduras for British Honduraneans [sic]."[67] A sleeping people had woken, he argued, to ask "for our rights." More challenging was his claim that "we interpret Government only as an Executive for the people." The petition did dampen its fire by portraying the people as loyal, law-abiding citizens of the Empire, desirous of friendship "with the White Men" even if they did not think of whites as being part of the native community. But when Kittermaster rejected the petition on the grounds that British charity was already substantial, Soberanis instantly dispensed with deference. "What we are receiving from England is only what belongs to us," he retorted, "we have for years been keeping things going."[68] He also denounced fifty or seventy-five cents per day as starvation wages for a man with a family, a rare reference to the male breadwinner model.

The LUA's anticolonialism and antimonarchism intensified after this bitter experience. Soberanis produced "a red and green flag . . . and said he had no King, and no Queen, nor no Prince."[69] Despite this native republicanism, the Garveyite *Independent* continued to cover the popular movement with some sympathy and the "new Labour Union" even participated in the 1 August emancipation parade led by the Black Cross Nurses. There is no evidence that LUA women marched at this time, but it would be surprising if they had not, considering their activism and the meaning of slave emancipation to a largely Creole group.[70] The meanings of the centennial were likely quite different for the British-identified respectably middle-class Garveyites and for the poor Creoles defining a national culture in the LUA. In the subsequent month all basis for joint LUA and middle-class celebration dissolved. In August the movement demanded the removal from office of H. D. Phillips, the magistrate of the Belize District,

FIG. 13. Antonio Soberanis and the Black Cross Nurses, probably taken on the occasion of the 1 August 1934 parade to mark the centennial of the abolition of slavery. Source: *Belizean Studies* 7:1 (January 1979): 3.

for incompetence and lack of popular respect. The LUA also picketed the big merchant stores that were refusing to donate to the movement's 10th celebration fund, enforcing a popular boycott.[71] Critique was turning into confrontation, precisely the transition that middle-class progressives consistently refused to make.

As a result, the LUA celebrated the 10th independently and with a distinctive intent. Refusing to pledge loyalty to government, Crown, and Empire, the LUA's 10th was a mammoth popular celebration of a rebellious native identity in which three thousand people participated. Women marched in the new colors of the LUA flag, wearing "white, red, and green aprons, and green caps," while the men wore the more traditional "red caps, blue shirt, white pants." Soberanis led the parade on horseback wearing a red cap that may have been worn at the turn of the century by working-class patriot Simon Lamb. Snubbing the acting governor by passing Government House without stopping, the LUA then marched through poor neighborhoods, as well as the main streets, and finished at Yarborough Green. Here

Soberanis laid a wreath on the grave of Colonel Thomas Paslow, a white slave owning hero of 1798, as the Friendly Societies had done in 1931. The honoring of Paslow, which seems so misplaced, probably stemmed from the LUA leadership's local patriotism and lack of knowledge about slave resistance. As a whole, the LUA's 10th challenged middle-class ownership of official history and reshaped the Battle of St. George's Caye myth by linking 1798 to national rebellion, though it did not reject the myth altogether. LUA women's aprons must have served them well that evening, for they ran at least six kitchens under the huge tent erected on the green. Winifred Flowers was there: "It's only the women cooking, then the men they go get the firewood." The women cooked conch soup, fried fish, rice and beans, and stewed pork—beloved Creole foods that had been rarely enjoyed since the hurricane—and fed twenty-five hundred people. Then bands began to play, and dancing lasted well into the night.[72] The LUA had pulled off a major organizational triumph, taken control of public space, and gained the confidence to take further independent action.

So fired up were the LUA leaders by the triumph of the celebrations and by a victory in their first strike—of Stann Creek stevedores—that on 29 September Soberanis told a Battlefield crowd that "if the Governor would not remove Mr. Phillips from the bench, he would," a remark that would land him in jail.[73] He also announced that on Monday 1 October the LUA would close down the BEC sawmill. The women of the movement—Elfreda Trapp, Amybell Pratt, and the rest—were about to come out from their kitchens and emerge as an independent force in the LUA's sharpest confrontation with the political authorities and economic powers of the colony.

At 6.30 a.m. on 1 October 1934 Soberanis and two hundred men and women marched to the gates of the sawmill. Forewarned, the entire police force lined up to allow the workers clear entry. At 7 a.m. Soberanis walked away, calling out to newspaper reporters: "strike fails."[74] He spent the rest of the morning negotiating with the acting governor at Government House. The crowd, particularly the women, opted for confrontation. "Supporters of the strike idea reflected grave disappointment, and the malcontents, chiefly women, significantly, commenced to disperse, but letting forth all kinds of unsavoury remarks about the workers. . . . Not one of [Tony's] lieutenants seemed to have appeared on the scene and some of the more fiery women, observing this, commented on it, calling their names and branding them 'damn cowards. '"[75] Disgusted, these angry women continued to discuss strategy as they returned to the market area. Two hours later they returned at the head of a five-hundred-person crowd armed with sticks, and "forced their way through the [sawmill yard] gate."[76] Ashdown's observation that "the strike leaders closed down the works" obscures the fact that at this peak moment of popular labor rebellion those leaders were women.[77] Tony Soberanis, Jr., then a young worker, remembers the pivotal role that women played in the events of 1 October 1934: "In every case the women have always taken the lead. It was the women who went there and shut down the sawmill. [The women were] more radical than the men. Men were afraid to strike. . . . The women went there with sticks and kitchen utensils, potspoons and kitchen forks."[78]

These were the tools of their domestic trades, used in September to feed the masses, now deployed as weapons against those defined as the people's enemies. Women left men to guard the gates and moved into the mill yard, scattering the workers before them and declaring that no white man would enter the yard. They blew the mill whistle to encourage other groups of picketers at other locations. Women were part of the crowd confronting workers and supervisors at the public works yard, and "300 men and women" armed with sticks confronted the town board chairman in Queen Street, the crowd soon ballooning to fifteen hundred.[79] Sarah Moore was arrested there for striking Superintendent Matthews with a stick. In court she was defiant, refusing to question the police (she appears to have been defending herself) or to pay a fine. "I have to go to prison," she instructed the magistrate, "just make out the paper."[80] The fight that Annie Flowers had been itching for in 1919 had finally arrived. Black women had led the popular takeover of the property of the largest private employer and landowner in the colony, warning off white men after decrying the cowardice of their own male leaders. Their actions and words together indicate an unevenly but passionately expressed political critique of class, race, colonialism, and of gender relations within and beyond the native community they were defending. Without their aggressive determination, the movement certainly would have been deflated rather than galvanized by the end of that pivotal day.

Soberanis certainly risked female wrath by abandoning the strike and playing a conciliatory role during the crisis, meeting with officials and defusing the Queen Street crowd at noon. But when he returned to the police station at 5 p.m. to bail out Moore and fifteen men, he was arrested for the earlier threats against Phillips. Any doubts about his leadership evaporated and the crowd outside the station swelled again to over two thousand, literally taking over Queen Street. At one point a snake charmer released two snakes into the station, causing the police to scatter in fear: "The crowd of spectators roared with laughter" at the spectacle.[81] The mood of rebellion remained strong overnight and on the morning of 2 October, when hundreds followed the police van from the station to the courthouse, which was packed and surrounded by at least a thousand people. A current of violence ran through the crowd when Soberanis was denied bail, and women, as the day before, "were the most virulent."[82]

During Soberanis's five-week incarceration, the rest of the male leadership began to fracture, its authority in the eyes of LUA women eroding further. Apparently a Sister Thurton of the Salvation Army kept LUA meetings going during Soberanis's absence, for she was praised for her work at the unofficial civic holiday and festival that greeted his release.[83] Otherwise the celebrations sidelined LUA women. They were run by John Lahoodie and Benjamin Reneau, who would soon split from Soberanis. These two men, who were among those whom women had deemed "damn cowards" during the riot, heroized Soberanis in biblically masculine terms, as Moses leading his children out of Egypt and as Daniel facing the lions of British colonialism on their behalf. Soberanis was willing to play the hero, but he would not tolerate Lahoodie's and Reneau's effort to make the nine-man executive's meetings confidential. Their move to centralize power, and their alleged theft of monies donated for the 10th festival, led Soberanis to repudiate them in early December. When he declared that he would continue as sole leader of the LUA, "Mr. Soberanis received cheers from a large number of his followers, mostly female."[84] The *Independent*'s female columnist, who generally wrote on manners and morals, was so impressed with LUA women at this Battlefield meeting that she devoted an entire column to describing them. "The other night when the big split occurred in the Soberanis committee they took a very bold stand for the leader, Tony. When Tony announced that he would carry on alone, women were the first to shout for joy. Women are so far his chief supporters. Tony is really popular among the women of Belize. . . . In the main women who attend the Battlefield meetings are sincere people. Indeed they are more sincere than the men. They support this claim by acts of chivalry and by their sincerity of purpose. What they now require is efficient and sincere leadership."[85]

But the women of the LUA had clearly chosen their leader, trusting Soberanis's more open democratic practices, rejecting Lahoodie's and Reneau's tendencies toward hierarchy and centralization. Women's support was the critical element in maintaining Soberanis's credible leadership, yielding them greater power and influence within the movement. Certainly after the October riot and the December split, they became better organized and displayed greater autonomy, ultimately forming the Women's League by February 1935, at which point they articulated a bold subaltern female vision of an implicitly national democracy without class, race, or gender hierarchies. Governor Alan Burns (1934–40), who arrived while Soberanis was in jail, announced the constitutional bill in January 1935, and it was passed in April after the unofficials defeated amendments to lower property restrictions and to lower women's voting age from thirty to twenty-one.[86] These amendments embodied the demands of Progressive Party men, like H. H. Cain, Calvert and Morrel Staine, shipwright and future labor leader Clifford Betson, and of Vivian Seay.[87] Middle-class men and women held public meetings in an attempt to gain popular support, but their refusal to embrace universal suffrage only further alienated the radicalized popular classes.

The Women's League of the LUA explicitly contested the colonial constitution and the middle-class amendments and specifically rejected Vivian Seay's assumed right to speak for them and to define women's political interests. Seay held two meetings to advocate lowering women's voting age to twenty-one, again earning the praise of the Cain's *Independent*, which did not want "a band of suffragettes" marring constitutional negotiations.[88] Both meetings were relatively small and dominated by male speakers, including Benjamin Reneau. Morrel Staine argued that "our Creole women are equal to us," and Cecilia Douglas, the deputy head of the Black Cross Nurses, maintained that "the women of British Honduras should be given equal rights." But Seay never extended her concept of "natural rights" to poor women, despite the fact that none of the Nurses qualified as municipal voters in the 1930s. Rather than find common political cause with the LUA women, the Nurses preferred the colonialist strategy of keeping the rowdy popular classes disenfranchised, relying on respectable social activism to guarantee their own political influence.

The LUA Women's League suffrage meeting was led by Elfreda Trapp, whose alliance with Seay during the divorce debate a year earlier was severed during the tumult of 1934.[89] By this point, Trapp had expanded her 1932 advocacy of working women's political rights to embrace universal suffrage. Soberanis supported the league's action, attending the meeting but remaining silent, exemplifying his ability to share leadership and to sanction women's public and militant politics and also his wisdom in cultivating strong female allies. The league clearly demanded universal womanhood suffrage, although the *Independent* disingenuously claimed that Seay's "ladies" and the LUA's "women" had the same goals. Mrs. Olive Blades criticized the constitutional bill's granting of "certain elective rights" to "certain women of the community," and pressed "for us women to decide as citizens" to claim "common rights" regardless of "the limited means of the mass of our women." She emphasized the importance of poor women in Belizean society as well as their "high standard of womanhood." Mrs. Christobel Usher, speaking for women under thirty, also defined "the daughters of British Honduras" as citizens who must unite for "proper representation." Implicit in their statements was a rejection of Seay's—and the entire middle class's—presumed authority over them and of the exclusionary middle-class project. Citizenship, not wealth, education, or literacy, should translate into political rights and power.

The league's petition reiterated this radical democratic vision. One of the very few surviving texts written by working women, it is a condensed expression of their consciousness after eleven months of open conflict with the racist colonial order, its vast class inequalities and patriarchal privileges. Addressing Governor Burns directly, their traditional tone and form belied the radical content of their petition:

(1) May it please your Excellency, Your Respectful Petitioners are the Female Natives of British Honduras, popularly known and classified as Negroes, Spaniards, Indians, etc. and whose proper and legitimate home was, is, and ever shall be British Honduras.

(2) We are a people who have suffered and are still suffering, owing to the fact that we, as the Government of British Honduras, have no voice in our country's affairs, and all sort of injustices are being meted out to us.

(3) We, your Humble Petitioners feel that the hour for such approach has come, and we humbly submit the following resolutions.

RESOLVED:

A. That the Franchise for Female Voters is too high, as there are only about 2 per cent of the Females of British Honduras who earns $25.00 per month. By which means the balance of 98% will have no vote, and also the age limit is too high, women should have equal rights as men.

B. Be it further resolved. That your Petitioners submit for Your Excellency's consideration, that we the women of Belize, British Honduras, humbly beg Your Excellency to put it before the members of the Legislative Council, and that it is the wish of the women of Belize, British Honduras, that the women be given womanhood suffrage in voting for the coming election of the Legislative Council, and the age limit be twenty-one years. And to further submit to Your Excellency that even though condition may change, that is, wages may go up, it will never reach $25.00 per month for the 98 per cent above mentioned.

We Your Excellency's humble Petitioners as in duty bound, do earnestly pray for a favourable consideration.[90]

Burns and the Legislative Council of course gave them no consideration at all, and womanhood suffrage arrived with manhood suffrage in 1954, after four years of intense nationalist struggle. But the petition remains one of the clearest surviving windows onto LUA women's identities, sharp analysis, and ideas about just and democratic government. They defined themselves as authentic native inhabitants of their country and, elaborating "nativeness" in racial terms, excluded whites while including the non-Creole groups located mainly in the districts.[91] This popular protonationalism stands in contrast to the Battle of St. George's Caye myth's emphasis on white male ancestry and also goes beyond the antiwhite virulence of the 1919 riot and the racial limits of Garveyism. Here was a group of urban Creole women, at the center of a movement that hoped to spread throughout the colony and that increasingly was achieving that reach, speaking as a multiracial female coalition and establishing *all* nonwhite women's claims to citizenship. While actual mestizo and Mayan women were not, for various reasons, able to participate in or accede to the league's suffrage petition, the important element was LUA women's inclusive vision and claim to representation. Seay acted to suppress already mobilized and vocal women, the league acted to include women who had not yet found political voice.

Flowing from the LUA women's claim to authentic native status was their self-definition as the government of their country—they never used the word "colony." Here the women spoke for an even larger community, that of all native men and women. Without political rights, the British Honduran people would continue to suffer injustice, the legitimate government would continue to be silenced. The rejection of colonial and class autocracy implied in this analysis was immediately backed up with quantitative socioeconomic data. League women knew exactly how much they earned and how few women could qualify, or would ever qualify, as voters. Thus they wove a condemnation of women's poverty and exploitation as workers into their characterization of the constitution as yet another injustice meted out to native women.

Notably, although the women's petition implicitly included native men as part of the "people" and "government" of the country, it did not mention manhood suffrage or take on men's struggles. League women were fighting for their own political rights in gender as well as class terms. On the age restriction, they rejected all gender inequality in voting rights. Elfreda Trapp's sister Virginia Stanford, in speaking to the resolution, vividly articulated the league's contestation of both gender and class privilege.

> The question before us tonight is the franchise for the new constitution. I want to impress upon the women that we are being jilted. Women of British Honduras you have heard the resolution; we women need womanhood suffrage. The new constitution is for us to select our own representatives for the Council Chamber. And yet we are not entitled to vote if we are not 30 years of age and if you are not getting $25.00 a month. . . . Now it's not so with men. . . . You see how they are keeping us out of it. Which one of us here in this hall tonight is getting $25.00 per month? Very few of us. We women do not get our rights. In this hard time especially where are we going to get the wages they are asking for; ladies that it to keep us out. I feel some of them are afraid of us. Now here is the injustice. . . . So tonight we want every one of you to vote in favour of this resolution. We want womanhood suffrage and if we are a body we must be in favour of it.[92]

Stanford, a market vendor, cast the political exclusion of working women as a deliberate policy rooted in fear, a policy intended to keep subaltern nonwhite women, and their concerns, outside the arena of formal politics. In contrast to the constitution's and to Seay's exclusionary politics, working women had found and made the LUA a markedly inclusive and relatively democratic arena, where their rights to speak for themselves and to vote were not questioned or limited.

In the LUA elections that followed women did not, as we have seen, seek any of the top leadership positions, just as they did not envision women as legislative leaders in their petition. They still defined ultimate political authority and responsibility as masculine, but they defined legitimate masculine leadership as fundamentally committed to the rights and welfare of

working women. Experience had taught them not to trust in colonial officials, middle-class mediators, or even some of their own movement leaders. Organized and vocal through the league, and linked to LUA women in
Dangriga, they were now in a position to command the attention of any
leader. Indeed, when Soberanis traveled south in May 1935 on an organizing tour, Virginia Stanford accompanied him, her presence indicative of
the league's interest in mobilizing women as the movement spread. When
they stopped in Dangriga, they were greeted by a massive throng—"the
seaside was black with people"—and Soberanis was carried shoulder-
high to the hall where he spoke long into the night. A week later, while
Soberanis and Stanford were in Toledo, where Stanford reportedly made
a strong impression on the local women, the Dangriga LUA mobilized a
labor action against the government railway, demanding that the workers
strike for higher pay. Women were present in the crowds of three to four
hundred, and one was among the six arrested.[93] The LUA and Women's
League seemed poised to widen and deepen the popular struggle, drawing in more and more of the rural communities that had protested colonial neglect and landlord oppression after the hurricane. Possibly Creole
and Garifuna women's militance in Belize Town and Dangriga would have
begun to legitimize public and collective women's politics in mestizo and
Mayan communities. But the trajectories of increasing popular anticolonial mobilization, and women's rising consciousness and self-organization, weakened in the second half of 1935 and collapsed in 1936.

Among the factors that contributed to the decline and disappear-
ance of the LUA was Governor Burns's rapidly developing reform project, which involved the Creole middle class and is the focus of the next
chapter. Other factors included an improving trend in the local economy
after 1934 and competition from Lahoodie and Reneau's British Honduras
Unemployed Association. The BHUA attracted two thousand people to a
Battlefield meeting in May 1935 and still existed in the summer of 1936,
when Soberanis devoted much of his energy to attacking it.[94] For many,
Soberanis had lost his ability to make the authorities cede ground and
implement change. But what most eroded Soberanis's popular cred-
ibility was Governor Burns's effective repressive strategy against him. In

September 1935 Burns barred the LUA from official 10th celebrations, but the movement held its own festivities as before.[95] They were large, and women undoubtedly played their usual organizing roles, but the did not achieve the size, emotion, and significance of the 1934 parade and celebration. Soberanis followed up with a series of very popular public meetings in Corozal in early October, to mark the anniversary of the sawmill riot.[96] Three weeks later Burns pushed through an antisedition law and charged Soberanis retroactively for his Corozal speeches. At the November trial in Corozal, he was convicted of abusive and seditious language. Burns's effort to prevent popular reaction by having Creole magistrate Ezekiel A. Grant conduct the prosecution proved futile. Support for Soberanis created "a state of civil commotion," forcing the government to ban public meetings in the north. Although his sentence was reduced in January 1936, the same month he was acquitted of the more serious charge of bringing the king into ridicule and contempt, he had lost momentum and no longer had a vibrant movement at his command.[97]

Women seem to have retained their level of organization longest as the LUA faded overall in 1936. There was no LUA role in the first legislative elections under the new constitution, which were held in early 1936. Popular interest was high despite the fact that, as the Women's League had predicted, only 1.8 percent of the population could register to vote.[98] In Orange Walk a heated public meeting attacked the candidacy of the BEC manager, who indeed lost to chicle merchant Robert S. Turton (the major backer of George Price in the 1940s and 1950s). In Belize Town the Garveyite PP endorsed native candidates L. P. Ayuso and Ricardo Meighan, and Reneau's BHUA as well as Cecilia Douglas endorsed black Creole lawyer Arthur Balderamos. Ayuso, a merchant, topped the polls.[99] Apparently Ayuso had made some campaign promises to women, for months later Soberanis claimed they were in revolt against him, threatening to "flog [him] with our underwear."[100] Women's conflicts with Ayuso remain obscure, although the evidence suggests a sexualized political critique designed to ridicule Ayuso's respectable masculinity. Much clearer is the action that LUA women took in July 1936, when they marched through Belize Town to present Burns with a petition for higher wages. It is quite possible that they made special demands for female workers, for the *Independent* commented: "Women today are feeling the pinch as much as the men."[101] With this final collective act of the LUA, women reasserted the movement's enduring praxis of political action on behalf of the colony's working people. Indeed, neither constitutional advance nor social and economic reforms could alleviate the disenfranchisement or grinding poverty of the majority. The women of the LUA as backbone and spearhead of the movement's campaign against the colonial order in the mid-1930s, learned a great deal about themselves, their leadership, and the strength of colonial power. They realized their own collective female strength in a moment of conflict, backed the movement's most democratic leader, who would not and could not contain their militance, and confronted the authorities with a clearly articulated vision of a society without privileges based on wealth or race or gender. The threat they posed to the legitimacy of colonial rule was extreme, and the next chapter will demonstrate that the imperial reform project was designed specifically to redomesticate poor black women.

The league subsided in parallel with Soberanis, never daring to dispense with male leadership altogether, and the reform project discouraged the labor mobilizations of the late 1930s from including women workers. The enduring effects of the league's gender-inclusive labor politics are suggested by Christobel Usher's pathbreaking election to the executive of Soberanis's British Honduras Workers and Tradesmen Union (BHWTU) in 1941.[102] But Soberanis went to work in Panama in 1942, and the following year the BHWTU was displaced by the more clearly reformist British Honduras Trades Union (BHTU), which emphasized male employment and activism. With the exception of a few rare moments of collective action, women's politics in the period from 1936 to 1949 were constrained by popular support for antiestablishment electoral candidates and by the rise of legal trade unionism, neither of which fostered or welcomed female participation.

Labour and Legislative Politics, 1939–41

The 1931 hurricane made constitutional reform possible, but it was the LUA's stormy mobilization that made the limited legislative elections at all meaningful. For in 1936, 1939, and 1942, progressive native candidates had to hold themselves at least somewhat accountable to an astute and organized public much larger than the tiny pool of voters. Calvert Staine and Ricardo Meighan, for example, who were respectively nominated and elected to the Legislative Council in 1942, cast the votes that in 1943 opened the way for legal union organizing. Important elements of that working-class public were Soberanis's BHWTU and Luke D. Kemp's British Honduras Federation of Workmen's Protective Association (BHFWPA), both organized in early 1939 during a period of renewed high unemployment and labor unrest.[103] Kemp had already accused Governor Burns of "fostering class hatred," and Soberanis had dubbed Robert S. Turton and Arthur Balderamos "the fighting cocks of the poor people," indicating organized labor's political retreat to reliance on elected, and thus propertied, native liberals.[104]

Although these unions focused heavily on the men working two-week rotations on the Public Works Department's road gangs and on mahogany workers, labor unrest also took place among women and rural people. Two moments of unusually autonomous female worker mobilization occurred in 1939 and 1940. In June 1939 six student nurses at the Belize hospital struck for higher pay, shorter hours, safer working conditions, and for greater respect from the nursing and medical authorities. With no allies, and facing Matron Roberts's intolerance of all insubordination, the strike failed and cost two young women their jobs and future careers.[105] Early the following year Miss Winifred Flowers, a former LUA member, and Miss Alphonsina Trapp organized a 320-woman petition for relief work, especially land settlement and farming. Notably, their demands were presented to the town board by John Lahoodie, suggesting that Flowers may have moved away from the LUA into his BHUA. As in the Women's League's suffrage petition, Flowers and Trapp used statistics for effect, claiming a female unemployment rate of 32 percent. The board members could not imagine women becoming farmers and spoke of starting a shirt factory or rock-breaking crews. But they took no action, and neither Lahoodie nor the women pursued the matter.[106]

Shortly after this, Gabriel Adderley, who had been an LUA leader in

Stann Creek in 1934 and had tried to mobilize labor in Cayo in 1937, collaborated with a local worker-peasant mobilization in rural Corozal.
Allying with a group of mainly Mayan working men, including representatives from Patchakan, Yo Chen, Xaibe, and Santa Clara, Adderley
formed the Corozal Knights of Labour, which had some female members.
In May 1940 a parade of the unemployed headed by Adderley and the
Xaibe village band delivered a two thousand-name petition for employment and education to the district commissioner, Ezekiel Grant, the same
Ezekiel Grant who had previously convicted Soberanis. Most signatories
were reportedly Mayan, arguing that without more government roadwork their families would starve, that boys and girls of the working class
deserved education, and, crucially, that the people should be able to own
land. They were "prepared to wage moral warfare for their future welfare," according to E. E. Cain, reporting for the *Independent*. The president
of the Knights of Labour was José Garcia, a self-identified Mayan, who
emphasized the need for land redistribution. This popular mobilization
was strong enough that Governor Sir John Hunter (1940–46) decided to
place the Northern District under special restrictions, akin to martial law,
in early June 1940.[107]

As the *milperos* of Yo Chen and Patchakan had warned in 1933, the rural
Maya were at last creating an organization through which to express their
collective political demands.[108] They had supported Soberanis in 1935,
entering the multiracial colony-wide project of the LUA in which Mayan
women had already been included as a result of the Women's League's
suffrage demands, and had been actively sought out during Soberanis's
and Virginia Stanford's trip to the Toledo District. Adderley's own trajectory, from a Creole childhood in Stann Creek to labor organizing in
Cayo to peasant-worker mobilization in Corozal, seemed to symbolize the
expanding potential of panethnic subaltern labor and anticolonial politics,
as did Soberanis's leadership of the Creole and Garifuna-based movement
in 1934–35. Still, neither the Maya mobilization of 1940, nor the thousand-
person unemployment march in Stann Creek Town in January 1941, went
beyond petitioning and marching to LUA-style direct confrontation.[109]

In 1941 Soberanis's BHWTU and Kemp's BHFWPA demanded universal

suffrage and a fully elected legislature; several progressive legislators supported the unions' stance in a historic break with middle-class politics.
Ricardo Meighan as secretary of the BHWTU seconded Kemp's motion, at
a huge Battlefield meeting, in favor of universal suffrage.[110] Joining him
in ending the Unofficials' long hostility to universal suffrage were lawyer
Arthur Balderamos and merchant Edward Usher, both elected to the legislature in 1939. The *Independent* too supported quick change, warning
that "the people will have to take such steps as will conclude the important matter in reasonable time."[111] Public meetings in Stann Creek Town
and Punta Gorda had already endorsed universal suffrage. The latter was
chaired by S. B. Vernon, the elected legislator for the Toledo District, and
heard from Mr. Claro Villafranco "on behalf of the Carib community,"
who endorsed universal suffrage. Governor Hunter privately favored a
return to crown colony rule but publicly supported both labor organization and adult suffrage in order to avoid renewed unrest.[112]

The alliance of organized labor and progressive legislators in 1941 was
not nationalist but was far more popular than the small proindepen-
dence group led by Lahoodie and Adderley. Named variously the British
Honduras Independent Labour Party, the People's Republican Party, and
the People's Nationalist Committee, and probably backed by Turton whose
chicle business was entirely with the United States, the group denounced
the British, called for the expulsion of all whites, the creation of a republic
linked to the United States, and the creation of a national flag.[113] They also
apparently threatened to have Japanese planes fly into the colony, perhaps with some idea of so gaining liberation from the British.[114] Governor
Hunter, facing this small nationalist threat and a much larger ground-
swell of support for universal suffrage, chose to detain Lahoodie and
Adderley in an internment camp through late 1941 and early 1942. Exactly
why Soberanis chose to ally in 1941 with middle-class progressives rather
than the nationalists remains unclear, but he may well have been loath to
trust Lahoodie a second time, relieved that some "intellectuals" had finally
found themselves capable of accomplishing "what the masses desired," or
simply reluctant to push the imperial reform project into repressing him
yet again. In 1973 Soberanis explained that he departed for Panama in 1942

because of the war and because he knew that "one could not give vent to their feelings."[115]

The rebellion of the LUA ultimately made a reform project, led by colonial officials but shaped by middle class progressives and their labor allies, both possible and urgently necessary. Unlike the radicals of 1941, the LUA was a massive popular movement, virtually an entire people in revolt against political and economic subordination. The British could not jail every man and woman who marched, struck, or denounced colonial rule, any more than they could in India during the salt march. Governor Burns targeted Soberanis in order to repress the entire movement, but even though the LUA disintegrated, its rebellion bred a democratic and inclusive protonationalist culture that had some impact on the late 1930s labor movement, progressive politicians' actions, and even the state-approved labor movement of the 1940s. The LUA itself could not withstand the colonial state's repression and reform, but the native identities it fostered, the gender-inclusive claims to labor and citizen rights it promoted, were its strongest contribution to the long struggle for a Belizean nation.

Without the militance of Elfreda Trapp and the hundreds of other LUA women the organization might have collapsed in late 1934. They certainly ensured the inclusion of nonwhite Belizean women in claims to and constructions of labor and citizen rights. And their militance undoubtedly shaped the deeply gendered local reforms of the late 1930s that aimed to incorporate popular demands for economic and social change, thus containing the movement and patching up colonial authority. The Women's League scared Governor Burns and the middle classes, just as Virginia Stanford had so perceptively claimed. Its militance had come out of a popular culture in which women were neither silent, dependent, nor domesticated. The reformers, who could not allow the league or the LUA to grow, were ambitious enough to think that they could transform the very culture that sustained—and grew with—the subaltern protests and rebellions of the 1930s.

4 Modernizing Colonialism

Development, Discipline, and
Domestication, 1935–1954

While the physical environment is thus being made wholesome and
productive, the people are made ready to react to it in a forceful, steady
and sustained upsurge of progress by educational, health, and housing
projects. [GOVERNOR SIR JOHN HUNTER, 1946]

A government must be made to suit a people, not a people to suit the
government. ["PRINCE DEE," 1940]

The British government launched an ambitious reform project in response
to the colonial labor rebellions of the 1930s, one intended to remove the
causes of discontent, modernize the colonies, and thus to save the empire
into the indefinite future.[1] The West Indian "disturbances" were particularly urgent, forcing British colonial policy makers to place the Caribbean
"center stage" for the first time since Jamaica's Morant Bay rebellion of
1865 and prompting reactions from them that "marked a vital turning-
point in colonial policy."[2] The West India Royal Commission (WIRC)
toured the region in 1938–39; its 1940 report, though not made public for
wartime propaganda reasons, confirmed the principles of the Colonial
Development and Welfare (CDW) Act of 1940, which created a £55 million
fund for social and economic development empire-wide. This was an initiative unprecedented in both scale and scope. To assess proposals and dis-
burse funds in the Caribbean, the Development and Welfare Organization
(DWO) was established with headquarters in Barbados. In addition, the
Colonial Office ordered the establishment of labor departments in all colonies and encouraged the formation of "responsible" trade unions. At the

same time, the British Trades Union Council became involved in training Caribbean labor leaders. DWO funding also made possible the formation of social welfare departments. Indeed, 60 percent of CDW spending from 1940–44 occurred in the Caribbean.[3] The second CDW Act of 1945, which had expanded funding, capped what seemed to be a period of unusually creative and comprehensive colonial reform.

The central flaw of the modernization project was its disciplinary, moralistic stance toward colonial peoples, which drained it of populist or hegemonic potential. Thomas Holt's analysis of this period emphasizes the extremely "hortatory and moralistic" language of the WIRC Report, which defined West Indians as "a people whose immature minds too often are ruled by their adult bodies" and that called for "an organized campaign against the social, moral and economic evils of promiscuity."[4] More broadly, both progressive Tories and the mainstream of the Labour Party embraced the new ideology of "development and welfare," an ideology that legitimated expanded, prolonged trusteeship, an essentially parental and paternalistic relationship cast as equal partnership.[5] As Holt has concluded, "The postponement of political maturity until the completion of an economic and social adolescence . . . appealed to British policymakers determined to retain . . . their classic compromise between democratic ideology and imperial ambition."[6] Thus, Caribbean people's political *and* economic fates depended on their own "moral regeneration." Despite occasional professions of guilt for a century of postemancipation poverty, most British leaders ultimately blamed the poor themselves for the conditions that led to rebellion, which was construed as evidence of ongoing political immaturity.

The critique of imperial moralism gains depth by connecting it to the feminist insight that "ideologies of gender and sexuality were foundational to the projects of colonial modernity."[7] This position roots moralism in the perceived gender and racial disorder of the rebellious West Indian popular classes, particularly as manifested in women's wage labor and political activism. More specifically, reformers blamed "promiscuity," or what they saw as the disordered sexuality, family life, and parenting of the West Indian popular classes. The remaking of the black working-class and peasant family—and in particular the domestication of its women—lay at the heart of colonial modernization.[8] Making the people "ready" for a modern infrastructure and economy meant, in practice, directing men's desires toward steady work and family headship, women's toward housewifery and motherhood, and children's toward attending and being obedient at school.[9] Social welfare in particular, as Rhoda Reddock has pointed out, was crucial to the reform project and overwhelmingly directed at women—a pattern also found in the spate of domestic science and mothering programs found in Africa and Asia.[10] The analysis of the DWO's social welfare advisor from 1941–45, T. S. Simey, thus applies generally: reform policy sought to break poor Afro-Caribbean women's significant sexual, economic, and political autonomy. Simey, an Englishman, saw in the Caribbean's high rates of illegitimacy, low rates of marriage, and high rates of female household headship a weakness—or outright absence—of family life and a low status for women. Until households "under the control of a woman" were eradicated, he argued, no advance in social development, economic prosperity, or local governance would be possible. By 1946 he had come to understand that many working-class women of the region chose "loose concubinage"—his disparaging term for common-law and visiting unions—but he still held to the doctrine that women must move from low-paid wage labor to homemaking. Only male-breadwinner households could be the basis for a moral prosperous Caribbean, one perhaps deserving of a measure of self-government, that coming-of-age gift for maturing colonial peoples.

Men and children were the other key players in colonial modernization. In the late 1930s the Colonial Office concluded that organized labor in the West Indies could not be suppressed but must be depoliticized and forced to accept state authority over labor relations. In this model, problems of men's "irregular attendance and avoidable absenteeism" would be overcome by "steady work at reasonable or agreed-on wage rates."[11] "Responsible" trade unionism—bread and butter unionism for employed men—was to be the classroom for the remaking of West Indian masculinity and was thus a central element in the development of colonial "competence." Its graduates were to stem the tide of nationalism and to join colonial authorities in domesticating women. More overtly pedagogical was reform policy toward the rising generation. Through vocational education—trades for boys, domestic science for girls—proper gender roles were to be inculcated and proper families, communities, and politics nurtured.

This chapter analyzes the colonial modernization project's labor, social welfare, and education policies in Belize through the local reform effort of 1934–39, which was a reaction to the LUA, and through imperially funded reform from 1940. In a concluding section, it also examines the intensification of social welfare efforts in reaction to the early nationalist movement of 1950–54. It argues that the gendered colonial modernization project represents both the culmination and collapse of the colonial-middle class political tradition in Belize. It was more ideologically and financially ambitious than the reform of the 1920s in that it addressed the labor question and expanded the role of the state in economic and social development, the latter occurring prior to imperial intervention. It also strengthened the alliance between officials and the middle class. Both defined poverty, rebellion, and immorality as the enemy, both supported agricultural development to dethrone the forestry elite, and the middle class was prepared to subordinate the goal of self-government to social reform when threatened from below. Their eventual leadership under a self-government arrangement depended on making the values of political compromise, sexual respectability, and cultural whitening hegemonic. But reformers simultaneously raised popular expectations of the state, expectations they could not fulfill, and in so doing stoked the fires of anticolonial popular culture. "The people" had already begun to define progress in terms of labor and citizen rights in the 1930s if not earlier, and in 1950 they would unleash an upsurge of "undisciplined nationalism," the kind neither created nor controlled by the agents of colonial modernization.[12]

If reform as a hegemonic project failed overall, it did strengthen middle-class women reformers—there were more of them, they had more authority, and they had greater security as state employees. Their collective self-consciousness also grew. In the 1940s veteran volunteers and newly trained professionals joined the Medical and Social Welfare Departments.

Activist female civil servants were as important to colonial modernization as respectable and responsible trade union leaders, and they certainly outnumbered the Labour Department staff. Female reformers did
not sustain their suffrage demands of the mid-1930s; instead they refocused on maternal and infant health and domestic science education. The
limits of their respectable activism ensured their legitimacy within the
colonial reform project.[13] They participated in the Loyal and Patriotic
Order of the Baymen (LPOB), founded in 1946 to dispute Guatemala's
renewed territorial claims to Belize.[14] The LPOB embraced colonial paternalism. In 1948 its leaders portrayed Britain as a "Guiding Mother," and
LPOB president Monrad Metzgen insisted: "We intend to remain British
until such time that we are competent to evolve a self-contained community."[15] LPOB women organized the new Queen of the Bay pageant, an
annual event designed to "bring up" the 10th celebrations by displaying
the well-bred, light-skinned, and loyal British femininity of the legitimate
daughters of the middle class. Akin to the Baby Exhibition, the pageant
sought to instill standards of "breeding and deportment," virtue and discipline into the colony's working class, particularly its women. The contestants united patriotism and empire loyalty and—as virginal young women
under paternal as well as maternal control—embodied proper family life.
The pageant thus promoted the middle class's fitness for political leadership.[16] Not until the outbreak of popular nationalism in the early 1950s did
female reformers expand the limits of their activism, both through participation in antinationalist party politics, and by founding the little-known
British Honduras Federation of Women (BHFW), a fascinating organization that will be analyzed in the next chapter.

The limited efficacy of female reformers' work clearly illustrates
Antoinette Burton's argument that colonial states were not able to fix
"with absolute authority the social and cultural conditions out of which
citizens and subjects could make and remake their relationships to the
state and civil society."[17] Female reformers as civil servants worked largely
to influence women of the popular classes to embrace housewifery, community volunteerism, and improved mothering, if not marriage. They did
succeed in cultivating a degree of popular dependence on state officials

and institutions but did not quell subaltern women's (or men's) anticolonial culture. Subaltern women's engagements with the modernization
project in the late 1930s and 1940s are not well documented, but existing
evidence all points toward a pattern similar to that of the 1920s in which
they negotiated for practical benefits such as health care while refusing the
project's moral critique of their families and culture.[18] Neither the Queen
of the Bay nor female civil servants became poor women's heroines. In
the colonial modernization project's last battle in the early 1950s, against
a massive popular labor-nationalist alliance, female reformers' efforts to
woo and control their unfortunate sisters proved no match for the appeal
of a nationalism free—at least temporarily—of a moral discourse of discipline and domestication.

Gendered state moralism was of course common in the new forms
of rule and alliance that emerged from the global crises that weakened
western Europe in the 1930s and 1940s. In Latin America's populist import-
substitution industrialization regimes, as well as in nationalist movements
worldwide, renegotiating the "proper" gender roles prescribed by the male-
headed nuclear family proved central to managing the popular classes'
demands for political inclusion. In Vargas's Brazil, for example, reordering the gender system to strengthen the family was an inherent part of
maintaining social order while reconfiguring the economy for renewed
growth.[19] And even in Popular Front Chile, state social workers perpetu-
ated some of the moralism that imbued earlier state projects aimed at
working-class women, such as vocational education.[20] Likewise, Indian
nationalist leaders created a moral ideal in which proper female behavior would safeguard the domestic sphere of the household as symbolic
of the nation. But in most *colonial* modernization projects, state moralism was more overt. Further, it was neither balanced by a solidarity with
labor, nor, of course, connected to the collective appeal of national liberation or regeneration. Colonial modernization projects therefore lacked
the populist element necessary to successfully containing subaltern rebel-
liousness. One exception was the successful renegotiation of U.S. colonialism in Puerto Rico, where local and U.S. reformers did connect with
the popular classes—including activist working women—in a hegemonic

alliance that went some way to addressing working mothers' political concerns.[21] Parallel efforts in the British Empire were certainly hegemonic in intent. But there was no common project uniting the British and local reformers of Belize with the restless working men and women who were the objects of policies designed to remake the colony's labor force, families, and communities. Responsible trade unionism and "social welfare" could not reweave the threadbare fabric rent apart by the LUA's anticolonial labor struggles.

Disciplining Men: Colonial Labor Policy and the General Workers' Union

While the censuses of 1931 and 1946 documented continued and slowly increasing female labor force participation, labor policy firmly ignored working women throughout the 1930s–50s period. In 1931 15.3 percent of females age fifteen and over were in the labor force overall; in the Belize and Stann Creek Districts, respectively, 21.9 and 24 percent were employed. In 1946 the figure was 16.6 percent for females age ten and over, and 47.8 percent for single women aged twenty-five to forty-four.[22] Officials made no attempt to capture the income-earning labor of the majority of women listed as engaged in "home duties." Nor did the colony's Labour Department, founded in 1939, ever bother to calculate female unemployment, even after female petitioners pegged it at 32 percent in 1940. Indeed, the department did not list female wages until 1944 and as late as 1950 continued to cast women as a secondary labor force performing only work of "a light nature which is not normally given out to men"—and thus, it implied, not worthy of serious attention.[23] The state's middle-class allies similarly avoided women's work and worker identities. The Black Cross Nurses in their 1938 presentation to the WIRC emphasized the plight of male breadwinners; more importantly, the General Workers' Union had only 7.5 percent female membership rate by 1948, a figure in all likelihood linked to the union leadership's adherence to the male-breadwinner ideology of responsible trade unionism. The 1937 government Nutrition Committee did attribute low rates of breastfeeding to many women's long hours of labor as housemaids and laundresses earning $1–$2.50 per week but simultaneously blamed "the high rate of illegitimacy" for creating a necessity for mothers to earn wages. If the Committee was unusual in hoping to solve the problem by "establish[ing] a crèche in Belize for the care of children whose mothers are away working all day," it was par for the course that no crèche came to be.[24] Links among women, motherhood, and social reform predated and shaped both the emergence of responsible trade unionism policy and that of the GWU.

Governor Burns's anti-LUA local reform project opposed all labor organization and so made no explicit link between men and unionism, but it certainly specified that men should be the laborers given government work building roads. There is no evidence that the kind of relief work for women that existed in 1932–34—rock breaking and cemetery cleaning—was revived after the LUA protests. British observer Major Orde-Browne, sent by the Colonial Office to tour the region, criticized Burns's road-building program precisely for its focus on male labor: "Such real suffering due to unemployment as exists in Belize falls more upon the women and children than upon the men, who in a regrettable proportion of cases shirk their responsibilities—a course with which the high percentage of illegitimacy existing in the town is closely connected."[25] But Burns never conceived of roadwork in narrowly welfarist terms, as mere "relief." Given the strength of the LUA when Burns arrived in late 1934, it is not surprising that he at first pleaded for imperial funding to slow the "steady decline in the physical and moral welfare of the inhabitants" and to stave off the revolt that malnutrition might incite: "[A]ny further delay will be dangerous," he wrote. "[The people's] temper is rising and matters must come to a head within a few months unless something is done."[26] But his long-term plan was to build roads in order to open up new land for agricultural development, thus breaking the power of the forestry elite and creating a new basis for colonial self-sufficiency. Men would thus become independent smallholders or wage laborers on corporate-owned plantations, able to provide for their families. Nor was Burns indifferent to women and children. Road building created the conditions for significant land settlement in the late 1930s, and in this arena the fundamentally gendered character of Burns's development project was realized. At the

Rockstone Pond settlement north of Belize Town, for example, male settlers received road work while their first crops matured, and the government built a school so that wives and children could leave Belize Town; it
also set up a mobile health service for the area.[27] As discussed in chapter
3, 320 women signed a 1940 petition asking to settle and farm in their
own right at Rockstone, demanding the work and land coded for men as
well as the health and education services coded for women and children.
Colonial reform could ignore women's worker identities, but those identities did not wither, and indeed the higher expectations of the colonial
state that women came to have were informed by these identities.

Burns's success in milking the CDF and in attracting investment set into
motion a structural shift away from forestry and toward export agriculture
as the basis of the colonial economy. But Burns did not plan the increases
in wage labor and commercial farming that occurred among Garifuna
women in Stann Creek. His efforts to attract foreign capital brought sugar
cane to the northern districts in the 1930s, but neither the construction
of the Libertad sugar refinery, opened in 1937 nor the field and factory
labor required by Plantations Ltd. drew local Mayan and mestizo women
into wage labor. The emergence of a tiny sugar smallholder sector in the
1940s affected a limited number of women, principally by putting unprecedented amounts of cash into their husbands' hands. In western Belize
and in Belize Town local economies changed very little, with the exception of some light manufacturing work that became available to urban
women.[28] But in the Stann Creek District local and foreign investment in
citrus created an expanding female wage labor force from the mid-1930s
on, although the Labour Department did not document this remarkable
change in female labor until 1946. Citrus work grew with the opening of
a grapefruit factory in 1935 and a juice plant in 1939, adding to seasonal
packing and harvesting work.[29] Even with significant slowdown during
the war, by 1947 almost every woman aged eighteen to fifty in the Garifuna
village of Hopkins, just south of Stann Creek Town, had wage labor experience and fully half were away working citrus five to six months a year.[30]
In the later 1940s the scale of citrus processing expanded further with the
installation of modern juice and canning plants, the latter in particular

becoming a stronghold of nationalist GWU support in the early 1950s.[31] Beginning in the late 1930s, then, a significant number of Garifuna and local Creole women in Stann Creek were earning their own cash incomes, a development that reinforced their traditions of personal and political independence.

The roots of autonomy for Garifuna women lay in their independent farming, which had fed the community during the Depression. Starting in 1936, hundreds of female Garifuna farmers were drawn into commercial cassava production with the arrival of the Empire Starch Products Company (ESPC) of Canada. The ESPC's plans to build a factory in the Stann Creek District were known as early as May 1936, and it chose its site soon after.[32] Estimating that there were eight hundred to one thousand cassava growers nearby, the Stann Creek Taxpayers' Association called for a decent price.[33] ESPC likely employed local men in clearing its own land and in setting up and running the factory, but women were the majority of those cassava farmers.[34] Production began by mid-1938, with plans to export twenty five hundred tons of starch annually to Canada.[35] Later that year, cassava growers had six hundred acres planted and were clearing two hundred more.[36] But the company faltered under wartime shipping restrictions and shut down in late 1942.[37]

Given the anomalous nature of women's citrus and cassava labor in Burns's gendered development plan, it is initially surprising to find that his very first grant application to the CDF in early 1935 was for a "Women's Land Settlement Scheme" that recognized women's unemployment and family headship. Originating with Vivian Seay in her capacity as a town board member, the scheme proposed to give twenty acres each to fifty unemployed women as well as houses, tools, seeds and training.[38] The scheme was almost certainly intended to weaken the LUA and its Women's League by removing part of their constituency from Belize Town and nurturing hopes for state-led amelioration among other women. Echoes of such hopes may have reverberated in the large 1940 women's petition for land settlement. The *Independent* approved of Seay's proposal with the seemingly inevitable reference to illegitimacy: "Really our women have a very hard time to exist and what is more many of them have to support fatherless children."[39] But the Colonial Office denied funding, and neither Burns nor Seay ever focused on female unemployment again. Rather than undermining Frederick Cooper's view that the creative impetus for imperial reform came from the colonies, this case suggests that the LUA's challenge had created a pragmatic exception to the common gender ideology informing both local reform and the beginning of Colonial Office reaction to Caribbean unrest.

Burns continued to enjoy good relations with Seay as well as with other middle-class reformers. In mid-1935, for example, he presented Seay with her award as a new Member of the British Empire, contrasting her to useless political agitators. The Black Cross Nurses were one of the local groups who addressed WIRC members during their November 1938 visit to Belize Town. Their presentation summarized an investigation into the shockingly bad housing, income, and diets of thirty-five "poor respectable families" in Belize Town, research carried out by twenty BCNs and introduced by Seay in a printed report.[40] The Nurses minimized female-headed households in the sample, and of the four mentioned (11.43 percent) only one woman was working—"very hard" for fifty cents a week.[41] By blaming men's inability to provide on general economic collapse and mass unemployment, the Nurses fortified the paternalism of Burns's reform project. While there may have been an element of the strategic in building up the image of a respectable victimized working class in need of imperial aid, the effect of the Nurses' presentation was to hide the realities of female employment, unemployment, and low pay.

Indeed, such interventions shaped WIRC's recommendations, which bolstered the two imperial initiatives emphasized at the beginning of this chapter: massive aid for "development" and the acceptance of trade unionism as a means to contain worker militance. The acceptance of trade unionism in Belize came with the establishment of the Labour Department in 1939 on Colonial Office orders, a step that Burns had long resisted. Staffed by Labour Officer E. P. Bradley, a middle-class Creole, and two office assistants, the department took over management of the road building gangs from the Public Works Department. Given that one of the department's original duties was "to assist and guide the labouring class in the formation of trade unions along the right lines," it had to contend directly with the new unions founded in 1939 by Soberanis and Luke Kemp as both employer and trainer.[42] In 1939 Bradley described Kemp's BHFWPA as not of the approved type, given its political agenda.[43] Kemp, in his guise as columnist Prince Dee, certainly earned official displeasure with his acute analysis of the Labour Department: "Government created Labour Department as a medium of smothering the ambitions of Labour and shaping the activities of labour to suit the convenience of government, rather than providing an instrument to aid labour in its fight for a fitting standard of life."[44]

The department's ability to nurture desirable unions was limited first by severe understaffing, for Bradley worked virtually alone for years. But wartime employment conditions, and the slow progress of modernizing labor legislation, also hampered efforts to shape union culture. The impetus to form unions subsided as male wartime employment boomed. From 1939–42 almost 2,000 men left to work in the Panama Canal Zone, while 855 shipped to Scotland in 1941 and 1942 to cut timber for the war effort. Many of those who returned home from both places in 1944 were absorbed into a group of twelve hundred men dispatched to the U.S. South as agricultural workers under a Wartime Manpower scheme.[45] The rest joined the pool of laborers working on the Belize-Cayo road, which numbered from several hundred to about one thousand.[46] Employment in chicle and mahogany was also relatively high during the war, totaling approximately three thousand men each season, although the seasons were not always long or lucrative, and employment levels in forestry dropped permanently after 1945. Further, although the Legislative Council passed a bill legalizing trade unions in March 1941, employers on it delayed action on a bill to decriminalize breach of labor contract until February 1943. The Employers and Workers Bill was finally passed in April that year, and the following month the first approved trade union registered, the British Honduras Trade Union (BHTU). Labor militance was curbed until the mid-1940s less by responsible trade unionism than by high employment, remittances from Scotland and Panama, price controls in effect from September 1939 to August 1946, and the passage of ameliorative labor laws dealing with workmen's compensation, minimum wages, and commissary prices. Ultimately, however, these laws, and the legalization of unions, jeopardized the reform project by dramatically raising workers' expectations of the state and of union leaders.

It is vital to establish the character of the BHTU, for it was *this* union that in 1944 renamed itself the General Workers' Union (GWU), the union that became the base of the nationalist movement in 1950. Bolland, in arguing against Ashdown's portrayal of the LUA as "stillborn," argues that the GWU grew out of Soberanis's British Honduras Workers Trade Union (BHWTU), founded in 1939.[47] But the BHWTU seems to have collapsed by 1943, a year after Soberanis left to work in the Panama Canal Zone, while the continuity between the BHTU and the GWU is clear. Crucially, the BHTU was founded in March 1943 by a group of "leading tradesmen" not in opposition to the reform project but as part of it. Most importantly, one BHTU founder was master shipwright Clifford Betson, who served as GWU president from 1944–50.[48] Betson was a war veteran who did not riot in 1919, a Garveyite, struggling homeowner and family man in the 1920s, and a successful Progressive Party municipal candidate in 1933. During the LUA crisis he supported Seay's proposals for a women's unemployment bureau and land settlement scheme and like her advocated broader but not universal suffrage in the 1935 constitution.[49] The first hint of Betson's interest in organized labor came in October 1941, after the Legislative Council had legalized union organizing. In a long letter to the *Independent*, Betson did not endorse the calls for universal suffrage just defeated but did mention the need to make "free education" available and to "form our unions."[50] He ran unsuccessfully for the town board elections the following month as a Progressive Party candidate.[51] Under his leadership, the imperial DWO included the GWU on its list of approved "responsible" trade unions.[52]

Those close to or involved in the BHTU in the spring of 1943 came overwhelmingly from the reformist, often Garveyite, middle class that Soberanis had denounced in 1934. Town board Deputy Chair and elected Belize District legislator Ricardo Meighan and UNIA leader Lionel Francis were the guest speakers at the BHTU's founding meeting of seventy-five tradesmen and laborers. As the vote on the Employers and Workers Bill approached, lawyer Simeon Hassock, who was the other elected legislator for the Belize District, and Calvert Staine, town board chair, appointed member of the Legislative Council and long-time Garveyite, both spoke to BHTU meetings. When Staine and Meighan voted with the officials in April 1943 to decriminalize breach of labor contract, thus opening the way for strike action, the BHTU was poised to register as the colony's first legal trade union the following month.[53] It changed its name to the General Workers' Union in September 1944 owing to membership pressure.[54] The *Independent* welcomed the BHTU as if no previous labor associations had existed. Indeed, the paper had recently dropped Kemp's column, and his BHFWPA union—which he claimed had been denied trade union registration under the 1941 law—had disappeared.[55] Notably, Henry A. Middleton, who had represented forestry workers in the BHFWPA in 1939, was one of the six men who founded the BHTU.[56] This was clearly a moment of triumph for the respectable middle class, including Garveyites. Their men had made it onto the Legislative Council and at last had the power—when in coalition with British officials—to defy the merchant-landowner elite. Governor Hunter counted on Staine and Meighan to support the modernization and increasing state control of labor relations, while the BHTU men counted on legal trade unionism to facilitate their leadership of the native laboring masses at a time when the Progressive Party was still split on the question of universal suffrage.[57] After 1947, however, the GWU leadership raised workers' expectations of change in ways that it ultimately could not control, and the union would soon become an arena for the resurgence of an anticolonial political culture whose roots did go back to the LUA.

That culture recognized women's legitimate labor and political claims as well as their domestic roles. The BHTU very briefly appeared open to a gender-inclusive and egalitarian politics, but female reformers soon returned to plowing the fields of social reform, and the GWU became predominantly male. Cecilia Douglas, deputy head of the Black Cross Nurses, spoke at a union meeting in April 1943, but more important was the intervention of Mrs. Gwendolyn Lizarraga (1901–73), who would become Belize's first female cabinet minister in the 1960s. A landowner and chicle contractor well known for treating her employees and their families with care, she was also a wife and mother.[58] As the invited guest speaker Lizarraga apparently attracted a number of women to the meeting. She described the injustice and degradation suffered by "poor working girls" and said that she had long intended "to form a Union for women" but had never received adequate support (there is no evidence that she supported the LUA's women). The assembled male leaders welcomed her stand, one claiming that "[n]o race, no community, can rise above the level of its womanhood" and arguing that a "girl" working from five in the morning to nine at night for a pittance could never "climb the social ladder," at least not honestly. He did not point out, as the LUA Women's League had, that this underpaid "girl" could not vote either.

Lizarraga's effort was not sustained and in June 1943 the BHTU excluded women from its minimum wage demands, apparently preferring that women adopt an entirely domestic female role. The BHTU discourse in fact turned women from sister unionists into sexual traitors, arguing that eroding wages were contributing to immorality and crime, including wives' infidelity, and to other forms of disrespect for authority.[59] For the rest of the 1940s, the GWU had nothing to say about women's chronically high unemployment or the wage disparities in jobs occupied by both men and women.[60] Like the Labour Department, it left questions of women's and children's poverty to the Social Welfare Department and the medical staff. Officially open to domestics and other female workers, in practice the union focused on raising the wages of key groups of men and never mounted a campaign to organize women or to link workplace, household, and political hardships. The union's retreat into a state-sanctioned masculine movement apparently had a chilling effect on women's participation. In late 1946 the GWU had a membership of 350, but phenomenal growth during 1947 boosted the number to 2,422 by May 1948; only 183 women (7.5 percent), however, were women.[61] The fundamental difference in gender politics between the LUA and the GWU perhaps best illustrates the latter's connection to the tradition of colonial reform.

Betson did take the GWU in a more militant direction in the later 1940s, pushing the progressive possibilities of reform to an unprecedented level, though not in the direction of gender inclusivity. But pressure from below seems to have played a part in this trend, and so I treat with caution Bolland's view that a "nationalist note" entered his politics. In July 1944 BHTU stevedores in Belize City staged an overnight strike and won pay hikes but were fired a month later over further wage demands. It seems probable that this setback prompted the members to exert the pressure that resulted in the BHTU renaming itself the GWU in September 1944, when Betson became union president. By the end of 1944 the GWU had 400 members. This membership had shrunk to 350 (267 of them paid up) two years later, at the end of the GWU's next strike of 22 ship's carpenters. A major turning point came in February 1947, when the GWU led a successful strike against the BEC sawmill. In true "responsible" fashion, the 250–300 strikers resumed work upon the appointment of a government arbitrator, who awarded them major raises three weeks later. During the stoppage, Betson exhorted a GWU crowd to end corporate exploitation: "It is only right that we should share in some of the profits of our land."[62] This rhetoric, and the favorable settlement, likely influenced nonunion workers at the Libertad sugar refinery to strike in May, earning them a 25 percent pay hike, and Belize City dockers in June, who suffered replacement by scabs just as they did in 1944. Possibly encouraged by the Libertad action to expand beyond Belize City, by year's end the GWU had three district branches. Indeed, growing unemployment, rising prices, and both union-led and independent job actions attracted droves of new members. Belize City membership rose from 267 in May 1947 to 1456 a year later, at which time there were 165 members in Corozal, 425 in Stann Creek, 200 in Punta Gorda, and 101 in the new Cayo branch.[63]

In January 1948 Betson called for "socialism in Belize," but his explanation revealed a faith in the British Labour government and a sense that Britain had legitimized increased militance against employers: "The scene in British Honduras is similar to the scene in England before the coming of Socialism. The same remedy must be applied . . . [A]ny programmes that have as their aims the social and economic development of the people of dependent territories and colonies must be sponsored by representatives of government, management, and labour. . . . [T]here must be a united front. The kind of united front that has moved forward under the banner of cooperative spirit in England. The evils that beset British Honduras call for three things—united labor front, the election of representatives of labor to the councils of the land, and the planning of a programme for cooperative action, probably on a smaller scale of the English model."[64] Two young reporters from the new *Belize Billboard* newspaper, Leigh Richardson and Philip Goldson, influenced by the American Jesuits at St. John's College, criticized Betson for endorsing communism.[65] Betson retorted that "socialism in England is not dictatorial, while communism in Russia is" and contrasted the Labour Party's commitment to the masses with "Tory dictators."[66]

Given the unique possibility reformers had of making trade unionism and empire loyalty consistent in the late 1940s, Betson's 1947 strike comment is better understood as a particularly forceful articulation of local patriotism rather than as a statement advocating a nationalist break with British reform. This interpretation is lent weight by the fact that Betson and GWU vice president Henry Middleton were both leaders of the Loyal and Patriotic Order of the Baymen.[67] The LPOB's cultural politics, focused on the Battle of St. George's Caye tradition and 10th celebrations, expressed the same compromised patriotism first articulated by middle-class Creoles in the 1890s. Consistent with this overlap between the LPOB and the GWU is the fact that the union's anthem was "Land of the Gods," the patriotic 10th song penned in 1925 by Samuel Haynes. The same month that he appealed for socialism, Betson named Ezekiel A. Grant as the GWU's choice for the Belize District in the upcoming legislative elections, at a meeting attended by other LPOB leaders and by reform stalwarts Monrad S. Metzgen and Vivian Seay. Grant, who as a district commissioner in the 1930s had cooperated with Burns's legal pursuit of Soberanis, received a law degree in Jamaica in the late 1940s and represented the GWU at the Caribbean Labour Congress meeting held there in September 1947.[68] Returning to a hero's welcome from the reform establishment, Grant quoted from "Land of the Gods" in urging unionists to "put on your armour" and declared himself a "democratic socialist." As unlikely as the idea of Belize as a democratic socialist colony within the British Empire may seem to modern readers, the GWU leadership was more comfortable with this than with outright popular nationalism.

During June 1948 constitutional hearings Grant and the GWU supported universal suffrage in elections for the colonial legislature, a position shared by an unusual number of establishment Creoles in the late 1940s, though not by veteran Garveyite Morrel Staine, who set the bar at an income of $25 per month.[69] Two years later, young nationalists took control of the GWU and its membership ballooned as thousands of women and unskilled forestry laborers flooded into it. It thus ceased to be a "responsible" trade union, both in terms of its membership and its explicit political agenda. Betson stepped down with dignity and was very quiet in withdrawing from the GWU, but the Creole middle class as a whole loudly ended its more superficial love affair with trade unionism. Metzgen and Seay helped to found an antinationalist political party in 1951, and in 1952 the constitutional commission, led by prominent Creole lawyer W. Harrison Courtenay, proposed changes that would block the nationalists' electoral sway in the rural areas where a majority of seats were at stake, and where nationalist strength depended on the GWU.[70] The union had become part of the nationalist foe. Ironically, Betson's own more aggressive British Labour-style politics of the late 1940s had nurtured the mass base of the GWU that ultimately showed more enthusiasm for the nationalist leadership than his own.

Tragically, nationalist leaders would prove to be more tactically committed to an independent labor movement than some colonial reformers and more paternalistic than Betson and his leadership ever were. One can only speculate that had Betson broken with the gendered ideology of colonial reform that dictated women's virtual exclusion from the labor movement and attempted to forge a populist coalition with working women, he might have given the nationalists some real competition for the crucial female political constituency. He might also have remained the champion of the GWU's increasingly nationalist male membership. What is certain is that the GWU's practice of "responsible" trade unionism, for all the reform establishment support that it garnered, was one factor allowing for a historic marriage of working women's political militance to the nationalist cause.

Domesticating Women, Disciplining Motherhood:
Health and Welfare Policy

In several ways social reformers were better equipped than their labor counterparts to pursue the common goal of reordering family life, laying the foundation for economic prosperity, and so modernizing the colony. In its attempts to promote a breadwinner-father-household-head identity among male workers, the Labour Department was hampered by under-staffing, the late development of a responsible trade union leadership, and then the unexpected radicalization of that leadership. Social reformers, by contrast, multiplied within the state and without, built on the reforms of the 1920s with early and sustained activism, and were free of respon-sible trade unionism's ambiguities. They aimed to remake working-class women as happy wives and mothers, and as grateful clients of state services, particularly maternal and infant health care. Poor black women were to be transformed from street agitators and labor militants to domesticated community volunteers—much as Baptist missionaries in Jamaica had sought to domesticate freedwomen in the aftermath of emancipation.[71] Local reformers largely avoided explicit references to race, although in 1937 labor critic Luke Kemp did note that "White prejudice is most ram-pant here among black and blackish citizens, " referring to middle-class reformers.[72] While many poor women welcomed the new state services, social reform's moralistic stance and the heightening of popular expecta-tions of the state caused it to founder. Although working-class women did not create any organizations or movements to parallel the GWU, by 1950 they did define health care as a basic citizen right. Not only did they politicize motherhood, itself a violation of the gender ideology of colo-nial reform, but they also continued to link their combative motherhood to issues of work, pay, unemployment, household headship, labor rights, and colonial rule. They brought these politics into the labor-nationalist movement of the 1950s.

Governor Burns, as we have seen, was not indifferent to the dire living conditions of the colony's laboring people during the local reform proj-ect of 1934–39; he especially feared that extreme hardship would further strengthen the LUA. With the Colonial Office's rejection of his and Seay's women's land settlement scheme in early 1935, state officials and female volunteers refocused on infant and maternal health.[73] The later 1930s witnessed a significant expansion of hospital maternity care and of the Infant Welfare League's clinic system and the beginning of a state takeover of the latter. But these changes could do little to combat the effects of unemployment, poverty, and malnutrition. The BCNS' own research in 1938 revealed the truly horrendous social condition of the urban working class, with a typical two-parent family subsisting on a few cents worth of bread, rice, sugar, and beans each day. When the Medical Department examined 2,297 schoolchildren in Belize Town in 1938, one fifth were anemic and one fifth had poor or bad nutrition.[74] These indices of social hardship were common even during "the periodic economic 'booms.'"[75]

The Infant Welfare League endorsed a modern state culture of maternal and infant health that was to remake unruly subaltern women by emphasizing their domestic identities and disciplining them as mothers. The IWL had continued to operate its Belize Town north side clinic through the bitter, conflictual years of the early and mid-1930s. In May 1934, for example, IWL health visitors reported decline in clinic attendance because many mothers had no clothing for their children. The public was asked to make clothing donations to Matron Roberts.[76] Lady Burns's early interest in the IWL resulted in a "Thrift Club," started in 1935, through which 350 clinic mothers deposited small sums, had 8 percent interest paid by Lady Burns, and received the money to pay for Christmas presents at a party where she also presented parcels of food donated by local merchants.[77] This was an activist, didactic model of charity very much at odds with the LUA Women's League's, which in 1935 argued that women deserved equal rights. League clinics became the central means by which the state sought to "squeeze out the dirty old "handy" women" and to replace these traditional midwives with professionally trained nurses.[78] In Stann Creek in 1935 an unlicensed midwife was held without bail for two weeks on charges of manslaughter by negligence of a pregnant woman, reportedly on the local Medical Officer's instructions.[79] In 1941 Vivian Seay was appointed inspector of midwives; her personal transition from volunteer to civil servant symbolized the modernization of colonial health policy.

It may well have been Governor and Lady Burns's visit to the BCNS' Stann Creek Baby Exhibition in May 1936 that provided the inspiration for establishing a colony-wide system of infant welfare clinics.[80] Through a combination of Lady Burns's interest and local initiative, a Stann Creek clinic opened in June 1936, staffed by a nurse trained under CDS auspices.[81] In August the Burnses toured the Orange Walk hospital with District Commissioner Ezekiel A. Grant and his wife Wilhelmina, who within two months had organized an infant welfare clinic in Orange Walk Town.[82] Burns budgeted $200 for the Belize Town clinic in 1936, its first government funding, and he ordered that every district establish a clinic.[83] Punta Gorda's opened in February, Cayo's in June of 1937, and Corozal's sometime in 1938.[84] That year the Orange Walk IWL briefly ran a second clinic in the large Mayan village of San Estevan, and Belize Town's south side clinic opened in the Mesopotamia neighborhood.[85]

The model of joint funding and staffing between the public and private sectors was followed in all clinics except Stann Creek, where a "native trained midwife" worked alone. Elsewhere, medical officers and staff nurses ran the clinics with the critical aid of voluntary workers. In Orange Walk, for example, Nurse Amy Card and later Nurse Kathleen Longsworth ran the clinic while Wilhelmina Grant headed a group of young ladies from the town's leading merchant families. Likewise, in Cayo Nurse Eleanor Haylock was supported by a troupe of young charity givers.[86] Volunteers raised funds to stock the clinics by organizing socials and entertainments. In addition, merchants made donations, as in Punta Gorda where Nurse Cora Pilgrim ran the clinic and in Cayo.[87] In Belize Town, Matron Roberts continued to receive aid from "certain ladies of the town," among them the BCNS, who during home visits directed women in need to the IWL.[88] No data on funding in Stann Creek exists, but it seems likely that the CDS made donations. By 1938 lady volunteers were still very active in Corozal and Cayo, barely so in Orange Walk, and not at all in Stann Creek.[89] In Cayo they were deployed to "keep behind the mothers [who are] inclined to gradually drop out," and in Corozal they were busy encouraging mothers to breastfeed. In Punta Gorda the number of infants seen weekly declined from sixty in early 1937 to less than thirty in 1938—in the other district clinics less than thirty were seen as well.[90] In Stann Creek the clinic nurse calculated that 65 percent of clinic infants had nutritional anemia and most of the mothers were also poorly nourished.[91] Mothers' reasons for "dropping out" probably included the clinics' very limited ability to end poverty-borne illness, and the volunteers' and nurses' assumptions about poor women's maternal intelligence and morality.

In Belize Town the Mesopotamia clinic opened in 1938 and both clinics continued to be in high demand, with about 230 infants seen weekly. In addition, a government nurse made over thirteen hundred home visits during the year.[92] The sustained urban demand may have been due to greater absolute poverty among women with no access to subsistence or new forms of wage labor, to higher rates of single motherhood, to a stronger popular culture of native rights, and to more familiarity with western medicine. By 1944, the infant mortality rate among Belize Town clinic babies was less than 15 percent of the colony-wide rate, or 24 per 1000 compared to 137.4 per 1000.[93]

Some of this dramatic improvement may have been due to the modest expansion of welfare services. When Governor Hunter arrived in 1940, he quickly ordered a survey of urban poverty among women and children, which found that even a doubling of outdoor relief would not begin to meet existing needs.[94] From 1937 to 1943 the direct welfare payments disbursed by the government's Outdoor Relief Committee (ORC) rose from $9,400 to $25,000, and the number of recipients from 376 to 743, most of them either children or over sixty years of age.[95] This represented an increase from $25 to almost $34 annually per person. By 1945 the ORC—now housed within the new Social Welfare Department—had determined that most of the indigent children on its rolls should have been receiving court-ordered maintenance from their fathers, prompting the revision of the Bastardy and Separation and Maintenance Ordinances that year.[96] The effect of this state effort to hold fathers accountable may well have been a reduction in welfare payments to the children of single mothers in the late 1940s. The ORC's other main activity was to jointly fund with the Belize Town Board the Gann's Rest House, a homeless shelter for men operated by the Salvation Army that opened in 1941.[97]

The Belize Town clinic babies' lowered mortality rate may also have been due to the welfare role taken on by the clinic staff. After 1940 the infant welfare clinics were completely professionalized and absorbed into the colonial state. A district visiting nurse service ran the weekly clinic and daily home visiting programs until 1945, when the last DVN resigned, and from 1941 on the clinics began to do antenatal checkups and to dispense powdered milk to indigent mothers. These latter measures undoubtedly encouraged attendance and directly improved maternal and infant nutrition. In 1944, 704 of 728 city newborns survived to one month of age, and of those 491 (70 percent) attended the postnatal clinics. Of these, 12 died before the age of one year, resulting in a mortality rate of just 24/1000. Of the 213 infants never seen at a clinic, 22 died, or 103/1000. Typically, the medical report mixed a heavy dose of moral condemnation with a trace of sympathy in commenting on these cases: "only one of these [22] families was in good economic circumstances; the others could be classed as . . . ignorant, careless, destitute or disunited," the last term apparently a veiled reference to fatherless or common-law families. The 24 mothers whose children died in the first month of life were all found to be suffering from "not solely . . . individual but [also] social pathology," primarily anemia due to malnutrition. The social conditions identified by the BCNs in 1938 may have been somewhat eased by increased outdoor relief, free milk powder, and the family allotments sent home by men working overseas, but in the later 1940s the last of those benefits ended, as did government price controls on staple imported foods. Colony-wide, infant mortality did not dip below 100/1000 until after 1950.

That 70 percent of new Belize City mothers used the infant welfare clinics in 1944 indicates that they had become an important arena of subaltern women's negotiations with and contestations of a state that never had enough to give. A shared experience inevitably developed in the clinic waiting room, just as it did in the water lines and at the market. Yet no evidence survives of urban women elaborating a collective praxis as "clinic mothers," perhaps because this was an identity tinged with shame, unlike working-class men's proud membership in the GWU.[98] Dependent on state services, but without any political control over them, poor mothers did not challenge the foundations of state paternalism.

Evidence of a collective "clinic mother" identity does exist for two rural communities. In 1944 the Medical Department began a new Rural Health Nurses (RHNs) program. The first four students enrolled in the program were all trained midwives and at least one of them, Cleopatra White, was a BCN. In 1945, as the urban visiting nurse program and regular nursing education collapsed, the new RHNs took charge of four village health posts, with immediate success. "They had been at work but few months," that year's Medical Report said, "when it became clear from the gratifying response of the villagers 'at risk' that the nurses individually and collectively had taken aid, comfort and encouragement to the isolated communities where the possibility of such help had formerly been outside their experience or even their hopes."[99] By 1948 there were twelve trained RHNs at work, and in 1950 fully nineteen "child hygiene clinic" sites existed. Because so many trained midwives entered the program, in 1945 the government initiated a state certificate in midwifery to replenish their numbers.

The RHNs evidently brought a new experience of state-provided health care to rural communities, an experience that not only raised villagers' hopes but also their expectations. Those expectations seem to have been most acute among women, to whom the RHNs' maternal and infant care was directed. Cleopatra White was in her mid-40s when she started work in Gales Point Manatee, a coastal Creole village south of Belize City, where she had an enormous impact. She set up the colony's first Village Council, which served as a model to colonial officials designing a colony-wide council system in the early 1950s, and she fostered a wide variety of cultural and social activities, especially for youth. When the government transferred her to Roaring Creek in 1953, two local women headed a petition to bring her back. White's devotees were still appealing for her return a year later, now led by Mrs. Albertha Hendy, but to no avail.[100]

RHN Evelyn Bell, who was stationed at Double Head Cabbage on the Belize River from 1947–53, was not so universally popular, although like White she had solid female support. When apparent clashes with the local telephone operator/linesman's family led to rumors of Bell's transfer in July 1952, five self-identified "clinic mothers" immediately wrote to the government demanding that she stay in the village.[101] They cited her

"good works and kindness," her "motherly way," and her record of achievement, which included setting up an infant clinic in 1947, supplying it with
milk powder for two years out of her own salary, paying for the burials of
three infants, and saving two mothers from childbirth death. Less than a
week later the women had collected 239 signatures from ten nearby river
villages, 101 of them from women.[102] The government assured them that
Nurse Bell would remain.

Colonial officials, however, reluctantly came to the conclusion that the
history of trouble between Bell and the linesman's family required her
transfer. The trouble had begun early on, when Bell failed to save the life of
his infant, and perhaps added insult to injury by paying for its burial. Even
saving his niece's life during childbirth did not improve relations. Then
Bell broke his wife's baking pot, donated for a clinic social, and was fined
$25 in April 1949 for using abusive words to this woman. In May 1952 the
director of Medical Services asked for police supervision in Double Head
Cabbage, as the linesman had reportedly wounded Bell's pig and threatened her life. It was this crisis that precipitated the clinic mothers' petition,
and ultimately saw Bell transferred to Progresso in Corozal District.

Without the clinic mothers' petition there would be no record of community support for Bell and her work, and we might conclude that she had
wielded her knowledge, skills, and authority in a manner alienating to all her
clients. Their support for her makes it clear that Bell and her clinic formed
an alternative site of state authority and funding in the community that,
combined with their intense personal interactions, led to friction between
nurse and linesman. Bell's community health work had empowered village
women with a new collective political identity, one that they brandished
in the face of a state that was supposed to look after them and their children, not cater to the "malicious feelings" of one faction. In defining their
interests as community interests, clinic mothers staked out a hegemonic
claim made possible by Evelyn Bell's perhaps unintentional politicization
of health care as an arena of female concern. And although the colonial
authorities stopped short of challenging the linesman's local power, they
did send another RHN to replace Bell. On some level, then, the clinic mothers had become a constituency to which reformers felt they must respond.

Women increased their demand for hospital obstetrical services in the late 1930s and 1940s, though the evidence of this is sparser. This trend is indicative of female expectations of state health care similar to those analyzed above. By 1938 all the district hospitals offered obstetrical services, although only Stann Creek had a maternity ward, which opened with four beds in late 1937. Whereas just eight births took place in the Stann Creek hospital in 1937, fifty-nine occurred there the following year. Medical officers in Orange Walk and Punta Gorda reported a growing demand for hospital births, and even Cayo reported that a "midwifery unit" was an urgent necessity.[103] Clearly the IWL clinics, although unable to offer more than palliative care, were fostering a widespread female demand for modern state-provided health care during pregnancy and childbirth. By 1944 over half of Belize City's babies were born in the hospital, a feat accomplished by jamming extra beds into the maternity ward, which still had the same official twelve-bed capacity as in 1927. Indeed, in 1946 there were still only twenty-two maternity beds colony-wide.[104] As with the town and village clinics, the state was simply unable to expand quickly enough to meet popular female demand for its health services.

A very similar dynamic developed around the issue of the urban water supply, an age-old problem, which, as we have seen, led to collective female protests in the 1920s and 1930s. Burns secured CDF funding for six huge water vats that opened in early 1937 in Belize Town, part of his wider concern to improve urban environmental sanitation. He had asked the town board for a comprehensive urban plan soon after his arrival, appointed a housing and slum committee in 1937, transferred sanitation work from the town board to the Medical Department in 1938, and hired a Jamaican as Senior Sanitary Inspector.[105] To accomplish these last changes, he had the Legislative Council suspend the town board, a violation of hard-won democratic rights that outraged columnist Luke Kemp, who already felt that a "united reactionary front" was at work in the colony.[106] As part of the slum committee's work, the Medical Department carried out a housing survey of 764 houses in Belize Town in 1938, finding disturbing rates of overcrowding, lack of sanitary facilities, and—despite the new water tanks—inadequate water supplies.[107]

During the early 1940 dry season water shortages prompted, as in the past, popular female action and elite male response. A deputation of women from Mesopotamia went to the Colonial Secretary, asking that the pipes be left open longer than 7 to 8 a.m.; a few days later a nasty knife fight among three women in a standpipe line put one in the hospital and was only broken up when men from the Defense Force intervened.[108] While the *Clarion* blamed women's disorderliness for slowing distribution, the *Independent* noted a decline in private vat capacity and thus greater pressure on the municipal tanks. The PP-dominated town board's response was a public meeting to mobilize support for demands for an imperially funded solution. A number of the labor leaders of the 1930s and 1940s spoke at this and other water protest meetings, including Tony Soberanis, Ricardo Meighan, Henry Middleton, Luke Kemp, and Clifford Betson. The only female voice was again that of Elfreda Trapp. The director of Public Works, representing the government, described plans to barge extra water from some miles up the Belize River.[109] Others, including Trapp, emphasized the need to improve order in the waiting lines, the cheapest option being for the town board to hire "ladies . . . as it did formerly" to collect tokens. Veteran PP leaders Calvert and Morrel Staine both suggested that there was a black market in tank water. Ultimately the board endorsed the barge plan, but no structural solution was implemented for another eight years.

Governor Hunter's 1940 survey of female and child poverty focused on health indices rather than housing, sanitation, and water, but he revived the Housing and Slum Committee in 1944, which produced a town plan at long last in 1946.[110] It confirmed the 1938 survey's findings that much of the south side, especially Mesopotamia, was overcrowded, congested, and underserviced. No slum clearance ever took place, but by late 1948 construction finally began on eleven miles of water piping, which, after several delays, reached Belize City in June 1949, at the very end of another parched dry season and just six months before the eruption of the nation- alist movement.[111] By then women had moved beyond the exceptionally polite deputation of 1940. In the 1944 dry season, for example, there was considerable agitation, and in April 1948 "a group of noisy women with buckets and pails invaded" city council offices, demanding water from one of the six tanks.[112] They had been waiting since 3 a.m. for it to open at 7 a.m., and had still not advanced to the front of the line by shut off time an hour later. The piped water system did not silence women's perennial water demands in the political uproar of the early 1950s. In 1954, fifty-seven residents of Cemetery Road—at least thirty-four of them women, led by Mrs. Maggie Pipersburgh—petitioned for an extension of the new pipes to their neighborhood.[113] Efforts by the reformist authorities to improve the urban water supply, particularly through the tanks of the late 1930s, did not solve dry season "water-famines" but did serve to focus popular hostilities on the state, a pattern that persisted even after the tanks disappeared.

In 1935 when she was made a Member of the British Empire, Vivian Seay gave a speech to a number of Creole girls, in which she acknowledged that "many in this community" were critical of the BCNs. She also argued to the rising generation that to be poor and black was no shame but to lack "decency, principle, and ambition [was] a thorough disgrace."[114] Her attempt to suppress the practices of combative motherhood, informed by race and class identities, and to replace them with those of respectable apolitical motherhood, embodied the spirit of colonial modernization policy toward women. By 1952 Seay was a founding member of the antinationalist political party and an LPOB activist, still promoting a colonialist model of proper womanhood that the working mothers of the colony had never accepted as hegemonic. Her entry into the colonial civil service as inspector of midwives exemplified the professionalization of social services but, like colonial social reform as a whole, had little effect on the human toll of dependent capitalist development or on anticolonial sentiment.

Making Good Boys and Girls:
Delinquency and Gendered Vocational Education

Elementary schools, most of them church-run, were a critical site of moral intervention by colonial modernizers, who defined all native children as potential delinquents.[115] While compulsory basic instruction, including hygiene classes, had aimed to improve the rising generation since the late 1910s, in the 1930s vocational education was added to the mix. The

Education Department itself largely eschewed the discourse of moralism in the late 1930s and 1940s, but its staff clearly viewed vocational education as a means of curbing delinquent tendencies by improving labor skills in a gender-divided manner. Its intent was to train men for the roles of family breadwinner and responsible trade unionist, women for those of house-wife and mother.

B. H. Easter, a Jamaican official who studied British Honduran educa-tion in 1933, was appalled that less than 10 percent of government spend-ing was going to education "when it [was] spending nearly 16 [percent] on its police and prisons."[116] Burns, limited by the exclusion of social spend-ing from imperial development grants before 1940, could do little about the education budget. He did however rapidly implement Easter's rec-ommendations that boys receive training in manual trades and that girls study domestic science and childcare.[117] In 1936 the government funded three trades workshops and two church-run domestic science centers in Belize Town. The latter amalgamated in 1939 and was taken over by the Education Department in 1948.[118] Throughout the late 1930s and 1940s roughly eighty girls each year from seven urban primary schools spent a full day every week at the centers, learning needlework, cooking, house-keeping, and childcare. Their teacher was Mary Wright, an active member of the LPOB, who went on to teach home economics at the new technical college in the early 1950s. The college's curriculum was built on the same gendered assumptions as elementary vocational training, i.e., that young men needed a trade to make a living, while young women needed domes-tic skills.

The 1946 report of the Development Planning Committee envisioned boys' trades and 4H education as serving the agricultural future of the colony, but—in a fine spirit of laissez faire—concluded that girls had such limited job opportunities that there was no point in offering them anything but infant welfare, nutrition, and cookery classes.[119] Domestic science would, the committee hoped, help to curb rising female juvenile delinquency. Others felt that more was needed. As early as 1943 the new British Honduras Social Services Council (BHSSC), a group of clergy, had spelled out the need for a government institution devoted to delinquent girls.[120] When the social welfare adviser from the DWO visited the colony a year later, both the BHSSC and the new Social Welfare Department's probation officer reiterated the urgency of the issue.[121] But the Development Planning Committee opted for research rather than action, recommending a five-year study of the problem and a continuation of domestic science education in the meantime.[122]

Girls' morality, and more broadly that of youth as a whole, was a concern of colonial modernizers throughout the 1940s. In 1940, for example, the BCNs proposed a curfew for young teenagers, needed, they suggested, to combat "lax parenting."[123] The idea was taken up in 1942 by the BHSSC, which evolved out of meetings in 1941 where the WIRC's call for a campaign against immorality was enthusiastically discussed.[124] The curfew may have been inaugurated during the BHSSC's first Social Uplift Week in late 1942, which BHTU leaders later referred to approvingly. The second such week was staged in November 1943 on the theme of "The Family and Parental Control," but activities were limited to a week of lectures on prayer, gambling, and parenting by clergymen and female reformers like Matron Roberts.[125] Only the concluding Battlefield meeting attracted a large crowd, quite possibly because the topic, "social diseases," promised "the spectacle of a church minister discussing" syphilis and gonorrhea in public. By then the BHSSC's curfew had proved a bust, as one "MRW"— possibly Mary Wright—lamented in a letter to the *Belize Independent*.[126] Like her middle-class forerunners of the late 1910s, "MRW" perceived a rising tide of juvenile delinquency, blamed the BHSSC for making the curfew voluntary, and doubted parents' desire and ability to control their adolescent children. Indeed, the curfew had been ridiculed and denounced "by the people it was most expected to help." Clearly, moral reform had little potential to attract popular support.

As the BHSSC and Development Planning Committee concerns suggest, domestic science training did not curb female juvenile delinquency. In 1948 the education staff indulged in a rare moment of moral critique when they described truancy as caused by a "lack of normal family life," "parental negligence," and "psychological upsets in the children." Mothers' "carelessness [and] irresponsibility" were to blame, not just the absence of fathers.[127] The Prison Department went even further, attributing the perceived rise in youth crime to "illegitimacy . . . and the carefree way so many fathers regard the offspring of these casual unions" as well as to the "calamitous upbringing" offered by unwed mothers."[128] Vocational education for prison inmates hewed to the same gendered assumptions as that for schoolchildren.

Very little vocational education was available in the districts aside from 4H clubs, ubiquitous needlework classes for girls, and the Pomona Industrial School's training for boys, mainly in farm work. Yet individual teachers could bring their own gender politics to bear in extracurricular activities. In Stann Creek, teacher Olivia Perriot led a Girl Guide troop that, like the movement colony-wide, emphasized domestic skills and ladylike morality and required fees beyond the capacity of most working-class parents. Perriot taught her guides to "smile and sing under all difficulties" and to bake bread. None of them ever went on to work in the Pomona grapefruit cannery, she recalled; instead they married and became housewives.[129] In the Mayan village of Yo Creek in the Orange Walk district, teacher Adolfa Garcia organized a successful girls' softball team, "Las Campesinas," as one way to draw the next generation of Mayan girls away from a life defined by kitchen work and endless childbearing.[130] Not surprisingly, given Garcia's contestation of both colonial reform and rural Mayan gender norms, she became one of the very few Mayan women to enter the nationalist movement independently of male kin.

Colonial education policy from the mid-1930s on was deliberately meshed with the gendered theory of colonial modernization as practiced through the Labour, Medical, and Social Development Departments. Like the infant welfare clinics, girls' vocational education aimed to break a perceived cycle of poor mothering, one that contributed to juvenile delinquency, family instability, and ultimately political immaturity. By training girls in undervalued domestic and maternal skills, the schools contributed to women's definition as at most a secondary labor force. Reformers' solution to female delinquency was not economic self-sufficiency and political rights but domesticity from which it was hoped a withdrawal from politics would follow as a matter of course. Economic, social, and political

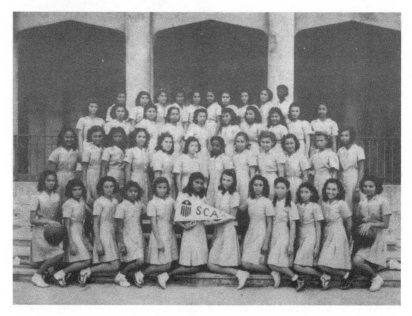

FIG. 14. St. Catherine's Academy Basketball Club, 1944. This well-groomed, orderly, modern image of young Belizean womanhood was central to the reform project of the 1940s. Source: *Belizean Studies* 7:1 (January 1979): 5.

progress for the colony would flow from women being within their households but not in control of them.

Fighting Nationalism: Cultural and Social Reform, 1946–54

In 1950 the young nationalist leaders wrested control of the GWU from the Garveyite middle class and hundreds of women joined up, invigorating the new labor-nationalist alliance as they had the LUA. No longer was labor an acceptable part of colonial modernization; as in the mid-1930s, it was the enemy. While elements of the middle class contemplated universal suffrage in the 1940s, and specifically during constitutional discussions late in the decade, by 1951 when the Courtenay Constitutional Report was released, the political calculus had completely changed. The commissioners, including Calvert Staine—veteran Garveyite and supporter of labor rights in the early 1940s—advised extremely limited change to keep the nationalists at bay.[131] Indeed, social elitism within middle-class culture was hardly eradicated during in the late 1940s. During constitutional discussions in 1948 Morrel Staine opposed proposals for universal suffrage, arguing that "you cannot give the riffraff the vote."[132]

An important though previously overlooked terrain in colonial reformers' hostile response to the nationalist movement was the clearly antinationalist intensification of social reform work aimed at poor women. The Social Welfare Department was renamed the Social Development Department in 1951, perhaps in response to the nationalists' discourse of independence as the key to economic development.[133] Through the Social Development Department British officials and middle-class civil servants, many of them female, tried to inoculate the masses against the contagion of popular nationalism. Between 1948 and 1951 the department grew from a staff of one to seventeen.[134] Of the ten male staff, three were the top administrators, two were office support, one was a probation officer, and three were cooperative officers. These three in the early 1950s were engaged in surveying each village in the colony and in setting up credit and savings unions and consumer clubs and housing, chicle, and farmers co-ops. By 1951 there were 4,122 members of these groups, with almost $135,000 in paid-up shared capital. The final male staffer was in charge of developing cottage industries and supervised three women—a "craft instructress" and two junior craft instructresses. Two other women worked as youth and women's organizers, and two others were office support. The junior craft teachers and the youth and women's organizers were hired in 1951. In 1953 a third woman was hired as a youth and women's organizer, and a female probation officer—Gwendolyn Lizarraga—also joined the department. Her work included efforts to reconcile marital disputes and, perhaps as a result, the social welfare officer claimed in 1953 that "there is every indication of a developing awareness of the value of stable family life among the masses."[135] While there was "a fair proportion of women" in the cooperative societies that male officers worked with, the female staff focused heavily on forming groups of village girls and women to produce woven grass products for sale in Belize City and to take short courses in housewifery skills.[136]

The cottage industries network was based mainly in Garifuna and Mayan villages where the staff viewed women as having "a natural aptitude" for craft work, though Creole villages like Gales Point, Placencia, and Burrel Boom also had craft depots.[137] Craft teachers ran intensive short courses; by late 1952 one hundred girls had been trained, and in 1953 four rural girls trained in the Belize City depot to teach crafts in their own communities.[138] Twenty-three girls finished the products in Belize City and at the Corozal depot and were paid by the piece. By 1954 there were ten girls in Corozal, seventeen in Belize City, fourteen in Punta Gorda, and twelve in Barranco, all supplying the materials for their work and all of whom were paid at piece rates.[139] Evidently the cottage industries never aimed to provide young women with a livelihood, only with an activity to fill their "spare time" and to earn them a small income, for in 1956 the department report criticized the people for being "interested only in making money" and for failing to "[catch] on to village craft."[140] The very nature of work in the cottage industry depots was ambiguous—paid, but supposedly reinforcing domesticity. Indeed, the whole idea of the cottage industries originated with a 1944 visit of the DWO social welfare advisor, and they were pioneered in state institutions: the prison, mental asylum, the Poor House, Gann's Rest Home, and the Pomona Industrial School.[141]

The program thus had as little potential for curbing the nationalist passions of subaltern women as had the vastly expanded infant and school feeding programs run through the Medical Department. Feeding programs, palliative like the Social Development Department's urban work program, sought to quell the urban political uproar with powdered milk, cod liver oil, yeast, and biscuits provided by UNICEF and the Red Cross, the latter headed by the governor's wife. By 1953 total government and nongovernment spending on these programs amounted to $23,000, and it was deemed politically impossible to cut back.[142] Just as poor women had been extracting urgently needed resources from IWL clinics since the late 1920s, so did they demand that the colonial state provide for their infants and children even as they agitated for an end to colonial rule.

Reformers battled valiantly against women's shedding of the guise of deferential client. In the government's new propaganda organ, *The British*

Honduran, Carol Campbell, veteran civil servant and active antinationalist, tried to woo women back to the Battle of St. George's Caye myth, arguing that it was women who made the settlement into a home worth saving from the Spaniards in 1798.[143] This was a clear allusion to anglophile accusations that the nationalist movement was pro-Guatemalan. And Mary Wright, now ensconced as the home economics teacher at the technical college, dispensed cheery advice to women about serving balanced meals by adding vegetables and dairy products to the menu. Oblivious to the realities of female unemployment and low wages and of the high cost of imported foods, Wright's columns are exemplary evidence of why the middle class lost even tenuous control of the laboring majority in the early 1950s.

The reforms of the early 1950s were no different in kind than those of the Burns era or of the 1940s. They continued to treat men as breadwinners and family heads, to promote a domestic destiny for women, and to attempt a fundamental but futile remolding of the gender, race, and class order. Trade unionism in the 1940s and maternal and child health programs throughout the 1935–54 period were always about depoliticizing subaltern demands and cultivating dependence on state mediators, power brokers, and aid givers. The project of colonial modernization was hegemonic in intent, and although it failed to erase popular nationalist and labor identities from popular culture, it nurtured a statist orientation in the popular imagination and a led to a loss of working-class autonomy. The reformist project of discipline and domestication shaped *how* nationalist struggle would take place, even though it could not prevent that struggle from erupting.

State and middle-class reformers never had guaranteed control over the arenas they themselves opened up in the late 1930s and 1940s. Most dramatically, responsible trade unionism became the vehicle for popular nationalism through the GWU, but less dramatically the infant welfare clinics also fostered a politicized citizen identity. As the clinic mothers of Double Head Cabbage demonstrated in 1952, female political identities and actions could take root in the soil of "domestic" amelioration. The nationalists, as they won control of the state in the 1950s, and aged in power in the 1960s and 1970s, would themselves spin a model of proper nationalist womanhood as conservative as the LPOB's Queen of the Bay. And they would learn that just as it took a concerted state-middle class effort to quell the LUA crisis, so would it require constant hegemonic work on their part to control how the nationalist women's rebellion against the patriarchal and racist prejudices of colonial modernization was interpreted.

5 A New Paterfamilias

The Creation and Control of
Popular Nationalism, 1949–1961

On New Year's Eve 1949 Governor Sir Ronald Garvey—on Colonial Office orders—used his reserve powers to override the Legislative Council and devalue the British Honduran dollar. Within hours a protest rally began on the Battlefield, the park in central Belize City where the LUA meetings of the 1930s had occurred. It was organized by the Open Forum, a small group founded in 1948 by labor veterans Antonio Soberanis and Luke Kemp, which by September of that year had earned the governor's disapproval for its hostility to British rule. In 1949 Soberanis and Kemp published a booklet that rejected the middle-class Battle myth, defined Belize as a black and Indian nation, and asserted its natives' right to national self-determination.[1] Joining them at the New Year's Eve rally were GWU president Clifford Betson and two younger men from the Catholic Social Action Group (CSAG), organized in the late 1940s by American Jesuits at St. John's College. These were John Smith, who had been elected to the Legislative Council in 1948, and George Price, who with Smith had been elected to the Belize City Council in 1947.[2] Belize's nationalist movement was born that night, for the protest quickly led to the formation of the nationalist People's Committee (PC), which in September 1950 became the People's United Party (PUP). In the period 1950–54 the PUP, together with a transformed GWU, confronted the colonial government, the colony's employers, and middle-class reformers—yet it was never anticapitalist or hostile to foreign investment, though more favorable to economic ties with the United States than Britain. The PUP won full-suffrage legislative elections in 1954, 1957, and 1961—and remained in power for twenty-four years after Britain granted internal self-government in 1964, though a major schism occurred in 1956 that ended the alliance with the GWU and made Price the chief leader of the PUP.

Elfreda Reyes, so prominent in the LUA and its Women's League in the 1930s, claimed to have spoken to the crowd that gathered on New Year's Eve 1949 to protest the Governor's devaluation of the British Honduran currency: "Give us back our dollar!" she remembered shouting. She also recalled having mounted the rostrum weekly in the tumultuous weeks that followed.[3] There were no women in the leaderships of any of the nationalist groups of the late 1940s and early 1950s, yet Elfreda's presence at the birth of Belize's nationalist movement would make sense, for the GWU and PUP became arenas for an enormous revival of the female activism that had characterized the LUA and to some extent of the LUA's gender-inclusive political culture. If Elfreda was a regular speaker at PC rallies in early 1950, she had a female audience: "It's only women would march and support those boys," recalled retired teacher and radio entertainer Gladys Stuart, referencing the youth of the male leaders. Elfreda herself responded warmly to my questions about women's attendance: "Ooo! More than the men. Some used to come with sticks." Dolores Balderamos Garcia, a niece of George Price and appointed leader of PUP women in the early 1990s, remembered growing up with the impression that "It was [the women's] mass support that gave the nationalist movement birth."[4]

These memories have survived despite the erasure of women from PUP manifestos and retrospectives, which have uniformly portrayed the male leaders, particularly Price, as the people's heroes—a self-serving narrative that easily succumbs to Marxist, feminist, and postcolonial critiques.[5] Scholarly accounts of the 1950s have nicely skewered PUP self-glorification, but only Cedric Grant has consistently recognized the power of the popular movement and the activism of women—even into the later 1950s—in a detailed account that yet remains heavily focused on the party leadership and its local and British opponents.[6] Nigel Bolland and Assad Shoman have certainly acknowledged the mass base of the nationalist movement. Bolland in particular has argued that PUP success would have been impossible without the GWU, which he tends to idealize as *the* authentic voice of Belizean workers, in part because he continues to see its origins in Soberanis's BHWTU. But they have tended also to mourn the popular movement as weak—lacking historical experience and political education and quickly falling victim to predatory middle-class nationalists who took over of the GWU in April 1950.[7] Shoman broke partially with this analysis in a 1990 article where he argued that in the early 1950s the PUP was "much too reliant on mass mobilization and support" to be acceptable to Britain, and that Price depended on grassroots action to pressure the British throughout the decade.[8] This chapter supports and complicates that argument by providing a fuller history of the popular movement and by distinguishing between the collapse of the GWU and ongoing, if hardly autonomous, popular pressure on the leadership.

As a history of nationalist women and gender politics, this chapter establishes the record of nationalist women's militant and continuous activism in both union and party but also demonstrates that women's alliance with the male leadership was central to nationalist populism, that their political importance broadened nationalist gender and labor politics, and that they wove core female demands into the fabric of nationalist hegemony. The chapter thus shows that the women and men who formed the mass base of the movement were never just the blind followers or unwitting tools of the leadership, and, crucially, that nationalist women outlasted the GWU as a group capable of challenging as well as supporting the leadership. At the same time, the chapter shows that the leadership sought to contain popular and female politics that, left undisciplined, could threaten the campaign to gain state power via negotiations with Britain. Ironically, the leadership's increasing domination of the nationalist alliance was facilitated by the electoral success that popular activism yielded, by the limits that women themselves accepted in not contesting the principle of ultimate male power in family life, the labor market, and politics, and by organizing entirely within the movement. Deniz Kandyoti's argument about the lure and risk of nationalist commitment for subaltern women worldwide fits Belize almost perfectly: "On the one hand, nationalist movements invite women to participate more fully in collective life by interpellating them as 'national' actors: mothers, educators, workers and even fighters. On the other hand, they reaffirm the boundaries of culturally acceptable feminine conduct and exert pressure on women to articulate their gender interests within the terms of reference set by nationalist discourse."[9]

In Belize, however, women were not so much invited into the nationalist movement as they were partners in forming it; moreover, their own activism helped to set the terms of reference within which they could articulate their gender interests. Thus, although they did not develop a self-consciously feminist politics, they did define a proud nationalist womanhood and did not accept a merely instrumental role in the forging of the nation. PUP leaders certainly took tactical advantage of women's political passions, but nationalist women brought a well-honed female political strategy to bear on the party brass. They not only expected the "new paterfamilias, the [national] state" to be a good patriarch, attentive to their needs and a guarantor of their rights, but demanded it.[10] As Elfreda Reyes recalled: "We began thinking the PUP was going to make us more independent[,] . . . to get from under the claws of this British Empire. . . . All we wanted—justice. It was for the children more than any other thing." Mrs. Eustaquia Galvez of Cayo was pithier: "The revolution," she told me, "was for the poor mothers and their little ones."[11] In supplying elections, education, health care, and housing, jobs, wages, lights, and piped water, that state would strengthen women in struggling with the problems that, unlike colonial rule, still seemed ineradicable: male neglect and abuse, women's status as a secondary work force, unwanted pregnancies and the responsibilities of single motherhood. They struck this historic compromise in part because the young nationalist leaders were willing to bargain with them, in part because no other viable allies existed.

As in other nationalist, populist, or revolutionary projects from India to Africa to Latin America, Belizean women were influential, enthusiastic participants at the same time that they were "becoming hostages" to or partially captured by such projects.[12] Maxine Molyneux's view of socialist projects as being able to meet some female demands to the extent that they benefited citizens and workers but being unable to emancipate women applies equally well to nonrevolutionary nationalisms.[13] In the short term, Belizean women were unable to demand inclusion in the family wage ideal promoted by nationalist leaders, to politicize the domestic gender conflict that so often made them responsible for family survival, or to build organizational autonomy within or beyond the movement. In the long term, they could not contest the economic development strategy that cast women as cheap labor in an export-led economy, or the increasing clientelism of party politics, and were able to manipulate but not prevent the growing gender conservatism of the leadership after 1954.

The core nationalist leadership of 1950–56 emerged from the CSAG and was thus socially distinct from the Protestant establishment, which had a tradition of allying with reformist British officials. Price, who was personal secretary to chicle magnate Robert S. Turton, was conspicuously different owing to his maternal connections to the white and mestizo elite of Orange Walk, to his white appearance, and to his studies as a Jesuit novice. Nicholas Pollard founded the Mercantile Clerks' Union in 1948, replaced Betson as GWU president when the nationalists took control of the union in April 1950, and then became its general secretary, but he was excluded from a political career until the late 1950s because of his Honduran birth. Also crucial were cousins Leigh Richardson and Philip Goldson, Catholic converts who gave up their jobs as schoolteacher and civil servant to write and edit the *Belize Billboard* newspaper in 1947. They would meet workers at the gates of the BEC sawmill, where they hawked copies of the paper. Herman Jex may have been one of their readers; via membership in the CSAG and PC he moved from hourly sawmill employee to GWU president in 1953. Like Price, Richardson, and Goldson, he was elected as a PUP legislator in the first universal suffrage elections in 1954.[14] Smith left the PUP in late 1951, Richardson, Goldson, and Jex in the historic schism of 1956, taking with them the GWU, and Pollard finally split with Price in early 1958.

From 1950–54 these leaders depended heavily on the popular movement, welcomed women's militant activism, and politicized women's roles as workers and consumer-housewives. Women joined the union and party, took part in and supported strikes, campaigned and voted, and organized demonstrations, celebrations, and fundraising. Repeated confrontations with the authorities—the 1951 dissolution of the PUP-dominated city council, the incarceration of Goldson and Richardson on sedition charges from late 1951 to mid-1952, and the late 1952 general strike—fueled popular mobilization. The strike fueled a wage and hours campaign by organized GWU domestics in early 1953, led by Elfreda Reyes and her sister Virginia Stanford. Exceptional in fighting specifically for women workers, this struggle received weak support from nationalist leaders, who were already focused on the April 1954 legislative elections. The PUP victory, and the incorporation of Richardson, Goldson, and Jex into the colonial administration, led to a more domestic construction of nationalist womanhood. Price distanced himself from these trends, emerging as the most "militant and personal" leader of the mid-1950s and retaining the bulk of female and general mass support after the 1956 schism. But he too emphasized female domesticity after sweeping the legislative elections of 1957 and establishing his own party newspaper.[15]

The tensions inherent in negotiating the claims of nationalist solidarity and gender interest were institutionalized by the late 1950s in the PUP's United Women's Groups (UWGs), founded by Gwendolyn Lizarraga, who probably joined the party in 1957. Though the UWGs worked for the party at election time, they began as a movement for female home ownership that thus manipulated the increasingly domestic ideal of nationalist womanhood to continue the fight for women's economic security. May Davis, a UWG leader, captured the delicate balance between women's leverage and dependence thus: "The women did a great job for the party, and in turn the party do things that we couldn't do on our own."[16] Like thousands of other female nation makers, she did not see the necessity of making some impossible, final choice between working toward women's rights and working toward nationhood. She and other nationalist women were a resistant presence—indeed, well after the collapse of the labor movement—but one deeply compromised by populist alliance.

Only one group attempted to break women's alliance with the nationalist leadership: the British Honduras Federation of Women (BHFW), founded in 1952, contested the PUP and GWU leaders' right to speak for Belizean women and articulated a bold series of demands for women's rights. The BHFW, however, never looked like a viable ally to working women, as its leaders were prominent antinationalist women, including Vivian Seay, who framed their arguments for women's equality within a class-bound charitable politics that stood little chance of weakening nationalist paternalism. Lizarraga, in leaving the federation to join the PUP and ally with working women in the UWGS, attempted to weaken it from within.

But once in the nationalist camp, Lizarraga had to contend with women's particular attachment to George Price. Many nationalist women personified their struggle in Price because he avoided premature accommodation with the British and because his celibate, ascetic, devout reputation created the image of a priestly man devoted to the female collective.[17] Price embodied the ideal state, a faithful substitute provider attentive to women's problems, but not one who would stifle their public political roles. Many women who spoke with me switched freely between arguing for their own creative role in the PUP's victory and attributing all change to Price. Their homes often boast photos of Price and his cabinet, which are sometimes hanging next to a picture of the Last Supper. Diane Haylock, as a young opposition campaigner in the 1970s, remembers being rebuffed by Miss Venancia Petillo, who had been the leading PUP woman of Punta Gorda since the 1950s, with the words: "George Price is like Jesus Christ come back to life for me." He was their Messiah, their Moses, their lucky charm, and they were his "support," willing "to do anything he would ask them to do," claimed Tharine Rudon, a middle-class woman who was the PUP office manager and held various elected posts within the party and GWU. When Price was acquitted of sedition in March 1958—a charge resulting from a November 1957 meeting with the Guatemalan ambassador in London—the PUP women of Belize City "picked up George on their shoulder and back him down until they back him over bridgefoot," recalled Elfreda Reyes. When he fell from power in the 1988 elections, they prayed novenas for his return. Even women like Arcelina Leiva and Teresa Orio of Orange Walk, both born in the late 1940s and both critical of corruption and paternalism in the PUP, retained in the 1990s a vision of Price as an honest man surrounded by corrupt machista advisors.[18]

Price and the PUP as a whole were like many other mid-century British Caribbean nationalist movements in gaining strong female alliance. As

Verene Shepherd has summarized, women were active in nationalist movements across the British Caribbean and have often enjoyed a reputation
as highly effective organizers and campaigners. Eric Williams, leader of
Trinidad and Tobago's People's National Movement (PNM) from 1955 until
his death in 1981, benefited greatly from women's prior political and social
activism and, as Reddock has argued, recognized that no popular movement in Trinidadian history had achieved success "without a large following of active and committed women." She shows that although the PNM's
Women's League was mainly supportive and did not challenge the sexual
division of labor within the movement, its "strength, loyalty, and single-
ness of purpose" yielded it at least limited autonomy. That loyalty, rooted
in the nationalist leadership's recognition of their needs, paralleled the
Belizean case, but in Belize the PUP's promises of change were clearly vital
to women. Female nationalism was also evident in many African cases,
such as that of Tanzania. There leaders sought to interpellate women even
as they invited them into the nationalist movement. These women were
comparable to typical West Indian nationalist women, except for being
Muslim, in their significant social and economic independence from men
and their strong presence in the informal economy. They too sought to
embed key female issues in the core nationalist agenda.[19]

Women, then, were active partners in many mid-century populist alliances, both projects for national independence and projects for national
renewal as in some Latin American countries. Women's trajectories into
these alliances varied: some had trade union—even leftist—identities;
others had been active in race-based movements; others still had no previous record of political activism. In Peronist Argentina, women connected
to the state principally through Evita and her institutions, while in other
cases male-dominated unions and parties mediated between the state
and women.[20] In Belize, as elsewhere in the Caribbean, women connected
more directly with populist nationalist leaders as members of union and
party. When those leaders corralled the strength of organized labor, then,
as in other populist projects, women suffered a narrowing of the popular
movement. But their autonomy from the union allowed them to launch
a new initiative through the UWGS, forcing the leaders to engage in a new

round of hegemonic work. While the overlapping groups of organized labor and organized women lost the kind of autonomy from the state that the LUA had enjoyed in the 1930s, they were nonetheless partners in creating new nation-states whose legitimacy rested in part on honoring these groups' popular, gender-inclusive origins.

Nationalist Women's Memories and Identities

Like the Tanzanian women nationalists Susan Geiger interviewed, Belize's nationalist women remember their actions of the 1950s, especially in the most dramatic moments, and understand themselves proudly as nation-builders. I had the following conversation with Elfreda Reyes the year before she died: Anne: "You campaigned for the PUP in 1954?" Elfreda: "1954? Then politics was just at its height." Anne: "Things were warm?" Elfreda: "Warm, you call that warm! And I enjoyed it you know, I really enjoyed it. Sometimes I lay down here, go right over it." May Davis, a Belize City activist a generation younger than Elfreda, remembered: "I think that's why this PUP progress—we [the women] were very aggressive. Mr. Price must thank the women of Belize. They are the stronghold of Belize."[21] Indeed, it is no secret among older Belizeans that nationalist women's activism was critical to the movement's strength and success. Again and again, women *and* men acknowledged as much to me, often without the question being posed.

Such memories usually constructed a contrast between women's militance and men's less passionate politics. May Davis claimed that "Men no do much in this place darling, they stay to the back. Oh men, the men were coward, but the women were brave." Elfreda responded to my questions about women's role in the movement with great energy: "Those men were so coward! When a thing is won the men want to take the best position. The women were more steadfast." Tharine Rudon was emphatic: "There were more women, there were more women every time. . . . Anytime if the men they are having any trouble . . . they come to women, [and] the women go right out. . . . The women always work more than the men, always." Philip Goldson likewise contrasted men's "reluctance to stick out their necks because of their jobs" with women's militance: "Women were very important from the beginning. They were to the forefront of the struggle, and the women were the most militant. . . . Women always seemed to understand these issues better than men. . . . When it came to the street action, there were the women, up in front you know." Tony Soberanis, Jr., an active party member in the 1950s, concurred: "The women were always more interested than the men, even in voting."[22]

In Stann Creek and Cayo, the story was the same. Alan Arthurs, who had been active in Dangriga since the late 1940s and was PUP mayor in the 1950s, recalled: "You had the men too but the women were always the leading force." Without them, change would have been impossible. Eduardo Espat, who ran against W. H. Courtenay for Cayo's legislative seat in 1948 and then had a checkered career with various parties, was a leading PUP organizer in the 1950s. In describing the early days, he recalled: "Women were the backbone of all this, not the men, because they were the ones to confront all the time. They do the work." Domingo Espat, a merchant and member of the Cayo Town Board from 1958 to 1969, concurred: "The women were more fighters than the men, more fanatical." These regional male leaders' female allies of the 1950s articulated the same memories in their conversations with me. Mrs. Lavinia Busano of Dangriga, a retired nurse and former PUP deputy mayor, explained the decline of the PUP Men's Marshals thus: "Dehn [Those] men can't handle it so it break through." Aurelia (Lela) Humes of San Ignacio summed the pattern up succinctly: "We womens used to push up the mens them."[23]

Written sources support these activists' memories. The *Belize Billboard* of the 1950s not only records the countless actions of women in the GWU and PUP but also reveals the same awareness of women's activism that my interviews found. For example, Domingo Ventura, a GWU leader from Stann Creek, urged a Belize City crowd in 1952: "It is up to the women to push their men into the GWU." In 1950 Cayo GWU committee member Mrs. Vicenta Gonzalez "appealed to the women to urge their husbands to become union members." And when Nicholas Pollard's wife Elizabeth spoke to organized GWU domestics in 1953, her claim that "in order to get anything done in Belize most of the time plans had to be pushed by women" must have rung true with the assembled female unionists.[24]

Memories that cast men as useless cowards are objectively untrue, but they do speak to nationalist women's perception that they were both the backbone and spearhead of the movement. At least in Belize City, women were even willing to risk domestic violence in order to remain politically active. May Davis and her friends paid little heed to the fact that "the husband fist we up" for attending rallies rather than preparing meals: "I never care 'bout that; I care 'bout me party." Some men supported their wives' activism and more tolerated it, but Rudon's reasoning that single women could be more active, "not having a husband to domineer them," is generally sound.[25] In Orange Walk and other areas of stronger domestic patriarchy, men more strictly controlled their wives' and daughters' political activities, and independent female involvement was exceptional.[26]

The prominence of outspoken, confrontational women, particularly in Belize City and Dangriga, linked the images of the bembe (in Creole) and suber (in Garifuna) to nationalist womanhood. Gladys Stuart defined the bembes as women who "were not afraid to fight or curse. . . . [T]hey would fight, they were abusive." In Belize City the term bembe had long been associated with women's jostling in the endless lines at municipal water standpipes. Rudon laughed when I asked her about the word and said "Yes, yes, bembes, because they don't give a hoot for anything." She identified Elfreda Reyes as one: she was "very saucy. . . . [S]he would stand up to any man." When Rudon stood as the first female PUP city council candidate, in March 1956, the party's bembes threatened her opponents, who had cast aspersions on Rudon's moral character. "I remember it so well. . . . I think it was on Canal Street they had a meeting . . . and they were talking all these kind of things, and the bloody women they move out, and they went around there, and they started to stone, [throw bottles] and Francis and Wilson couldn't come out, because they were going to beat the hell out of them if they had come out."[27] Nationalists' admiration for the bembes, however, did not completely erase the connotation of indecency inherent in the term. One woman, for example, described PUP women to me as "the dregs of society." Because the term is so laden with middle-class judgments about poor women's sexual morality and general worth, nationalist women's identification with it speaks to their collective consciousness. To be a bembe, fighting for one's country and children, *was* to be respectable and self-respecting.

In the Stann Creek District, the mainly Garifuna women who worked as sectionizers at the Pomona grapefruit cannery from 1949 were often known as "subers," a word with connotations similar to those of bembe. Most of these women were staunch nationalists, and many were also active in the annual Garifuna Settlement Day celebrations of 19 November, which began about this time. Mrs. Juanita Joseph captured the tension inherent in the term, describing the subers as responsible working women who nonetheless were not seen as decent. They were noisy and merry, singing Garifuna songs in the company trucks that carried them from Dangriga to Pomona, treating each other "like sisters" but also competing to get at the incoming hot peeled fruit. Many of them built houses and saw their children through high school on their Pomona paychecks, which also gave them a feeling of independence that probably fuelled the "sexually hot" connotation of the word suber.[28]

The combative femininity of the bembe and the suber was a critical element of nationalist culture, but it was not the only acceptable way of being a nationalist woman. Many PUP and GWU women did not relish campaigning or picketing. Miss Caroline Flowers of Belize City, for example, contributed by donating money from her weekly earnings, and Mrs. Canuta Flores of Dangriga preferred to organize party fundraisers rather than canvass door to door. But regardless of their level of militance, the majority of nationalist women developed their political identities out of their reality as income earners with family responsibilities, often as single mothers and/or family breadwinners. Goldson's memories confirm this: "Now when you say women were not employed you have to put it in quotes, because traditionally Belizean women might be employed in the informal trade, selling Creole bread, making cut 'o brute and tableta. They bake bread for sale, they wash clothes. They might not be employed by a regular employer . . . but they nevertheless ma[k]e their living." Mrs. Petrona Briceno in Cayo described her activism as being rooted in this reality: "From 1950 we start our journey. We was fighting for our independence. . . . We was all slaves, we had it hard: twelve hours for seventy-five cents. We had it hard with our kids: no education. . . . The mother is the one. She have to think and think." For all, conventional respectability, although hardly irrelevant, was less important than ending British rule and the hardships it represented.[29]

Goldson told me that women were identified with "this cause for the betterment of poor people as a whole" and indeed, two women who wrote to the *Billboard* in the early 1950s expressed themselves in such ungendered terms. Mrs. Emma Martinez wanted the country to "be free and self-governing," while Mrs. Rosita Phillips of West St. in Belize City wrote that Belizeans wanted to be "ourselves. We want self-government."[30] Yet the memories elicited during my interviews strongly suggest that nationalist women maintained within the movement a proud awareness of their activist womanhood, a particularly female agenda, and a critique of men's limitations, although they did not contest ultimate masculine authority in the struggle against colonial rule.

Nationalist Women in Action, 1950–56

The nationalist movement erupted in Belize City, as had all major uprisings since the 1890s. There may have been an early antidevaluation march in Dangriga, which was certainly the second focus of popular mobilization, as in the 1930s.[31] A GWU branch existed there from the late 1940s, although its relations with the national executive were contentious.[32] The Belize and Stann Creek districts had the colony's highest rates of female gainful employment and of single adult women and not surprisingly gave rise to the strongest organizations of nationalist women.[33] But in Cayo, too, women served on the local GWU's founding executive in 1948, and an organized group of women campaigned for the PUP in 1954.[34] A nationalist and specifically female organization developed later in Orange Walk. The GWU did not organize until after devaluation but was soon able to reach BEC's mahogany workers at Gallon Jug and Hill Bank. George Flowers, local GWU leader, remembered only two women in the Orange Walk Union—domestic Violet Gill and seamstress Domitila Alvarez.[35] Local organization for the 1954 election was weak, and it was not until 1957 that a coherent group of PUP women was involved in election campaigning.

In the first six weeks of 1950 the working women of Belize City participated enthusiastically in frequent rallies and marches—some jointly sponsored by the GWU and PC—that protested devaluation, the resulting 30–40 percent rise in the cost of living, and "colonial exploitation" as a whole. On 12 February ten thousand people marched on Government House. May Davis, who identified proudly as a bembe, was in the thick of the action: "At that time I was a brave woman . . . right out there with all those riot!" She recounted with glee how people exclaimed when they saw the PC women approaching during street actions: "The bembe di come [The bembes are coming]," they would call, and she would respond, "Mek dehn arrest all a wi [Let them arrest all of us!]!" Gladys Stuart recalled women wrecking lawyer, businessman, and Legislative Council member W. H. Courtenay's car during the peak of street violence in mid-February, when the police teargassed crowds and secured Smith and Price's cooperation in calming and dispersing thousands of protestors.[36] On 14 February the colonial government imposed a state of emergency, banning all public meetings in Belize City until 1 July 1950.

Even before the state of emergency shut down possibilities for street action, women were turning to the GWU as a forum for their anticolonial politics: "In all parts of the country working men and women and in some cases housewives, are proudly pinning on the GWU red and green button of honour," reported the *Billboard*. Women joined as workers and housewives, as far away as Orange Walk. In February men and women formed a new GWU branch at Garbutt Creek in rural Cayo and raised the issue of low female wages with visiting union leaders, who then established a committee to demand jobs for women "at proper wages," in the words of GWU vice president James Middleton. By early March the GWU had established both housewives and domestics sections to accommodate a flood of new female members. In Cayo, the union's most active female member was Emilia Galvez, "a very intelligent and clever woman" who had campaigned for Eduardo Espat in 1948 legislative elections. In March 1950 the "spicy-voiced lady unionist" called for unity at a Cayo union meeting. At the GWU's annual meeting in April 1950, Mrs. Harriet Durante was elected as shop steward for domestics, Virginia Adolphus was elected to the GWU Council, and Ena Gabb became assistant secretary on the executive, now headed by Nicholas Pollard.[37] It is not clear what role women played, if any, in ending the leadership of Clifford Betson at that point. By the end of 1950, according to colonial officials, the GWU had 2,629 members, 212 of them women (8 percent). By April 1952 membership had risen to 6,171, with 3921 (63.5 percent) in Belize City, where 337 women (9.4 percent) were members, and in September that year the Stann Creek branch boasted 237 women (18.2 percent).[38] Women thus never approached the 50 percent mark as they had in the LUA, although unofficial female support was strong.

GWU meetings outside Belize City kept nationalist momentum going during the state of emergency, but more important was the PC dissolving itself to become the PUP in September 1950. Leigh Richardson, who was on a one-year Colonial Office journalism course in London until late July 1950, sent editorials home to the *Billboard*, frequently urging the formation of a nationalist political party. In July, for example, he wrote that "the day of the Battlefield is past" and pressed the same message to a crowd of ten thousand in August—ironically, at the Battlefield![39] But the founding of the PUP only clarified the tension between mass action and the leadership, which consisted of Richardson (chairman), Smith (leader), Price (secretary), and Goldson (assistant secretary). Membership ballooned. Rudon, who ran the PUP office, recalled that "The party was so big . . . you couldn't get to know everyone," and Goldson reported in the *Billboard* at the time that the PUP was having trouble keeping up with the demand for membership cards.[40] By 1954, according to Price, the party had about three thousand members, mostly in Belize City; it is unclear what proportion were women, but it was probably greater than the proportion of women in the GWU.[41]

The party won five of nine city council seats in November 1950, a victory largely due to women campaigners. Philip Goldson vividly remembered the prominence of women as neighborhood canvassers: "mainly women who were at the grassroots level, uneducated but very loyal. They were good campaigners. It was women who carried the message from house to house." Indeed, by all accounts, party fund-raising, canvassing, and campaigning were female domains. The Clarion, appalled by what it saw as mob politics, denounced the PUP's particular targeting of female voters.[42]

The advent of party politics did not blunt nationalist women's labor activism. In October 1950 "female adherents" of the GWU picketed through a rainy night in support of striking Belize City stevedores, "with the approval of the public." Some of these women may have been among the 150 "women domestic servants" who in late November 1950 responded to a call by the GWU to attend a union meeting. Two women spoke at this meeting—in addition to GWU secretary Henry Middleton and Leigh Richardson—though only the second cast women as independent workers and union members. The first, a "housewife-teacher," condemned birth control as a method of dealing with poverty and claimed that "it is the duty of every housewife, domestic servant, and other working woman to join the GWU, to back up our men, to protect ourselves against overwork and unjust wages." The second, Mrs. Enid Panting, outlined the advantages of union membership, citing sickness and death benefits and increased leverage with employers. "Ladies," she concluded, "let us get together and form a strong chain with good links. Let us leave our footprints on the sands of time."[43] The trajectory of female labor activism through 1950 very likely fueled the increase in individual complaints by domestic servants to the Labour Department in 1951, although its staff made no headway in improving working conditions in private homes where labor law did not apply.[44]

The PUP held internal elections in April 1951, during which Elsa Vasquez—who older Belizeans repeatedly identified as a bembe and die-hard Price loyalist—was voted onto the party council.[45] But women also maintained their historic presence on the streets. That same month demonstrations erupted in reaction to the Courtenay constitutional report, which sought to thwart mass nationalism in a variety of ways. In July, when the governor dissolved the PUP-dominated city council, Elfreda Reyes apparently led a huge crowd to the gates of Government House to protest. "We heard that she was right up at the gate shaking her fingers at Government House you know," recalled Gladys Stuart, "Had they broken the gate you would have had maybe a riot." In early August women helped mobilize a twelve hundred name petition in half a day to protest the dissolution.[46] PUP women were no doubt prominent in the five thousand-strong crowds that turned out to a party meeting in mid-August and to the party's 10th celebrations in September. Only three hundred people attended the traditional middle-class-led parade, and the governor stayed at home.[47] The National Party, formed in 1951 by veteran middle-class reformers including Vivian Seay, was proving ineffective at holding back the nationalist tide.

The colonial administration became even more repressive in the fall of 1951 when it charged Leigh Richardson and Philip Goldson with sedition for publishing favorable articles about Guatemala, then experiencing progressive democratic rule. Nationalist women raised money for the Billboard Defense Fund—Elsa Vasquez presented the funds to Richardson's wife and Goldson's mother—which paid their legal costs, and turned out in force at the jail entrance to welcome Richardson and Goldson upon their release in July 1952. The spontaneous rally for Goldson was dominated by women–this is clear from the fact that GWU vice president Herman Jex cut the speeches short in recognition "that many of the women had yet to prepare their mid-day meals for their families (although some had done that from as early as four o'clock this morning)." During their incarceration, Tharine Rudon had been GWU councilor for clerks and office workers and women had again campaigned during the March 1952 city council elections. The PUP ran an all-male slate and won only three seats, largely because Goldson's and Richardson's nominations were rejected, but Floss Casasola won on the NP ticket. For the GWU's May Day fiesta, Elfreda Reyes led nationalist women in celebrating at the Barracks in Belize City, staging a maypole dance, organizing a singing group, and setting up food stalls: "It wasn't a demonstration, it was a beautiful march and we were singing. . . . We took up there foods to sell," she recalled.[48] In September 1952, when the PUP began to call the 10th "National Day," Reyes spoke to the three thousand-strong nationalist crowd, exhorting mothers to teach their children patriotism. Women led the PUP's march and seem to have outnumbered men. The women's singing group again performed for the PUP's second anniversary celebration at the end of the month.[49]

Scholarly accounts of this period have focused much attention on the general strike of October to December 1952 but have said little to nothing about women's role in it or in a smaller strike that preceded it by a few weeks. In early October the GWU struck the Pomona citrus plant to protest manager Frank Sharpe's posting of antiunion signs, and the sectionizers joined in. At this time there were 1121 men and 297 women (20.94 percent) in the Stann Creek GWU branch, and most of the women were probably sectionizers. Andrea "Nucu" Nunez, a longtime sectionizer, participated in the walkout, although she was never a union member.[50] The general strike, intended by the leadership to be a two-day affair, began on 20 October, gathering popular momentum and lasting for weeks. It halted work at the BEC sawmill, the Public Works Department, the construction site of the Fort George Hotel, and on the waterfront and extended to Public Works Department road gangs in rural Belize district and in Cayo. In addition, four waitresses were fired when the GWU protested their wages and working conditions by boycotting the Belize City saloon where they worked.[51]

Most women, however, participated as supporters, not strikers. Idolly Erskine, then a market vendor, donated food to strikers' families, as did many district farmers, including Garifuna women. Tharine Rudon and Elfreda Reyes distributed groceries weekly to strikers' wives while Adeline Patnett, Estelle Bevans, Lucille Hall, and others aided in fund-raising and running a free lunch kitchen for striking men. Most dramatically, hundreds of women marched and picketed through the long weeks of the strike in Dangriga as well as at the main strike sites in Belize City.[52] By late November all affected employers except BEC had begun negotiations; at that point, therefore, thet GWU focused its attention on the BEC sawmill. As in 1934, anticolonial women came out in force: "They wanted to stone the BEC," recalled Reyes. Clashes between picketers and a few scabs resulted in arrests. Nine women, all reportedly leading bembes, were charged with following the scabs, while twelve more were charged with "watching." Overall, one third of those charged with strike-related offenses were women, though many more may have had charges thrown out by sympathetic magistrates. The BEC wore the strikers down by early December, but by that time the GWU membership had risen to eighty two hundred and had two separate sections for women—one for garment workers, the other for domestics.[53]

Women's militance during the general strike, and perhaps also a general rise in domestics' wages during it, galvanized organized domestics to launch a struggle for their own rights as workers, although Reyes recalled that the process of organization began with the May 1952 festivities.[54] Days after the end of the general strike, one hundred GWU domestic servants gathered. Elfreda Reyes led the meeting. "We must see that better wages are given to our women," she argued, "there is nothing to fear." Her sister Virginia Stanford assured the assembled women that the female union leaders would do all they could to improve wages and working conditions.[55] The meeting bore fruit, for in January and February 1953 the GWU Domestic Workers' Department DWD grew to a membership of 450, all of whom backed demands for written contracts, a minimum of $5 per week, and a maximum of forty-eight hours per week.[56] This was clearly a high point of nationalist women's labor activism.

Acting GWU general secretary Philip Goldson pledged the union's full membership to back the DWD campaign, but he was unable to deliver institutional support. This, combined with domestics' well-grounded fear of being fired, made the campaign difficult. Reyes claims that Goldson did accompany individual domestics in meetings with their employers but attributed her own pay hike to $5 per week to her aggressive confrontation with the dentist's wife who was then her employer.[57] In early March, at another DWD meeting, Virginia Stanford urged the domestics to continue "organizing themselves into an aggressive force." When the DWD held elections in early April, Tharine Rudon, by then a GWU trustee, tried to keep the women's spirits up: "Who shall be able to stop us if we, like a marching army, keep on as we have started? An orderly, united, determined body, asking, no demanding the right to be independent and self-supporting."[58] Her emphasis on female economic self-sufficiency in 1953 was echoed in her conversation with me, when she insisted that single women could be more militant than most married women.

The importance of GWU women, in particular the organized domestics, was reflected in the election of Reyes to the GWU's General and Executive Councils later that month.[59] The DWD seems to have been the most independent kind of nationalist women's politics, but it had less momentum than the LUA Women's League in the 1930s, and faded with the approach of full-suffrage legislative elections. Many GWU women, particularly domestics and sectionizers, were certainly family breadwinners if not also single mothers. But they organized as workers, consumers, and voters, never as single mothers/family breadwinners, and were thus unable to denounce $5 per week as a travesty of the family wage idea constantly trumpeted by nationalist leaders.

The British announced historic constitutional changes in January 1953 and by mid-year had set April 1954 as the date for the first adult suffrage elections to a majority elected Legislative Council. As nationalist energies focused on the elections, women's activism as workers within the GWU diminished. Still, in Belize City wage-drive meetings continued until September 1953, and in October Rudon was elected PUP treasurer and four women were elected to the ten-person party council: Hazel Gentle, Enid Panting, Elfreda Reyes, and Elsa Vasquez.[60] These leading bembes and countless others actively campaigned in the early 1954 from within both the GWU and PUP. The *Billboard* recorded that Reyes, for example, spoke at a rally in the Pickstock district of Belize City, and a Dorothy Bradley campaigned in rural Belize District. Women's, and specifically the bembes', importance was further recognized when Price, Goldson, and Richardson each chose at least one woman to sign his nomination papers in 1954.[61] The PUP swept the April 1954 elections, with women turning out strongly. One of the thousands of Belizean women who voted for the first time in April 1954 told the *Clarion*: "I come prepared to vote; I put my rice on from six o'clock this morning."[62] Domestic duties, whether performed with resentment or pride, would not hamper this woman from exercising her new political rights.

With the exception of Stann Creek, town boards were entirely appointed until 1955, so for most nationalist women in the districts, the April 1954 legislative elections and the 1955 municipal elections were their first experiences of voting if not campaigning.[63] As in Belize City, "grassroots" women were vital campaigners in most towns. Alan Arthurs of Dangriga agreed with Goldson's view of women canvassers, describing the mostly Garifuna women, led by Evelyn Avila, as "a force to be reckoned with."

Avila "had an art to organizing women" and was crucial to Arthurs's election as mayor in the 1950s and as district representative in the 1960s. Avila's squadron—including Henrietta Mejia and Stella Avilez and perhaps also Miss Ida Partiss, who was on the local GWU executive in 1952, and Frances Castillo, a 1954 member of the GWU district council—certainly campaigned for GWU-PUP candidate Nathaniel Cacho in the 1954 legislative elections.[64] In Cayo Enrique De Paz benefited from the labors of women led by Maria Samos, who went on to serve on the Cayo Town Board in the 1960s. The Cayo group included Petrona Briceno, Mariana Lisbey, Maria Martinez, and Lela Humes, who spoke proudly of her party activism from the early 1950s: "We [women] was the people who walked the villages from the beginning."[65] They would especially reach out to Mayan women in the river villages, telling them that a national government would see their children through high school: "To be just like the ones with money." In Orange Walk, the earliest and best known PUP woman activist was Adolfa Garcia, by then a teacher in her home village of Yo Creek. Not only did she promote nationalist values in her school, but she was secretary of the village council and confronted the governor himself over a broken promise to provide Yo Creek with water: "I was never a coward woman. So how was I going to be coward of a white man?"[66] The PUP candidate in Orange Walk in 1954 was GWU leader George Flowers, who won more because of union than party organization.

From April 1954 to September 1956, divisions within the nationalist leadership grew.[67] On the one hand, Richardson, Goldson, and Jex became members with portfolios within the colonial government, tilted in favor of West Indian Federation, and began to use the *Billboard* to argue that the state should be the primary agent of social change and that women should be good Christian mothers. On the other hand, Price accepted only an associate member position, sustained his opposition to federation, and, as Grant has argued, maintained a vital connection to the mass nationalist movement. There was little popular action in this period, though GWU workers did strike Sharpe's Citrus Company at Pomona in the Stann Creek District in November 1954 and February 1956. In 1954 120 female sectionizers struck to protest the firing of one female worker, who had argued they should all get an afternoon off to prepare for Settlement Day festivities. In 1956 sectionizers were among six hundred strikers and were touted as "loyal GWU women" impervious to scabs.[68] The possibility of female street action had not disappeared, as Rudon's female defenders showed in March 1956 when they threatened her opponents with violence.

In July 1956 Pollard was suspended as GWU secretary for misuse of union funds. In August Richardson's house burned down, with arson suspected, and Mr. Robert Stansmore, PUP auditor, and Miss Thelma Stansmore, PUP councilor, resigned. In September, at the PUP's annual meeting, debate led to violence, and finally the resignations of Reyes, Rudon, Richardson, Goldson, Jex, and eight other male leaders. Elfreda remembered that when the first fighting broke out, Price "brought a group of women outside in the street to create a sensation. . . . There was Elsa Vasquez [and] . . . Hazel Gentle. Those were his support to do anything he would ask them to do." Grant confirms that those who left claimed Price had packed the hall with his own supporters, and the *Clarion* reported that Richardson had a police escort. Indeed, the vast majority of Belize City's nationalist women sided with Price, who became "undisputed leader of the party" for the next thirty years.[69] While Price went on to build a markedly undemocratic party machine, in 1956 most women contrasted his continued responsiveness to their experiences and demands with the other leaders' growing emphasis on state policy and action.

The Leadership's Gender Politics to 1956

Judging by the gender politics of the *Belize Billboard* in the late 1940s, the young men of the CSAG were unlikely candidates for the leadership of a gender-inclusive labor-nationalist movement, for the paper endorsed the principle of female domestication at the heart of the colonial modernization project. Its women's column, "Powderpuff and Paint," consistently advocated moral regulation, motherhood, and housewifery for women, in defense of "the sacred home," and men's command of the labor market. Single mothers, career women, flirts, and lazy housewives were condemned as violators of the nuclear family ideal as were users of birth control.[70] Like Pedro Albízu Campos, Puerto Rico's nationalist firebrand, the young Catholic critics emphasized social justice over contraception as the solution to poverty.[71] Yet social justice did not encompass progressive labor politics. When Clifford Betson issued his call for socialism in Belize, Goldson and Richardson (the *Billboard*'s main writers) mounted an overblown anticommunist response centered on the defense of a conservative gender order. While the proreform *Clarion* supported Betson's demand that labor have political representation, the *Billboard*'s red scare tactics linked socialism to prostitution, venereal disease, adultery, juvenile delinquency, and incest. It was only safe and proper for women to leave the domestic arena in the name of "making our national lot a bit better" as social welfare and credit union volunteers.[72]

In August and September 1949, when rumors of devaluation were beginning, the *Billboard* carried two articles that hinted at a new attitude toward women. First, it published a letter defending Garifuna women starch vendors, who were forced to travel from home and sell on the streets. The writer made no mention of any domestic norms that these women might have been violating but instead criticized the colonial government for failing to develop a reliable market for their starch. Then, in a brilliantly satirical article, the paper described a creative housewife's recipe for making rice and beans with neither ingredients nor money.[73] Women's unpaid labor was suddenly stripped of its romantic gloss and connected to harsh economic conditions. Marital bliss and maternal love were no longer enough to stave off hunger; only the end of colonial rule would do.

With the eruption of popular nationalism at the beginning of 1950, and especially because of working women's rapid, massive, and militant alliance with the GWU, PC, and then PUP leaderships, the young leaders transformed their gender politics. At a time when devaluation directly cut working-class spending power, and when mass mobilization was needed against the British and local middle class, nationalist women were recognized as consumers, workers, and voters and embraced as union and party members, fund-raisers, campaigners, even street fighters. Particularly in the period before the PUP's victory in the April 1954 legislative elections, nationalist leaders all but suspended moral critique of popular culture and particularly female behavior. Instead, they embedded women's core demands in the nationalist agenda. As a *Billboard* article said of the PUP, GWU, and Billboard in 1951: "These three institutions are out to get . . . more than the three teaspoons the Belize hospital had a few months ago and to end the parade of women . . . [who] dump body waste in the Belize canals at night."[74] This shift was historic, for it created the conditions for, indeed symbolized, the interpellation of world views at the heart of populist alliance, accommodated popular definitions of respectability, and permanently made nationalist hegemony dependent on some recognition of women's rights in nationalist culture and policy.

Yet even at their most inclusive, the leadership's gender politics always sustained a tension between mobilizing and responding to women on the one hand, and containing, condescending to, and domesticating them on the other, a tension symbolic of its ambivalence about popular and particularly female mobilization. Leaders did not stigmatize single mothers or female heads of households, but they also did not attack colonial stigmas of these overlapping groups or even acknowledge that many women were breadwinners, not simply workers. Even before April 1954, the nationalist embrace of activist women sat uneasily next to a discourse of the "living family wage" demanded for working men. In tracing the tensions between the leaders' openness to women's nationalist activism and their efforts to quell female militance and to privilege male workers, I will deal first with the early months when Clifford Betson was still president of the GWU, then the period April 1950 to April 1952—when a middle-class member of the Federation of Women castigated the union's treatment of women—then the periods of the general strike and domestics' wage drive and the legislative campaign, and finally the conservative turn after the 1954 legislative victory.

In January 1950, as we have seen, Price and Smith cooperated with the police to quell popular attacks on property, actions in which women were reportedly prominent. The problem with these actions was their spontaneous "wildcat" nature, for in February the *Billboard* applauded women for joining the GWU and called on "every man and woman in British Honduras" to unite. It also publicized the new Garbutt Creek branch's concern about women's low wages in rural Cayo, and the GWU's for-mation of a high-level committee to investigate the issue. The People's Committee's first memorial to the king, sent in February 1950, raised issues of keen interest to women: housing conditions and malnutrition as well as unemployment and low wages. Yet union rhetoric also invoked "the brotherhood of man" and the need for all members to "obey and trust" the leadership.[75]

The same tension between inclusion and containment of women emerged in an article by Betson published in early March. Addressing "the female domestic servants and female mercantile clerks" of the colony—some-thing he had not specifically done since 1944—he approached them as exploited low wage workers who should fight back by joining the GWU rather than as mothers. By contrasting female clerks' wages with those of their male counterparts, he made one of the most daring arguments of the 1950s: "Why should not the principle of equal pay for equal work be adhered to?" Yet he also maintained a reformist moralism, arguing that the women would be irreligious not to fight for better working condi-tions, and that their low wages put them "in danger of losing [their] moral code." Crucially, he assured them that "You need not resort to violence. We have passed that stage." A week later, the *Billboard* launched the "living family wage" discourse by analyzing the weekly budget of a male govern-ment manual worker earning $10 per week, then just half of the Labour Department's official cost of living. The following month, the *Billboard*'s Corozal correspondent lambasted "a certain local official and a business-man" for paying their maids $1.50 per week for seven nine-hour days.[76] During these early months, nationalist leaders were willing to recognize women's participation in the labor force, and readily blamed colonial rule for their low wages, yet they were unsettled or perhaps divided on whether to treat them as a secondary labor force or as meriting a family wage.

After Betson's ouster, the *Billboard* again cast the GWU as belonging to "working men and women" in May, reported on Price defining social jus-tice as being for men, women, and children to a Battlefield crowd in July, and expressed concern about domestics' low wages in August. That same month the People's Committee prayer included the phrase: "Grant . . . to young girls the gift of purity," though the new PUP welcomed women's campaigning in city council elections in October, raising no questions about their respectability.[77] The GWU recruitment meeting for female domestics held soon after the PUP's electoral victory attracted one hundred women. GWU secretary Henry Middleton began the evening by laying out the facts about the appalling wages and working conditions of domestic servants, which were undoubtedly crystal clear to the women. Then PUP party chair Leigh Richardson, newly elected to the Belize City Council, rose to speak. He exhorted the women to join the union in terms that were strangely paternalistic for a man in his twenties: "If any one of you take back, I will count you not only a traitor to yourself and your country, but what is worst, a traitor to your children."[78] This idea of women's union membership and wage demands as a moral duty rather than as vehicles for an expansion of their rights speaks to the leadership's ongoing difficulty in treating nationalist women as equal political partners or as deserving of a living family wage.

The ambivalence of the leadership's gender politics persisted in 1951. Their serious, respectful, and inclusive approach to women was revealed in recognition of women's lower wages and of women's presence in the lumber industry behind the "Green Curtain" that kept GWU organizers off BEC property in the Orange Walk District. It was also revealed in its reporting on a domestic servant who was fired for belonging to the GWU. In February the GWU included domestics in its demand for a minimum wage and maximum hours law and asked domestics to report to the GWU office about their pay and conditions. In July and August, when PUP women were so active in protesting the dissolution of city council, the GWU followed up, first by calling on "working men and women" to join the GWU and by trying to establish a job placement agency for female domestics, clerks, and seamstresses, then by including domestics in its 40 percent wage hike campaign. Throughout 1951, when postdevaluation food subsidies ended, the *Billboard* returned to its politicization of the housewife's problems. Repeatedly, she was portrayed as burdened and stressed by the impossible task of both finding and affording basic necessities, and both the colonial government and greedy merchants were blamed.[79]

Yet the leadership also continued to treat women as a secondary labor force. The living family wage discourse was carried on throughout the year, repeatedly defining the worker as a male head of household maintaining a wife and two children. This ideal family's living wage was calculated at $22 per week in July and at $24 per week in October. This ideology became concrete in the GWU's negotiated contract for Stann Creek citrus cannery workers in late 1951, which established a lower hourly wage for women.[80] Worst, the woman's column "Powderpuff and Paint" was reintroduced in 1951, casting women's lives as a comic struggle to catch a man while maintaining one's reputation.

No women were included on the PUP's slate for the March 1952 city council elections, though the opposition National Party candidate, Floss Casasola, did win, becoming the first elected female municipal politician. Women had maintained their slight presence on the PUP and GWU governing bodies, but this was not enough to satisfy Gwendolyn Dunn, the invited speaker at the GWU's annual national conference in April 1952. Dunn was an odd choice considering her clear alignment with antinationalist forces as a government craft teacher and volunteer with the BHFW and the BCNS.[81] True to the outspoken tradition of middle-class reformism that Vivian Seay had pioneered, Dunn delivered a stinging critique of what she saw as the union's failure to organize women and to promote them to leadership positions. "If it is correct that the hands that rock the cradle rule the world, then why is it that in Trade Unions women are seldom given positions that are above the subordinate ones? . . . The GWU certainly has a golden opportunity to improve the standard of our working women. You do not mean to say truthfully that you are unaware that domestic servants are paid as low as $1.00 per week for seven days work. . . . I must say that the field for female members in your organization is ripe and the harvest would be great if you concentrate in planning a drive for membership. . . . This is a colony where the dependence of working women on their men folks is far from attractive." Dunn, however, tainted the appeal of her message to nationalist women by linking their poverty to juvenile delinquency, unwed motherhood, and child malnutrition. She thus failed to weaken women's support for the GWU and PUP, as would the Federation of Women during the summer of 1952. Nor did Dunn dislodge the nationalist leaders' privileging of male workers: the GWU's late 1952 memorial to the Colonial Office reiterated the living family wage discourse without any reference to the specific problems or struggles of female workers.[82]

It was less complicated for the *Billboard* to applaud women's support during the general strike of October to December 1952 and to castigate their treatment by employers. The paper favorably covered women's picket line support, their fund-raising, and their organization of food distribution to strikers and their families. Although the GWU executive had planned only a two-day strike, its continuation by the rank and file resulted in a major confrontation with the authorities in which women's activism was again welcome. Even the women charged for the early December incident at the BEC sawmill had not violated proper nationalist womanhood. Still, when the union began negotiations with the Public Works Department, the living family wage for male workers was central to its demands.

The starkest example of the gendered limits of the living family wage discourse is that of the leadership's response to the GWU Domestic Workers' Department's wage drive of late 1952 and early 1953. The DWD came closest to replicating the LUA Women's League within the nationalist movement of the 1950, and may indicate an effort by some nationalist women to develop a more autonomous base than the leadership was willing to tolerate. Certainly at the first organizational meeting in December 1952 male leaders did not remain silent as Soberanis had at LUA Women's League meetings. GWU vice president Herman Jex exhorted the women "to play a greater part," making the future of their children and the country dependent on their efforts. Leigh Richardson, GWU education secretary and leader of the PUP, then stated what must have been painfully obvious to the gathered women: "You cannot build a sound life upon 5 cents an hour." The male leaders behaved as if women were ignorant of their own economic hardships and as if women should treat the wage drive as a moral duty to others. In early March, with the wage drive underway, GWU president Nicholas Pollard "called upon [the women] to flock to the GWU for protection and guidance" at another DWD meeting, while Richardson urged them to vote for nationalist candidates in the legislative elections, still a year away. Apart from Philip Goldson, none of the leaders made the DWD a priority, at a time when women were needed as party campaigners. But Goldson's efforts to make a virtue of the fact that $5 per week was not a high or unreasonable wage was equally disturbing, for it completely ignored the nationalists' own insistence on $20–$25 per week as a living family wage. As discussed above, however, the DWD women did not politicize this inequality, perhaps because $5 per week would be at least a doubling of their wages for most female domestics.[83]

From mid-1953 on, as the nationalist leaders moved into electoral gear, their at least discursive support for women's right to work at higher if not breadwinner wages, and their right to have union representation, subsided markedly and never really revived. The enduring strength of the living family wage discourse, by contrast, was made possible by both leaders' and women's almost complete silence, after devaluation, about single motherhood. The living family wage became a mantra, perfectly compatible with the claim that "a nation begins with a family."[84] Eschewing colonial reformers' critique of popular class families, the nationalist leadership nonetheless idealized the male-headed nuclear family as the norm. Nationalist women did not directly contest this, perhaps because they could read the family wage discourse as reinforcing the social expectation of male responsibility.

Nationalist leaders, as mentioned above, sought symbolic legitimacy from the movement's women by having their election nomination papers signed by notable bembes or by female kin. And, though they made little of women finally gaining equal voting rights, they again welcomed their voluntary labor during the campaign. The *Billboard* recognized these myriad female organizers with a tribute to Dorothy Bradley, who was busy mobilizing PUP support in the villages north of Belize City. Praising her good looks and quiet dynamism, the paper described her as a "handy woman on a farm, in the kitchen or round the house." The opposition *Clarion*, in contrast, printed a letter from a woman conscious of the significance of women's suffrage: "Let us be aware of our numerical strength as voters, as taxpayers, or *breadwinners*," she wrote, for "until policy makers become convinced that life is more important than power, power will continue to destroy life."[85] This was one of the few moments when the full extent of working women's economic responsibilities was acknowledged, though not from within the nationalist movement.

Hard on the heels of the PUP-GWU's electoral victory, the *Billboard* broke the PUP's silence on the subject of single motherhood in a Mother's Day editorial. It attributed the rise in the numbers of "husbandless mothers" to a decline in "parental supervision." This "erratic family set up" was also the fault of employers who paid wages too low for men to fulfill their role as provider. National progress required "less and less illicit motherhood and more and more enlightened capitalism."[86] The moralistic language of imperial reform, marginalized for five years, was reentering nationalist discourse, casting single mothers as the enemy of the nation. The shift was so sudden that it cannot simply be attributed to Richardson and Goldson being influenced by their new involvement in the colonial administration. The Mother's Day editorial of 1955 was a paean to British Honduras's Christian mothers, valiant and sacrificing guardians of the Christian nation, who were asked to contribute yet more by raising industrious children. By then the GWU had been used for the first time since the nationalist takeover as a conduit for imperial reform directed at domesticating women, union domestics having been shown a film on infant care. Member for Social Services Philip Goldson very likely facilitated this screening. He also gave speeches prioritizing government-subsidized housing for "young men with families," for social planning would be useless "if men [did] not have jobs to support their families decently." Goldson's role as a moral regulator encompassed even banning a private women's boxing match. His goal of reclaiming the "Baymen's heritage" as "democratic government . . . and sound family life" no longer entailed a confrontation with colonialism but a process of negotiation in which behavior and relationships were to be reformed. The idea that women needed protectors rather than allies, prevalent even in the early discourse on women workers, appeared again in Goldson's speech at the opening of the YWCA in 1956.[87] The *Billboard* even explicitly condemned abortion, virtually unmentioned since the late 1940s, in a 1956 column. The paper's comparison of abortion with murder contrasted sharply with its 1953 coverage of the trial of a woman charged with performing an abortion on another woman. Then, the nationalists covered the trial in all its shocking detail, but implied that the women's fates—one dead, one sentenced to five years—constituted a double tragedy.[88]

George Price maintained a deliberate distance from the colonial administration and continued to "campaign chiefly among the ordinary Creole women in the market square in Belize City and among the peasants in the outdistricts."[89] As Richardson and Goldson became advocates of the West Indies Federation, he mobilized the nationalist base against it with a march in 1955 and a petition in 1956. At the kickoff of the city council campaign in early 1956 he told the thousand-strong crowd: "Four years of active political life had made the people of British Honduras graduates of the College of Politics, and the men and women in the streets held degrees in Political Science. Four years of politics had made BH people responsible, intelligent and sharp."[90] Tharine Rudon was the first woman to stand for the PUP in those elections, with strong female support. But loyalty to Rudon was conditional on her loyalty to Price. When she left the party in September 1956, the only other prominent woman to join her, Goldson, Richardson, and Jex was Elfreda Reyes. The rank and file, including most of the prominent bembes, remained with Price. Rudon indicated that she quit the party because she believed in the West Indies Federation, while Elfreda Reyes "wanted to give George Price a good whipping for what he was doing to women."[91] The women who stayed believed in Price's continued hostility to the colonial authorities, a hostility that necessitated ongoing popular mobilization, albeit of less intensity than during 1950–54. They would stay with him even when his PUP became as elitist and conservative, in gendered and other terms, as Richardson and Goldson had become after the 1954 elections.

The British Honduras Federation of Women

After the schism, Elfreda joined the British Honduras Federation of Women (BHFW), founded in early 1952 by a formidable group of middle-class reformers who early on came to the conclusion that Price was arrogantly manipulating women for his own selfish purposes. By the end of

1952 the BHFW had articulated a relatively modern and progressive gender politics that contrasted with PUP and GWU ambivalences and that challenged both colonial officials and nationalist leaders. Yet the BHFW failed to win the allegiance of the women of the popular classes. Nationalist women may have appreciated its messages, but they rejected the organization itself.

The reasons for this are two. First, although the BHFW was officially autonomous, it was linked to antinationalist forces and embraced neither universal suffrage nor self-government. As such, it remained within the paradigm of colonial reform that had been embraced by the Creole middle class ever since 1898 and that had been elaborated on after the crises of 1919 and 1934–36. Second, its ideas were articulated and its projects organized in the elitist, moralistic, and implicitly race-conscious manner of colonial reform. The BHFW was a class-bound group that, like the middle class as a whole, was unable to turn its politics of charity into a politics of alliance. The story of the BHFW is not simply a dead end, however, because its clashes with the nationalists revealed the importance of the female constituency to both political currents and the continued gender inequality within the GWU and PUP. Additionally, the first leaders of both parties' women's branches, founded in 1959, were former presidents of the BHFW. In this section, I analyze the BHFW's challenge to nationalism in 1952 and the development of its day care project from 1952 to 1959.

Mrs. Wilhelmina (Mina) Grant, the founding president of the BHFW, and her vice presidents, Mrs. Gwendolyn Lizarraga and Mrs. Vivian Seay, were very much part of middle-class women's tradition of voluntary community welfare activism. Of these women, Lizarraga was clearly the most liberal and least attached to the cultural politics of the middle class, while Seay was most vehemently antinationalist. In 1943 Lizarraga had attempted to make the BHTU as much a union for women as for men, and in 1948 she invited the new Maskall Farmers' Association to cultivate as much of her land as they could, rent free. Lizarraga had been born in Maskall, just north of Belize City, in 1901, and had inherited her father's seven thousand acres of prime chicle and mahogany lands. Throughout the 1930s and 1940s she developed a reputation as a liberal businesswoman who treated her workers and their families particularly well.[92] From 1953–57 Lizarraga worked for the colonial government as a female probation officer in the Social Development Department, her departure just preceding her leap into the PUP.[93]

Mina Grant had founded the Orange Walk Infant Welfare League in 1936 as the wife of Ezekiel Grant, then-district commissioner of Orange Walk, and before that had supported Seay's prodivorce stance. Ezekiel went to study law in Jamaica in the 1940s, and Mina, who accompanied him, was influenced there by the Jamaica Federation of Women, a group founded in 1936 with the governor's wife as its patron that concerned itself with the welfare of children and unemployed girls. As the GWU's lawyer in the late 1940s, Ezekiel favored a constitution that would balance universal suffrage with a minority of nominated legislators, thereby assuring the power of what he called the "dark-skinned aristocracy" to lead a controlled process of decolonization. He led the Unemployed Citizens' Association demonstration of September 1949, but he did not build on that to oppose devaluation in 1950. His views on the modern woman can be read as similar to and influenced by Mina's.[94] Women, he argued in early 1948, should take a "public interest," for their place "was no longer in the home exclusively"; he maintained that women should be able to pursue careers in teaching, science, and politics. Even after the nationalist takeover of the GWU divorced Grant from the labor movement and curbed his middle-class liberalism, he denounced the mistreatment and neglect of female domestic servants and called for a minimum wage: "No nation can rise above its women." Popular disinterest eroded his sympathies over the next few months. When he ran with other independents in the November 1950 municipal elections their platform referred to "acts of subversion" that had excited the "uninformed element of the community."[95]

Vivian Seay served on the executives of the BHFW and the National Party, organized in July 1951 by "a collection of old empire loyalists" whom Shoman correctly sees as "more concerned with protecting [their] own class privileges than developing a nationalist movement in which the poor majority would have a voice."[96] Indeed, at the time of the federation's founding, Seay was sitting on the appointed city council that replaced the majority PUP council dissolved by Governor Garvey in 1951. Through the NP, the federation was also linked to the culturally conservative LPOB, which labeled the PUP anti-Creole and claimed it intended to sell out the British heritage to Guatemala. In 1953, the federation had a float in the LPOB's September 10 parade.[97]

The BHFW held its first meeting in February 1952 and invited the colonial social development officer who deemed it a "responsible body of organized women" deserving of state support. The government had already given the BHFW access to its radio station, which Lizarraga used to make the first of three challenging statements that BHFW leaders made in the spring of 1952. She argued that women "will be paramount in shaping the new destinies of Nations" and countered the PUP's prevailing discourse of the family wage: "the man of a family will no longer be the economic unit." Women should get career and job training and should win equal pay for equal work through "organized feminine industrial units." Despite the flood of working women into the GWU, and perhaps because of their silence about equal pay, Lizarraga argued that "realization of the power of organization has not yet dawned extensively" among women.[98]

Lizarraga switched her attention to women's collective political power in her second statement.[99] Women could only make gains in a time of rapid global change, she argued, by together winning representation on city council, on government committees regulating work conditions and pay, and on the Executive and Legislative Councils. Change would come when women became a "force," educating their society through personal networks and the press. The PUP had never articulated any such goals, and this piece could be read as a gendered critique of the nationalist movement. But instead of advocating universal suffrage or self-government, Lizarraga called for research on housing conditions and on the relationship between domestic workers and their "gainfully employed" female bosses. While these were issues of keen interest to urban working women, Lizarraga's effort to articulate and extend the spirit of popular mass politics fell short. Gwendolyn Dunn was also a founding member of the BHFW and her speech at the GWU's 1952 convention advocating working women's rights in the labor movement was compromised by a moralism taboo in the nationalist movement of 1952. Dunn had linked female labor organization to the colonial discourse of development and welfare, not to the nationalist discourse of political change and social justice.

The summer of 1952 saw the BHFW come into direct conflict with the GWU over "organized feminine industrial units," specifically the female sectionizers at the Pomona cannery, who had recently become the first women to be covered by a GWU contract. What was at stake was the right to speak for and define the interests of the working women of Belize. There is no evidence that working women themselves intervened in this argument between male union leaders and middle-class women's advocates, though it is conceivable that the debate contributed to the thinking of those who launched the GWU domestics' wage drive later that year.

In the *Billboard* of 27 May 1952 George Price made some critical remark about the BHFW. In response, the BHFW invited Price to a meeting at Mina Grant's home, but he did not attend. The *Clarion* then printed a letter from a BHFW supporter, condemning Price's arrogance in speaking for "all the women of British Honduras, or even Belize [City]." The following day the BHFW denied that they were using his name to recruit members: "As this is a female organization we do not need Mr. Price's personal influence in order to exist." It seems that the PUP was taking the initiative to counter the BHFW's potential threat.[100] By this time, according to later nationalist claims, Mina Grant was already in touch with the Citrus Company in Pomona concerning the recruitment of "girls" to work in the strongly pro-GWU sectionizing plant.[101] Showing its antinationalist agenda behind its support for working women, the BHFW seems to have colluded with manager Frank Sharpe to dilute union support there. On 11 June the *Clarion* published a notice from the BHFW inviting applications from married or single women for 150 jobs at the Stann Creek cannery, at $2 a day plus free lodging and sick benefits.

GWU president Nicholas Pollard's attack on the BHFW for acting as an employment agency was acid.[102] He labeled the women "cunning, unladylike and malicious," a petticoated cover for the NP leaders, and accused them of being well aware of the GWU's hard bargaining for the sectionizers' contract. He dismissed the BHFW as an "archaic" group of at most fifty members, who were deceiving women with false promises, and called on working women to come to the GWU in search of work. He did not mention that the contract paid men $2.25 a day, but women only $1.80.[103] Yet the BHFW proved itself less interested in unequal pay than in ridiculing the union leadership. Carol Campbell of the BHFW wrote a delightfully barbed rebuttal of Pollard's position.[104] She questioned the GWU's monopoly claim to represent the interests of Belizeans, and defied Pollard's definition of women's business: "Surely nothing can be more quaintly archaic than this concept of a woman's business. Since the question of women's employment is NOT in a woman's sphere of activity, presumably he thinks that a woman's sphere of activity should be restricted to our being nice, placid little females who sit by the fire and spin, only taking time off to produce infants and attend to the needs of their lords and masters. That view might have held water in the horse and buggy days, Mr. Pollard, but this is the 20th century—the atomic age!" Having asserted middle-class women's right to concern themselves with working women's problems, Campbell proceeded to deny any affiliation to the NP or conspiracy with the Citrus Company and concluded that it made no difference whether women got cannery jobs through the GWU or the BHFW. Working women, it seemed, were faced with a choice between a union that maintained unequal pay and a federation that had no real respect for a collective agreement.

Pollard bit back by printing Sharpe's alleged 24 May letter to Grant to prove the insincerity and inaccuracy of the BHFW's promises. It is conceivable that Price had somehow found out about this letter, prompting his 27 May comments and setting the BHFW up to be exposed. We do know that at a September 1952 BHFW meeting with the group of women who answered the call for citrus workers, tension erupted within the leadership. An anonymous letter to the *Billboard* claimed that "one of the officers" of the group encouraged the women to join the GWU once they got to Pomona, and that Grant became angry "and tried to reprimand her."[105] The dissident was most likely Gwen Lizarraga. The following week the GWU struck the cannery to protest Sharpe having posted antiunion signs.

Finding that working women did not leave the GWU or even criticize it, the BHFW launched two new projects in the summer of 1952. First was a resolution demanding that the colonial government further the modern democratic age by hiring women police officers, appointing women jurors, raising maintenance support so that illegitimate children would not grow up to be criminals, and increasing housing.[106] Colonial officials balked. The superintendent of police simply dismissed the need for women officers. The attorney general was willing to consider women jurors once Grant assured him that only propertied women should qualify, but the chief justice vetoed even this, arguing that there was no pool of suitable women in the colony. Governor Renison concurred: "All sorts of complications about domestic duties and care of children . . . would arise." The social development officer viewed increased maintenance as impractical, for most fathers were ordered to pay minimal amounts and still fell into arrears. Renison agreed with an acting magistrate's sympathy for these men: "many of the mothers are equally guilty as the fathers in these casual liaisons."[107] The federation, precisely because it shared the government's definitions of fit and unfit women, had no mass membership to pressure the government for action.

The second and longer-term project of 1952 was the plan to build a low-cost day nursery for working mothers. Again, an idea that could have appealed to many nationalist women was framed in alienating terms, as a means to improve poor single mothers and their children. Proper day care, the federation believed, would save poor children from substandard care in their own communities. They invited Mrs. Hone, wife of the colonial secretary, to announce their plans: "When I first came to Belize I was amazed at the number of unmarried mothers with not only one child but two or three. Although such conditions were strange to me, they are accepted here and will continue until such time as a proper home and family life is established." Mary Wright, supervisor of domestic science in the Education Department and member of the BHFW as well as the LPOB, spoke in a similar vein during the September celebrations of 1952. At the LPOB's annual Patriotic Meeting, Wright linked the problem of juvenile delinquency, so threatening to the Baymen's heritage, to Belize's "matriarchal state."[108]

Lacking popular support, the day nursery project proceeded slowly, with sporadic aid from city council, middle-class donors, and ultimately the Official Charity Fund. Philip Goldson as member of social services from 1955 until 1957 tried to send government funding to the BHFW, but a lapse in its registration and an internal dispute held up the money. Lady Renison laid the foundation stone in July 1954, but the finished building was not opened until November 1958, by Governor Thornley and his daughter. By then, Lizarraga was in the PUP and the BHFW's president was Winil Grant Farr, Mina and Ezekiel's daughter, who also envisioned the nursery as replacing "unsuitable" childcare provided within the working-class community. Its treasurer was none other than Elfreda Reyes, who took on the job of petitioning the government for more money through 1959 and 1960, the same years that Lizarraga was building the United Women's Groups as a mass movement within the PUP that Reyes had rejected.[109]

The Mina Grant Day Nursery, like the citrus recruitment effort of 1952, and like Lizarraga's and Dunn's speeches, failed to give the BHFW political legitimacy in the minds of nationalist women. Federation women presented their care and concern not as equal allies in working women's struggle to support their households but as enlightened representatives of all women's interests. Their critique of the GWU for claiming the same authority over working women was well placed, but because the federation stood with the colonialists and against the nationalists, its assertion of women's rights had no discernible popular support. Unable to articulate a cross-class feminist politics, or a less paternalistic nationalism, the BHFW facilitated the emergence of two opposing factions of women, each primarily identified with a political party.

The United Women's Groups and PUP Conservatism, 1959–1961

Those factions took on institutional form in early 1959 with the founding in February of the PUP's United Women's Groups (UWGS) and in April of the National Independence Party's (NIP's) Women Pioneers. The NIP itself had been born in July 1958 of a merger of the NP and the Honduras Independence Party (itself formed in 1957 by Richardson and Goldson) and it boasted more female leaders than the PUP had ever had; the Pioneers' first president was Stephanie Jones, a former president of the BHFW. Acknowledging PUP women's "intense and passionate loyalty" to the nationalist cause, the now pro-NIP *Billboard* alleged nonetheless that they were merely the "degrad[ed] instruments" of Price, "a political dictator and traitor."[110] But PUP women had not been reduced to militant marionettes. With the founding of the UWGS and under the leadership of Gwendolyn Lizarraga, they engaged in a renewed mobilization in support of their own interests, albeit one framed by party membership. In organizing for female home ownership through 1959 and 1960, Lizarraga's UWGS manipulated and slowed the leadership's tack toward more narrowly conservative gender politics in the late 1950s, thus challenging nationalist paternalism. The story of the UWGS shows the continued capacity of the nationalist rank and file—and specifically women—to pressure the PUP leadership even at a time of critical negotiations with the British.

Yet it also shows the degree to which nationalist women had been captured by party politics in under a decade. Lizarraga was never able to destabilize women's intense devotion to Price as party leader or to mount an open critique of the leadership's gender politics by publicly stating that home ownership offered women security against male abuse and neglect and against low wages and unemployment. Indeed, the UWGS may have also masked the growing elitism and conservatism of the PUP brass, just as the formation of weak party-run unions was meant to do. Though more women than ever before became official members of the nationalist movement during the mobilization of 1959–60, it did not force a progressive resolution of the historic tension between inclusion and control in Belizean nationalism, but it did, at the very least, renew the principles of women's rights and activism in nationalist culture.

Lizarraga's leadership was critical to the scale and influence of the UWG mobilization. She had spent most of the 1950s as a Social Development Department employee and a member of the BHFW, but she probably joined the PUP in the second half of 1957, for she resigned her job in March of that year and by December 1958 was prominent enough to be a PUP candidate in the Belize City Council elections, which she lost.[111] There can be little doubt, then, that her victory in the March 1961 legislative elections was attributable to her rise to national popularity and power at the head of the UWGs. The timing of her job resignation coincided with the PUP's clean sweep of the 1957 legislative elections; we can thus speculate that she decided she could best serve women's interests not by fruitlessly opposing the nationalists but by working within their camp.

There is little doubt that Lizaragga's priority in founding the UWGs was to improve the living conditions and rights of working women. Her career had shown her to be primarily interested in the welfare and, more than other middle-class women—the empowerment of women and children. As a chicle and mahogany contractor, she had given sympathetic aid to her workers and their families. Her daughter-in-law Rita Lizarraga, interviewed by Silvana Woods, remembered: "[W]hen she had to pay the workers who were living in the city and in poorer areas like Card Alley—when she went there she would see a lot of poverty and she was touched by that. . . . She would go to the hospital and tell the . . . people that there is a woman with a baby who is dying."[112] She would even give money to men who had drunk their pay away so that they would have something to bring home: "she was only thinking of the wife and kids." As a probation officer, the hardships of women without any male support became her responsibility. In 1956 Lizarraga was visiting and trying to find proper shelter for Mrs. Catherine Penglass, 62, and her two young granddaughters, who were living in a tiny windowless box intended as a chicken coop.[113] In 1943 she had urged the BHTU to organize working women and through the BHFW had argued for equal pay and education.

By leaving government service and the BHFW, joining the PUP, and founding the UWGs, Lizarraga demonstrated her resolve to address the issues of female poverty and vulnerability at a national level and in a way that would mobilize women collectively despite the decline of the labor movement. "Her overriding goal . . . was . . . to encourage women to become independent economically." As such, she broke with the majority of middle-class women in Belize, not only by abandoning antinationalism but also by committing to fight for working women's interests without lacing her politics with moral critique. Still, like other middle-class feminists in twentieth-century Latin America and the Caribbean, such as Beatrice Grieg in Trinidad and Ofelia Dominguez Navarro in Cuba, Lizarraga did not develop a clear relationship of solidarity with the UWG membership.[114] She was their "Madame Liz," a *patrona* as much if not more than an ally.

The UWGS' founding agenda was not to win elections or raise money for the PUP but to promote national development and particularly to organize women to obtain their own homes. Woods speculates that Lizarraga's focus on women gaining home ownership stemmed from the pre-1954 property restrictions on the vote, but more enduring problems of low wages, unemployment, domestic violence, and male neglect likely also informed her program for the UWGS. In launching them, Lizarraga announced the groups' intentions to combat not only housing problems but also the rising cost of living, including rental rates and food prices, using petitions and demonstrations if necessary.[115]

She began recruiting women in Belize City at PUP divisional meetings and by the end of March 1959 there were nine hundred members, the number rising to fourteen hundred by May. In April Lizarraga began to recruit in the districts, and branches were founded first in Stann Creek and Cayo (both in San Ignacio as well as in a half dozen villages), where groups of PUP women had been mobilized since at least 1954. Soon after branches formed in Maskall and Orange Walk, then in Sand Hill, Benque Viejo, and Punta Gorda. By November 1959, when membership had reached five thousand (thirty-five hundred outside Belize City), only Corozal lacked a branch.[116] It formed in May 1960. At these recruiting meetings, in Belize City and the districts, Lizarraga was coming into contact with hundreds of women who had defined a nationalism of social and economic justice as the solution to their problems and who had been local organizers long before 1959.

The UWG president in Cayo was veteran PUP organizer Maria Samos. She, like her counterpart in Dangriga, Stella Avilez, worked with the established party women in their communities. In Punta Gorda, the zealously loyal Venancia Petillo organized the UWGS, recruiting among others Modesta Norales. In Orange Walk, the original leader was Mrs. Leonie Vega, the wife of a leading PUP town counselor, Ignacio Vega. The female kin of the powerful Urbina men also headed the original group. When Ignacio split from the PUP in 1960, Leonie became the leader of the NIP

Women's Pioneers. Adolfa Garcia was then elected president of the uwg, although soon the sisters of the new pup frontman, Victor Orellana, took it over.[117] All of these district branches started with memberships of several hundred and retained several dozen active members. At least two of these leading women, Samos and Avilez, were elected in the 1950s and 1960s as town counselors, and others served on the local pup branch executives as well.

The pursuit of housing was not the focus of every uwg branch, although all were concerned to provide mutual aid to their members and to extend aid to the wider community of women and children in need when possible. Outside Belize City, housing was most important to the uwg in Dangriga, where Evelyn Avila and Winifred Flowers were early settlers in the Bowman's Square/Unity Zone area in the late 1960s.[118] Initially, then, housing efforts were concentrated in Belize City. May Davis was a founding member of the uwgs and was one of several hundred women who received house lots in the Queen's Square area in 1963, the most successful case. By October of 1959 there were twenty-five groups of twenty women each, pressuring the government for training in its aided self-help housing policy.[119] Here the accuracy of Cedric Grant's characterization of this period in terms of "two parallel systems, the colonial and the emergent Belize regime" becomes apparent.[120] It was a colonial bureaucrat, the social development officer, who received the uwgs' "urgent and persistent requests." He perceived his pup boss, the member of social services, as sympathetic to and seeking to encourage a demand for housing that the department could not meet: "I deem it unwise and undesirable to orient [housing] groups unless I know what is the connection with Government. This matter is becoming increasingly important and I would be pleased to have an interview with you and the Associate Member." Soon after, a *Belize Times* editorial called on the government to meet the uwgs' demands for land and training.[121] By March 1960 uwg groups in Belize City had stockpiled twenty-eight thousand cement blocks, and the pup paper again berated the colonial authorities for their failure to move forward.

But pup leaders were not unambivalent supporters of the uwgs. This revival of the nationalist base began just after the pup's sweep of twenty-nine of thirty-three municipal seats colony-wide in December 1958 and coincided with Price's realization that his popular strength would lead nowhere if he did not accede to the British model of decolonization.[122] His powerful place at the negotiating table could benefit from the UWG mobilization only if it was contained. The party brass thus launched the United Men's Groups, which met to discuss political issues but undertook no direct action or practical projects and never developed into a mass organization.[123] Nevertheless, this was a response to the disproportionate mobilization of women—and their enduring capacity of self-organization—at a time when Price was promoting a model of beneficent paternalism. More serious is Philip Goldson's claim that after 1961, the PUP leadership deliberately limited the gains of the UWGs in order to "quell" Lizarraga's "expanding influence" and out of a fear of autonomous organized female strength: "So here was Mrs. Lizarraga organizing women[,] . . . first of all, their economic power! I mean 25 cents a week didn't seem like much, but that was all that these poor women could afford in those days. . . . Now, at 25 cents, or 50 cents taken out of their little earnings, put aside toward their idea of women owning their own house one day, for women having economic power and borrowing power, now this seemed like a dream. Mrs. Lizarraga began to give foundation to this dream and I think they probably felt that she was going too far." C. L. B. Rogers, one of Price's key ministers through the 1960s, also remembers that there was a latent fear of the UWGs, of their being a gun with Lizarraga's hand on the trigger. But he disputes Goldson's claim, saying that Lizarraga herself made promises she could not keep, and turned the UWGs into a mutual aid society.[124]

Such claims cannot be proven, but it is clear that in the 1960s the UWGs lost momentum as a force within the party and, with the exceptions of those groups that gained housing, focused on electoral campaigning. As I will discuss in the next chapter, even the Queen's Square house lots came at a time of marked female challenge from the NIP, suggesting that nationalist women's leverage within the PUP depended to some degree on outside pressures. The UWGs' supportive role was presaged in 1960 when they backed up the PUP members of the bipartisan committee, which included

Lizarraga, that began constitutional negotiations in London.[125] In January 1960 the UWGS as a whole pledged loyalty to Price as he left for London, in February the executive sent a telegram of support, and in March a mass UWG meeting approved a telegram to the secretary of state for the colonies supporting the Joint Committee's demands and protesting the government's stalling on the allotment of land for housing.[126]

While the latter element of the telegram may have been a way for the UWGS to enable Lizarraga to push the housing campaign during decolonization talks, it was far too weak a gesture to prevent the PUP leadership moving official party discourse about women in an increasingly conservative direction in 1960. The 1960 party manifesto, for example, discussed labor issues exclusively in terms of a family wage for "the worker and his family," thus refusing to even include women as a secondary labor force. The *Belize Times* began to cast women in morally absolute terms, either the source of all evil or the only bulwark against the evil of Communism, and even printed St. Paul's instructions to women to obey their husbands.[127] But Lizarraga refused to let the idea of women having their own safe havens and equity die. She could talk, as in the 1961 electoral campaign, about housing as part of the dominant domesticating discourse and demand that women have decent homes of their own to defend from the nation's enemies.[128] In some measure, then, the UWGS prevented the total abandonment of nationalist women's original agenda of social justice and represented a renewal of the popular origins of the movement as well as an institutionalization of women's loyalty to the party. Indeed, when Assad Shoman launched a movement for democratic renewal from within the PUP in the 1970s, he found his strongest allies in the UWG women of the Cayo District.

Conclusion

March 1961 witnessed two signal events in the history of Belizean women: Gwendolyn Lizarraga was elected to the Legislative Assembly, and the Williamson-Dickie garment factory opened its doors under the new Development Incentives Ordinance passed by the PUP-dominated legislature.[129] Lizarraga's candidacy and victory were expressions of the importance of the UWG constituency to the party leadership and the popularity of her platform of social reforms, but it was hardly the "true revolution" touted in the PUP's *Belize Times*. Indeed, as "the new leaders invited neo-colonialism rather than had it imposed on them," women began a new phase of underpaid work for foreign capital, even while they disappeared from official PUP labor policy.[130] None of Lizarraga's efforts with the UWGs could make a dent in this process. Williamson's made clear the terms of the new era, tolerating no hint of labor organization among its largely female Creole workforce.

Subaltern women in Belize in the 1950s did not feel compelled to choose between nationalist solidarity and gender interest, in part because the PUP leadership welcomed women into the movement, in part because the BHFW's arguments for equal pay and equal rights were framed within a moralistic antinationalist politics. Price, Richardson, Pollard, Jex, and Goldson never extended the "living family wage" discourse to women—a fact that attracted Williamson-Dickie in the first place—but they recognized women as workers in the early 1950s. When that recognition was largely withdrawn later in the decade, Lizarraga played key role in renewing female mobilization within the party for their own economic interests, not as wage earners but as homeowners. For the working mothers of the PUP, who agitated throughout the decade for independence with social and economic justice, the UWGs represented their importance to the party, and the party's commitment to them. As many women emphasized to me, the reason women participated in the nationalist struggle was to create better lives for their children. As gendered agents in the construction of the nationalist state, they established real, if limited, commitments to women's rights and well-being. Those limits would be questioned by the next generation's feminist pioneers, even before Belizean independence in 1981.

Zee Edgell set her acclaimed 1981 novel *Beka Lamb* in the early 1950s when her generation was entering adolescence amid the exhilaration and anxieties of nationalist struggle. Fourteen-year-old Beka's Granny Ivy, an elderly Creole woman, is an enthusiastic nationalist, carrying her stool to sit front and center at all the Battlefield rallies. Edgell honored the antico-

lonial passions of women like Granny Ivy but also portrayed their historical praxis of party-based activism as a problematic inheritance. Beka, for
example, watches nationalist speakers exhort a crowd to unity, but they
have nothing to say about the deep gender divisions that allow Toycie,
her best friend, to be cut off from the promises of education and national
independence when her pregnancy becomes obvious to the nuns at her
convent school, while Toycie's boyfriend goes on to university.[131] Beka's
search for an authentic way forward for her life, beyond Granny Ivy's loyal
nationalism, mirrored Edgell's own sensitive questioning of the relations
between Belizean women and the nation-state so long in the making.

6 Negotiating Nationalist Patriarchy

*Party Politics, Radical Masculinity, and the
Birth of Belizean Feminism, 1961–1982*

Nora Parham, the first woman ever executed by the state in Belize, was hanged on 5 June 1963, in a rare display of the hybrid colonial/neocolonial state's capacity for sovereign violence.[1] The jury, entirely male, as were all juries until 1970, had wrestled with the evidence for four hours before handing down both a guilty verdict and a mercy plea, evidently in an effort to balance the state's demand for justice and the public's strong sympathy for Parham. Mercy was denied by the Executive Council—led by the British governor but stacked with PUP legislators—three days before the execution. A clemency petition from Parham's relatives the day before her death swayed neither the governor nor First Minister George Price. The PUP's paper, the *Belize Times*, had already made the ruling party's position clear in an editorial denouncing National Independence Party (NIP) accusations that the PUP was taking partisan revenge by letting Parham die. The authority of the state, it argued, not party interests, required such harsh punishment: "If sympathy can change court rulings, then the respect and authority of the courts would start on its slow flow to nil; the prestige would be lost. And we would be entering into nationhood without the advantage of our one stable institution: the court."[2]

Belize entered into self-government under a new constitution hammered out in London in July 1963 and implemented from January 1964 to March 1965, when the PUP won new elections and George Price became premier.[3] The Nora Parham case faded from public memory, invoked only when other women resorted to burning their husbands to death.[4] The act itself explains why the family, the PUP's usual guardian of national security, was at this moment displaced by the court as the new nation's only stable institution. Parham's unusually harsh treatment is explicable only in the context of the transition to self-government and her husband's status as an agent of state authority.

Ketchell Trapp was a police constable in Orange Walk, and although Parham set him on fire at home, when he was off-duty, and in the immediate aftermath of him beating her—as he admitted on his deathbed—the state dealt with her as a "cop slayer." Another woman who committed the identical crime just a few weeks later received only an eight-year sentence, for her husband did not embody the masculine authority of the emerging nation-state.[5] No policemen were killed by men during this moment of transition, so we cannot claim that Parham was punished specifically as a woman. But by ignoring allegations and evidence of Trapp's physical abuse of Parham, by refusing to treat the pair as wife and husband, not just cop slayer and cop, the government deepened its own highly political silence about domestic and community gender oppression and violence and added a threatening element to its re-call to "domestic womanhood."[6] PUP women, however sympathetic privately, adhered to that public silence.

On the eve of full national independence, eighteen years later, the young feminist Cynthia Ellis argued that in Belize, as in other decolonizing nations, "the situation of women has often been submerged by the question of national liberation . . . and when considered at all, it has been seen as a secondary and insignificant problem."[7] Between 1963 and 1981 a small space, "a space in which we women" were able to "communicate . . . without feeling threatened,"[8] was created outside the dominant system of party politics. In 1963 Gwendolyn Lizarraga and her United Women's Groups had neither the autonomy nor the motivation to defy Price in order to politicize domestic violence, and NIP protests about Parham were easily dismissed as partisan. In 1981 Ellis's critique appeared as part of the work of the independent Belize Committee for Women and Development (BCWAD), whose middle-class members—almost all with secondary or even postsecondary education—carefully maintained the group's partisan neutrality in order to work *with*, not under or inside, the state to combat women's cultural, economic, and political oppression.

This chapter traces the shifting possibilities for and forms of female political activism in the 1960s and 1970s, arguing that both fault lines within and challenges to nationalist hegemony contributed to the birth of Belizean feminism in the two years before national independence.[9] Export-led economic growth and mildly redistributive policies—dubbed the "peaceful, constructive Belizean revolution" and justified in terms of Walt Rostow's theory of modernization—as well as the postponement of independence owing to the Guatemalan claim, helped Price and his cabinet *patrones* maintain the loyalty of the UWGs in the 1960s. The PUP's share of the popular vote in general elections declined, however, from 63.4 percent in 1961 to just under 58 percent in 1965 and 1969 to 51.3 percent in 1974.[10] The PUP's own promotion of both growth built on cheap labor and higher education drew women into the paid labor force at all levels, gradually eroding domestic patriarchy and women's own patience for PUP paternalism and promises of prosperity as well as their tolerance of partisan quarrels over negotiations toward national sovereignty.

Although the opposition NIP could not contest the PUP's electoral strength in the 1960s, it did challenge it in the arena of popular culture. With its roots in the gender order of the Creole middle class that had been shaped by female activists since the 1920s and as much in need of a mass base as the PUP had been in the 1950s, the NIP nurtured a strong female leadership and articulated a more progressive policy on women's rights and power than the PUP, albeit within the paradigm of party rivalry and female respectability. The NIP's indeed obsessive focus on the Guatemalan threat actually fostered a discourse of women as the Anglo-Caribbean nation's militant (not domesticated) saviors against the PUP and Guatemala. The NIP's Women Pioneers and the PUP's UWGs were each subordinate within their respective parties in the 1960s, but the former had the freedom of autonomy from the state.

A second challenge to PUP gender politics emerged in the 1969–74 period, when young leftist and Black Power radicals garnered phenomenal support among young Creoles and Garinagu in Belize City and Dangriga by denouncing the entire party system as a smokescreen for capitalist neocolonialism.[11] This was the "Hattie generation," teenagers and young adults who had come of age since the immensely destructive Hurricane Hattie of October 1961. One poet linked their political disaffection and distinctly un-Victorian sexual politics: "half-educated, frustrated, desperate/they roam the streets and stay out late/young girls with forced-ripe developments/do things their mothers never dreamt."[12] Black Power leader Evan X Hyde, son of a civil service family, articulated and defined the feeling of those Belizeans in their teens and twenties most evocatively in his own poetry and fiction. His movement, the United Black Association for Development (UBAD), created an explicitly sexualized but also antifeminist politics, casting the nation's redemption as depending on the recuperation of black masculinity from the womanish leaders of female-dominated political parties. Neither UBAD nor its leftist counterpart, the Political Action Committee of Assad Shoman and Said Musa, founded women's branches, but UBAD did attract a few female activists, who subordinated gender conflicts to racial unity. The radicals prompted both parties to return to grassroots organizing—a process pushed vigorously by Shoman and Musa after joining the PUP in 1971—and while all leading radicals were pulled into party politics to some degree by 1974, UBAD's gender politics in particular eventually legitimized public discussion of sexuality and domestic gender oppression.

That discussion coincided with unprecedented opposition electoral strength from 1974 on, and the beginning of the UN Decade on Women in 1975, both of which put pressure on the ruling PUP to develop a "women and development" policy and ultimately to create the government Women's Bureau in 1981. The PUP administrations of 1974–79 and 1979–84 depended on the Caribbean Community (CARICOM, created in 1973) nations as their best allies in the fight for support at the UN for Belizean independence; this may have put additional pressure on the PUP to cooperate with the UN and CARICOM's regional plan for combating gender inequality.[13] The government thus endorsed a "women and development" discourse, which defined the cause of women's inequality as their exclusion from the development process. On one level this argument simply updated the party's original emphasis on social and economic progress as the solution to poverty and oppression, but it also provided an opening for early Belizean feminism. Although the late 1979 elections did not yield the expected victory for the United Democratic Party (formed in 1973 of the NIP, its offshoot the People's Democratic Movement, and the new Liberal Party), causing an acrimonious leadership change, they did weaken the PUP, which won just 51 percent of the popular vote and faced a briefly resurgent and independent labor movement.[14] Within that weakened PUP, leftists Shoman and Musa had finally won seats, defeating the UDP's leader and deputy leader, and became ministers of health and education respectively. They joined Elaine Middleton, the non-PUP head of the Social Development Department, as at least passive government allies of the new BCWAD.

BCWAD was not free of the lure of party politics in the intensely partisan and delicately balanced run-up to independence in 1979–1981 period, during which the committee formed, built a small membership, and began to develop its feminist analysis and program. None of its middle-class members came out of the PUP, but several were prominently linked to the UDP; the committee thus survived by working within the moderate "women and development" paradigm already officially blessed by the PUP. The committee staged no women's liberation demonstrations or marches and organized no petitions or even a public festival until March 1982, when it celebrated the first International Women's Day since national independence in September 1981. Yet it quietly challenged the primacy of the national question, insisting that improvements in women's lives should not await independence or general economic development. The most public and politically pointed aspect of its work was the publication of three issues of *Network*, one each in 1980, 1981 and 1982, where the analyses of sisters Cynthia and Zoila Ellis were particularly important.

Given the political context, the committee's work lacked the drama and scale of the popular labor-nationalist tradition in twentieth-century Belize, exemplified by Annie Flowers's denunciation of colonial rule and black manhood in 1919, LUA women's labor and suffrage struggles in the 1930s, and even the UWGS' housing campaign of the late 1950s and early 1960s. It also maintained a lower profile than its more direct political foremothers in the middle-class reformist tradition—the BCNs, the Federation of Women, and the Women's Pioneers—each of which received some support or at least approval from British officials and/or middle-class men. Not all committee members were comfortable with even such a moderate, low-key feminist politics, and many dropped out in the 1980s and 1990s as the committee became the Belize Organization for Women and Development (BOWAND), an increasingly working-class "grassroots" women's space. Yet despite its internal contradictions, by 1981 the committee had begun to elaborate a female consciousness of the state not as women's and the nation's savior but as a necessary yet dangerous ally in a self-directed struggle in civil society. Equally important, it had broken with the dominant twentieth-century pattern of women organizing within larger male-led movements. As such, it challenged both nationalist gender politics and the hegemony of party politics.

The committee's members—like women in Caribbean, Asian, and African national movements, Latin American revolutionary and prodemocracy movements, and North American and European civil rights and antiwar movements—were powerfully disillusioned by enduring patriarchy in both theory and practice. Belize in the 1970s produced no female politics as gripping as those of the Mothers of the Plaza de Mayo, the Central American *guerrilleras*, or the women activists within Grenada's New Jewel Movement and Jamaica's "democratic socialist" experiment. Belizean women were struggling with enemies more nebulous than military dictatorship—party politics, older generations' commitment to what those parties had once represented, and sometimes their own hostility to the PUP—and without a major ally like Maurice Bishop or Michael Manley. Like the Women in the Caribbean Project of 1979–82, carried out by academics within the University of the West Indies, the committee sought a "woman-centered" approach to analyzing and changing Belizean women's reality.[15] It achieved a measure of autonomy from the state and party politics at a time when Sandinista women, for example, were embarking on a decade of disillusioning struggle within a leftist national revolution. Yet perhaps early Belizean feminists' autonomy was not hard-won enough, for clientelist party politics—however discredited on principle—has continued to compete extremely effectively with civil society activism in independent Belize.

The Gender Politics of the Party System in the 1960s

The PUP dominated the legislature from 1954 to 1974, shutting the NIP out completely in 1961, losing just two seats in 1965, and only one in 1969. Yet Cedric Grant, while acknowledging that the PUP was never threatened electorally in the 1960s, describes it as a "weak government incapable of commanding national unity" on the Guatemalan issue.[16] Price and his cabinet *caciques* worked hard to channel all initiative and change through government, particularly the cabinet, rather than through the party or worse, independent organizations. Grant and Shoman agree that after 1961 the PUP became markedly centralized and undemocratic, strongly empha-sizing patron-client relations with the relatively unorganized (compared to 1950–54) rank and file.[17] Shoman's view that from 1961 forward "PUP leaders . . . consciously promoted the idea that they were the country's natural and legitimate leaders; that they were the government rather than the party in government" is supported by the claim in the party's news-paper just prior to the 1965 elections that "the one-party system, with the PUP as the governing party," is "fit and proper."[18] Yet their control even within the party was hardly complete. Internally, legislator Jesus Ken of Xaibe in the Corozal District, whose great-grandfather was a leader of the Santa Cruz Maya in the Caste War, continued to act as a representative of his cane worker and farmer constituency rather than as an enforcer of the party line.[19] Even after being relegated to the Senate in 1965, Ken continued to expose the costs of export-led capitalist growth, issuing his *Manifiesto Cañero* in March 1967, during a season of cane field fires. His replacement in the legislature, Florencio Marin, challenged not party col-lusion with foreign capital but the centralization of power in Belize City.[20] And in the mid-1960s PUP backbenchers challenged cabinet supremacy, forcing the institution of the Parliamentary Committee and public hear-ings system.[21]

Outside the ruling party, the NIP was the party wing of an array of opposition groups rather than the dominant force of the opposition. The Public Officers' Union (POU), for example, which was overwhelmingly of middle-class Creole origins, could have a direct impact on government regardless of the NIP's legislative strength. In June 1966 the POU struck when NIP leader Philip Goldson claimed publicly that the British Foreign Office was sympathetic to an American negotiator's very pro-Guatemala proposals for the resolution of the territorial dispute.[22] Female civil servants had some clout within the POU, but women were more powerful in the LPOB and the NIP itself. Grant argues that Philip Goldson's NIP was "narrow, negative, and reactive,"[23] in the 1960s, owing to the party's emphasis on Creole identity and the British connection to counter the PUP's perceived policy of "Central American or Latin Integration."[24] But it was precisely that siege mentality, and the party's electoral weakness, which nurtured women's prominence in both cultural and political opposition activism. In terms of gender politics, the NIP of the 1960s was *more* liberal and progressive than the ruling PUP.

Both parties of course relied on their women's organizations for fundraising, campaigning, and the round of social activities that sustained a party culture and commitment. And neither had any official policy of including a certain number of women as party councilors or candidates. Yet the NIP included women—middle-class Creole women from Belize City—on the party executive and as legislative candidates far more often than the PUP. Gwendolyn Lizarraga was reelected in the Pickstock constituency in 1965, and served as minister of education and housing from 1965–69, but she was never part of Price's inner circle, and despite her leadership of the UWGS, she had at most a minor influence on PUP labor, development, and social policy. No other PUP women ran for national office prior to independence.[25] In the NIP, several women ran for the Belize City Council and the Legislative Assembly, a group that overlapped with the women who, through the LPOB, vehemently rejected the PUP's cultural politics, which promoted "a sense of Maya and Spanish heritage" via government radio broadcasts and in the design of the new capital's government buildings.[26]

The Save Our Country movement of 1961–62 was the most coherent example of respectable opposition women's cultural mobilization. Soon after the March 1961 elections the one-party legislature voted to rename September 10 "National Day," a move that provoked Miss Helen Taylor, daughter of a district commissioner's son and a white *corozaleña*, to launch the Save Our Country movement, probably before Hurricane Hattie.[27] Together with Vivian Seay, Calvert Staine, and his niece Leotine Gillette, Taylor organized an enormous petition and parade, demanding the retention of the name "Battle of St. George's Caye Day."[28] This anti-PUP mobilization was galvanized in early 1962 by an incursion into southern Belize by a small force of Guatemalans.[29] Taylor's effort ultimately failed, for the PUP legislature voted to maintain the name change.[30] She and three other NIP women were among the nine opposition candidates for city council in late 1962, but the PUP swept those elections as well, with two female candidates, Lizarraga and teacher Lois Encalada.[31]

Two of Taylor's female colleagues on the NIP slate were teachers Floss Casasola, who was Luke Kemp's sister and had first been elected to city council in 1952, and Leotine Gillette, daughter of veteran Garveyite Morrel Staine. The fourth female candidate was Mrs. Rosita Williams, a woman lacking their respectable middle-class credentials. Her brief but fiery journey in the political limelight coincided with the Save Our Country campaign, but there is no evidence that she integrated into the established cadre of NIP women activists. After all, she was a longtime PUP supporter and secretary of a UWG housing group when she dramatically defected in March 1962, claiming that Price had used her as a courier to his contacts in Guatemala. Worse, she made no apologies for her status as an unattached mother of five with two marriages behind her, and she cast a shadow of doubt over Philip Goldson's marriage to Hadie Goldson, who was then in England studying law. Whatever the opinions of Taylor, Gillette, Seay, and Casasola, Goldson unleashed Rosita Williams on the PUP, and the effect she had on PUP gender politics seems to have been more dramatic than anything she could have accomplished had she remained within the ruling party.

Williams denounced Lizarraga as "a good woman who got in with the wrong crowd" and claimed that the United Women's Groups' sole function was to win votes for the PUP. Price, she maintained, had no intention of granting women house lots or houses.[32] She thus wove together two key opposition themes, that of the PUP's betrayal of women and its betrayal of the nation to Guatemala. The UWGS, meeting at their annual convention just days after Williams's allegations, duly expelled her.[33] But Goldson had embraced her as Belize's Joan of Arc, and her political career was on the ascendancy. Together they traveled to Cayo, where Williams challenged PUP representatives Santiago Perdomo and Hector Silva to disprove her allegations about Guatemala, and over the months they appeared on rostrums in almost every district.[34] When they addressed an open air NIP meeting in Belize City in May, a verbal and physical scuffle broke out with PUP hecklers, who labeled Williams a "weedsmoker," a "drunkard," and "Goldson wife," according to police testimony.[35] She in turn called them "happy cows and happy hogs from Cattleville," a reference to the strongly PUP politics of the village of Hattieville, set up for the homeless after the 1961 hurricane. More daringly, and completely violating middle-class women's dependence on respectability for public legitimacy, Williams accused George Price of homosexuality: "George does not want me. He wants a man. What the hell is he going to do with me?"[36] Apparently the hecklers had been suggesting that Williams had switched parties as a woman scorned, a woman determined to attach herself to one party leader or the other.

When Williams was found guilty of disorderly conduct, Goldson declared her to be a "Heroine of British Honduras" and inaugurated the sale of "Rosita ribbons" as a symbol of women's determination to defend the nation. Williams in turn announced that Goldson had asked her to organize the women of British Honduras "for the defense of their country." As a PUP activist, she implied, she had purchased women's votes with promises of housing, but now she would promise only "security for yourself and your children."[37] In short order Williams emerged as the national president of the Women Pioneers and continued to travel and campaign with Goldson, while Seay, Taylor, and Gillette staged the Save Our Country movement parade.

Rosita Williams embodied a kind of street politics, language, and sexuality that was both threatening and repugnant to respectable middle-class women. At the time of the September 10 celebrations of 1962, Williams declared from the rostrum in Belize City that she was not ashamed of her two marriages: "I am a woman and as a woman I should have had loves, and I had them but I have done nothing to be ashamed of."[38] Established NIP women were in no position to ice Williams out, and she won her place on the municipal slate by internal party vote. Defeated with the others, she was apparently removed as president of the Women Pioneers in February 1963,[39] although she was part of a high level NIP delegation to the governor in 1968.

PUP reactions to the Rosita phenomenon were initially retaliatory; she was expelled from the UWGS and denounced as Goldson's "dirty mouthpiece."[40] But she endured, a constant thorn in the party executive's side and a threat to their authority over party women. Soon enough, more constructive responses emerged, including the first fruits of the UWGS' four-year struggle for women's housing lots. Lizarraga began by calling on women to fight sexual corruption in defense of the nation's morals.[41] More significant was the founding of the United Women's Credit Union in October 1962, with 208 members and $4,000 in assets. Jane Robateau, one of the UWG councilors, was the secretary of the credit union, and May Davis—active in the Queen's Square housing group and elected national president of the UWGS in 1973—was also on the governing board.[42] This formalization of the process by which women saved and struggled for home ownership countered Williams's accusations that the UWGS were simply tools of the PUP patriarchs.

In February 1963 the government granted one hundred house lots in the new Queen's Square area to UWG women, announcing the move in a highly unusual editorial praising women's struggles for equality, jobs, and political voice.[43] Just before this, the PUP-linked Christian Workers' Union (CWU) founded a women's branch that it disingenuously claimed was the first women's union branch in Belizean history. Jane Robateau was elected president, a role that complemented her leadership positions in the UWGS and UWCU, while her fellow councilors Virginia Stanford and Enid Panting—both PUP veterans—became secretary and vice president.[44] There is no evidence that this women's labor organization contested the PUP leadership's faith in a Rostowian process of capitalist growth leading to a "plateau of plenty," women's position as cheap labor within that economic model, or labor's subordination to party politics. At most,

CWU women kept up a rather private pressure on government to include domestic servants in the labor law by 1965.

Robateau, Stanford, and—crucially—Elfreda Reyes of the NIP were all appointed in 1962 to the Labour Department's new Domestic Servants Committee, a major advance in the department's attention to female workers.[45] Reyes had carried her lifelong concern for working women into the Federation of Women after leaving the PUP in 1956 and had organized the federation's training program for women aiming to get jobs as domestics in Canada. In May 1962 the first women were at last departing for Canada, and the *Billboard* warned that there would be trouble if the federation's sixty trained women were not chosen.[46] When the uniquely bipartisan committee, which reunited Reyes and her sister Virginia, reported, it was to recommend extending all of the 1959 Labour Ordinance rights and protections to domestics working in commercial establishments and private homes. The gradual process of effecting this began in January 1963 and was completed by 1965 when full hours and overtime regulations were applied to domestics. Such measures were rendered virtually meaningless, however, as labour inspectors still could not visit private homes without prior permission from the owner-employer.[47]

In early 1963, however, as Price and the cabinet prepared for negotiations for a self-government constitution, the establishment of the CWU branch, the United Women's Credit Union, and the Queen's Square housing lots appeared to have effectively countered Rosita Williams' extralegislative challenge to the party. And then news of Nora Parham's killing of Ketchell Trapp broke, becoming the focus of public attention until June, when she was hanged. This fresh crisis gave Goldson, who marched in Parham's funeral procession, another opportunity to accuse the PUP of treating women callously.[48]

In the late 1963 town Board elections the NIP achieved its first victories of the decade, winning the Benque Viejo and Orange Walk Town Boards, although with all-male slates. Every one of the five PUP town boards had female representation, an unprecedented situation that reflected nationalist women's long years of party activism across the country. Stella Avilez was elected in Stann Creek, Maria Samos in Cayo, Erminda Vansen and Angelina Avila in Monkey River, Venancia Petillo in Punta Gorda, and Amy Watson in Corozal.[49] Just two women ran for the NIP, Maria Martinez Arellano in Cayo and Matilda Leon Zetina in Corozal, but both were defeated. For the PUP the numerical strength of female candidates in city council and town board elections was comparable; it was only at the legislative level that women virtually disappeared. For the NIP, the lack of female candidates in the districts was likely due to an overall weakness in organization, while their marked strength in Belize City politics at the municipal and legislative levels was a pattern with roots in middle-class Creole women's long-term development of public legitimacy.

In the March 1965 legislative elections the PUP ran Lizarraga, while the NIP's Helen Taylor contested the wealthy Fort George constituency and Tharine Rudon, who had left the PUP in 1956, ran against George Price in the Freetown division. Adding to this drama was the return of Hadie Goldson as Belize's first female lawyer, an event heralded by the *Billboard* in late 1964: "[A]ll women of British Honduras are thrilled, proud and happy that British Honduras now has its first woman Barrister. Years ago, Dr. Bernice Hulse became the first woman doctor of our country. The women are slowly but surely moving into the medical and legal professions, prepared to play their part in the building of our country."[50] The obvious subtext of this modern take on women's capacities was that educated women were NIP women, and that the country they would build would not be the Central American republic that the party regularly accused George Price of pursuing, but a British Honduran nation within the British Commonwealth. The NIP had already declared in its party manifesto that military training would be mandatory for men and voluntary for women and that it would appoint female magistrates to new juvenile courts.[51]

Tharine Rudon accompanied the reunited Goldsons on a campaign tour of the country, during which Hadie's higher education and Tharine's head-to-head fight with Price combined in an open discourse of activist women and nation-building. The tour kicked off in Benque Viejo, one of two NIP-controlled towns, where hundreds of local women, mainly mestizo and Mayan, came out to get a look at Hadie. But it was Rudon who electrified the crowd. "The women of British Honduras . . . made Price and the women must break him," she exclaimed. And when the tour reached Stann Creek, Rudon elaborated: "From the Hondo to the Sarstoon I am carrying the message—that the women must save our country. We women outnumber the men. We women are fighters when we understand an issue. We women don't beat around the bush. If we women go out and vote and bring out the men, British Honduras will be saved."[52] The popular imagination, according to NIP claims, had been captured by "the idea that the downfall of George Price should come about through a woman." For Yvonne Usher of Burrell Boom in rural Belize District, it was equally important to have a woman lawyer. In her welcome speech to the Goldsons she told Hadie: "Now that the women of this country have at last someone to come forward, and take over our problems and troubles, we will in the future get some kind of justice and peace."[53] Here was a popular longing not for an ideal patriarch, but for a female protector, another Madame Liz, implicitly coded as maternal.

Hadie, however, did not stay long in Belize to practice law or politics. Years later the *Times* contrasted the Rudon-Goldson tour of 1965 with Philip Goldson's unchaperoned campaigning with Rosita Williams in 1962 and accused him of "using [Hadie] to win votes during the 1965 campaign."[54] In this she was not much use, for both Taylor and Rudon went down to defeat, and Goldson's victory in the Albert division on Belize City's south side was likely due in large part to the heavily female leadership of his constituency organization. Its chair and vice chair were men, but Miss Theola Pinks was the secretary, assisted by Miss Valerie Pipersburgh, and the treasurer was Mrs. Sarah Perry. All five members of the divisional council were women, including Vivian Seay.[55] The victorious PUP named one woman, veteran Price loyalist Elsa Vasquez, to the Senate.[56]

The PUP rebounded from its slight legislative losses to again sweep the city council elections of December 1966, although the NIP won 46 percent of the popular vote.[57] Gwendolyn Lizarraga, now elevated to the cabinet, did not run, and Lois Encalada was the sole female in the municipal government. NIP candidates Helen Taylor, Leotine Gillette—by now one of the deputy leaders of the party—and Claire Gill were all defeated. Gillette, who was nominated by young NIP lawyer Dean Lindo and ran on the platform "democracy before independence," was described as "carry[ing] on the family tradition of fighting fiercely and stubbornly for the British Honduran heritage—the heritage of law and order and political stability and the Commonwealth link."[58] The PUP hailed Lindo as the leader of the "new intellectuals" within the NIP, those who felt that the emphasis on the Guatemalan threat was weakening the party's appeal to the general public.[59]

From 1966–68, however, that emphasis was reinforced rather than contested, for American mediator Bethuel Webster's distinctly pro-Guatemala recommendations were leaked in June 1966 and formally released in April 1968. Only then could the PUP officially reject them. NIP women were in fact prominent in January 1966 demonstrations to mark a visit to the colony by Webster, demonstrations which landed twenty-nine people in court for parading without a permit. These included Goldson, Taylor, Gillette, and other women.[60] In June when Goldson leaked the Webster proposals, a NIP crowd rioted in Belize City over two days, targeting Radio Belize, the homes of Price and cabinet ministers, and that of the Guatemalan consul.[61] In the aftermath, the Public Officers' Union staged a one-day strike that kept 70 percent of civil servants at home.[62]

In March 1968, with the final Webster proposals expected to recommend an independence fundamentally compromised by Guatemalan control, a twelve-woman NIP delegation went to the governor to demand electoral reform, elections before independence, a referendum on the Guatemalan issue, and an end to Radio Belize's monopoly of the airwaves.[63] They "informed his Excellency that as citizens, wives, mothers, sisters, and daughters they are deeply concerned with the future of their country," but he could do little for them. One, Mrs. Thelma Goodin, denounced his inaction by reiterating the typical 1960s NIP gender politics: "We women have taken the lead and we will continue to fight for our country and we are asking the men to follow."[64] Once Webster's proposals were made public and rejected by both parties as well as the LPOB, the Black Cross Nurses, and the remnant of the UNIA, the immediate threat of a Guatemalan takeover receded. It then became possible for Lindo to contest Goldson's leadership and, when defeated, to form his own People's Democratic Movement (PDM), just before the December 1969 national elections.

By that point, both parties were focused on controlling an unprecedented internal threat—young university-educated radicals returned from Britain and the United States who had entered the political fray at New Year's in 1969 by picketing the film *The Green Berets* as a protest against the Vietnam War. In February the Black Power group UBAD formed, and in May the leftist People's Action Committee (PAC) was established. Throughout 1969 UBAD and PAC mobilized particularly young people, with UBAD meetings in Belize City and Dangriga drawing huge crowds of young men and women disillusioned with party politics, the stymied struggle for independence and prosperity, and the PUP's rhetoric of "Christian Democracy" and the "peaceful, constructive Belizean revolution." When UBAD and PAC joined together in October 1969 and gained Senator Jesus Ken's allegiance, George Price was moved to quote Frantz Fanon in a speech urging the rising generation to channel its energy into the "peaceful constructive Belizean revolution."[65] And one of his cabinet ministers commented that the people were no longer looking for a Messiah: "They seem to want participation. . . . I think Mr. Price senses this change in the country."[66]

Party women were galvanized to counter the threat. In the late 1960s the UWGs had grown moribund, like the party base as a whole, the only area of positive activity being in Dangriga, where UWG women finally got homes in 1967–68. But in June 1969 Lizarraga led a rousing UWG public meeting denouncing UBAD and PAC as dangerous and unpatriotic. The following month Hadie Goldson, visiting from the US, led a reorganization of the Women Pioneers, beginning with elections that made her president, Helen Taylor second vice president, and Elfreda Reyes, now one of the party's deputy leaders, the representative from the Pickstock division.[67]

The young radicals bit back, suggesting that a marriage between Reyes and George Price would be a suitable symbol of the two parties' shared neocolonial conservatism and that Lizarraga's role in the PUP was to give the illusion that party women had power.[68] For the generation raised on nationalist promises and expectations of continuing economic growth and redistribution, women's incorporation into and importance within the PUP and NIP were simply signs of the party system's corruption and emasculation of the nation. Yet party competition, particularly in the period 1962–63 marked by Rosita Williams and the Save Our Country movement, had given women some leverage, and in the case of the NIP a pattern of female leadership and activism that endured. It was Goldson's female-dominated Albert division of the NIP that proposed the inclusion of women on juries, a policy that the party's 1968 convention endorsed.[69] In 1970 the PUP legislature finally made this proposal law. This was classic cooptation, like the ruling party's countering of Rosita Williams with the United Women's Credit Union, the Christian Workers' Union women's branch, and the Queen's Square house lots. In the early 1970s, Price would try the same strategy of dynamic control on the leftist radicals of PAC, encouraging fault lines within the radical coalition.

The Radical Challenge: Masculinity and the Politics of Protest

"The world intrudes," wrote V. S. Naipaul of Belize in 1969. "The sons of people once content with the Premier's benediction go away to study and come back and curse both parties. They talk of Vietnam and Black Power. They undermine the Negro loyalty to the slave past."[70] Like Charles Sutherland, who came home from World War One full of antiwhite and anti-imperialist rage, the Black Power and leftist radicals of the late 1960s and early 1970s confronted Belizean society with their passionate subversive analysis of neocolonialism. Unlike Sutherland and his coconspirators of 1919, these modern radicals went beyond rioting to build a fractured social movement that would, despite its brief existence, fundamentally alter Belizean political culture. Its gender politics, particularly those of UBAD, broke the sexual taboos of respectable Belizean society in a vigorous revindication of black manhood against white imperialism. This project embraced women as "sisters" and celebrated black women's beauty but also insisted on the primacy of male-led racial struggle as the path to national liberation for all. The radicals' connection of masculine power with political power was celebratory and intolerant of feminist critique.

Party politics, dominated by "she men and old women," was emasculating the nation.[71] The old women of the NIP and PUP were, like Susan
Sutherland, part of the problem, but the "bad, beautiful, Afro-Honduran
sisters" envisioned by UBAD were not to be like Annie Flowers, with her
biting critique of black manhood.[72]

The radical challenge had two factions, UBAD and the more openly
leftist PAC, formed in May 1969, which fiercely criticized the neocolonial
political economy and tried to politicize what it saw as UBAD's weaker
cultural emphasis on race. PAC, which gained the support of PUP Senator
Jesus Ken, was most active in the districts among Spanish-speaking peas-
ant-proletarians and sought to revitalize the labor movement as the base
of renewed nationalist struggle. PAC's principal leaders, Assad Shoman
and Said Musa, were both sons of male Palestinian immigrants to Belize
and both also returned from England in 1968 with law degrees. Musa won
the presidency of the Public Officers' Union in 1969, using his position to
raise a middle-class labor consciousness in preaching against civil service
elitism as well as government corruption.[73] But PAC did not talk about
women's role as cheap labor in the export-led economy, nor did it consciously encourage a gender-inclusive labor mobilization for independence and social justice. Its focus was rather narrowly on class. The PAC-
UBAD unity of October 1969 to February 1970 in the Revolitical Action
Movement (RAM) was always tenuous, and although Musa and Shoman
successfully defended UBAD leaders Evan X Hyde and Ismail Shabazz on
sedition charges in July 1970, UBAD condemned their subsequent joining
of the PUP as a betrayal of the people.

UBAD's politics were more unpredictable than PAC's—one former activist claimed that "nothing was thought out"[74]—but did employ a provocative gender analysis of PUP rule, party politics, and civil society that had
strong elements of homophobia and antifeminism. Neocolonial politics
were cast as those of weak men leading blind women like sheep to the
slaughterhouse.[75] After a PUP parade marking the party's nineteenth anniversary, the UBAD paper, Amandala, commented: "The new black generation stood quietly on the sidewalks and in the drains watching their mothers and grandmothers following the tune of the PUP piper. Our mothers

and grandmothers marched and gyrated and we watched because the sins of the fathers will be visited on the children."[76]

One of those sins was apparently allowing women such a prominent role in politics, for UBAD claimed radical change required the leadership of strong black men reclaiming their stolen power: "all non-white societies recognize the biological and spiritual need for men to exercise leadership."[77] Feminism was defined as a white middle-class movement— justifiably so in 1969—irrelevant to black women with national freedom and racial justice to win. In 1973, on the eve of UBAD's third Miss Afro-Honduras pageant, *Amandala* insisted that there was no need to apologize for the fact that "the UBAD Party has been a political party dominated by men."[78] While a private critique of leading UBAD men's sexual and social behavior seems to have been carried on among UBAD women, publicly they made the most of what space they had to serve their community and reshape their own identities.[79]

Only two women ever held executive positions in UBAD, both for brief periods. Penny Casasola served as assistant secretary from UBAD's founding in February 1969 to about June of that year.[80] Lillette Barkeley was elected secretary general of the new UBAD Party, formed immediately after the sedition acquittals in July 1970. She had studied in Jamaica at the University of the West Indies until 1969 and left Belize for the United States in February 1971, so both her tenure and her involvement in UBAD were brief.[81] As secretary general she wrote UBAD's letter protesting the government's treatment of hospital ward maids, who struck in September and October 1970. UBAD gave strong support to the strikers through *Amandala*, for once portraying women as rights-bearing citizens and the backbone of society.[82] With Barkeley's departure the executive reverted to its all-male state, with Evan X Hyde, Ismail Shabazz, Norman Fairweather, Rufus X, and Charles X Stamp, and Galento X Neal dominating.

They had apparently tried to organize a women's section within the movement as early as August 1969, but it never took institutional form.[83] There was, however, a cadre of "sisters" whose work for the movement and in the community provided a less visible kind of continuity. Among these was Eleanor Gill, who ran UBAD's breakfast program for poor children from July 1969, when it started, to at least August 1970.[84] Blossome Peters was working in the UBAD bakery in August 1969, Alva Vansie and Jane Spanish were preparing the newspaper in April 1970, and Ursula Sabal had done office work for UBAD prior to June 1970.[85] Women also "worked long, smoky hours without pay preparing food for the different party functions."[86] Bert Tucker recalls Eleanor Reneau, an X-ray technician at the hospital, as a strong and ongoing force within the organization, as a mobilizer and political educator.[87] She was the organizer of the third and final Miss Afro-Honduras pageant in August 1973.

Lillette Barkeley had organized the original pageant in September 1970, leading the Miss Afro-Honduras Committee, which was composed of "UBAD Party sisters."[88] It was the first project UBAD women fully controlled, selecting and preparing the contestants, designing the African-style clothing made at Galento X Neal's tailor shop, and pulling together a panel of judges that included Assad Shoman. The second staging of the pageant was in May 1972, when Sandra Fairweather, wife of UBAD secretary general Norman Fairweather, was the principal organizer, and the majority of contestants sported Afros.[89] When Eleanor Reneau took on the organization of the third pageant, *Amandala* commented: "At this time of year . . . when the UBAD Party is preparing for the Miss Afro-Honduras pageant, it is the women who take over direction of the party. The Miss Afro-Honduras pageant is our sisters' thing: through this medium they will express their beauty, culture, fashion and creativity in a distinctively Belizean way."[90]

Lillette Barkeley recalls that the pageant provided a forum in which black girls, shut out from the rival September pageants of the political parties, could develop positive self-esteem in both personal and racial terms. While there is no doubt that this was a radical challenge to enduring colonial standards of female beauty, it remained a ritualized form of physical and sexual competition among young women. Barkeley, Fairweather, and Reneau were hardly breaking new ground either, as women in the LPOB and both political parties had been organizing pageants for years. On a very personal level, the pageant did not alter the power dynamics defining life as a black woman in Belize. Barkeley, Fairweather, and the first two pageant winners all followed the distinctly Belizean strategy of leaving for the United States.[91] Tragically, the third winner was murdered in 1981, reportedly at the hands of her husband.[92] Even then, seven years after UBAD ceased to exist except as invoked by Hyde in the pages of *Amandala*, the paper maintained the movement's defense of men, suggesting that the husband was provoked by an affair between his wife and a younger man. Indeed, UBAD women's acceptance of men's alleged biological and spiritual need to be in charge had never been assumed by UBAD leaders, whose attitude to female power was always deeply ambivalent.

Hyde expressed this ambivalence in explicitly sexual and racial terms in his account of his undergraduate years at Dartmouth College, in which he dismissed "white man dregs" as below his sexual standards, while making it clear that he had conquered his share of pretty white girls.[93] If Malcolm X could satisfy his lust for white women, *Amandala* implied, why not UBAD's leading men?[94] This account was written in 1971, the year of Hyde's divorce from his Creole wife, and the same year that *Amandala* cited Shoman's marriage to a white English woman as evidence of his capacity for cooptation by the PUP, which Shoman had just joined.[95] Black women had to be convinced that feminism was a foreign, imperialist, white poison, produced by women whom Hyde denigrated as sexual objects.

Feminism was a threat to the movement's claims to represent black women's sexual and political needs. An early article titled "Woman in Islam," probably of North American origin, argued that women's fundamental need was to be under male control or else they would become "treacherous, disloyal, unrighteous."[96] Appearing at a time when UBAD was reasserting its Black Power credentials after the unhappy union with PAC, this piece clearly defined the movement's dominant gender ideology. UBAD also denounced women's use of birth control as genocidal and instructed them to stop straightening and processing their hair. "Woman" was repeatedly cast as the supporter of her man, working with him but remaining his sexual and political subordinate. UBAD's strongest attack on feminism argued that it was trivial, unnecessary for black women's freedom and full self-realization. Their struggle was for racial equality, a "man-sized" task leaving no time to worry about "whether men see her as just a plaything with which to satisfy their sexual desires [or] to worry whether men purposely made her into a house drudge."[97]

Beginning in 1973, UBAD toned down this kind of rhetoric and began to open up *Amandala* to a variety of opinions on issues of sexuality and gender relations. But as late as 1979 Hyde made room in his paper for Rufus X, former vice president of UBAD, to articulate the movement's foundational obsession with male authority and power. Rufus X began to publish a men's magazine, *Fun and Games*, in 1979, the first issue featuring black female models in swimsuits. A woman named Lois Bower wrote to *Amandala* denouncing the magazine as a perpetrator of "black sexism," only to be labeled "frigid and mentally insane" by Rufus X. He argued that his magazine was "a stepping stone for black women's liberation in Belize. Exposure is what our women need in Belize."[98] Bower then questioned this concept of liberation in explicitly feminist terms:

> I understand [liberation] to signify freedom of choice and opportunity in the political, economic, and social spheres of life, and for women to share this freedom equally with men. Social stigma and stereotypes are difficult to erase, the inclusion of scantily-clad models perpetuates the sexist image of the primary role of women. Journalism of this type can only reinforce society's pictorial view of women and in so doing deny them credibility as equal participants in the workforce. This denial limits their job opportunities to the less intellectually demanding and less responsible positions. More injuriously, it lowers their own expectations and inhibits their aspirations and self-confidence. How can this negation of social progress be a vision of a "liberated society wherein a black woman will be most proud to set foot?" I urge . . . the editor of *Fun and Games* to expose the strivings and achievements of Belizean women in a manner which encourages their recognition as equally valuable and capable members of society. In so doing, you will help to dispel the myth that women's most important asset is the sensual form of her body.[99]

Rufus X's response to this feminist onslaught was to insist that racial struggle would liberate women as well as men, backing away from his earlier claims to be promoting women's liberation: "If someone wants to publish a woman's liberation magazine, that's cool with me. I'm not a woman, and I'm not a woman's liberationist. I respect the beauty, talent, brains and guts of quite a few women, but women's liberation is not the solution to the black community's problems in Belize. The WHOLE COUNTRY needs liberation, then everybody will be fine." In fact, he claimed, "ghetto man" was more oppressed than his female counterpart, "to the point where he is a man kept by a seamstress"—this last comment a reference to the Williamson-Dickie garment factory. And harking back to the movement's earliest denunciation of party politics as an emasculation of Belizean men, he concluded: "So please do not bring the problems of women and the white middle class woman liberation movement to me. If you sisters believe that you are oppressed, then you work on the problems of women in a colonial society. I'm a man and I know that I'm being suppressed. I'm working on the problems of being a man in a colonized, claimed, and castrated society."

In the last years of colonial rule, however, both Belizean women like Lois Bower and Evan X Hyde himself had begun to discuss gender oppression as one of the problems of women in a neocolonial society. From 1968–74, while mobilized as the UBAD movement and party, Belizean Black Power had primarily politicized gender relations in terms of masculine leadership and female support, women's African beauty and men's approval of it. With the demise of the UBAD Party in the 1974 legislative elections, coinciding with the beginning of the UN Decade on Women, *Amandala* became probably the most important forum in the country for discussion of gender issues. Lois Bower could not have aired her views in the PUP's newspaper in 1979.

As early as 1973 Hyde allowed, in an editorial endorsing the PUP's pronatalist population policy, that birth control was acceptable at an individual level, if only to prevent the worse crime of abortion. Soon after, the Mercy Sisters of St. Catherine's Academy announced their decision to allow pregnant high school students to remain in class. Assad Shoman's spirited defense of the policy against its moralistic critics was not the only voice of progress.[100] Hyde published Garifuna artist Philip Lewis's condemnation of "this society's false sense of propriety and delicateness" and urged a greater discussion of "the enormous problem of sexual ignorance and abuse in Belizean society."[101] Unwed motherhood, Lewis argued, extended well beyond St. Catherine's gates and was compounded by men's pride in biologically fathering many children. He alluded to the physical and emotional toll of illegal abortions and advocated sex education geared to increasing girls' use of contraception. Lewis's critique of male behavior, mild as it was, posed an implicit challenge to UBAD's gender politics as well as to PUP policy.

By 1975 Hyde, although still opposed to population control as a national antipoverty policy, acknowledged that a Belizean feminism had taken root and perceptively identified its fundamental task as being to resolve the contradiction between rampant male chauvinism in sexual terms and Belizean women's political militance and clout.[102] This was no call for an extension of male dominance but rather a late-blooming appreciation of the female activism previously dismissed as party-bound and emasculating. Heeding his own call for open political discussion between the sexes, Hyde invited public views on abortion in late 1975. "Liberated Woman" wrote to argue for contraception over abortion, the latter being a "crime and a sin." Two responses to her position appeared, one arguing that abortions were sometimes necessary, the other actually advocating the legalization of abortion in Belize. This writer, also a woman, did not consider a first trimester fetus to be a person and defined the real crime as dangerous illegal abortions.[103] Evidently the absence of any independent women's organizations did not mean that feminist opinions were not gaining ground among young Belizean women.

Always sensitive to shifts in popular culture, Hyde wove the issue of abortion into his unfolding serialized soap opera, "Ros'lin," in 1976–77. This was an immensely popular story in pretelevision Belize, for it captured and exaggerated the urban youth culture that UBAD's early 1970s supporters had created and were living. Ros'lin, a young woman living with her grandmother, became pregnant by her handsome, irresponsible boyfriend, Dorian, and with a girlfriend's help took bush medicine, successfully terminating the pregnancy.[104] Her subsequent trials included surviving an attempted rape by her mother's boyfriend and a beating by Dorian after they finally married, but Hyde never portrayed her as suffering for her sins. Indeed his fiction increasingly suspended moral judgment as the 1970s wore on.

By 1977, during a brief period of supporting the PUP, Hyde was ready to admit on the editorial page what was already common knowledge: that illegal abortions occurred every day in Belize City, and that some of them were fatal to the women involved. "The law condemns and the churches condemn but our women continue to find it necessary and in fact urgent to flout the law and defy the churches. . . . Personally and instinctively we are against abortion but we respect the opinion of the individual pregnant woman."[105] Hyde went down to defeat as a PUP city council candidate in 1977, but continued to be moved by women's persistence in seeking illegal abortions, as in this editorial responding to groundless rumors that the PUP was on the verge of legalizing abortion. "[T]he volume of its incidence, the plaintive cries of abandoned mothers-to-be, the belligerent brutality meted out to unwanted children—these factors have led us to the unpopular opinion that negative dogmatic opinions on this matter may have to be revised."[106]

This fell well short of an endorsement of women's reproductive rights, of course, and Hyde never criticized UBAD's definition of birth control as genocide or its fetishizing of black female beauty in the Miss Afro-Honduras pageants. In the Rufus X-Lois Bower dispute he provided space to both opinions, offering, as in the "Ros'lin" saga, a nonjudgmental airing of the issues.

UBAD women mounted no public or organized feminist critique of the movement. Like the PUP for its female supporters, UBAD created a strong and proud identity, although in racial rather than partisan terms. Even the three pageants served on one level to counter the self-doubt and insecurity fostered by mass media images of white beauty and by local colonial standards of Belizean beauty. But the Miss Afro-Honduras pageant, when compared to the LUA's Women's League, with its multiracial female identity and fight for women's suffrage and labor rights, or to the

Black Cross Nurses' enduring community activism, stands as a symbol of Black Power's dominant *machismo*. The movement politicized sexuality and gender oppression, defining an arena that emerging feminist voices could then enter and transform, but was never feminist in itself. UBAD from 1969–74 and *Amandala* from 1969 to independence and beyond confronted the party system with a radical masculinity, as Soberanis had done with the colonial regime in the 1930s, but unlike him they defined their project in terms of that masculinity. They delegitimized traditional party paternalism without directly nurturing, as Soberanis had, a semiautonomous female mobilization.

The Birth of Belizean Feminism

Like Lois Bower, the women of the Belize Committee for Women and Development found that Evan X Hyde's *Amandala* was open to their analysis of women's oppression in Belize. In late 1980 they placed three features in the paper, one on women's oppression as consumers of imported goods, one advocating a national family planning policy, and the third linking women's poverty to the myth of the male breadwinner and to gender bias in education.[107] And in August 1981 the paper hailed committee coordinator Zoila Ellis, just admitted to the bar, as "a positive social action sister."[108] Cynthia Ellis's sister, Zoila was running the new Legal Aid Centre, where she helped mainly female clients during the day and hosted BCWAD meetings after work.[109] The women who came to those meetings at the end of their own workdays were almost all middle-class women with secondary or postsecondary education and with white collar or professional jobs. None of them were in the PUP.

The committee's first coordinator was in fact Bette Lindo, then wife of UDP leader Dean Lindo, and older sister of former UBAD leader Norman Fairweather.[110] Dean Lindo emerged as party leader after six UDP candidates won seats in the 1974 elections, but when the party lost the 1979 elections, he was replaced by Dr. Theodore Aranda of Dangriga, who had little control of Belize City UDP women. Another early committee member was lawyer Cynthia Pitts, whose mother Eudora Pitts, daughter of Calvert Staine, was part of the victorious UDP slate in the 1977 city council elections.[111] Gwynneth Gillett, an active UDP member, also belonged to the committee in its early period. Zoila Ellis's direct participation, and Cynthia Ellis's ongoing support while in Holland pursuing graduate studies, fortified the group's independence from party politics as well as its feminist critique. Garifuna, and daughters of a career civil servant, they had both freedom from the cultural influence of the Belize City Creole establishment and the experience of studying in Manley's Jamaica in the 1970s. They had the keenest awareness of the limits of party politics in general, not just the nationalist project, for women and were most interested in going beyond the class and ethnic boundaries of the original membership.[112] These women were bound loosely together by an unevenly shared hostility to the PUP and an equally uneven commitment to challenging the political and cultural limits on women's rights and freedoms.

When the UN Decade for Women began in 1975, the PUP had difficulty in finding the language to make the "women and development" paradigm mesh with the record and policies of the nationalist project. The issue was handled in the women's column of the *Belize Times*, where "Cousin Alma" was accustomed to holding forth on fruit preserves and household decoration. At first Alma interpreted International Women's Year as a formal tribute to the women who had sacrificed to build a better Belize, reproducing the PUP's standard discourse on mothers as the bulwark of the nation. But soon she saw the need to fend off potential critiques of the PUP, first by asserting that "the Belizean woman . . . has been liberated for many years," then by attributing any residual inequalities to "years of slavish colonialism" and the colonialist activities of the new Women's Action Movement (WAM) of the UDP, whose members Alma attacked as "black backras."[113] Possibilities for a gendered self-critique within the ruling party seemed very slim.

By 1977 the government had settled on the argument that women's liberation was about harnessing all of women's energies and talents for national development. Sewing groups run by the Social Development Department in rural Belize District, for example, were "broadening [women's] horizon and their inputs to their society."[114] Women and development policy would encourage "the full utilization of women's human and material

potential in the development process."[115] Existing limits on women's freedom had not been put in place by "chauvinists" but were coincidences
of "circumstance, financial and educational." In fact, not until the nation
reached a higher level of economic development would women be able
to go beyond the traditional female professions of nursing, teaching, and
social work. Women, like all workers, were to wait for the inevitable downfall of barriers to national development.

Mrs. Elaine Middleton, who had been head of the Social Development
Department since the late 1960s, did not accept her political bosses' self-
serving argument. Her dissent may have emerged as early as 1968, when
a study by the British Honduras Christian Social Council, which the
department actively supported, criticized the PUP government's under-
staffing of the department, general disregard for social work, and hostility to family planning.[116] In the 1970s she seemed to become increasingly
frustrated with the PUP's unchanging program of home economics for
women's groups across the country. In 1971 she wrote a scathing critique
of the child maintenance system, portraying it as a burden on women
rather than a benefit to them and their children.[117] In 1975 she attended the
Caribbean conference on women where the regional response to the UN
Decade was first discussed, the beginning of a process culminating in an
official regional plan in 1978.[118] Cynthia Ellis, whom Middleton hired that
year as a community development consultant, maintains that Middleton
pioneered women and development programs in Belize.[119] Certainly the
pair's two-week workshop in June 1979, titled "Participatory Techniques
for Working with Women," funded by the University of the West Indies'
new Women in Development Unit, had a very different emphasis from the
typical courses on fruit preservation and needlework.[120]

One of Middleton's goals for the workshop was very likely to acceler-
ate the establishment a Women's Bureau within the state, an aspect of the
regional plan being implemented in other CARICOM nations. Legislation
passed in 1980, but the Women's Bureau did not become functional until
mid-1981, when Zee Edgell was hired as its first director.[121] In her novel
based on this experience, Edgell made it clear that neither PUP politicians
nor the male elders of the civil service had any intention of allowing the

bureau to serve or mobilize women outside of partisan and administrative channels. Indeed, she suggests that Middleton hired her against the PUP brass's wishes and without consulting the UWG leadership.[122] Early BCWAD member Cynthia Pitts recalls that the government was pressured into opening the bureau: "We really forced the government to consider opening up a Women's Desk . . . because here was this NGO showing them up."[123] Edgell acknowledged as much at the time of her appointment: "Women have always been involved in development. Those [non-government] organizations were the foundations of the Women's Bureau."[124]

Indeed, the June 1979 workshop's first result was the formation of the Belize Committee for Women and Development as a nongovernment organization. In March 1980 the committee's coordinator, Bette Lindo, traced its origins to the June workshop and described it as in an "embryonic stage."[125] Its functions were, in her words, "to act as a clearinghouse of information and ideas about women's issues, concerns and activities[,] . . . to enhance co-ordination and co-operation of existing women's groups and non-government organizations[,] [and] to sensitize society at large about women's problems and the need to involve women totally in the development process."

By then Middleton had already invited the committee to review the International Year for Children committee's ten-year plan for Belizean children and had included the Ellis sisters, Pitts, and Sadie Vernon from the Christian Social Council on a committee to review laws on women and children.[126] Out of these processes came the 1980 Status of Children Ordinance, which equalized the inheritance rights of legitimate and illegitimate children. The government's own propaganda magazine acknowledged that the legal change was urgently needed "in a society like so many others in this region where the 'macho' image is strongly asserted and continues to prevail," although it encouraged "the establishment of the stable family unit where mother and father are legally married to each other."[127] Zoila Ellis commented on the new law in BCWAD's first issue of *Network*, pointing out the tension reproduced in the official coverage: "There is . . . a serious contradiction between the ideal we claim to live by and the standards which we do, in fact, live by."[128] Unlike the PUP, she refused to judge common-law marriage, simply insisting that so widespread and accepted an institution deserved legal protection and praising the erasure of illegitimate children's legal disabilities.

Bette Lindo attempted to define the committee's collective purpose in the first issue of *Network* as a search for "an indigenous programme which is relevant to the needs of Belizean women."[129] In 1981 the committee was apparently concerned with its middle-class profile, for it insisted that its "collective aim is to cover a wide cross-section and [it] tries very hard not to be elitist in nature. The hope is, that we will be able to develop a mix that will be representative of the needs of the widest cross-section of women in Belizean society."[130] But until December 1981, when the committee organized a rural women's health workshop in the village of Sand Hill, the group's main activity was the publishing of two issues of their journal, issues that revealed the ongoing diversity of opinion among BCWAD members.

The first issue included a short life history of Black Cross Nurse Cleopatra White, clearly as an attempt to give women's organizing some historical roots, a review of Esther Boserup's *Woman's Role in Economic Development*, and an account of the July 1980 Copenhagen conference on women. These were written by, respectively, Shelmadine Faux, Kay Tillet, and Velda Aguet. Tillet, the issue's editor, was one of the more conservative members. In 1983 at a BCWAD self-evaluation workshop, she asked that the group stop using the word "sister," as its communist associations disturbed her.[131] Aguet, née Fairweather, was Bette Lindo's second cousin and worked at the Council of Voluntary Social Services, a coalition of charity and community service agencies dependent to some degree on government funding but politically oriented toward the opposition.[132] Neither Tillet nor Aguet remained in the group after about 1984, when the UDP finally won national elections.

The boldest analyses in the first issue of *Network* came from the Ellis sisters. Zoila, as discussed above, wrote on the new Status of Children Ordinance, a topic suited to her legal training. Cynthia, then in a master's program in Development Studies in Holland, contributed a broad analysis of the causes and dimensions of women's oppression in Belize, based in part on dependency theory.[133] But like Zoila she offered a cultural analysis as well, arguing that the colonial ideal of the male-headed nuclear family meant that "although the woman is given the heavy responsibility of reproduction and nurturing of the species, she is not given full recognition for this." Belizean education channeled women into home economics, nursing, and teaching, where, defined as nonbreadwinners, they earned low salaries; "male-dominated" Belizean trade unions made no effort to argue or organize against this situation. The government, "for religious and cultural reasons," refused to implement family planning programs, "yet it is believed that illegal abortions are performed, and contraceptives are available at pharmacies for those who can afford them." She concluded by questioning the very idea that bringing women into the development process was the solution, for clearly women's work was the glue holding the national economy together.

In the second issue of *Network* Cynthia Ellis proposed her own solutions to women's oppression in Belize. Building women's unity across ethnic, generational, party, and class divisions was fundamental as was organizing outside the state. Ellis defined both revolutionary and reformist women's politics, concluding that: "Since Belizean women do not at this point in history see it necessary to break down the existing system, the reformist approach seems to be more suitable."[134] Yet even reformist feminism should work against politicians' harnessing of women's political talents in a party rivalry divisive of female unity. Belizean women, she argued, "have struggled and supported each other. . . . As long as women remain atomized and separated and view each other as competitors they remain weak."

But the committee itself was less than unified. Most members were comfortable with the discourse of "women and development" as it allowed a kind of modernization of the politics of charity, but they remained wedded to class division, respectability, and the importance, if not primacy, of party politics. During the unrest of March and April 1981, caused by the PUP administration's and Guatemalan dictatorship's agreement on a list of topics for discussion and that resulted in the declaration of martial law, Bette Lindo was arrested for picketing a government building, presumably as a UDP supporter. Years later Cynthia Ellis was still bitter about the government's stifling of popular dissent at that time, and its "imposition" of independence.[135] Judging by BCWAD's lack of activity for much of 1981, it seems that the political crisis temporarily returned women's energies to partisan politics and the politics of independence, but neither did they completely abandon the committee's work.

Perhaps even more difficult to deal with was the politics of class within the committee, for not only did they make it hard for middle-class women to ally themselves with "grassroots" women, but they made many women reluctant to mobilize around the issues of abortion, violence, and single motherhood raised by the Ellis sisters. Zoila Ellis recalls that most of the membership was uncomfortable with even private discussions of sexuality or domestic abuse. She found her work with female clients at Legal Aid far more intense and interesting, for it forced her to grapple in a very direct way with real problems of unpaid maintenance, unhappy marriages, and domestic violence.[136] She persevered, however, and recruited her client Rita Garcia as the first working-class women in the group. Garcia, a laundress, factory seamstress, domestic, and shop clerk at different times, came to Ellis for help in securing court-ordered child maintenance from her exhusband. But she emphasized that Ellis was her ally, not her savior: "I was woman enough to stand on my own and take him to court."[137] At her first committee meeting, Lynda Moguel encouraged her to "talk up," but no other members were overtly friendly until Diane Haylock joined a few months later, the first of the middle-class women besides Ellis to ask Garcia about her life and visit her at home, and the only one to become a "soul sister." Other "grassroots" women who joined at about the same time were Olivia Rhaburn and Yvonne Jeffries.

Among the more conservative group were, as mentioned, Kay Tillet and Velda Aguet, as well as Sadie Vernon and teachers Gwynneth Gillet and Jennifer Smith. Cynthia Pitts remembers Vernon and Aguet as the founders of the committee, while Lynda Moguel, then principal of St. Hilda's College, the Anglican girls' high school, remembers Elaine Middleton and the Ellis sisters as the driving force.[138] Apparently Aguet, who "could not take this group of professional women," was particularly at odds with

Moguel and the Ellises.[139] Of the original group, only Moguel, Garcia, and Gaynor Palacio, an office worker and cultural activist with Square Peg Players, who joined in 1981, maintained an uninterrupted commitment to BOWAND in the 1980s, along with former UDP organizer Diane Haylock, who joined in 1983.[140] While the Ellises branched off into other areas of activism and professional work, most early committee members drifted away entirely as the small activist core continued to emphasize cross-class unity and an approach to sexuality and reproduction that, while moderate, eschewed moral judgment.

The committee's first community workshop, in Sand Hill in December 1981, emphasized the theme "Women Working Toward our own Solutions" and was cosponsored with the Belize Agricultural Society and the Extramural Department of the University of the West Indies. Sixty women from twelve villages attended and told the Belize City feminists about their problems: a lack of health care in the villages, the difficulty of communication among the villages, and their problems of getting their farm produce to the Belize City market.[141] The committee, finally released from the pressures of the independence struggle, held five rural women's health workshops in 1982, in rural Belize District, in Orange Walk, and in the Stann Creek District.[142] Returning to Sand Hill in February 1982 with government nurses, an agricultural officer, an education officer, and a magistrate, the committee provided village women with a forum for discussing divorce, women's land ownership, contraception, and gender-biased school texts. In her letter thanking Shoman as minister of health for his help with the workshop, Zoila Ellis emphasized the importance of improving rural women's health as part of national development and hoped for an ongoing relationship of mutual cooperation and respect between BCWAD and government.[143]

The committee also elaborated a three-year plan in 1982, set up a booth at the popular Agriculture Show, and pursued its Urban Food Project, started in late 1981 and funded by Canadian University Services Overseas. This was never successful, for the twelve women who participated had never been asked about their needs and were not really interested in urban gardening as a form of income-generation.[144] More impressive was the

March 1982 Cultural Market Day, a Belizean celebration of International Women's Day. Through their contacts with village women, committee members Zoila Ellis, Lynda Moguel, Cynthia Pitts, and Regina Martinez organized a festival featuring women's cultural, agricultural, and business talents.[145] Its highlight was the performance of "Mantenance," a play about women's struggles with the state's child maintenance system and with their children's fathers. Planning for the second Cultural Market Day began in January 1983; three BOWAND representatives, two Women's Bureau staff, and other civil servants from various cooperating departments and programs were on this committee.[146] A newsletter was produced just for the celebration that featured contributions from BCWAD-linked women's groups in the villages of May Pen and Hattieville.[147]

By this time Zee Edgell had left the Women's Bureau, which PUP supporter Dorla Bowman was running with Regina Martinez as her only staff member. The government also appointed the National Women's Commission in early 1983 to direct and guide the Women's Bureau.[148] Its members included Jane Usher, deputy minister of health, housing and coops (and George Price's sister) and younger PUP activists Phyllis Cayetano from Dangriga, Natalia Moguel from Orange Walk, and Lilia Zaiden from Cayo. Zaiden was active in Shoman's large and vibrant Cayo North PUP branch from the late 1970s, at once a party dissident and devotée. Adding to the mix were Elaine Middleton and Charles Hunter S. J. Middleton was very likely dismayed by Edgell's departure and by the PUP's determination to curb nonpartisan state action against women's oppression.

Yet she must have taken some satisfaction in the committee's survival and evolution into BOWAND by 1983, four difficult dramatic years after its beginnings. It had not resolved issues of class—indeed problems arose as some members hired others as domestic help. Rita Garcia commented on this situation later in the 1980s: "That has been a problem and is still a problem. Even though you and that individual meet in one room, talk, yet still that person has that certain instinct in her that she is still beyond you at the point that she is making more money than you and you is her maid! . . . If we could get the majority of women in my rank we would have to build a . . . stronger foundation."[149] BOWAND was not some mythical, purely feminist organization, magically free of the divisions of class, culture, and party that had shaped all previous women's mobilizations in twentieth-century Belize. It was, however, by the time of Cultural Market Day on 8 March 1982, a small but energetic space autonomous of all male leaders, a critic of the labor movement, the political parties, the schools and the churches, a voice that kept on arguing that women's problems and women's rights were of crucial importance in Central America's and the Caribbean's newest nation.

Conclusion

From 1961 to 1982, women outside the PUP had the greatest motivation and ability to politicize gender inequality and oppression. In the civil service and the NIP, in PAC and UBAD, and finally in the Belize Committee for Women and Development, women—some of whom came to call themselves feminists—analyzed and criticized the limits and abuses of the nationalist project. Only with the emergence of the committee did those critiques become significantly autonomous from the demands of racial and partisan solidarity, although class divisions continued to be potent. The committee's survival from 1979–1981 and its postindependence transformation and growth as BOWAND contrast with the limited ability of the Women's Bureau (now the Department of Women's Affairs [DWA]) and the party women's groups to change the state and the two political parties from within. Mobilization in civil society—as in 1919, 1934–36, 1950–54, 1969–70—again proved more effective in promoting democratic practice and provoking state reform.

   Challenges from outside the PUP in the 1961–1982 period, like the Save Our Country movement and Rosita Williams's accusations, gave the PUP's United Women's Groups some leverage with the centralized party elite. The UWGs had to be courted, and house lots proved a fairly effective antidote to the NIP's surprisingly liberal gender politics of the 1960s. When the radical challenge emerged, PUP women stood with Price and the party and were mocked for their blind trust by the new generation. UBAD's own gender politics proved equally complex, not enabling of a black Belizean feminism within the movement but ultimately promoting public discussion of thorny gender issues.

The women who formed BCWAD in 1979–81 came out of the partisan opposition, the civil service and teaching professions, university education, and to some extent the radical period, but not out of the PUP. The struggles of women in the popular-nationalist tradition did help to forge a nation in which a cadre of educated, employed, middle-class women could organize, but with the nation *still* to be won, thirty years after the eruption of popular nationalism, PUP women maintained their public silence about gender oppression within the nation. In 1963 Gwendolyn Lizarraga and her UWGS made no public protest against Nora Parham's execution. The hopeful emergence of BCWAD sixteen years later, while tremendously significant, should not blind us to the fact that, for all PUP women's creative and critical activism within their party, they continued to place their hopes in national independence and in patron-client relations within the party. BCWAD, on the other hand, disillusioned with the nationalist project and with partisan and radical challenges to it—reversed the statist orientation of almost all women's activism in twentieth-century Belize—and began to forge a postindependence Belizean feminism even before the lowering of the Union Jack at midnight on 21 September 1981.

Conclusion

Gender and History in the Making of Modern Belize

You have to know them (the ancestors) and you have to know that these were the problems and this was how they dealt with them, you have to know that this was how the women of your past, or your race or of your nation have dealt with it, and you have to look and you have to shake their hands still and know that this was their way of coping. But it does not necessarily mean that you have to do it this way. I'm making the same claim for the history of the nation—that you have to go back and look at it, no matter how distressing, no matter how dirty, no matter how your myths have to be destroyed, you have to decide whether you're going to live with it, whether you're going to forget it, or—hopefully—you say, well it's so it go and let me do my piece and claim it.

[ERNA BRODBER in Evelyn O'Callaghan, *Woman Version: Theoretical Approaches to West Indian Fiction by Women*]

In 1991 female employees at Civic Textiles, a foreign-owned garment factory in Belmopan, formed the Women Workers' Union (WWU) to fight poor working conditions. When management fired the WWU's leaders, the all-female labor force went on strike. A coalition of nongovernment organizations, including BOWAND, supported the WWU and eventually shamed the Labour Department into upholding the labor laws (a success unfortunately not repeated in 2001–04 with regard to environmental laws by those attempting to stop the Chalillo Dam on the upper Macal River). The late Elizabeth Waight, a WWU leader, was later hired by BOWAND to research the garment industry countrywide.[1] According to the Department of

Women's Affairs (DWA), the Civic Textiles strike—the first ever action by an *independent* female union—prompted the PUP administration to pass a minimum wage law in 1992, making $2.25 per hour the standard.[2] BOWAND campaigned against the exclusion of domestics from that law and then the setting of $1.50 per hour as their minimum wage. In early 1993 the government responded by raising domestics' minimum wage to $1.75 per hour, still unsatisfactory, but evidence that organized women outside the party system could have some political impact.[3] Simultaneously, the Belize Women Against Violence organization (WAV), founded in 1985, was, with the collaboration of BOWAND and DWA, lobbying for the passage of the Domestic Violence Bill. In 1993 it became law, and WAV opened a shelter for abused women in Belize City. A year later DWA condemned government's "failure to put in place the necessary mechanisms to avoid domestic and other physical violence, and failure to take due legal action to prevent repeat offences."[4]

The early 1990s were a high point of postindependence feminist activism in Belize. A loose coalition of groups politicized women's ongoing subordination in the labor market as well as domestic violence (though less so the ongoing criminalization of abortion that results in unsafe illegal abortions). That civil society groups could ally with the DWA, and that the DWA could articulate such a strong critique of the government, indicates the growth and diversification of Belizean feminism after independence in 1981. That government could still get away with legal discrimination against domestics and with making a mockery of the domestic violence law suggests that Belizean feminists were fighting an uphill battle against politically entrenched male power and state paternalism. A full history of women's organizing in the 1980s and 1990s, and of various groups' and leaders' connections to the two political parties, is beyond the scope of this book.[5] But the history it offers of the seven decades of women's political activism and gendered state policy that shaped Belize's two main political traditions—that of colonial-middle-class reform and that of popular labor-nationalism—as well as the making of this improbable nation-state provides the groundwork for further study. Transformative as much as additive, this book enables scholars and students to incorporate Belize into their comparative analyses of gender, race, colonialism, and national-ism in Latin America, the Caribbean, the African diaspora, and the British Empire. It can also enable Belizeans to claim the inseparable histories of colony, nation, women and gender, to appreciate and critically examine them, even while creating their own ways of coping with and changing the present.

Unlike any previous political history of Belize, this book has established that women were active in both political traditions—indeed, in their nineteenth-century precursors—starting the 1910s, often as pioneers and leaders, always as critical alliance partners. Female activism, whether lim-ited to Belize Town or emerging countrywide, had clear effects on the nature and legitimacy of state formation, first colonial, then national. In turn, both colonial officials and reformist middle-class men on the one hand and nationalist leaders on the other recognized the importance of cultivating but also controlling female allies. Women's dominant politi-cal strategy was to choose alliances with male leaders, not as blind dupes but in order to make masculine authorities answerable to their dis-tinctly female agendas. They sustained complex identities and, until the late 1970s, sought to pursue gender interests as part of reformist, labor, nationalist, or partisan movements. Without autonomous organizations, activist women risked a partial containment by the colonial and then, more firmly, the national state. Although neither reformist nor nationalist women suffered a complete loss of agency, Belizean feminists did choose a new political strategy, one that combined building an autonomous orga-nizational base and allying with specific state actors and other nongovern-ment organizations.

Middle-class women's tradition of charitable and community ser-vice has not previously been understood as political, an expression of the reformism practiced by the Black Cross Nurses, the Infant Welfare League, the Federation of Women, and the Women Pioneers. This study shows that their interventions in the name of proper motherhood and even women workers' rights were not purely altruistic acts performed out-side the dynamics of power but rather racialized efforts to control subaltern women and to detach them from their alliances with anticolonial leaders and movements. Yet middle-class women also firmly rooted the legiti-macy of women's political voices and activism within the colonial reform current in Belizean politics. Indeed, reformist women were key allies of both middle-class men and colonial officials, from the crisis of the late 1910s on. While colonial projects of the 1920s and 1940s were hegemonic in intent, they were unable to forge the populist connections necessary to establishing hegemony. The very weakness of colonial-middle-class hege-monic projects in the 1920s and 1940s may have increased the importance and autonomy of women within those alliances. Certainly conventionally respectable middle-class women were acceptable allies in a way that the women of the popular classes, perceived as morally and racially disor-dered, were not.

The strength of the popular labor-nationalist tradition, both in the LUA of the 1930s and the PUP-GWU of the 1950s, was due in no small measure to the activism of popular class women. As early as their looting during the 1919 riot, these women linked family and community economic hard-ships to employers' political as well as economic power and to colonial officials' indifference or incapacity. They negotiated continuously with colonial authorities to fulfill popular expectations of paternal state care but also mobilized for citizen and worker rights and for a national state that would meet their demands. Rooted in a popular respectability that made it honorable to be a struggling working mother, anticolonial women developed proud politicized female identities. They were crucial partners in the populist alliance that yielded nationalist hegemony. While they partially succumbed to paternalistic party clientelism, particularly in the 1960s, they also made nationalist legitimacy in part contingent on recog-nizing women's rights and working to solve their problems. The failure of successive PUP administrations to do this contributed to the emergence of Belizean feminism.

Women in twentieth-century Belize carried ethnic, racial, or cultural as well as class identities into their political activism. The powerful reform-ist middle-class tradition remained overwhelmingly Creole, from Vivian Seay to Wilhelmina Grant to Leotine Gillette, although political parties hostile to the PUP have grown more multiethnic since the 1960s. The popular labor-nationalist tradition, by contrast, was multiethnic almost from the start. The Creole working women of Belize Town were joined early on in protesting the abuses of colonial rule by Garifuna women from Stann Creek. Their activism was connected to traditions of female wage labor and farming and a relatively flexible domestic patriarchy. In 1935 women from both ethnic groups joined in the LUA Women's League, demanding womanhood suffrage for "Negro, Indian and Spanish" women, and efforts to organize both Garifuna and Mayan women in Toledo district were made. The inclusive vision of 1935 became reality in the 1950s, as the PUP organized across the country, but perhaps most forcefully in the UWGS of 1959–60, a huge women's federation that sought to strike a better bargain with the emerging nationalist patriarchs. Discussions of race were suppressed by the PUP in the 1950s and 1960s, however, as divisive to national unity. It was not until the rise of the Belize Rural Women's Association in the 1980s that an autonomous coalition of Creole, Garifuna, mestizo, and Mayan women developed, one in which ethnic differences could be addressed deliberately and openly. Still, the pernicious legacy of gendered imperial racism, which linked labor and anticolonial protest to disordered black sexuality and family life, especially to black women's family headship and wage earning, has yet to be squarely attacked in Belizean society or politics. It is worth remembering that in 1935 LUA women asserted not only the rights of Belizean women, regardless of income or race, but also their dignity and worth.

Grant Jones has recuperated a sixteenth- and seventeenth-century history for Belize, contesting the myth of the Battle of St. George's Caye as *the* moment of Creole national creation.[6] This book likewise makes available new histories of and for Belizeans, demonstrating that the nation was not a masculine creation either. In so doing it overturns several key aspects of the existing historiography of Belize from Peter Ashdown's view of the 1919 riot as incited by male war veterans' anger alone to Eleanor Krohn Herrmann's view of the Black Cross Nurses as beloved volunteers to Ashdown's views of the UNIA as founded by radicals and as hostile to British rule and of the LUA as weakened by its large female membership. Crucially, this study has also shown that the GWU originated in the reform project of the 1940s, when Britain finally sanctioned responsible trade unionism in its colonies, not in Soberanis's BHWTU, as Nigel Bolland's most recent work still argues. By attending to women's activism in the nationalist movement of the 1950s, and in party politics during the 1960s, I complicate Bolland's and Shoman's more pessimistic views of the Belizean "masses" being reduced to a manipulated audience by party elites. While women were a key part of the GWU during its nationalist alliance with the PUP, their capacity to effectively bargain with the nationalist leadership did not collapse with the GWU. I also challenge Shoman's and Grant's views of the opposition National Independence Party as monolithically conservative in the 1960s by documenting its strong middle-class female leadership and its relatively progressive gender politics. Finally, I show that the Black Power challenge to party politics in the 1970s was explicitly sexualized, if antifeminist, and that it facilitated the emergence of a Belizean feminism that defied the primacy of party politics even in the intensely partisan run-up to national independence.

In transforming the Belizean historiography—in particular by recognizing the political agency of subaltern men and women and by refusing to either celebrate rebel heroes or to condemn the compromises of both reform and nationalism—this book sheds light on several issues relevant to comparative study of hegemonic projects and processes and of women's political strategies. My discussion of colonial reform makes it clear that the failure of colonial hegemonic projects requires historical explanation, and that the gendered, racialized moralism of reform in Belize was common throughout the West Indies and elsewhere. Afro-Caribbean women's particularly visible public roles and political record may have intensified this moralism in the region, erasing any possibility of populist connection with men and women of the popular classes. That same reality meant that when hegemonic, populist connections were established within the nationalist movement, women became direct partners in the alliance. The discourse of the male breadwinner had to be diluted and to some extent displaced, far more so than in the leftist politics of Popular Front Chile, for example, even as the female household head/single mother went officially unmentioned.[7] Nor could a domestic space of home, coded female, become central to rejecting colonial rule as alien, as in India.

Both the colonial reform and labor-nationalist traditions in Belize were primarily oriented toward gaining greater control of the state—through a middle-class-dominated legislative assembly in the former, an independent state in the latter. This commonality nurtured in both popular and middle-class cultures growing expectations of the state that could yield either protest or devotion. While the postponement of national independence, and thus the postponement of disillusionment with national state promises, was specific to Belize, disappointment with postcolonial states has been ubiquitous. Black Power activists in Belize certainly felt this acutely and pioneered a postcolonial strategy of civil society organization even before independence. Yet this book has treated nationalism not as an opiate of the masses, but as their authentic choice, their way of coping with the inadequate scale and pace of colonial reform in meeting their basic needs and recognizing their basic rights. That the national state has fallen short of their expectations, both in its efforts and achievements, reflects most harshly on the nationalist leaders and the global capitalist economy that they have embraced. Moreover, the Belizean state's official commitment to improving the quality of life of the popular classes and women stems not only from multilateral pressures that have been exerted since the 1970s but from the older, persistent demands of the nationalist grassroots.

As Cedric Grant argued in the 1970s, the nationalist struggle of the 1950s "climaxed a long period of gestation," indeed one longer, and more inclusive of middle-class women and popular class women and men than he allowed for.[8] During that period, women in both of twentieth-century Belize's political traditions established the legitimacy of women's political presence, voice, and demands and made the state responsible for at least some women's rights and needs. Middle-class female reformers guarded their social status within the colonial order by pursuing only propertied voting rights and an empowered colonial legislature and by adopting a didactic stance toward poor women. Yet by negotiating with and increasingly working within the colonial state, they pushed the process of constructive reform that raised popular expectations of the state as a provider of health care and other services. At the same time, labor-nationalist women agitated outside the state, mounting personal and collective challenges that articulated a popular gender-inclusive conception of labor and citizen rights, even as they made female reformers' work more urgent. As hostile as these two groups of women were to each other, their combined record of pressuring the state from within and without, and their common experience of becoming hostages to party politics and the national question, provide Belizeans—especially the women's movement, which has faltered since the 1990s—with crucial lessons and tools for confronting the challenges of the past and present.

Notes

Introduction

The subtitle to the introduction comes from Mrs. Adolfa Garcia of Orange Walk who declared to me in our 1993 interview that "I was never a coward woman!" when she was describing a youthful confrontation with the British governor over a promised village water supply.

1. In Belize, the Creoles are descendants of British settlers and/or the Africans they imported as slaves during the seventeenth and eighteenth centuries. Later West Indian immigrants, like Elfreda's Barbadian father, George Stanford, became part of the group, which was markedly stratified by class and color as early as the late 1700s. For more on the 1894 riot see Assad Shoman, *13 Chapters*, 175–78.

2. On the creation of the annual ritual, and the origin myth it was based on, see my "Imagining the Colonial Nation."

3. My interviews with Elfreda Reyes, 10 and 11 July 1991, focused mainly on the 1950s and 1960s. I later learned from documentary sources about her activism in the 1930s. She has been mentioned in two previously published books, both drawing on my research: Shoman, *13 Chapters*, 211 and 312, and Verene Shepherd, comp. and ed., *Women in Caribbean History*, 165–66.

4. On the British Caribbean see O. Nigel Bolland, *The Politics of Labour in the British Caribbean*, chs. 3 and 4.

5. On suffrage movements see María de F. Barceló-Miller, *La lucha por el sufragio femenino en Puerto Rico, 1896–1935*; June Hahner, *Emancipating the Female Sex*; Francesca Miller, *Latin American Women and the Search for Social Justice*; Asunción Lavrin, *Women, Feminism, and Social Change in Argentina, Chile, and Uruguay, 1890–1940*; and K. Lynn Stoner, *From the House to the Streets*.

6. The Garifuna are descendants of Africans and Windward Islands "Caribs," who were deported by the British to the coast of Central America at the end of the

eighteenth century. They are phenotypically African and linguistically Arawakan; their traditional religion combines elements of West African, Arawakan, and Roman Catholic practices.

7. Belize's Mayans have pre-Columbian and modern origins within Belize's borders and are concentrated in the north, west, and inland south. Mestizos (mixed Spanish and Mayan) arrived largely in the mid-nineteenth century, fleeing the Caste War in the Yucatan. The American Jesuit influence on the Belizean nationalist movement is discussed in Cedric Grant, *The Making of Modern Belize*, 92–6, 115–17.

8. Stuart Hall's conclusion that "in spite of the fact that the popular masses have never been able to become in any complete sense the subject-authors of the cultural practices of the twentieth century, their continuing presence . . . has constantly interrupted, limited, and disrupted everything else" speaks to Elfreda's experience. See Lawrence Grossberg, "On Postmodernism and Articulation: An Interview with Stuart Hall," 140.

9. Joan Wallach Scott, ed., *Feminism and History*, 2–5, distinguishes between additive and transformative forms of feminist historical practice as stages in the development of the discipline.

10. Verene Shepherd, Bridget Brereton, and Barbara Bailey, eds., *Engendering History*. Both the editors' introduction, xiv, and Patricia Mohammed's essay, "Writing Gender into History," urge the further development of transformative feminist historiography. Kumkum Sangari and Sudesh Vaid, eds., *Recasting Women: Essays in Indian Colonial History*, 3; Anne McClintock, *Imperial Leather*, 4–9; and Joan Wallach Scott, *Gender and the Politics of History*, 46.

11. Scott, *Gender*, 45; R. W. Connell, *Gender and Power*, 125–32.

12. Key works in the historiography of the 1970s and 1980s are articles by Peter Ashdown, including "Antonio Soberanis and the Disturbances in Belize 1934–1937" and "Marcus Garvey, the UNIA and the Black Cause in British Honduras, 1914–1949"; O. Nigel Bolland, *The Formation of a Colonial Society* and *Colonialism and Resistance in Belize*; Bolland and Assad Shoman, *Land in Belize, 1765–1871*; Angel E. Cal, "Anglo-Maya Contact in Northern Belize" and "Rural Society and Economic Development: British Mercantile Capital in Nineteenth-Century Belize"; Grant, *The Making of Modern Belize*; Grant Jones, *Maya Resistance to Spanish Rule*; and Assad Shoman, *Party Politics in Belize, 1950–1986*.

13. The anthropological literature includes Laurie Kroshus Medina, *Negotiating Economic Development*; Mark Moberg, *Citrus, Strategy, and Class* and *Myths of Ethnicity and Nation*; and Richard Wilk, *Household Ecology*. Feminist anthropology on Belize is discussed in n. 16.

14. Bolland, "Race, Ethnicity and National Integration in Belize," in *Colonialism and Resistance in Belize*, 198.

15. Matthew Restall, "'He Wished It in Vain,'" shows evidence of Mayan women's resistance to both Spanish and Mayan male dominance.

16. This scholarship includes several fine anthropological monographs: Peta Henderson and Ann Bryn Houghton, eds., *Rise Up*; Virginia Kerns, *Women and the Ancestors*; Irma McClaurin, *Women of Belize*; and Wilk, *Household Ecology*. Zee Edgell's novels *Beka Lamb*—a classic of Caribbean women's literature—and *In Times Like These* portray two key periods in Belizean political history from female perspectives. My book generally confirms the nature of the processes that Edgell approaches through fictionalized personal memory. The broader women's studies literature on the Caribbean includes Olive Senior, *Working Miracles*, and Consuelo López Springfield, *Daughers of Caliban*, both of which illuminate specific areas of postemancipation women's history.

17. Antonio Gramsci, "Notes on Italian History," in *Selections from the Prison Notebooks*, 55.

18. Rosalind O'Hanlon, "Recovering the Subject," 197. O'Hanlon's critique is focused on the early Subaltern Studies scholarship; the school's later work is more careful of constructing rebellious subalterns and emancipatory metanarratives.

19. For criticism of the strongly postmodern position see Fernando Coronil, "Listening to the Subaltern: The Poetics of Neocolonial States," 648; Nancy Fraser, "False Antitheses"; and Hall, "On postmodernism and articulation," 148.

20. Mrinalini Sinha, "Gender in the Critiques of Colonialism and Nationalism," 479.

21. Fraser, "False Antitheses," 71–2, and Florencia Mallon, "The Promise and Dilemma of Subaltern Studies," 1500 and 1510. On Fanon see Homi Bhabha, *The Location of Culture*, ch. 2; Drucilla Cornell, *At the Heart of Freedom*, 155–6; and Anne McClintock, "'No Longer in a Future Heaven': Nationalism, Gender, and Race," 265–71. On African American feminism see Evelyn Brooks Higginbotham "African-American Women's History".

22. Evelyn O'Callaghan, *Woman Version*, 51, 69, 80. The historical development of these stereotypes in the British Caribbean is analyzed in Barbara Bush, *Slave Women in Caribbean Society, 1650–1838*, ch. 2. On the impossibility of a pure authentic Caribbean identity see Stuart Hall, "Negotiating Caribbean Identities."

23. Mimi Sheller, "Quasheba, Mother, Queen," examines slave women's manipulation of dominant stereotypes. For other examples of slave women's resistance see Hilary McD. Beckles, *Natural Rebels*; Bush, *Slave Women*, ch. 5; and my "Viragoes, Victims, and Volunteers."

24. Middle-class West Indian women's political activism is discussed in Rhoda Reddock, *Women, Labour, and Politics in Trinidad and Tobago*, chs. 6–9.

25. Mohammed, "Writing Gender into History." The concept was first articulated by Deniz Kandyoti in "Bargaining with Patriarchy."

26. Scholars working with Gramsci's conception of hegemony include Raymond Williams, *Marxism and Literature*; Ernesto Laclau and Chantal Mouffe, *Hegemony and Socialist Strategy*; Stuart Hall, "Gramsci's Relevance for the Study of Race and Ethnicity," in *Stuart Hall*, 421–25; O'Hanlon, "Recovering the Subject"; and Mallon, "The Promise and Dilemma of Subaltern Studies." By some interpretations, Michel Foucault could also be included.

27. Connell, *Gender and Power*, 106–9, 125–32. I adopt Connell's view of the modern nation-state's patriarchy as historically constructed rather than, as Carole Pateman's analyses suggest, essentially or inherently so. For critiques of Pateman see Nancy Fraser, "Beyond the Master/Subject Model"; Joan Landes, "The Performance of Citizenship"; and Chantal Mouffe, "Feminism, Citizenship and Radical Democratic Politics." On sexuality and nation building in nineteenth-century western Europe see George Mosse, *Nationalism and Sexuality*. The importance of empire building to this process is more thoroughly established in Ann Laura Stoler, *Race and the Education of Desire*.

28. On Caribbean women's tradition of activism see Reddock, *Women, Labour, and Politics in Trinidad and Tobago*, 255. McClintock, *Imperial Leather*, 31, presents her contrasting pair as a warning against making global generalizations about "the gendering of imperialism." On lower-class Indian women see Partha Chatterjee, *The Nation and its Fragments*, 127.

29. On populism and hegemony see Ernesto Laclau, "Towards a Theory of Populism"; Alan Knight, "Populism and Neo-populism in Latin America, Especially Mexico"; and Jon Beasely-Murray, "Peronism and the Secret History of Cultural Studies." Gender analyses of Latin American populisms include Marjorie Becker, *Setting the Virgin on Fire*; Karin Rosemblatt, *Gendered Compromises*; and Joel Wolfe, "'Father of the Poor' or 'Mother of the Rich'?"

30. I discuss the British Caribbean failure of colonial hegemony in "Citizens vs. Clients."

31. Partha Chatterjee, *Nationalist Thought and the Colonial World*, 48–50; Chatterjee, *The Nation and its Fragments*, esp. xi, 6, 12–13, 18, 21, and "Was There a Hegemonic Project of the Colonial State?"; and Ranajit Guha, *Dominance without Hegemony*, esp. xii, 25, 63. For Mallon's critique of Guha see "The Promise and Dilemma of Subaltern Studies," 1512. Peter Ashdown has tended to treat Belize's popular classes as

inherently anticolonial, while Cedric Grant portrays the colonial state as sitting atop a politically unconscious and mostly quiescent population until the 1940s. Neither view allows for any historical explanation of the failure of colonial hegemony.

32. Lata Mani, "Contentious Traditions: The Debate on Sati in Colonial India"; and Chatterjee, *The Nation and its Fragments*, chs. 6 and 7.

33. This paragraph draws on Michael Banton, *Racial Theories*, 52–60; Ivan Hannaford, *Race*, 147; McClintock, *Imperial Leather*, 22–23, 43–54, 113; George Mosse, *Toward the Final Solution*, 1, 70; Nancy Leys Stepan, *"The Hour of Eugenics,"* 22, 44–6; George Stocking, *Race, Culture, and Evolution*, 48–49; and Robert J. C. Young, *Colonial Desire*, introduction and chs. 4–6.

34. Stoler, *Race and the Education of Desire*, 9; David Theo Goldberg, *Racist Culture*, 3; Hannaford, *Race*, 5–6; Thomas Holt, *The Problem of Freedom*, xix–xx; and Young, *Colonial Desire*, 118–19.

35. In addition to works cited in n. 23 above, see Antoinette Burton, "The White Woman's Burden: British Feminists and 'The Indian Woman,' 1865–1915"; Catherine Hall, "Gender Politics and Imperial Politics"; Claire Midgely, "Anti-slavery and the Roots of 'Imperial Feminism'"; Melanie Newton, "Dirty Trollops and Matron Ladies"; Swithin Wilmot, "Females of Abandoned Character?"

36. Macpherson, "Imagining the Colonial Nation," 111.

37. Stepan, *"The Hour of Eugenics,"* ch. 3; Lourdes Martínez-Echazábal, *"Mestizaje* and the Discourse of National/Cultural Identity in Latin America, 1845–1959," 27–30. On the gendered constructions of the Cuban nation, see Ferrer, *Insurgent Cuba*, 126–27, and Jean Stubbs, "Social and Political Motherhood of Cuba: Mariana Grajales Cuello." On the inclusion of "white wives and mothers" as instigators of the Puerto Rican autonomists' *gran familia* see Eileen Suárez Findlay, *Imposing Decency*, 54–59, 85–87.

38. See my "Imagining the Colonial Nation," 111. On the West Indian middle class see Patrick Bryan, *The Jamaican People 1880–1902*, 254, who argues that Jamaica's "black intellectuals were alienated from the Creole society which gave them birth." On British policy, see Young, *Colonial Desire*, 144.

39. On the construction of the Battle of St. George's Caye Myth see my "Imagining the Colonial Nation." On the politics of racial uplift see Higginbotham, "African-American Women's History," 199–200.

40. Antonio Soberanis Gomez and Luke D. Kemp, *The Third Side of the Anglo-Guatemalan Dispute over Belize or British Honduras.*

41. My argument about folkloric nationalism is confirmed by Moberg, *Myths of Ethnicity and Nation*, 13 and Medina, *Negotiating Economic Development*, 41, 48–49.

42. Medina, *Negotiating Economic Development*, 50–53; Moberg, *Myths of Ethnicity and Nation*, 14.

43. The literature on the Belize-Guatemala dispute includes Wayne M. Clegern, *British Honduras*; Grant, *The Making of Modern Belize*, ch. 10; Tony Thorndike, "The Conundrum of Belize"; and Alma H. Young and Dennis H. Young, "The Impact of the Anglo-Guatemalan Dispute on the Internal Politics of Belize."

44. Prasenjit Duara, *Rescuing History from the Nation*, 7.

45. Stephen Howe, *Anticolonialism in British Politics*, 10–11, is critical of the Subaltern Studies school for dismissing formal decolonization as merely a continuation of the politics of state dominance. See also Laura Chrisman, "'Journeying to Death.'"

46. See for example Gilbert M. Joseph and Daniel Nugent, eds. *Everyday Forms of State Formation*; Rosemblatt, *Gendered Compromises*; Ada Ferrer, *Insurgent Cuba*.

47. Mallon, "The Promise and Dilemma," 1495.

48. John French and Daniel James, "Squaring the Circle," 15; Thomas Miller Klubock, *Contested Communities*, 7; Rosemblatt, *Gendered Compromises*, 269. See also Lowell Gudmundson and Francisco Scarano, "Conclusion: Imagining the Future of the Subaltern Past."

49. Holt, *The Problem of Freedom*; Frederick Cooper, Thomas Holt, and Rebecca Scott, *Beyond Slavery*; Sheller, "Quasheba, Mother, Queen"; and Sheller, *Black Publics and Peasant Radicalism in Haiti and Jamaica*. Unfortunately, O. Nigel Bolland's recent synthesis of British Caribbean labor politics does not adequately integrate questions about or findings on gender, especially in the twentieth century. See Bolland, *The Politics of Labour in the British Caribbean*. Shepherd, *Women in Caribbean History*, 164–70, summarizes some of the published material, while Reddock, *Women, Labour, and Politics in Trinidad and Tobago*, has thoroughly documented the gender dimensions of labor mobilization in Trinidad and Tobago. Scholarship on gender and labor in Puerto Rico is strong for both centuries. See for example Eileen J. Findlay, "Free Love and Domesticity"; Blanca Silvestrini, "Women as Workers: The Experience of the Puerto Rican Woman in the 1930s"; and Altagracia Ortiz, ed. *Puerto Rican Women and Work*.

50. Peter Ashdown, "Race Riot, Class Warfare, and Coup d'Etat."

51. Eleanor Krohn Herrmann, "Black Cross Nursing in Belize."

52. Ashdown, "Antonio Soberanis and the Disturbances in Belize 1934–1937."

53. Bolland, "The Labour Movement and the Genesis of Modern Politics in Belize," in *Colonialism and Resistance*, 180. He reasserts this argument in *The Politics of Labor*, 630. It seems to stem from a confusion between two labor unions with almost identi-

cal acronyms, one founded in 1939 by Soberanis, the other—the one that became the GWU—founded in 1943 by reformist tradesmen within the colonial reform project.

54. I thus move beyond Shoman's analysis in *Party Politics*, pt. 1.

55. Shoman, *Party Politics*, pt. 1, and Grant, *The Making of Modern Belize*, ch. 9.

1. The Making of a Riot

1. On Annie Flowers see CO 123/296/65699, "Riot at Belize." BA, Minute Paper Collection 3506-1919, contains the Riot Report without appendices. On the 22 July riot see BA, Minute Paper Collection 3547-1919, "Report of the Commissioners appointed . . . to inquire into the cause and origin of a disturbance . . . on the night of the 25th day of July, 1919," and Ashdown, "Race Riot, Class Warfare, and Coup d'Etat," 9–11. Author's interviews with Kathleen Soberanis, 15 September 1993, and Winifred Flowers, 22 April 1994. Flowers is a common Creole surname; Annie and Winifred were not necessarily related.

2. William Hoar served as keeper of prisons from as early as 1909 until 1920. One of the reformist voices in the state during the 1910s, he is unlikely to have simply invented Annie Flowers's words, although he may have substituted "live with" for a more openly sexual phrase.

3. Ashdown, "Race Riot, Class Warfare, and Coup d'Etat," 10. Haynes worked with another officer, F. H. E. McDonald, to restore order.

4. Ashdown, "Race Riot, Class Warfare, and Coup d'Etat," 13.

5. *Belize Independent*, 18 June 1930. Hereafter cited as *Independent*. The *Independent* was a local Garveyite paper started in 1914 by Hubert H. Cain, a middle-class black Creole (Ashdown, "Marcus Garvey, the UNIA and the Black Cause in British Honduras, 1914–1949," 46).

6. *Independent*, 4 June 1930. Haynes authored the article with this headline.

7. Ashdown, "Race Riot, Class Warfare, and Coup d'Etat," 12; Ashdown, "The Growth of Black Consciousness in Belize 1914–1919"; Winston James, *Holding Aloft the Banner of Ethiopia*, 51–66.

8. CO 123/295/48749, Hutson, "Causes and Handling of Outbreak."

9. Ashdown, "Race Riot, Class Warfare, and Coup d'Etat," 13–14, and "Marcus Garvey, the UNIA and the Black Cause in British Honduras, 1914–1949," 46–47.

10. In addition to works cited in nn. 33 and 34 of the introduction, see Ferrer, *Insurgent Cuba*, 4, on the gendered character of biologized racism.

11. On the politics of other West Indian middle classes see Bridget Brereton, "The Development of an Identity"; Patrick Bryan, "The Black Middle Class in Nineteenth Century Jamaica"; Reddock, *Women, Labour, and Politics*, chs. 3 and 6; and Bolland,

The Politics of Labour in the British Caribbean, 165. Though these authors empha-size different characteristics in defining the West Indian middle class—occupations, wealth, education, culture, skin color—all find a strong emphasis on respectability.

12. Hart-Bennett served from April to August 1918, when he died from injuries he received fighting the fire that razed the government buildings (*Clarion*, 5 September 1918).

13. Bolland, *The Politics of Labour in the British Caribbean*, 132–34.

14. On Mexico see Ana Macías, *Against All Odds*, and Elizabeth Salas, *Soldaderas in the Mexican Revolution*. On Cuba see Aline Helg, *Our Rightful Share*; Ferrer, *Insurgent Cuba*; Alejandro de la Fuente, *A Nation for All*; and Stoner, *From the House to the Streets*, 54–57.

15. See Bolland, *The Politics of Labour in the British Caribbean*, 173–209, on early labor mobilization in the British Caribbean, and 192, 194, 199–204, on Trinidad in particular.

16. On unemployment see BA, Minute Paper Collection 269-1918. In early 1918 the district commissioner of Belize gathered statistics on employment to provide to the new Food Control Committee. His numbers were 1,717 hired in the 1913–14 hir-ing period, between Christmas and New Year's, and 714 for 1914–15. Wages dropped from $16 per month to about $9 per month. These figures are higher than those cited by Grant, *The Making of Modern Belize*, 40. The employment level of 1913–14 was not exceeded until 1924–25, the beginning of the late 1920s boom. On debt ser-vitude see BA, Minute Paper Collection 3179-1909. In 1909 Collet supported Slack's proposal to reform the advance system. Improvidence, he believed, was responsible for workers bringing home $10 at the end of an entire season in the bush. On price inflation see Ashdown, "Race Riot, Class Warfare, and Coup d'Etat," 9, BA, *Blue Book*, 1917, and Minute Paper Collection 1406-1917 and 1519-1918. *Blue Book* prices were far from truthful, listing rice at seven to eight cents per quart, beans at eight to twelve cents per quart, and pork at twelve to fifteen cents per pound, when in reality the prices were triple those levels. Details of the Bradley family are found in BA, Supreme Court Actions, Summary Jurisdiction Suits 22 and 23 of 1914–15, Gertrude and Estella Bradley vs. Karl Heusner. These suits were ultimately combined.

17. Heusner was married to one of the seven daughters of John James Usher, a cousin of prominent Creole businessman and politician Archibald R. Usher, but also had children with her sister Elsie May Usher. Karen Judd notes that these off-spring "are not part of the family history" ("Elite Reproduction and Ethnic Identity in Belize," 243 and 272 n. 32).

18. BA, Minute Paper Collection 1795-1916 (31 May 1916). Thirty-five (5.4 percent) of the 650 petitioners were women.

19. *Clarion*, 15 April 1915 and 4 May 1911. The editor presented these comments as examples of "Creole humour."

20. Bolland and Shoman, *Land in Belize*, 77–78, explain the origins of BEC.

21. *Clarion*, 15 May 1915, reported increased *milpero* corn planting in San Roman, in northwest Orange Walk District near the Mexican border. Thomas Gann, *The Maya of Southern Yucatan and Northern British Honduras*, 15–28, noted that the colony's Maya were significantly enmeshed in the cash economy, but it appears that with effort they were able to reverse this process during the war.

22. On the rising price of flour see BA, *Blue Book*, 1917, and Minute Paper Collection 1406-1917 and 1519-1918. On the stolen shipment see BA, Minute Paper Collection 2804-1918 (13 September). The *Clarion* voiced its fears of female larceny on 24 May and 6 September 1917. On mahogany cutters' changing diets see BA, Minute Paper Collection 302-1918 (19 January). BA, Minute Paper Collection 595-1918 (16 February), describes the coconut oil demand. A large bottle cost thirty-five cents, as compared to forty cents for a pound of lard.

23. The 1911 and 1921 censuses did not calculate marriage and legitimacy rates by ethnic group, but given the concentration of particular groups in each district, a rough correlation is possible. In 1911 the Belize and Stann Creek Districts, dominated by the Creoles and the Garifuna, had the lowest female marriage rates of the six districts (36 percent and 44 percent, respectively, vs. 51.6 percent in Orange Walk). See British Honduras, *Report on the Result of the Census of the Population of the Colony of British Honduras Taken on the 2nd April, 1911*, table 4, 24–29. In 1915 and 1916 the Registrar General found the highest illegitimacy rates in those same two districts (46 percent and 47 percent in Belize District, 49.6 percent and 50.2 percent in Stann Creek District) vs. 31.5–32.5 percent in Orange Walk and 41.35–41.56 percent colony-wide. See British Honduras, *Annual Report on the Vital Statistics of British Honduras*, 1915 and British Honduras, *Annual Report on the Vital Statistics of British Honduras*, 1916, paragraphs 13 and 14 in both reports.

24. The 1911 census found that 56 percent of women over fifteen in the Belize District (town and rural) were over thirty. Assuming that this was also true of the municipal voting area, there were 2200 women over thirty. Of these, 467 or 21.23 percent, qualified to vote in 1912. In the elections of 1915, 1918, 1921, 1924, 1927, and 1930 the numbers were, respectively, 577, 565, 532, 513, 471, and 538. The female voter lists can be found in the British Honduras, *Government Gazette*, 31 July 1915, 20 July 1918, 26 October 1921, 16 August 1924, 13 August 1927, and 9 August 1930. An annual income of $300 was required to qualify, according to the *New Edition of the Consolidated Laws of British Honduras*, ch. 118, 704, originally an ordinance passed 25 July 1911.

25. In 1901 Belize Town had a population of 9113, 5051 of them women. There were 740 female domestics in the Belize District, most of them in town, as well as 87 in Orange Walk, and 28 each in Corozal, Stann Creek and Toledo (British Honduras, *Report on the Result of the Census of British Honduras Taken on the 31st of March, 1901*, 5 and 22).

26. Interviews with Winifred Flowers, 22 and 25 April and 12 and 20 May 1994. Her father Benjamin Flowers worked as a mahogany cattleman at Northern River for a wealthy Creole family. Her mother was Marina Webb Flowers, whose brother Joseph Webb was head attendant at the Poor House. Their short rung above the unskilled laboring population was not enough to afford Winifred other opportunities, although she pointed out that she never worked for "coloured people."

27. *Blue Book*, 1912, AA1. Subsequent *Blue Books* repeated this data, as did *Peace Handbooks*, vol. 21, "North, Central and South America," 30. The 1918 petition can be found in BA, Minute Paper Collection 1519-1918 (6 May).

28. *Clarion*, 3 August 1916, carried Williams's description of her plight. BA, Orange Walk District Court Records, Suit 16 of 1916, lists Bacab's effort to secure her income. On Smith see BA, Minute Paper Collection 1035-1920. Even twenty years later laundry work was still very poorly paid. Mrs. Florence Herrera of Orange Walk Town was washing a dozen pieces for thirty-five cents in the 1930s (interview with Mrs. Florence Herrera, 15 November 1993).

29. The midwives' suits are: BA, Orange Walk District Court Records, Suit 12 of 1916, Catherine Morter v. Samuel Twiss; Suit 45 of 1916, Macedonia Perez v. Cristino Cabanas; Suit 60 of 1916, Bernalda Flowers v. Francisco Torres. On midwives' voting rates see BA, Minute Paper Collection 2367-1916 and British Honduras, *Government Gazette*, 31 July 1915. Just 7 percent of registered midwives in 1909 (Minute Paper Collection 74-1909) qualified to vote in 1912, while 14 percent of those listed in Monrad Metzgen and H. E. C. Cain, *Handbook of British Honduras*, 116, qualified in 1924. On store and saloon owners see BA, Miscellaneous Collection, Sologaistoa Brothers, compilers, *Guide to British Honduras*, 127.

30. The four seamstresses who qualified by income were Ella Lord, Miss Minnie Faber, Rose Harrison, and Mrs. Sarah Wallace. Details of Lord's living situation come from BA, Judges Notes, 15 October 1915. In this trial, the clerk at Woods, Slack and Franco's law offices was prosecuted for skimming off rent that was owed to the firm's landlord clients. Among the tenants who testified were Ella Lord and Diana Gladden, whose rent was significantly higher than that of the other witnesses. The Arnold petition gave poor people's rents at $3–$6 per month; policemen generally paid about $5 per month. On Meighan's participation in the contingent see BA, Minute Paper

Collection 446-1917. Three kin groups comprised nine of the twelve propertied petty bourgeois seamstresses. Alice, Margaret, and Emma Belisle of Prince St. were the widow and daughters of baker and grocer Samuel F. Belisle who died in 1912, leaving them the Prince St. property (BA, Probates, number 3 of 1912). Matilda, Elfreda, and Estella Haylock of Daly St. were the wife, daughter, and possibly daughter-in-law of grocer and civil leader Wilfred A. Haylock. Agnes, Ella and Sarah Craig of Albert St. were all piano teachers as well as seamstresses (Metzgen and Cain, *Handbook of British Honduras*, 442).

31. *Clarion*, 4 December 1913.

32. Recent works on gendered conflict in court records include Steve J. Stern, *The Secret History of Gender*, and Sueann Caulfield, *In Defense of Honor: Sexual Morality, Modernity, and Nation in Early-Twentieth-Century Brazil*.

33. For Myvett v. Dawson see *Clarion*, 16 August 1917. McLiverty's suit is BA, Supreme Court Actions, 1917, number 3. The northern cases are BA, Orange Walk District Court Records, Information and Complaints, numbers 23 and 36 of 1916. Gann, *The Maya of Southern Yucatan and Northern British Honduras*, 16, confirms that Mayan women were just as likely to use sexualized language as Creole and Garifuna women: "When quarrelling among themselves [they] use the most disgusting and obscene language, improvising as they go along . . . pouring out a stream of vituperation . . . to meet each case."

34. BA, Orange Walk District Court Records, Information and Complaints, number 18 and 121 of 1918, Catalina Malic v. Alfred Blair and Apolonia Rodriguez Ak v. Agapito Ak. Both of these were maintenance cases, as was that of Caroline James v. George Welsh in Belize Town (*Clarion*, 23 August and 25 October 1917). Jane Hamilton, an enfranchised woman who signed the Arnold petition in 1918, took Alfred Pitts to court a year earlier for assaulting her son (*Clarion*, 30 August 1917).

35. BA, Judges Notes, 1914–1915, Rex v. Moore, describes Louis Nathaniel Moore's knife attack on his wife Margaret in January 1915, who had left him in Cayo. He followed her to Belize Town, where the incident took place. BA, Judges Notes (Criminal Sessions), Rex v. Chable, 31 July 1914 recounts Bernable Chable's assault and attempted rape of Angela Moralez at Calla Creek in Cayo. BA, Judges Notes (Criminal Sessions), Rex v. Ruiz, 25 October 1914, is the trial of Solomon Ruiz for assaulting Felicila Tessacum in Cayo. The latter two did twelve and nine months in jail respectively. BA, Judges Notes (Criminal Sessions), Rex v. John Shepherd, 24 April 1914, and Rex v. Christopher Cherrington, 31 July 1914, both deal with cases of men attacking their former common-law wives in the Cayo lumber camps. On the Guzman case see *Clarion*, 6 November 1913.

36. Rosemarie M. McNairn, "Crime and Punishment in British Honduras," provides a rare window onto nineteenth-century court battles in Belize.

37. In places as different as Brazil and Egypt, higher education bred female nationalists and suffragists during this period, but there was no postsecondary education for women in British Honduras, and no male-led anticolonialism to foster female politics. See Margot Badran, *Feminists, Islam and Nation*, and Hahner, *Emancipating the Female Sex*. For information on girls' high school curricula, see the *Blue Book*, 1912, w4, and Metzgen and Cain, *Handbook of British Honduras*, 369–78. Anglican women were active in charity work long before the founding of the Women's Auxiliary in 1918. The first all-female branch of a friendly society opened in 1898, but most had mixed memberships from their beginnings. BA, Minute Paper Collection 407-1920 (3 February), reports on government inspections of the six female-owned schools. *Handbook of British Honduras*, 429, lists the boardinghouse owners. Ashdown, "Race Riot, Class Warfare, and Coup d'Etat," 8 and 13 n. 24, describes events at Staine's boardinghouse.

38. British Honduras, *Government Gazette*, 31 July 1915.

39. Judd, "Elite Reproduction and Ethnic Identity in Belize," 206 and 294, claims that there was a strict gender divide in Creole public culture and ethnic identity, while my evidence suggests a more flexible and changing gender order.

40. Mark Moberg, "Crown Colony as Banana Republic," 371.

41. *Clarion*, 28 February 1907. It was Haylock who was the real driving force behind the campaign for a municipal franchise (Judd, "Elite Reproduction and Ethnic Identity in Belize," 252).

42. Moberg, "Crown Colony as Banana Republic," 361 and 370.

43. On the Woods-Usher family connections see Judd, "Elite Reproduction and Ethnic Identity in Belize," 279.

44. For Slack's biography see *Clarion*, 27 January 1916.

45. *Clarion*, 5, 12, and 19 September 1912. Ashdown, "Race Riot, Class Warfare, and Coup d'Etat," 10. Usher ventured out to read the Riot Act, only to be jeered and jostled.

46. *Clarion*, 25 April and 25 July 1912.

47. *Clarion*, 8 August and 7 November 1912.

48. Lillian Guerra, *Popular Expression and National Identity in Puerto Rico*, ch. 6.

49. *Clarion*, 7, 21, and 28 March, 11 and 18 April, 25 July, and 29 August 1912 and 6 March and 1 and 8 May 1913.

50. *Clarion*, 27 June 1912. Thompson reinforced the message that women's political involvements should be carefully limited when he had Keziah express her disgust with the masculine vulgarity of electoral competition (*Clarion*, 5 December 1912).

51. *Clarion*, 8 May 1913.

52. *Clarion*, 22 May and 12, 19, and 26 June 1913.

53. *New Edition of the Consolidated Laws of British Honduras*, ch. 118, "The Belize Town Board," stipulated that while propertied men could vote at twenty-one, women had to be thirty.

54. *Clarion*, 27 June 1912.

55. *Clarion*, 10 October 1912.

56. *Clarion*, 5 December 1912.

57. Alfonso A. Tzul, author of *After 100 Years*, is the grandnephew of these Tzuls. His grandfather described them to him as a very strong group of brothers who refused the San Antonio alcalde's authority and set up bases at Monkey Falls and Chorro in Cayo, as well as at Yal Och in the Petén. They stole women because Mayan parents were reluctant to marry their daughters to them. According to Don Alfonso's father-in-law's uncle, Hernandez was a mostly Mayan but part-Spanish chicle contractor who began his exploits after R. S. Turton, the Wrigley agent, and his local agent Alvaro Habet refused to pay him (interview with Don Alfonso Tzul, 21 June 1994). In the *Clarion*'s coverage, however, Hernandez led the Tzul "bandits." For Keziah's quote see *Clarion*, 6 June 1912. For Woods's attacks see *Clarion*, 29 February and 28 March 1912.

58. On the 1907 debacle see D. N. A. Fairweather, *A Short History of the Volunteer Forces of British Honduras (now Belize)*, 21–24. *Clarion*, 7 March 1912. *Clarion*, 20 and 27 February 1913. *Clarion*, 12 April 1913.

59. *Clarion*, 16 May 1912.

60. *Clarion*, 11 November 1915.

61. Moberg, "Crown Colony as Banana Republic," 379, cites Ashdown, "Race, Class, and the Unofficial Majority," 273, in arguing that P. S. Woods backed off because Collet, despite his ongoing advocacy of the UFCO, allowed the unofficials free reign.

62. The Minute Paper Collection in the Belize Archives is patchy for the pre-1916 period, which biases my analysis here toward the later 1910s.

63. Ashdown, "The Growth of Black Consciousness," 4. Grant, *The Making of Modern Belize*, dispenses with the 1910s in a few sentences.

64. Ashdown, "The Growth of Black Consciousness," 3. He cites CO 123/279, Collet to the Colonial Office, 24 September 1914, on the Young Belize Party. Nobody was ever charged for the 1918 fire, but, he notes, it was "obviously the work of an arsonist" (3).

65. *Belize Billboard*, 20 September 1958.

66. *Clarion*, 4 February 1915.

67. BA, Minute Paper Collection 1318-1916 (Annual Report for Cayo 1915). The district commissioner reported that "a considerable number of people came from Belize to El Cayo. These people were generally able to obtain employment." The British Honduras Contingent consisted of 533 men, the highest per capita rate of World War 1 volunteers in the British Caribbean (Bolland, *The Politics of Labour in the British Caribbean*, 196).

68. BA, Records 128, Despatches Out, 1913–1915. Collet to the Secretary of State for the Colonies, 15 July and 27 August 1915, 339–40 and 353.

69. *Clarion*, 28 October 1915.

70. *Clarion*, 14 October 1915.

71. *Clarion*, 28 October, 1915. This was a speech Woods gave at a Belize Town recruiting meeting.

72. *Clarion*, 30 December 1915.

73. On Mrs. Slack's volunteers see *Clarion*, 4 February, 3 June, 7 October, and 4 November 1915. On fundraisers see *Clarion*, 4 February, 29 July, 7 October, and 4 November 1915. One lady cricketer, Carmen Pears, signed the Johnston clemency petition. On the ladies' auxiliary see *Clarion*, 11 November 1915 and 7 December 1916. McField and Cain were, respectively, the president and secretary of the UNIA's founding female executive (*Clarion*, 29 April 1920). On elite women in Stann Creek and Corozal see *Clarion*, 9 and 16 December 1916. The 1915 photograph of fifteen Benque girls appeared in *Belizean Studies* 5:1 (January 1977): 13. Mrs. Armandina Simmons, née Castellanos, identified her two aunts, whose father was a bookkeeper. Both women married and never worked outside the home. Coleman's father was a carpenter, and she later worked as a seamstress. Mendez, of humbler origins, never married and was known for her religiosity (interview with Nurse Armandina Simmons, 15 August 1994).

74. Ashdown, "Marcus Garvey, the UNIA and the Black Cause in British Honduras, 1914–1949," 44 quoting *Clarion*, 27 January 1916.

75. *Clarion*, 27 January 1916.

76. Eleanor Krohn Herrmann, *Origins of Tomorrow*, 35 n. 92.

77. BA, Minute Paper Collection 1795-1916 (31 May 1916).

78. BA, Minute Paper Collection 2186-1916 (11 July 1916) contains Wyatt's report.

79. For example, Wyatt dismissed as nonsense fears of a growth in child prostitution. BA, Minute Paper Collection 3395-1918 (26 November 1918).

80. BA, Minute Paper Collection 1246, 1356, 1432, 1537, 1606, 1718, 1886, 1953, 3362, and 3364 of 1916.

81. *Clarion*, 11 January and 22 February 1917.

82. BA, Minute Paper Collection 3036-1916 (28 September).

83. BA, Minute Paper Collection 692-1917 (16 February).

84. BA, Minute Paper Collection 2988-1917 (8 September 1917). Colonial officials named her husband as Henry Flowers. She may have omitted this detail in order to avoid revealing that theirs was a common-law marriage.

85. BA, Minute Paper Collection 3559-1917 (6 November). The Pomona Industrial School, finally opened in 1927, had its origins in this preriot committee.

86. *Clarion*, 7 June 1917.

87. *Clarion*, 5 July 1917.

88. BA, Minute Paper Collection 1581-1918 (*Annual Report of the Medical Department*, 1917).

89. BA, Minute Paper Collection 277-1918 (15 January 1918).

90. BA, Minute Paper Collection 147-1920. The villages of Yo Creek, Trinidad, and San Lazaro were named.

91. Judd, "Elite Reproduction and Ethnic Identity in Belize," 186, citing *Clarion* 3 and 17 December 1914, finds that in late 1914 a group of farmers who petitioned the government for a loan to start cultivation was turned down. *Clarion*, 5 September 1918, gives the date of Hart-Bennett's arrival as 5 April 1918.

92. BA, MPS 527-1918 (8 February), and 584-1918 (12 February).

93. BA, Minute Paper Collection 2308-1918 (7 September 1918).

94. BA, Minute Paper Collection 263-1918 (14 January).

95. BA, Minute Paper Collection 334-1918 (23 January) and 344-1918 (24 January).

96. BA, Minute Paper Collection 347-1918 (25 January).

97. BA, Minute Paper Collection 3534-1918 (17 December).

98. BA, Minute Paper Collection 3538-1918 (21 December).

99. BA, Minute Paper Collection 514-1918 (4 February). The FCC set the price of flour at eleven cents per pound, almost 300 percent higher than the official *Blue Book* price of 1917, and even higher than the price quoted in Arnold's petition three months later.

100. BA, Minute Paper Collection 517-1918 (1 February).

101. BA, Minute Paper Collection 2697-1918. This brought forth a petition of protest from the merchants (Minute Paper Collection 2942-1918).

102. BA, Minute Paper Collection 2573-1918 (20 August).

103. BA, Minute Paper Collection 525-1918 (21 January).

104. BA, Minute Paper Collection 1519-1918 (6 May 1918).

105. *Clarion*, 22 August 1918. Two months later, on 31 October, the paper reprinted an article from 1854 on that year's fire in Belize Town, which condemned the laborers who were happy to see "backra's" goods burn.

106. *Clarion*, 31 October 1918, announced the committee's formation. There were already seventy cases in the village of Bomba near Belize Town by that time. On female work during the epidemic see BA, Minute Paper Collection 534-1919 (19 February), Influenza Committee Report. All told, 19,000 people came down with influenza and 1,014 died from it (BA, Records 136, Despatches Out, 26 February 1919, 143).

107. BA, Minute Paper Collection 3218-1918 (29 November), 3426-1918 (2 December), 3433-1918 (3 December), 3445-1918 (4 December).

108. BA, Minute Paper Collection 3304-1918 (16 November).

109. BA, Minute Paper Collection 3219-1918 (2 November).

110. BA, Minute Paper Collection 534-1919 (Report of the Influenza Relief Committee, 1918). The three voters were Edith Brown, Maria Davis, and Henrietta Allen. The twelve nonvoters, aside from Ann Flowers, were Violet Adolphus, Emmeline Allen, Clarissa Barrow, Jane Ferrel, Ethel Gill, Susan Hughes, Henrietta Lawless, Irene Phillips, Harriet Pitts, Sarah Rodgers, Julia Smiley, and Ellen Trapp.

111. The lady workers bore names such as Eyles, Grabham, Gahne, Usher, Franco, and Belisle, indicating their status as wives or daughters of colonial officials or merchant-landowners.

112. Ashdown, "The Growth of Black Consciousness," 4.

113. BA, Legislative Council Minutes, 24 April 1919; Despatch Out, 25 March.

114. BA, Minute Paper Collection 964-1919 (8 April) and 1126-1919 (5 May).

115. BA, Minute Paper Collection 1353-1919 (7 June).

116. *Clarion*, 24 April and 10 July 1919. The association's members were John P. and C. R. Usher (cousins of A. R. Usher, the latter being married to P. S. Woods's sister), P. S. Woods, H. H. Vernon, W. A. Haylock, H. E. C. Cain (brother of Hubert H. Cain), L. A. Smith, and Frans Dragten. Dragten was the only witness before the Riot Commission who emphasized the disparity between stagnating wages and rising prices during the war years (BA, Minute Paper Collection 3506-1919, Riot Report, 25).

117. BA, Minute Paper Collection 3093-1920, "The Petition of Charles H. Sutherland of Albert Street, Cabinetmaker, 20th October 1920," and "Inquiry into Charges against Benjamin Peon, Prison Warder, before the Executive Council, November 1920."

118. BA, Minute Paper Collection 3506-1919, Riot Report, 22.

119. *Clarion*, 18 September 1919, testimony of Major L. A. Jeffrey of the contingent.

120. BA, Minute Paper Collection 3506-1919, Riot Report, 1, 5, 10, 11, 22.

121. *Clarion*, 18 September 1919.

122. *Clarion*, 18 September 1919, testimony of Major Jeffrey.

123. As Temma Kaplan has argued in "Female Consciousness and Collective Action," urban working-class women have frequently taken such direct action in the cause of community survival. In this case there was clearly a more pointed political consciousness, as Creole women looted in defiance of white rule.

124. BA, Minute Paper Collection 3547-1919 ("Report of the Commissioners . . ."), 1.

125. BA, Minute Paper Collection 3036-1919 (30 August), on the Labour Bureau, and 3817-1919 and 3818-1919 (10 and 11 November), on Jane Flowers's, Theodosia Reyes's and Nancy Goff's applications for relief.

126. Bolland, *The Politics of Labour in the British Caribbean*, 202.

2. A Fragile Peace

1. BA, Minute Paper Collection 199-1920, 15 January, "Riot Commission Report."

2. The quote is from Ashdown, "Marcus Garvey, the UNIA and the Black Cause in British Honduras, 1914–1949," 46. On prison sentences for rioters see CO 123/299/9789, "Re riots July last [1919]. Report of trials: Table of cases tried in the Supreme Court 10th Nov. 1919 to 22 Jan. 1920," dated 29 January 1920 at Government House. On the founding of the Belize City UNIA see *Clarion*, 29 April 1920.

3. Hutson's efforts did little to shift the distribution of wealth in the colony. In 1927, for example, 96.86 percent of freehold land was owned by 96 owners with over 1,000 acres each. The remaining 3.13 percent was divided among 1,556 freeholders. The BEC owned half of the private land and one-fifth of the colony's territory (Sir Alan Pim, *British Honduras, Financial and Economic Position*, 217, cited in Grant, *The Making of Modern Belize*, 36).

4. The Labour Bureau operated from October 1919 to August 1920, paying out just over $10,000 in relief wages (BA, Minute Paper Collection 2485-1920 [August 1920]). Details of the weekly unemployment reports are in BA, Minute Paper Collection 1764-1920 (4 June).

5. Frederick Cooper, *Decolonization and African Society*. On Trinidad see Bolland, *The Politics of Labour in the British Caribbean*, 138–40, and Reddock, *Women, Labour and Politics*, 121–24. The only hint of labor organizing in Belize during the 1920s was one statement by the otherwise obscure British Honduras Workers' Union, emphasizing "personal responsibility" and arguing that "the true Worker's Unionist will at all time endeavour to develop healthy, manly, robust characteristics." (*Clarion*, 2 October 1924). The statement was dated 1923.

6. Theodore G. Vincent, *Black Power and the Garvey Movement*, 175.

7. Vincent, *Black Power and the Garvey Movement*, 36, 128, 175, contributes to the false link between the riot and the UNIA, as do Tony Martin, *Race First*, 12, 58, 95, and

James, *Holding Aloft the Banner of Ethiopia*, 51–66. The notes following "Report of a Meeting" in *The Marcus Garvey and Universal Negro Improvement Association Papers*, 303, give the same impression (cited hereafter as *The Garvey Papers*). On the founding of the UNIA local see Ashdown, "Marcus Garvey," 46, and *Clarion*, 29 April 1920. The female executive comprised Miss Ann R. McField, a Methodist schoolteacher (president), Mrs. Uetta Campbell (1st vice president), Mrs. Elizabeth Joe, a friendly society leader (2nd vice president), Eliza Lammy (3rd vice president), Miss Eva Cain, a Methodist schoolteacher and head of the women's brigade during the epidemic (secretary), and Mrs. Vivian Seay, founder of the Black Cross Nurses (treasurer). The male leaders were C. H. Mortley (president), W. A. Campbell (1st vice president), Benjamin Adderley (2nd vice president), Calvert Staine, an elected town board member from 1921–24 (3rd vice president), David Belizario (executive secretary), Samuel Haynes (general secretary), B. Reneau (associate secretary), and J. E. Vernon (treasurer). On the UNIA's exhibitions see *Clarion*, 5 January and 27 April 1922, and 20 December 1923. For Hutson's suspicions see Ashdown, "Marcus Garvey, the UNIA and the Black Cause in British Honduras, 1914–1949," 47 citing Foreign Office 371/4567, Hutson to Milner, 10 May 1920. His meeting with Garvey is transcribed in "Report of an Interview, Belize 5th July 1921" in *The Garvey Papers*, 508–509. Haynes's departure is described in *Clarion*, 7 and 14 July 1921.

8. Barbara Bair, "True Women, Real Men." At the 1920 and 1922 UNIA conventions in the United States, women protested against both a male authoritarianism that consigned them to voluntary community service and a lack of male responsibility and respect. The Black Cross Nurses always celebrated their anniversary in March, a month ahead of the UNIA founding.

9. For Usher's speech see *Clarion*, 9 April 1925. For middle-class opinion see *Clarion*, 5 March 1925. The BLDC voted for "half a loaf" on 27 February. Those present included P. S. Woods's son Eric, H. H. Vernon, H. H. Cain, Morrel and Calvert Staine, Monrad Metzgen, and J. O. B. Menzies. Peter Ashdown, "A Democracy Too Soon," 27–30 and Grant, *The Making of Modern Belize*, 60, both rely on the "flood of democracy" quote made in 1933 by Colonial Office figure S. E. V. Luke (CO 123/342: 15539). Bolland, *The Politics of Labour in the British Caribbean*, 137, suggests a similar pattern in Trinidad, where pre-WWI reformism failed to attract the disenfranchised masses.

10. For Dragten's proposal see *Clarion*, 3 November 1921. Dragten's interest in representative government dated to at least 1919, when he was a founding member of the British Honduras Elected Representation Association (BHERA). It seems likely that Hutson appointed him to the Legislative Council knowing that he would use

his position to lobby for this change. On the unofficials' vote see BA, Minute Paper Collection 3315-1921 (8 November), "Resolution re: Representative Government."

11. On the Franchise Commission members see *Clarion*, 26 June 1924. *Clarion*, 31 October 1918, mentions the PP. W. A. Campbell, a UNIA leader in the 1920s, and W. A. Wagner won seats for the PP, and possibly also A. Balderamos. For BHTA criticism of the PP see *Clarion*, 24 November 1921. On the BHTA's inaugural meeting see *Clarion*, 20 October 1921. The founding officers of the BHTA were A. R. Usher (president), H. H. Vernon (vice president), D. B. Evans (treasurer), and H. H. Cain (secretary). Members included P. S. Woods, W. C. F. Stuart (a merchant), and possibly W. A. Haylock, who attended an early meeting.

12. *Clarion*, 7 and 14 June 1923. In 1920, a mahogany cutter's top wage was $17 per month for a maximum of eleven months, or $187, so Cain's proposed franchise would not have amounted to universal suffrage (Great Britain, *Annual Report on the Social and Economic Progress of the People of British Honduras*, 1920, 17.)

13. The BHTA meeting was attended by just twenty-seven people. (*Clarion*, 24 July 1924). On the BLDC proposals see BA, Minute Paper Collection 2010-1924 (12 July). On the PP meeting see Ashdown, "A Democracy Too Soon," 27, citing the *Independent*, 16 July 1924. Staine and Longsworth's description comes from a letter they wrote to A. R. Usher (*Clarion*, 17 July 1924).

14. For Hutson's comments on women voting see *Clarion*, 26 June 1924. Clarion, 17 July 1924 reports the unofficials' debate. The expatriates were George Grabham, manager of the BEC and Charles Beattie, manager of the Royal Bank of Canada branch.

15. For the Staine brothers' comments at the BHTA meeting see *Clarion*, 12 March 1925. Their letter to Hutson, dated 6 March, appeared in *Clarion*, 26 March 1925.The PP set the bar at an income of $360 per year, which a male laborer earning $7 per week year round could meet. The *Blue Books* of 1923 and 1925 list laborers' wages at $1.50/day, or $7.50/week, but official figures were highly optimistic and did not account for casual and seasonal labor patterns. Even officially, women earned at best $2/week. On the district meetings of the BHTA see *Clarion*, 12, 19, 26 March and 2 April 1925.

16. Ashdown in fact cites the *Independent*'s coverage of July 1924 as evidence of PP activities in March 1925 (Ashdown, "A Democracy Too Soon," 27 n. 14).

17. See chapter 3 for discussion of this confrontation.

18. *Clarion*, 20 October and 3 November 1921.

19. BA, Minute Paper Collection 3097-1920 (20 October 1920) and Minute Paper Collection 2654-1921 (7 September 1921).

20. On elements of the celebration see *Clarion*, 20 September 1923 and 10 September

1925. Disapproval of popular festivities appeared in *Clarion*, 20 September 1923, 10 September 1925, and 13 September 1928. On funding in 1924 see BA, Minute Paper Collection 2073-1924 (July 19). On Orange Walk in 1928 see *Clarion*, 26 July 1928.

21. For Hutson's speech see *Clarion*, 13 September 1923. For Cain's editorial see *Independent*, 3 September 1930. My analysis supports the view of Judd, "Elite Reproduction and Ethnic Identity in Belize," 205, that the Garveyite interpretation of 1798 was one strain of middle-class culture rather than a radical threat to it.

22. For lyrics to "Land of the Gods," see Lita Hunter Krohn, Fr. M. Murray, S.J., and Lena Ysaguirre, eds. and compilers, *Readings in Belizean History*, 289.

23. *Clarion*, 27 September 1923, reported that Metzgen was the new club's vice president. In February 1924 the officers included Metzgen and W. Harrison Courtenay, then at the beginning of a remarkable civil service and political career (*Clarion*, 21 February 1924). Metzgen and Cain, *Handbook of British Honduras*, 1–29. Governor Hutson supervised the compilation of data in the book but had no hand in this historical essay. Metzgen's proposal to the Board of Education is in BA, Minute Paper Collection 3262-1924 (5 December). Sir John A. Burdon, *A Brief Sketch of British Honduras Past, Present and Future*, 18 and 21. The *Clarion* echoed his "birthday of the colony" argument on 13 September 1928.

24. Monrad Metzgen, *Shoulder to Shoulder*. Peter D. Ashdown, "The Colonial Administrator as Historian". On Burdon's hostility to the UNIA see BA, Minute Paper Collection 1-, 52-, 522-1928, and 824-1929; "John Burdon, Governor, British Honduras, to L. C. M. S. Amery, Secretary of State for the Colonies," 3 March 1928, in *The Garvey Papers*, vol. 7, 134–35; *Clarion*, 26 April 1928 and 12 and 19 February 1930.

25. For an account of both celebrations see *Independent*, 24 September 1930.

26. Lavrin, *Women, Feminism, and Social Change*, 98; Leys Stepan, "The Hour of Eugenics," 85; Ann Stoler, "Making Empire Respectable," 54; Molly Ladd-Taylor, *Mother-Work*, 49–52.

27. Samita Sen, "Motherhood and Mothercraft"; Marouf Arif Hasian, Jr., *The Rhetoric of Eugenics in Anglo-American Thought*, 64; and Higginbotham, "African-American Women's History."

28. Macpherson, "Colonial Matriarchs," 508. On the Garveyite leadership's ideal of black womanhood see Barbara Bair, "Pan-Africanism as Process:," 122; Honor Ford-Smith, "Women and the Garvey Movement in Jamaica," 73; Robert A. Hill, "General Introduction," in *The Garvey Papers*, vol. 1, l–li; Judith Stein, *The World of Marcus Garvey*, 246. Bair, "True Women, Real Men," 156, discusses the Garveyite desire to penetrate Victorian culture. On Garvey's criticisms see Bair, "Universal Negro Improvement Association"; Bair, "True Women, Real Men," 154–66; Ford-

Smith, "Women and the Garvey Movement in Jamaica," 76; and Honor Ford-Smith, "Making White Ladies," 65.

29. Krohn Herrmann, "Black Cross Nursing in Belize." Seay was eulogized in the *Belize Times*, 18 July 1971, and *The Reporter*, 23 July 1971. Although no Miss Myvett or Mrs. Seay was mentioned as being involved, Empire Day was celebrated in Xcalak in 1907 by a mixed group of Mexicans and British Hondurans, among whom was Mr. David Belizario, a founder of the UNIA in Belize Town in 1920 (*Clarion*, 13 June 1907). *Independent*, 26 June 1935, reported Seay's MBE award. Stoler, *Race and the Education of Desire*, 8, argues that imperial discourses of self-discipline and self-mastery were concerned with defining whiteness as against colonial degeneracy. As with other mixed-race colonials seeking racial improvement through respectability, the Black Cross Nurses bought into what Stoler refers to as an "implicitly raced" biopolitics (11, 92).

30. Governor Hutson's introduction to the British Honduras, *Annual Report of the Medical Department*, 1923, dated 13 May 1924.

31. On the children's ward, see Great Britain, *Annual Report on the Social and Economic Progress of the People of British Honduras*, 1920, 5. On Roberts's assessment of the hospital see BA, Minute Paper Collection 505-1920 (12 February) and 651-1920. On Mrs. Georgina Smith see BA, Minute Paper Collection 1035-1920 (2 April). On the ward maids' duties and turnover see BA, Minute Paper Collection 2182-1920 (July) and 1406-1921 (30 April).

32. On the nursing staff see BA, Minute Paper Collection 715-1920 (2 March). The character of desirable probationers was laid out in *Clarion*, 29 November 1923. See British Honduras, *Annual Report of the Medical Department*, 1920, for Dr. Simon's report on the Cayo District. See BA, Minute Paper Collection 1406-1921, for the Orange Walk District report. See BA, Minute Paper Collection 1406-1921 (30 April), and British Honduras, *Annual Report of the Medical Department*, 1920, for Gann's views. Hutson picked up on these in 1921's *Annual Report on the Social and Economic Progress of the People of British Honduras*, 23, in which he attributed infant mortality to parental neglect. See Herrmann, *Origins of Tomorrow*, 40, citing *Independent*, 19 March 1941, on the 1920 housing survey.

33. BA, Minute Paper Collection 1348-1921, letter from Gann to the colonial secretary dated 23 May. Cecilia Douglas, Seay's longtime second-in-command, recalled that practical training began in July 1921, a date that matches archival documentation (*Independent*, 26 June 1935). See BA, Minute Paper Collection 3531-1921 (25 November), for Gann's vision of the Black Cross Nurses' future.

34. On the infant mortality rate see Great Britain, *Annual Report on the Social*

and Economic Progress of the People of British Honduras, 1922, 10. Krohn Herrmann, "Black Cross Nursing in Belize," 42, citing *The Reporter*, 1 November 1968, mentions Hutson's request to the Black Cross Nurses. On the Liberty Hall inauguration see *Clarion*, 5 January 1922. On the Nurses' Health Crusade see *Clarion*, 27 April 1922.

35. On Seay's initial instructions see the retrospective by Cecilia Douglas, *Independent*, 26 June 1935. BA, Minute Paper Collection 1348-1921 (26 April), contained a flier titled "Don'ts for Mothers" that was based on Gann's research into the practices of the Guyanese medical staff and the Trinidadian Baby League. The water protest is described in *Clarion*, 11 May 1922.

36. On the first Baby Exhibition see *Clarion*, 20 December 1923. The standard view that the first Baby Exhibition began in 1922 comes from a retrospective article, "The Black Cross Nurses' Activities in Social Work and Otherwise," published in *British Honduras Agricultural Journal* (1942). In 1932 only 150 of 200 infants entered were "found to be in a proper state of health to participate" (*Independent*, 21 December 1932). The Nurses may not have performed this weeding out role from the beginning but clearly began to do so as they deemed it necessary. They definitely did so in 1937 and 1943 (*Clarion*, 1 September 1937, 14 August 1943, *Independent*, 26 June 1935). On the clinic effort see BA, Minute Paper Collection 2302-1924 (16 August) and 3046-1924 (24 October). The government decided to convert the Hart-Bennett children's ward into a maternity ward in 1926 (British Honduras, *Annual Report of the Medical Department*, 1926, 10), and it opened in 1927 (British Honduras, *Annual Report of the Medical Department*, 1927, 11). *Clarion*, 1 November 1928, listed Vivian Seay and four other Nurses as having completed the midwifery course in March. British Honduras, *Annual Report of the Medical Department*, 1927, 11, mentioned that the course had begun.

37. British Honduras, *Annual Report of the Medical Department*, 1927, 11, discusses the opening of the VD ward. Both the medical report for 1927, 5, and the report for 1926, 14 and 18, indicate the prevalence of gonorrhea especially in Cayo and Orange Walk Districts. The heavy use of the ward is mentioned in British Honduras, *Annual Report of the Medical Department*, 1929, 4, and British Honduras, *Annual Report of the Medical Department*, 1930, 4. The description of venereal disease in Orange Walk District comes from British Honduras, *Annual Report of the Medical Department*, 1929, 19.

38. BA, Minute Paper Collection 2629-1926 (12 October). The bill was gazetted in February 1927.

39. On government support for the league see BA, Minute Paper Collection 522-1928 (6 March). Roberts's concert was reported in *Clarion*, 26 April 1928. The $50 gift is mentioned in "The Black Cross Nurses' Activities in Social Work and Otherwise."

40. For details of the league's clinics see *Clarion*, 26 July, 9 August, 27 September 1928, and British Honduras, *Annual Report of the Medical Department*, 1929, 6. On continued demands see *Clarion*, 19 February 1930.

41. *Independent*, 12 and 19 February 1930.

42. BA, Minute Paper Collection 1795-1930 (29 September). The obituary of Mrs. Rafaela Garcia McField (1896–1995) appeared in the *Times*, 23 July 1995, listing James McField as her husband from 1913 until his death in 1971. She had come to Belize Town from Cayo in the early years of the century under the care of her older sister, after her parents died. She was described as "a kind and loving person who was a consummate peacemaker." Some of that good-heartedness comes through in her quietly, almost apologetically assertive 1930 petition.

43. For the Cayo petitions see BA, Minute Paper Collection 376-1921 (24 January), 1322-1921 (16 April), and 1368-1921 (27 April). Susana Cowo and Felipa Torres were the only female signatories of the first of these petitions. BA, Minute Paper Collection 1315-1920 (20 April), includes a special warrant dated 14 November 1921 allowing expenditure beyond the 1921–22 estimates for the construction of the Cayo hospital. On the hospital's completion see British Honduras, *Annual Report of the Medical Department*, 1923, 13. The district medical officer also noted that there had been dramatic improvement in sanitation since his last posting there in 1919. The screening of the hospital is reported in British Honduras, *Annual Report of the Medical Department*, 1930, 21.

44. *Clarion*, 29 August and 4 September 1913.

45. John Everitt, "The Growth and Development of Belize City." For an excellent study of urban sanitarianism in the British Caribbean see Juanita de Barros, *Order and Place in a Colonial City*.

46. BA, Minute Paper Collection 1781-1919 (July), contains one of the first versions of these hygiene lessons. The annual reports of the Medical Department from the late 1920s specify that they remained the principal form of hygiene education in the colony.

47. On income tax see BA, Minute Paper Collection 3713-1920 (Great Britain, *Annual Report on the Social and Economic Progress of the People of British Honduras*, 1920). Details of more vigorous local tax collection can be found in BA, Minute Paper Collection 560-1920 (10 February) on Toledo, 638-1920 (24 February) on Corozal, 3566-1920 (30 November) on Cayo, and 2743-1924 (6 October) on Cayo.

48. On the organization of the Central Board of Health see British Honduras, *Annual Report of the Medical Department*, 1923, 6. On Hutson's frustration see British Honduras, *Annual Report of the Medical Department*, 1923, 2. For budget numbers see

Blue Book, 1911, C3; *Blue Book*, 1916–17, 33; *Blue Book*, 1925, 65, and *Blue Book*, 1927–31, 47. On Hutson's pessimism see BA, Minute Paper Collection 1117-1920 (9 April).

49. On Cayo latrines see BA, Minute Paper Collection 1939-1920 (22 June). The Guinea Grass petition is in BA, Minute Paper Collection 992-1920 (21 March), while mention of Corozal villagers' emigration is in BA, Minute Paper Collection 3417-1920 (20 November).

50. Prosecutions for sanitation infractions are detailed in the British Honduras, *Annual Report of the Medical Department*, 1923, 17, the British Honduras, *Annual Report of the Medical Department*, 1929, 22, and the British Honduras, *Annual Report of the Medical Department*, 1930, 28.

51. The original petition is in BA, Minute Paper Collection 3189-1920 (November). The petition leader was Ramon Martinez, a barber, who was a CDS trustee in 1925 (BA, Minute Paper Collection 1089-1925 (3 April), "Constitution and Rules of the Carib Sick-Aid and Development Society"). Other signatories were Thomas V. Ramos, Gervasio J. Norales, and Thomas Petillo, all CDS officers. The CDS had just over one hundred members in the late 1920s (BA, Minute Paper Collection 574-1927 (8 March) and 229-1928), and was thus not much more representative than the UNIA. The CDS constitution treated men as members and women and children as members' dependents and beneficiaries. Unlike the UNIA, it had no female executive. Two other significant CDS founders were civil servant C. J. Benguche and Zacharias Flores, who was a labor activist in the 1930s. On the 1927 crisis see BA, Minute Paper Collection 1247-1927 (24 June) and 1963-1927 (2 November). Ramos and another CDS officer, shopkeeper B. C. O. Blanco, were on the town board in 1927, as was Benito Guerrero, a middle-strata Garifuna (BA, Minute Paper Collection 454-1927 [14 February]).

52. The Stann Creek Town thatch controversy is documented in BA, Minute Paper Collection 3576-1919 (28 October), 1225-1920 (14 April), and 378-1921 (29 January).

53. On Camal see BA, Minute Paper Collection 147-1920. On Ramsey and Latchman see BA, Minute Paper Collection 307-1921 (25 January). On Cocom and Loj see BA, Minute Paper Collection 3186-1924 (November).

54. Everitt, "The Growth and Development of Belize City," 83. Belize Town's population rose from 12,423 in 1921 to 16,687 in 1931.

55. See British Honduras, *Annual Report of the Medical Department*, 1930, 28, on septic tanks.

56. BA, Minute Paper Collection 2722-1924 (10 October).

57. BA, Minute Paper Collection 1226-1928. One of the final lists in this large file, dated 21 October 1930, named sixteen individuals who had still not met sanitation standards, of whom nine were women.

58. *Clarion*, "Mespotamia Paragraphs," 27 September and 1 November 1928.

59. Water vat regulations and the Belize Town Board's price for water appear in British Honduras, *Annual Report of the Medical Department*, 1923, 7.

60. *Clarion*, 1 June 1922.

61. *Clarion*, 5, 12, 26 July and 2 August 1923.

62. Details of Hutson's piped water efforts of 1924 come from British Honduras, *Annual Report of the Medical Department*, 1923 (Hutson's introduction), and from Great Britain, *Annual Report on the Social and Economic Progress of the People of British Honduras*, 1924, 10. On continuing shortages see British Honduras, *Annual Report of the Medical Department*, 1927, 9.

63. BA, Minute Paper Collection 2986-1924 (19 July).

64. The Cayo District was an early target for compulsory education. See BA, Minute Paper Collection 1095-1918 (25 March), Report on the Cayo District for the Year 1917. On the reach of the act by 1919 see British Honduras, *Annual Report of the Education Department*, 1919, 1.

65. CO 123/296/65699, "Riot at Belize."

66. BA, Minute Paper Collection 508-1921 (11 February) and 2394-1921 (15 August), and Great Britain, *Annual Report on the Social and Economic Progress of the People of British Honduras*, 1924, 18.

67. *Clarion*, 29 April 1920.

68. *Clarion*, 19 January 1922.

69. *Clarion*, 28 December 1921.

70. *Clarion*, 5 January 1928. Reverend Harvey of the Methodist schools raised this issue.

71. *Clarion*, 21 November 1918. The report was submitted 28 August 1918.

72. BA, Minute Paper Collection 1923-1919 (15 August).

73. BA, Minute Paper Collection 2582-1920 (24 September).

74. The education budget jumped from $26,487 in 1916–17 to $54,424 in 1922–23 to $72,509 in 1927–28 (BA, *Blue Books*).

75. BA, Minute Paper Collection 2127-1921 (16 July).

76. BA, Minute Paper Collection 3177-1921 (25 October). Unlike the Brazilian mothers in Susan K. Besse, *Restructuring Patriarchy*, ch. 4, Martin and Moray did not blame themselves for their children's weaknesses.

77. BA, Minute Paper Collection 903-1921 (20 March). Martin did not appear on the police's truancy lists.

78. BA, Minute Paper Collection 1323-1921 (25 April) and 1324-1921 (15 February).

79. BA, Minute Paper Collection 1920-1924 (June 23). Twenty-eight men and 14 women signed the petition.

80. The Industrial School Committee was appointed in March 1918, comprised of William Hoar (the keeper of prisons), George Grabham (manager of BEC), J. B. Brindley (a clergyman), and Frans Dragten. BA, Minute Paper Collection 3559-1917 (6 November). Woods applauded it in *Clarion*, 28 November 1918. Hutson referred to "vagrant children" and "vagrant boys and juvenile offenders" in BA, Despatches Out, 30 April and 24 May 1919, before the riot. Young Creoles were characterized as hooligans in BA, Minute Paper Collection 702-1920 (2 March).

81. BA, Minute Paper Collection 353-1921 (Prison Report for 1920).

82. BA, Minute Paper Collection 3537-1920 (3 December).

83. BA, Minute Paper Collection 2623-1920 (25 August).

84. BA, Minute Paper Collection 1500-1927 (8 June) and 1883-1927 (26 July). These were quarterly reports submitted by the district commissioners, who before 1927 had written only annual reports. British Honduras, *Annual Report of the Medical Department*, 1927, 29, gives the year-end figure for 1927, as does Great Britain, *Annual Report on the Social and Economic Progress of the People of British Honduras*, 1929, 9, for that year. Legislation to create the school passed in the early 1920s, but revenue shortfalls delayed its establishment (ch. 69, The Government Industrial Schools Ordinance, *New Edition of the Consolidated Laws of British Honduras*, 475–82, consolidated ordinances 28 of 1920 and 42 of 1923).

85. British Honduras, *Annual Report of the Medical Department*, 1930, 24.

86. The superintendent of prisons' views are in British Honduras, *Annual Report of the Prison Department*, 1922, 4, and *Annual Report of the Prison Department*, 1923, 3–5. The red-collar system is outlined in BA, Minute Paper Collection 3325-1921 (7 November). Commentary on the UNIA exhibition is in *Clarion*, 5 January 1922.

87. BA, Minute Paper Collection 1292-1920 (April 22).

88. Cran was a physician in private practice and for the militia, which was renamed the Defence Force in 1928, with the motto "Shoulder to Shoulder." Fairweather, *A Short History*, 43. For Cran's speech, given on the same occasion as Lady Burdon's, see *Independent*, 12 March 1930.

3. Hurricane from Below

1. Ernest E. Cain, *Cyclone!*, 6, cast the hurricane in biblical terms. Details of the damage can be found throughout Cain's book and in Everitt, "The Growth and Development of Belize City," 101; *Independent*, 16 and 30 September 1931, 7 and 14 October 1931, and Bolland, "Labour Control and Resistance in Belize in the Century after 1838," in *Colonialism and Resistance*, 169. On the crowds gathered at the police station see Cain, *Cyclone!*, 24. On George Price see *Independent*, 7 October 1931.

2. Lady Burdon, "Hurricane Housekeeping."

3. On trade statistics see Bolland, "Labour Control and Resistance in Belize in the Century after 1838," in *Colonialism and Resistance*, 162, and Norman Ashcraft, *Colonialism and Underdevelopment*, 48. On declining government revenues and wages see Great Britain, *Annual Report on the Social and Economic Progress of the People of British Honduras*, 1931, 29, and Pim, *Report of the Commissioner*, 30–31. *Independent*, 7 June 1932, reported that BEC was paying the few remaining mahogany workers only $6 per month, less than during the World War One trade depression.

4. Dr. V. F. Anderson's report on the Belize District in BA, Miscellaneous Collection 1677, *A Report of the Committee on Nutrition*, 24–26.

5. Grant, *The Making of Modern Belize*, 67, contrasts the political retreat of Belize's middle class with the alliances the middle class in other Caribbean colonies during the 1930s made with labor.

6. Soberanis Gomez and Kemp, *The Third Side of the Anglo-Guatemalan Dispute over Belize or British Honduras*, 10.

7. Cain, *Cyclone!*, x, 6, 129–30.

8. *Independent*, 15 July 1931, 7 December 1932, 12 July 1933, 21 February 1934.

9. Grant, *The Making of Modern Belize*, 79–81, and Bolland, "The Labour Movement and the Genesis of Modern Politics in Belize," in *Colonialism and Resistance*, 176.

10. Bolland, "The Labour Movement and the Genesis of Modern Politics in Belize," in *Colonialism and Resistance*, 171; Ashdown, "Antonio Soberanis and the Disturbances in Belize 1934–1937," 62. The LUA's independence from middle-class leadership confirms Judd's argument that "the broad vision of creole solidarity" definitively fractured in the 1930s, although she attributes this to economic hardships rather than political choices (Judd, "Elite Reproduction and Ethnic Identity in Belize," 306).

11. Soberanis and Kemp, *The Third Side of the Anglo-Guatemalan Dispute over Belize or British Honduras*, 10.

12. Bolland, "The Labour Movement and the Genesis of Modern Politics in Belize," in *Colonialism and Resistance*, 176. For the key distinction between a limited movement and a blossoming struggle, see Ranajit Guha, "On Some Aspects of the Historiography of Colonial India," 6.

13. Bolland, "Race, Ethnicity and National Integration in Belize," in *Colonialism and Resistance*, 200, suggests that processes of political integration deepened and accelerated in the 1930s. Bolland, *Belize: A New Nation in Central America*, 36, refers to the struggles of the 1930s as "the crucible of modern Belizean politics."

14. Ashdown, "Antonio Soberanis and the Disturbances in Belize 1934–1937," 70, contrasts the LUA with the People's National Party in Jamaica.

15. Bolland, "The Labour Movement and the Genesis of Modern Politics in Belize," in *Colonialism and Resistance*, 180.

16. Eric Hobsbawm, *Age of Extremes*, 214–22.

17. See Frederick Cooper, *Decolonization and African Society*, 58. Reddock has pushed the date back to 1934 to include the National Unemployed Movement's "hunger marches" in Trinidad and Tobago.

18. Bolland, *The Politics of Labour in the British Caribbean*, 368.

19. Franklin Knight, *The Caribbean*, 286–87 and Bolland, *The Politics of Labour in the British Caribbean*, 365.

20. Bolland, *The Politics of Labour in the British Caribbean*, 513–30.

21. BA, Miscellaneous Collection 27, Antonio Soberanis, "This is my life history and background."

22. *Independent*, 9 September 1931.

23. *Times*, "Tribute to Antonio Soberanis G.," 23 February 1975.

24. Soberanis "This is my life history and background."

25. Reddock, *Women, Labour, and Politics*, 108–11, 135–42, 156–61. See also Verene Shepherd, *Women in Caribbean History*, 165–67.

26. The Belize Archives' collection of colonial Minute Papers includes these petitions up to the year 1934.

27. On male unemployment and early unrest see *Independent*, 31 January 1932 and 22 April 1931; Pim, *Report of the Commissioner*, 150. On female political debates see Pim, *Report of the Commissioner*, 12 April 1933.

28. Pim, *Report of the Commissioner*, 18 March 1931.

29. BA, Miscellaneous Collection 1677, *A Report of the Committee on Nutrition*, 25.

30. BA, Minute Paper Collection 382-1932 (6 February). In 1938 a special syphilis clinic was opened at the Belize Hospital, with 1,456 cases treated (British Honduras, *Annual Report of the Medical Department*, 1938, 5).

31. BA, Minute Paper Collection 1050-1932 (11 May).

32. On proposals to legalize trade unions see Bolland, "Labour Control and Resistance in Belize in the Century after 1838," in *Colonialism and Resistance*, 163, and *Independent*, 10 and 24 August 1932. On export tax cuts see Ashcraft, *Colonialism and Underdevelopment*, 48. On the land tax increase see Grant, *The Making of Modern Belize*, 64–66. Large landowners simply refused to pay, while smallholders petitioned for tax relief and ended up working off tax debt through "relief" jobs.

33. Bolland, "The Labour Movement and the Genesis of Modern Politics in Belize," in *Colonialism and Resistance*, 170, argues that women, children and the elderly bore "the brunt of the poverty" and overcrowding. *Independent*, 8 June 1932, cast these

pregnant women as dependents of men who should be hired instead—"to save the woman and her offspring"—but they were likely single mothers. Interview with Aurelia Humes, 7 July 1994. Humes went on to become a PUP activist in Cayo from the 1950s.

34. For coverage of the Jobless Workers see the *Independent*, 7, 14, and 28 December 1932, 4, 11, and 25 January 1933, 1 and 8 February 1933, 15 March 1933, 19 April 1933, 3 and 10 May 1933, 5 July 1933. The original deputation to Kittermaster comprised James Pipersburgh, J. A. Campbell, J. Bulwer, and the brothers Simon and Solomon Trapp. Soberanis donated $1, an amount similar to that given by various officials and merchants. Soap testimonials came from a multiethnic group in Corozal, including those with East Indian names (Williams, Gilharry), mestizo names (Peraza, Chavarria), Mayan names (Bob), and Creole names (Catthouse, Neal).

35. The large community petitions included BA, Minute Paper Collection 2068-1932 (Cayo), 388-1932 (Benque Viejo), 1081-1932 (Ambergris Caye), 1912-1932 (Orange Walk villages), 576-1933 (11 April) (Patchakan and Yo Chen). This last document contains the Mayan tenant farmers' stated plan to organize. They were tenants of BEC, which was refusing to grant leases for 1933 unless all rent arrears and all 1933 rents were paid in full, in cash or corn. The district commissioner asked his superiors to fix the price of corn in order to ease the burden on the indebted men, to no avail. BEC's local agent, merchant Cornelio Lizarraga, did not want to carry out management's orders to evict: "Owing to the depression . . . they find it very hard even to live. Every day they come and . . . beg me to help them." On these villages' support for Soberanis see Bolland, "The Labour Movement and the Genesis of Modern Politics in Belize," in *Colonialism and Resistance*, 175. On the *chicleros'* wage protest see BA, Minute Paper Collection 1975-1930 (District Commissioner's Quarterly Report on the Cayo District, July to September 1930). The proeducation petitions are in BA, Minute Paper Collection 338-1933 (Corozal Town) and 331-1933 (Benque Viejo).

36. Interview with Adolfa Garcia (née Cal), October 1993. District reports of the period indicate a surge in crop production, so much so that local market prices collapsed, depressing family's cash incomes. See BA, Minute Paper Collection 99, 322, 332, 1032, 2352 of 1932, and 304-1933.

37. On the vital farmwork of Garifuna women see BA, Minute Paper Collection 289-1932 (26 January), District Commissioner to Colonial Secretary. The *Census of British Honduras, 1931*, Table 2, 52, listed 324 women small farmers in the colony, 265 of them in the Stann Creek District; probably the large majority were Garifuna. H. T. A. Bowman's observation comes from his life story, *Emerald Valley and Twinkling Town*, 18. His father, W. A. J. Bowman, was the pioneer and king of Stann Creek cit-

rus and won election to the Legislative Council in 1936. On the packing shed see BA, Minute Paper Collection 2085-1933. Women were easily hired at cheap wages to wash, wrap, and pack the fruit. The petition against a land tax, BA, Minute Paper Collection 289-1932 (January), was signed by 348 men and 165 women. Belize City officials dismissed most petitioners as nontaxpayers who had been engaging in less acceptable forms of protest: threatening local officials and derailing cars in the valley. But the district commissioner supported the petition, citing Garifuna women's vital food production. On Garifuna women's meeting with Kittermaster see *Independent*, 31 August 1932. On their relief work see BA, Report on the Stann Creek District for 1932, and MP 1434-1934 (10 October). Men were paid seventy-five cents per day.

38. See BA, Minute Paper Collection 2075-1932 (22 August), for the petition. Reminiscent of the UNIA-BCN relationship, the CDS nurses' training was a key element in the political self-construction of the small cadre of Garifuna shopkeepers and tradesmen. Eventually just two young CDS women were trained. One of these was Mrs. Juanita Joseph's mother Paula Sabal Castillo, who did not work as a nurse after her marriage (interview with Juanita Joseph, 7 April 1994). On the CDS in 1931 see Cain, *Cyclone!*, 127–28.

39. BA, Minute Paper Collection 1167-1932 (5 April).

40. Lifelong teacher Isoleen Straughan remembers the 1930s and 1940s as a period when women took on much of the family breadwinner role, although the structural and conjunctural crises in forestry employment also revealed women's existing work more starkly (interview with Isoleen Straughan, 6 October 1994).

41. Bolland, "The Labour Movement and the Genesis of Modern Politics in Belize," in Colonialism and Resistance, 170, describes the municipal hutments. On Hill see BA, Minute Paper Collection 115-1933 (6 February). Hill was receiving $1 per week from the father of one of her daughters and food from her brothers. This file contains a large number of individual petitions from men and women. On Moses see BA, Minute Paper Collection 1252-1932 (11 May). In April and May 1932 there were one hundred women on the Magazine Road rock-breaking gang (BA, Minute Paper Collection 1050-1932 [5 May]). On the roof removal see *Independent*, 7 September 1932.

42. On the East Indian woman see *Independent*, 13 January 1932. Almost the entire Belize Town East Indian community perished in the hurricane. On Hewitt see BA, Minute Paper Collection 115-1933 (13 May). On Ocean see BA, Minute Paper Collection 1236-1932 (29 April) and 115-1933 (20 June).

43. Of twenty-six female compensation claims approved (BA, Minute Paper Collection 1955-1932), five women's applications survive: Minute Paper Collection

166, 196, 253, 609, and 1579 of 1932. For Diamond's protest see BA, Minute Paper Collection 115-1933. John Lahoodie was one of Soberanis's chief associates until late 1934, when he and Benjamin Reneau, a UNIA officer in 1920, split from the LUA, forming the BHUA. Lahoodie was also in the small radical nationalist group of 1940–41. Detained in a government camp in 1941–42, he moved to Guatemala after his release (Bolland, "The Labour Movement and the Genesis of Modern Politics in Belize," in *Colonialism and Resistance*, 171, 174, 179). For Lahoodie's housing protest see BA, Minute Paper Collection 2069-1932 (9 September). It is unclear whether this wife was Henrietta Diamond.

44. Coverage of drought conditions can be found in *Independent*, 5 February and 23 April 1930, 6 January, 2 and 30 March, 6 April 1932, 1 February, 5 and 12 April 1933, 21 February 1934. William Henry Arnold, organizer of the 1918 petition for political change and economic development, wrote in April 1932 that the town had suffered water shortages for fifty years. Details of the water tickets and lineups come from my interview with Miss May Davis (26 October 1994). A teenager during those years, she remembered six water tickets, enough for three kerosene cans of water, costing five cents. Women would carry the water home on their heads: "I wouldn't want those days to come back," she said. On criticism of the authorities see *Independent*, 19 April 1933. On the Easter 1933 actions see *Independent*, 19 and 26 April and 3 May 1933.

45. *Independent*, 20 January 1932. Grant, *The Making of Modern Belize*, 107.

46. Grant, *The Making of Modern Belize*, 102, citing CO 123/337, File 94670, Governor to Secretary of State, 21 April and 28 October 1933.

47. *Independent*, 2 November 1932. Manhood and universal suffrage were normally invoked at public meetings by PP leaders, but in their official proposals to colonial authorities they always limited the franchise by requiring low property qualifications to vote.

48. *Independent*, 2 November 1932. Elfreda Trapp was born Elfreda Stanford in 1900 and became Elfreda Reyes upon her remarriage in the 1940s. I interviewed her in 1991 before learning of her exploits in the 1930s.

49. Property qualifications were $300 income, $500 real property, or $96 rent per year (Bolland, "The Labour Movement and the Genesis of Modern Politics in Belize," in *Colonialism and Resistance*, 176, and Grant, *The Making of Modern Belize*, 106).

50. *Independent*, 15 February 1933.

51. "The Black Cross Nurses' Activities in Social Work and Otherwise," *Independent*, 19 July 1933.

52. *Independent*, 8 and 22 November 1933. One of the six PP men elected to the board was Clifford Betson, future president of the General Workers' Union

(GWU). Meighan would go on to run in the 1936 and 1939 legislative elections with Soberanis's support and finally won in 1942, when he had taken over the leadership of Soberanis's BHWTU).

53. On the Employment Bureau proposal see *Independent*, 3 January 1934. On the Palace Unemployed Women's Fund see *Independent*, 21 February and 11 April 1934.

54. *Independent*, 31 January, 7 and 14 February 1934.

55. Research in British Honduran legal records on legalized divorce and working-class women is still to be done.

56. Reddock, *Women, Labour, and Politics*, 129–32. Seay's counterpart in Trinidad was Audrey Jeffers, who founded the Côterie of Social Workers in 1921 for "black and coloured women" (Reddock, *Women, Labour, and Politics*, 57). The Côterie was not part of the Trinidad UNIA. *Independent*, 31 January 1934, reported on a mass meeting of Catholic women in Belize Town.

57. On the Cleopha Perdomo attack and Perez's trials see *Independent*, 13 September, 29 November, and 6 and 13 December 1933. On the Tessecum and Brown cases see, respectively, *Independent*, 1 February 1933 and 27 February 1935. Tessecum's partner Alfonso Galves was found guilty of maiming and Brown's—Bartolo Gongora—of wounding. For other examples from across the colony see *Independent*, 27 January 1932, 30 March 1932, and 13 and 20 November 1935. On the William Johnson case see *Independent*, 21 January 1937. The column critical of unsympathetic wives appeared in *Independent*, 18 April 1934.

58. *Independent*, 9 January 1935. Only unofficials Alexander Hunter and Henry Melhado, both Catholics, voted against the bill.

59. On the Unemployed Brigade march see *Independent*, 14 February 1934, and *Clarion*, 15 February 1934. On unemployed relief see Bolland, "The Labour Movement and the Genesis of Modern Politics in Belize," in *Colonialism and Resistance*, 171.

60. BA, Minute Paper Collection 1666-1934, *Report regarding the Disturbances in Belize on 1st and 2nd October*, 1934, 2–3 (written by Police Superintendent Matthews, and hereafter cited as Matthews), and *Independent*, 21 March 1934.

61. *Independent*, 20 March 1935. The elections were held the night before. The all-male executive consisted of Soberanis as president, James "Bangula" Barnett as vice president, James Daly as secretary, Archibald Lodge as assistant secretary, and Fred Allen as treasurer. The six male committee members were Charles Lovell, Hubert Lopez, James Livingston, Wilfred Vernon, Edward Franklin, and John G. A. Stamp.

62. Bolland, "The Labour Movement and the Genesis of Modern Politics in Belize," in *Colonialism and Resistance*, 186 n. 29, cites Soberanis to Burns, 23 September 1935, CO 123/353/66571, as evidence of the LUA nursing group of twenty-two women, but

it clearly existed earlier. Letters of appreciation to the LUA nurses appeared in the *Independent*, 2 September and 23 October 1935. *Independent*, 15 November 1933, announced Trapp's thanks to those who supported her after Solomon Trapp's death. In my interview with Adelia Dixon, September 1993, she mentioned the group of LUA women who met at Pratt's home. Dixon, who was never part of the LUA, also recalled that a woman named Esner Rose was part of the core group. Another possible member was Mrs. Christobel Middleton (interview with Eduardo Espat, June 1994). She was married to Henry A. Middleton, who was Clifford Betson's second-in-command of the GWU in the 1940s. When she died in 1950, scores of GWU members attended her funeral (*Billboard*, 29 October 1950). Eliza Brooks was the cook at Government House in 1933, raising six children alone. She petitioned the authorities to give one of her sons a job (BA, Minute Paper Collection 1137-1933 [29 May]). The Stann Creek delegation included Susan Cacho, Antonia Gutierrez, Ofonia Genio, Petrona Enriquez, and Cecilia White, none of whom appeared on E. E. Cain's list of CDS women in 1931. Soberanis almost certainly traveled to Cayo at some point, for Eugenio and Eustaquia Galvez remember him visiting the district's villages and *ranchitos* and holding lamp-lit meetings in downtown San Ignacio, which women attended. They were twenty-four and twenty in 1934 and described Soberanis as a bilingual barber who was "for the poor"(interview with Don Eugenio and Doña Eustaquia Galvez, 15 June 1994).

63. Matthews, 4, on LUA women and the length of Battlefield meetings. On the frequency and size of LUA meetings see Bolland, "The Labour Movement and the Genesis of Modern Politics in Belize," in *Colonialism and Resistance*, 171. On women's particular enthusiasm see *Independent*, 12 December 1934.

64. *Independent*, 21 March 1934.

65. Details of this general period are in Matthews, 3–5, and *Independent*, 16 May 1934. BEC's manager had been living in Government House since the hurricane. For Soberanis's threat against Matthews see Matthews, 4, and *Independent*, 25 April and 2 May 1934. Matthews, then a police officer, had been assaulted during the 1919 riot.

66. BA, Minute Paper Collection 700-1934 (17 May), Soberanis to Kittermaster, also printed in *Independent*, 30 May 1934.

67. Matthews, 4, merely described him as claiming authority as "the chosen leader of the unemployed."

68. BA, Minute Paper Collection 700-1934.

69. Matthews, 5. At some point a LUA song, "Arise Ye Belizeans from Starvation," was created and became popular. It was revived in the early days of the popular nationalist movement in 1950, forming a link with the popular culture of the 1930s anticolonialism.

70. *Independent*, 8 August 1934. It was probably on this occasion that the photo of Soberanis with Vivian Seay and the Black Cross Nurses was taken. The photo also appears in the nationalist elementary history text *Belize: A Nation in the Making* (Belize: Sunshine Books, 1983), 50. Reddock, *Women, Labour, and Politics*, 291, notes that by the 1930s 1 August had been forgotten by most Trinidadians, but that from 1939 the Negro Welfare Cultural and Social Association tried to revive it.

71. Matthews, 5–6, and *Independent*, 26 September 1934.

72. For general descriptions of the LUA's 10th see Matthews, 7, and *Independent*, 12 September 1934. *Independent*, 5 September 1934, reported that a descendant of Lamb's gave the cap to Soberanis. Soberanis's son Tony Jr. recalled that the red and green colors of the LUA came from the cap of a mahogany laborer (interview with Antonio Soberanis Jr., 5 July 1991). On the 1931 wreath laying at Paslow's grave see Cain, *Cyclone!*, 3. Details of women's work during the feast come from sources cited above and from my interview with Winifred Flowers, 22 April 1994.

73. On the stevedores' strike see Bolland, "The Labour Movement and the Genesis of Modern Politics in Belize," in *Colonialism and Resistance*, 173. Their pay rose from eight to twenty-five cents per hour. On Soberanis's threats against Phillips see Matthews, 7. Another man arrested for using threatening language at this meeting was Simeon White, a very recent Jamaican immigrant, who advocated overthrowing white rule by covering the streets in "blood, fire and water." At his trial he testified that he was referring to a prophecy made during the 1894 riot that had been repeated to him by elderly Belize residents after he arrived in the colony. James Pipersburgh, Thomas Livingston, and Caroline Clare all confirmed that they had been in the 1894 riot and had heard the prophecy (*Independent*, 31 October 1934).

74. For a description of the strike scene at 6:30 am see Matthews, 8. Soberanis's remark appears in *Clarion*, 4 October 1934.

75. *Clarion*, 4 October 1934. *Independent*, 3 October 1934, perhaps more concerned to play down popular disorder, merely reported that "[t]he crowd left disappointed."

76. *Clarion*, 4 October 1934, and *Independent*, 3 October 1934.

77. Ashdown, "Antonio Soberanis and the Disturbances in Belize 1934–1937," 65.

78. Interview with Antonio Soberanis Jr., 5 July 1991. Among these women was Amybelle Craig with her granddaughter Idolly (interview with Idolly Erskine, 8 October 1994).

79. *Clarion*, 4 October 1934; *Independent*, 3 and 24 October 1934.

80. Matthews, appendix 1: Return of offences committed on Monday 1st October, 1934, and dealt with summarily; *Clarion*, 11 October 1934.

81. Matthews, 14.

82. Matthews, 15. Of thirty-two rioters arrested, twenty-six were convicted. Besides Sarah Moore, at least three others were women: Mavis Brakeman, Elma Petillo, and Elfreda Millings. The government responded to the unrest by promising $3000 in immediate relief (Bolland, "The Labour Movement and the Genesis of Modern Politics in Belize," in *Colonialism and Resistance*, 174).

83. *Independent*, 14 November 1934.

84. *Independent*, 12 December 1934. Three of the eight male leaders remained with Soberanis: James "Bangula" Barnett, Charles Lovell, and Fred Allen.

85. *Independent*, 12 December 1934.

86. *Independent*, 9 January and 3 April 1935.

87. Luke D. Kemp reacted to the constitutional bill with a strong call for universal suffrage (*Independent*, 9 January 1935), but the PP took the position that the poor majority did not need the vote to get proper representation (*Independent*, 23 January 1935).

88. *Independent*, 6 and 13 February 1935.

89. *Independent*, 13 February 1935.

90. *Independent*, 13 February 1935.

91. The absence of "Carib" from the petition's list of racial groups is not as meaningful as the overall exclusion of whites from the category "native." The term "Negro" may have included both Creole and Garifuna women, for the latter were already active in the LUA in Stann Creek and soon would be even more so.

92. *Independent*, 13 February 1935.

93. On the southern tour see *Independent*, 22 May 1935. Details of the Stann Creek visit come from my interviews with Mrs. Alexandrina Martinez, 9 May 1994, and with Joe and Canuta Flores, May 1994. On the labor disturbances that followed that visit see Bolland, "The Labour Movement and the Genesis of Modern Politics in Belize," in *Colonialism and Resistance*, 175, *Independent*, 29 May 1935, and CO 123/353/66568, which names Patricia Ramos as the woman arrested.

94. Bolland, "The Labour Movement and the Genesis of Modern Politics in Belize," in *Colonialism and Resistance*, 175.

95. *Independent*, 11 September 1935.

96. Bolland, "The Labour Movement and the Genesis of Modern Politics in Belize," in *Colonialism and Resistance*, 175.

97. *Independent*, 29 January 1936. He allegedly referred to the king as a "crook."

98. Grant, *The Making of Modern Belize*, 107, citing W. H. Courtenay (chairman), *Report of the Commission of Inquiry on Constitutional Reform 1951* (Belize City: Government Printer, 1951), 26.

99. *Independent*, 18 and 25 December 1935, 5 February 1936.

100. *Independent*, 29 July and 2 September 1936. In July, Soberanis as well as PP leader Morrel Staine were campaigning in Stann Creek for Ricardo Meighan. Meighan lost the by-election to citrus king W. A. J. Bowman, who was supported by leading Garifuna men.

101. *Independent*, 22 July 1936.

102. *Independent*, 12 March 1941.

103. Bolland, "The Labour Movement and the Genesis of Modern Politics in Belize," in *Colonialism and Resistance*, 177–78. Unrest began again in 1937, when in Cayo hundreds signed a petition for higher wages organized by Gabriel "Nehi" Adderley (*Independent*, 23 June 1937), and when Belize stevedores struck a United Fruit steamer. In 1938, mahogany workers struck in Toledo, Soberanis held large pro-labor meetings in Belize and Dangriga, and unrest among unemployed men on the relief rolls resulted in expanded road work from November until January of 1939. In 1939, unemployment in Belize remained in the twelve hundred to two thousand-man range, and the BHWTU built a membership of seven hundred. In June Stann Creek road workers struck.

104. *Independent*, 9 December 1936 and 30 August 1937; Bolland, "The Labour Movement and the Genesis of Modern Politics in Belize," in *Colonialism and Resistance*, 176.

105. *Independent*, 12 July 1939 and Herrmann, *The Origins of Tomorrow*, 56 and 61.

106. *Clarion*, 7 and 16 February 1940. When I interviewed Winifred Flowers, which was prior to reading these documents, she did not bring up either her association with Lahoodie or this incident.

107. *Independent*, 15, 22, 29 May and 12 June 1940. Garcia was joined on the Knights of Labour executive by Guerre Acosta, Angel Vera, and Santiago Arjona, who was definitely Mayan. The village representatives named were Aniseto Ku from Yo Chen and Alejandro Acosta, John Cano, Crescencio Zapata, and Tomás Santana from Xaibe.

108. BA, Minute Paper Collection 576-1933 (11 April).

109. On the Stann Creek demonstration see *Independent*, 8 January 1941.

110. The BHWTU now had branches in Dangriga, Corozal, and San Ignacio (Bolland, "The Labour Movement and the Genesis of Modern Politics in Belize," in *Colonialism and Resistance*, 178, and *Independent*, 26 March 1941). In 1942, when Soberanis left for Panama, Meighan became president of the BHWTU and was elected to the Legislative Council as a representative of the Belize District.

111. *Independent*, 27 August 1941.

112. CO 123/380/10, Hutson to Secretary of State for the Colonies, 8 February 1943.

Hutson classified this document as secret and in it argued that adult suffrage, while less desirable than a return to crown colony rule, was the only politically feasible strategy.

113. Bolland, "The Labour Movement and the Genesis of Modern Politics in Belize," in *Colonialism and Resistance*, 178–79 and 187 n. 50, Governor Hunter to Lord Moyne, 24 October 1941 and n. 52, Governor Hunter to Viscount Cranbourne, 5 March 1942, both BA 174.

114. *Independent*, 27 August 1941, from minutes of a Legislative Council meeting. Like Pedro Albízu Campos in Puerto Rico, the Belizean radical nationalists seem to have been open to extreme right-wing influences.

115. Soberanis, "This is my life history and background."

4. Modernizing Colonialism

1. The epigraphs come from Great Britain, *Annual Report on the Social and Economic Progress*, 1946, 3, and *Independent*, 27 March 1940, respectively.

2. Howe, *Anticolonialism in British Politics*, 90.

3. Bolland, *The Politics of Labour in the British Caribbean*, 387.

4. Holt, *The Problem of Freedom*, 390; *West India Royal Commission Report*, 220–21 and 60.

5. See D. K. Fieldhouse, "The Labour Governments and the Empire-Commonwealth," in *The Foreign Policy of the British Labour Governments, 1945–51*, 86, 103, 105–106; D. J. Goldsworthy, *Colonial Issues in British Politics, 1945–61*, 14–20, 118–21, 132; P. S. Gupta, *Imperialism and the British Labour Movement, 1914–1964*, 11, 55, 131, 260; and Howe, *Anticolonialism in British Politics*, 44–45, 98–99, 138–39.

6. Holt, *The Problem of Freedom*, 398.

7. Antoinette Burton, *Gender, Sexuality and Colonial Modernities*, 2.

8. Reddock, *Women, Labour, and Politics*, 237, makes precisely this argument, though she defines colonial modernization in terms of social and economic development without making explicit the way that political rights were made contingent on "moral regeneration."

9. Reddock, *Women, Labour, and Politics*, 183, on housewifization.

10. See, for example, La Ray Denzer, "Domestic Science Training in Colonial Yorubaland, Nigeria"; Susan Geiger, TANU *Women*, 28–29; Nancy Rose Hunt, "Domesticity and Colonialism in Belgian Africa; and Margaret Jolly and Kalpana Ram, eds., *Maternities and Modernities*.

11. Annette Baker Fox, *Freedom and Welfare in the Caribbean*, 120, and Mary Proudfoot, *Britain and the United States in the Caribbean*, 231.

12. Baker Fox, *Freedom and Welfare in the Caribbean*, 139.

13. Besse, *Restructuring Patriarchy*, 5, argues that Brazilian feminists gained a lady-like legitimacy with liberal male politicians by limiting their demands.

14. The territorial claim was renewed in the 1945 Guatemalan constitution, during the tenure of Juan José Arévalo. See Grant, *The Making of Modern Belize*, 110, and James Dunkerley, *Power in the Isthmus*, 139. The claim was supported in 1947 by the Arevalista *Unión de Mujeres Democráticas* at a hemispheric feminist congress held in Guatemala City. Ironically, these women shared a social reform perspective with the women of the LPOB. See Miller, *Latin American Women and the Search for Social Justice*, 125–32.

15. BA, Miscellaneous Collection 4901, "Programme of the September 10th, 1948 Celebrations"(published by the Publicity Committee). This was probably the "illustrated brochure" prepared and sold by Mr. T. Keating, mentioned in *Crown Colonist* (November 1948): 649.

16. BA, Miscellaneous Collection 4901. On the intent to "bring up" or raise the cultural tone of the 10th celebrations through the pageant see Richard Wilk, "Connections and Contradictions," 220–21.

17. Burton, *Gender, Sexuality and Colonial Modernities*, 2–3.

18. The rich Minute Paper Collection in the Belize Archives has not survived for the 1935–49 period.

19. Besse, *Restructuring Patriarchy*, 5.

20. On social workers during the Popular Front period in Chile see Rosemblatt, *Gendered Compromises*, 125 and 131. On earlier vocational education see Hutchison, *"Labors Appropriate to their Sex"*, 144.

21. Macpherson, "Citizens vs. Clients".

22. Jamaica Central Bureau of Statistics, *West Indian Census, Part E*, xxxi.

23. British Honduras, *Annual Report of the Labour Department*, 1950, 12.

24. BA, Miscellaneous Collection 1677, *Report of the Committee on Nutrition*.

25. Major St. G. Orde-Browne, *Labour Conditions in the West Indies*, 200. Grant, *The Making of Modern Belize*, 70, echoes this sentiment in arguing that relief should have been given directly to women and children.

26. CO 123/349/35604, Burns to the Secretary of State for the Colonies, 29 November 1934, cited in Graham Hurford, "The Moyne Commission in British Honduras," 5; PRO, CO 123/352/66554, Burns to the Secretary of State for the Colonies, 31 March 1935, cited in Hurford, 6.

27. British Honduras, *Annual Report of the Medical Department*,1938, 17–18. The service was for the entire ribbon of agricultural settlements along the new Belize-Maskall-Orange Walk road, serving twenty-five hundred people three days each month.

28. British Honduras, *Annual Report of the Labour Department*, 1945, 4, appendix 2. Manufacturing jobs paid $3–$4.80 per week for women, $4.75–$7.80 per week for men.

29. Frank G. Sharp, "Activities of the Citrus Company of British Honduras."

30. Douglas MacRae Taylor, *The Black Carib of British Honduras*, 55.

31. Medina, *Negotiating Economic Development*, 63.

32. *Independent*, 6 May 1936. The news may even have spread earlier, for in February a large number of Garifuna women banded together to clear the paths to their farms, angry that men were not carrying out this traditional task (*Independent*, 19 February 1936).

33. *Independent*, 26 August 1936.

34. *Independent*, 8 January 1941, reported that a massive Stann Creek petition for employment mentioned that hundreds of women were ready to expand commercial cassava production. In 1939 workers at the plant staged a strike for higher wages (*Clarion*, 8 January 1940; the *Clarion* at this point became the *Daily Clarion* but will still be referred to here by the short form *Clarion*). Medina, *Negotiating Economic Development*, 146, interviewed a small citrus farmer whose husband had worked at the cassava plant and who remembered that the plant workforce was all-male.

35. *Crown Colonist* (June 1938): 343.

36. *Crown Colonist* (October 1938): 561. They also had two thousand acres in cassava for local consumption.

37. *Independent*, 18 November 1942. The company received a small Colonial Development and Welfare loan in 1945 but never restarted production (*Crown Colonist* [February 1945]: 45).

38. *Independent*, 21 November 1934 and BA, Minute Paper Collection 1628-1934 (22 December).

39. *Independent*, 28 November 1934.

40. BA Miscellaneous Collection 164, Black Cross Nurses, *Compendium of the Living Conditions and Dietary Statistics of the Labouring Classes in the Town of Belize, British Honduras*.

41. The 1946 Census found that 18.7 percent of all mothers in British Honduras were single mothers, while another 18.7 percent were in common-law unions (Jamaica Central Bureau of Statistics, *West Indian Census 1946, Part E*, xxiii.

42. British Honduras, *Annual Report of the Labour Department*, 1947, para 3.

43. British Honduras, *Annual Report of the Labour Department*, 1939, para 20.

44. *Independent*, 27 March 1940.

45. British Honduras, *Annual Reports of the Labour Department*, 1939–45. Both

the Scottish and U.S. labor programs required that the men remit family allotments, which were substantial enough to ease poverty at home during the war.

46. British Honduras, *Annual Report of the Labour Department*, 1946, 8, lists 350 men as public works road laborers.

47. Most recently Bolland has made this argument in *The Politics of Labour in the British Caribbean*, 439.

48. *Clarion*, 13 March 1943.

49. Bolland, *The Politics of Labour in the British Caribbean*, 440, sketches a briefer biography of Betson.

50. *Independent*, 15 October 1941.

51. *Independent*, 5 and 26 November 1941.

52. Sir Frank Stockdale, *Development and Welfare in the West Indies, 1943–44)*, 71, included the GWU on a list of approved responsible unions.

53. *Clarion*, 8 April 1943, reported that Cayo's elected legislator, chicle contractor J. S. Espat, voted against the bill, while his fellow unofficials (citrus king Henry Bowman of Stann Creek, chicle magnate Robert Turton of the Northern District, and S. B. Vernon of Toledo) did not attend the session. British Honduras, *Annual Report of the Labour Department*, 1948, table 10, gives the GWU's registration date as 13 May 1943.

54. British Honduras, *Annual Report of the Labour Department*, 1944, paragraph 32.

55. *Clarion*, 27 May 1942.

56. Bolland, "The Labour Movement and the Genesis of Modern Politics in Belize," in *Colonialism and Resistance*, 183 and 187 n. 69.

57. CO 123/380/10 27103, "Memorandum on the Constitution of British Honduras," 9.

58. *Clarion*, 17 April 1943; Silvana Woods, *Mothers of Modern Belize*, 13–18.

59. *Clarion*, 29 June 1943.

60. British Honduras, *Annual Report of the Labour Department*, 1945, 4, appendix 2, lists shop assistants' wages at $2.50–$10 per week for women, $3–$30 per week for men. The comparable figures for office clerks were $5–$15 and $5–$30 per week respectively. In the grapefruit cannery, men earned three times women's wages.

61. *Belize Billboard*, 2 May 1948 (hereafter cited as *Billboard*). It is not clear who the 183 female unionists were. Some may have come out of the labor associations of the 1930s in Belize City, and there were very probably female citrus workers in the active Stann Creek branch. There were three women on the executive of the new Cayo branch: Annie Barber, Vicenta Gonzalez, and Margaret Catthouse (*Billboard*, 25 April 1948). None of the people whom I interviewed remembered these women.

62. Bolland, "The Labour Movement and the Genesis of Modern Politics in Belize," in *Colonialism and Resistance*, 181, citing *Billboard*, 2 February 1947.

63. *Billboard*, 25 April and 2 May 1948.

64. *Billboard*, 3 January 1948.

65. *Billboard*, 25 April 1948.

66. *Billboard*, 18 January 1948.

67. For evidence of Betson's and Middleton's LPOB leadership, see BA, Miscellaneous Collection 4901.

68. *Billboard*, 18 January 1948

69. *Billboard*, 20 and 27 June 1948.

70. Grant, *The Making of Modern Belize*, 149–51.

71. On Jamaica see Hall, "Gender Politics and Imperial Politics."

72. *Independent*, 15 December 1937.

73. British Honduras, *Annual Report of the Medical Department*, 1935, 4–5, gives a rate of 170.1 infant deaths for every 1,000 live births, whereas a rate of 124 per 1,000 was more typical.

74. British Honduras, *Annual Report of the Medical Department*, 1938, 12.

75. BA, Miscellaneous Collection 1677, *Report of the Committee on Nutrition*, 24.

76. *Independent*, 16 May 1934.

77. *Independent*, 15 January 1936.

78. British Honduras, *Annual Report of the Medical Department*, 1938, 37.

79. *Independent*, 27 March 1935.

80. *Independent*, 6 May 1936.

81. British Honduras, *Annual Report of the Medical Department*, 1938, 37.

82. *Independent*, 12 August and 9 December 1936.

83. BA, Miscellaneous Collection 1677, *Report of the Committee on Nutrition*, 38.

84. *Independent*, 28 April and 26 June 1937. The 1938 *Annual Report of the Medical Department* indicated that every district town had a clinic.

85. *Independent*, 22 June 1938 and the 1938 *Annual Report of the Medical Department*, 11.

86. *Independent*, 10 November 1937 and 22 February 1939.

87. *Independent*, 28 April and 11 August 1937.

88. BA, Miscellaneous Collection 1677, *Report of the Committee on Nutrition*, 38, and BA. Miscellaneous Collection 164. Black Cross Nurses. *Compendium*, Families A1 and A4.

89. British Honduras, *Annual Report of the Medical Department*, 1938, 27, 30, 34, 37.

90. Ibid. Cayo, Orange Walk, and Corozal saw twenty-nine, twenty, and twenty-eight infants weekly, on average, respectively.

91. BA, Miscellaneous Collection 1677, *Report of the Committee on Nutrition*, 32.

92. British Honduras, *Annual Report of the Medical Department*, 1938, 11 and British Honduras, *Annual Report of the Medical Department*, 1937, 10.

93. British Honduras, *Annual Report of the Medical Department*, 1944, 3.

94. *Crown Colonist* (March 1941): 149.

95. *Independent*, 21 June 1944.

96. *Independent*, 14 March 1945, and BA, Miscellaneous Collection 1726, British Honduras, *Report of the Development Planning Committee*, paragraphs 135–36.

97. British Honduras, *Annual Report of the Medical Department*, 1941, para 16.

98. Indeed, the gap from 1935 to 1949 in the Belize Archives' Minute Paper collection means that even individual clinic mothers' demands remain a matter of speculation.

99. British Honduras, *Annual Report of the Medical Department*, 1945, 1.

100. BA, Minute Paper Collection 1315-1952. The leaders were Mrs. E. Smart and Mrs. M. Wade. Of 152 petitioners, 73 are identifiable as women.

101. BA, Minute Paper Collection 756-1952 (12 July). The five women were Amy Jones, Bernice Belisle, Olga Jeffords, Marie Frass, and Christine Kelly.

102. BA, Minute Paper Collection 756-1952 (12 July). This list had a majority of Creole surnames, a minority of Spanish, and one Mayan surname.

103. British Honduras, *Annual Report of the Medical Department*, 1938, 32, 34, 44.

104. British Honduras, *Annual Report of the Medical Department*, 1946, 3.

105. *Clarion*, 6 December 1934.

106. *Independent*, 26 May and 15 December 1937. Kemp's testimony to the WIRC in November 1938 was a direct protest against the suspension of the town board (PRO, CO 950/330, "Working People of Belize, Oral Evidence," 35–36, cited in Hurford, 30–31).

107. British Honduras, *Annual Report of the Medical Department*, 1938, 8.

108. *Clarion*, 29 February and 6 March, 1940.

109. *Clarion*, 8 March, 1940 and *Independent*, 13 March 1940.

110. BA Miscellaneous Collection 191, "A Town Planning Scheme for Belize" (1946).

111. *Crown Colonist*, issues from late 1948 to late 1949.

112. *Independent*, 2 August 1944; *Billboard*, 4 April 1948.

113. BA, Minute Paper Collection 37-1953 (7 October 1954).

114. *Independent*, 13 November 1935.

115. Stoler, *Race and the Education of Desire*, 161, defines the school as a key site for maintaining the morality of white children raised in the colonies, but here the focus was on Belizean children.

116. B. H. Easter, *Report of an Enquiry into the Educational System of British Honduras, 1933–34*, 11.

117. Easter, *Report of an Enquiry into the Educational System of British Honduras, 1933–34*, 34.

118. I. E. Sanchez, *The Easter and Dixon Reports*, 24.

119. *Report of the Development Planning Committee*, paragraphs 10, 11, and 43–44 on agriculture, paragraphs 73 and 124–25 on boys' and girls' education.

120. *Clarion*, 8 May 1943.

121. *Independent*, 21 June 1944.

122. British Honduras, *Report of the Development Planning Committee*, paragraph 138.

123. *Clarion*, 24 February 1940.

124. *Independent*, 4 March and 26 August 1942; *Clarion*, 8 May 1943.

125. *Clarion*, 23 and 30 October and 2, 3, and 6 November 1943.

126. *Independent*, 2 June 1943.

127. British Honduras, *Annual Report of the Education Department*, 1947, n.p.

128. British Honduras, *Annual Report of the Prison Department*, 1947, 1.

129. Interview with Mrs. Olivia Perriot, 26 April 1994.

130. Interview with Mrs. Adolfa Garcia, 9 October 1993.

131. Grant, *The Making of Modern Belize*, 148–53.

132. *Billboard*, 27 June 1948.

133. Medina, *Negotiating Economic Development*, 39 and 44, emphasizes the centrality of the development discourse from the inception of the nationalist movement.

134. British Honduras, *Annual Report of the Social Development Department*, 1951, 1.

135. British Honduras, *Annual Report of the Social Development Department*, 1953, 10.

136. British Honduras, *Annual Report of the Social Development Department*, 1952, 11, on female membership in credit unions and co-ops.

137. British Honduras, *Annual Report of the Social Development Department*, 1952, 12–13.

138. British Honduras, *Annual Report of the Social Development Department*, 1953, 2.

139. British Honduras, *Annual Report of the Social Development Department*, 1954, 7.

140. British Honduras, *Annual Report of the Social Development Department*, 1956, 10.

141. British Honduras *Annual Report*, 1946, 29.

142. BA, Minute Paper Collection 1397-1952.

143. *The British Honduran* (September 1954): 8.

5. A New Paterfamilias

1. See Bolland, *The Politics of Labour in the British Caribbean*, 632–33, on British hostility to the Open Forum. See my "Imagining the Colonial Nation," 126, on the rejection of the Battle of St. George's Caye myth in Soberanis and Kemp, *The Third Side of the Anglo-Guatemalan Dispute over Belize or British Honduras*.

2. Grant, *The Making of Modern Belize*, 5 and *Clarion*, 12 June 1948.

3. Interview with Elfreda Reyes, 10 July 1991.

4. Interviews with Elfreda Reyes, 10 July 1991, Gladys Stuart and Diane Haylock, 25 July 1991, and Dolores Balderamos Garcia, 10 July 1991.

5. For examples of PUP documents that fail to mention women, see BA, Miscellaneous Collection 694, PUP Manifesto 1960, and BA, Miscellaneous Collection 744, *The Manifesto for the New and Progressive Revolution, 1979–84* and *25 Years of Struggle and Achievement, 1950–1975*.

6. Grant, *The Making of Modern Belize*, mentions nationalist women on 126 and 171 and the importance of the popular movement on 126, 134–35, 153, 166, 171, and 177. Shoman does not mention women in "The Birth of the Nationalist Movement in Belize, 1950–1954" or in *Party Politics*. Most recently, Bolland, *The Politics of Labour in the British Caribbean*, 637, mentions women once in passing in a twenty-two-page discussion of Belizean nationalism, apparently drawing on Grant, 126.

7. See Bolland, "The Labour Movement and the Genesis of Modern Politics in Belize," in *Colonialism and Resistance*, especially 183, and *The Politics of Labour in the British Caribbean*, 630, 633, 635, 638–39, 641; Shoman, "The Birth of the Nationalist Movement in Belize, 1950–1954," 201, 204, 229, *Party Politics*, 24–25, 87, and "Belize: An Authoritarian Democratic State in Central America," 51.

8. Shoman, "Belize: An Authoritarian Democratic State in Central America," 52–53.

9. Deniz Kandyoti, "Identity and its Discontents," 380.

10. Lucille Mathurin, "Reluctant Matriarchs," 6, describes the independent states of the former British Caribbean in these terms. For a similar argument about the relationship between Indian nationalism and its female supporters, see Maria Mies, *Indian Women and Patriarchy*.

11. Interviews with Elfreda Reyes, 10 and 11 July 1991, and Don Eugenio and Doña Eustaquia Galvez, 15 June 1994.

12. Kandyoti, "Identity and its Discontents," 378. On India see Partha Chatterjee, "Colonialism, Nationalism and Colonialized Women," 629. On Africa see Susan Geiger, "Woman and African Nationalism," 236, and *TANU Women*; Nina Emma Mba, *Nigerian Women Mobilized*; and La Ray Denzer, "Toward a Study of the History of West African Women's Participation in Nationalist Politics." On Mexican women's unfulfilled hopes of the Cardenas regime in the 1930s, see Macías, *Against all Odds*, ch. 6.

13. Maxine Molyneux, "Mobilization without Emancipation?"

14. Price's father W. C. Price was a white Creole, his mother Irene Escalante of Orange Walk a *mestiza*. On Pollard's noncitizen status, see Grant, 178, 219. On the MCU, see *Billboard*, 25 July 1948. Two women, Betta Hoy and Pearl Kemp, served on the first MCU executive. Interview with Philip Goldson, 3 July 1991. On Jex see Grant, *The Making of Modern Belize*, 114, 163, 169, 170.

15. Grant, *The Making of Modern Belize*, 171, on Price in the mid-1950s.

16. Interview with May Davis, 25 October 1994. Davis replaced Gwen Lizarraga as national president of the UWGS shortly before Lizarraga's death in 1975 (Woods, *Mothers of Modern Belize*, 14).

17. Besse, *Restructuring Patriarchy*, 202, casts Getulio Vargas in a similar light, arguing that he consciously promoted his image as "the father of the poor[,] ... [a] benevolent ... infallible ecclesiastical father." As late as 1979 Price was referred to as the "father-confessor" of the nation (Don Bohning, "Bargain Price," 5).

18. Interviews with Gladys Stuart and Diane Haylock, 25 July 1991, Tharine Rudon, 28 July 1991, Elfreda Reyes, 11 July 1991, and Mrs. Arcelia Leiva and Teresa Orio, October and November 1993.

19. Shepherd, *Women in Caribbean History*, 170–71; Reddock, *Women, Labour, and Politics*, 303–308; and Geiger, *TANU Women*, 31–43, 57.

20. Nicholas Fraser and Marysa Navarro, *Evita* , 114–25.

21. Interviews with Elfreda Reyes, 11 July 1991, and May Davis, 25 October 1994.

22. Interviews with Elfreda Reyes, 16 July 1991, May Davis, 25 October 1994, Philip Goldson, 3 July 1991, and Tony Soberanis, Jr., July 1991.

23. Interviews with Alan Arthurs, 18 May 1994, Eduardo Espat, 1 July 1994, Domingo Espat, 4 August 1994, Mrs. Lavinia Busano, 11 April 1994, Aurelia Humes, 7 July 1994, and Mrs. Petrona Briceno, 14 June 1994.

24. *Billboard*, 30 July 1952, 25 June 1950, and 12 April 1953.

25. Interviews with May Davis, 25 October 1994 and Tharine Rudon, 28 July 1991. Harriet Durante, first GWU shop steward for domestics, enjoyed her activist husband's support, as Juanita Joseph of Dangriga still did in the mid-1990s. Louis and

Idolly Erskine remembered that women generally came to PUP meetings as a group, not with their men (interview, 8 October 1994).

26. Interview with Victor Orellana, November 1993.

27. Interview with Gladys Stuart and Diane Haylock, 25 July 1991. In March 1956 drama school students created and performed a Creole play dealing with "the stand-pipe gossip of the bembes and treating the immortality of illegal lotteries" (*Billboard*, 21 March 1956). Interview with Tharine Rudon, 28 July 1991 and *Billboard*, 20 March 1956.

28. Interviews with Mrs. Juanita Joseph, 7 April 1994; Mrs. Petrona Blanco, 8 April 1994; Agnes Avila, 15 April 1994; Dymples Wesby, 15 April 1994; Lorenzo Benguche, 21 April 1994; Clarene Gabourel, October 1994; and Regina Martinez Lewis, 19 April 1994.

29. Zee Edgell does not define her grandmother Inez Webster as a *bembe*, for example (interview, July 1992). Still, during the national strike Webster was arrested for "watching" outside BEC's sawmill (*Billboard*, 5 December 1952). Interviews with Miss Caroline Flowers, July 1991, Mrs. Canuta Flores, May 1994, and Mrs. Lavinia Busano, 11 April 1994. D. H. Romney, ed. *Land in British Honduras*, 33–34, discussed women's irregular, informal wage-earning.

30. Interview with Philip Goldson, 16 July 1991. *Billboard*, 17 and 24 August 1950.

31. Interview with Juanita Joseph, 7 April 1994.

32. In May 1948 the Stann Creek branch had 425 members and rebelled at the GWU annual convention against Belize City's financial control (*Billboard*, 9 and 23 May 1948). In 1950 Catarino Benguche broke away from the GWU with the water-front workers, establishing the rival British Honduran Development Union, which amalgamated in 1960 with the now opposition GWU to form the General Workers Development Union (Interview with Lorenzo Benguche, 21 April 1994 and Medina, *Negotiating Economic Development*, 76–78).

33. Jamaica Central Bureau of Statistics, *West Indian Census 1946, Part E*, xxi–xiv, xxxi. In the Belize District 22.2 percent of females over age were employed, 23.8 percent in Stann Creek. These were more than double the next highest rate. In Belize District 46.3 percent of females over 15 were single, 35 percent in Stann Creek District. Single and common-law mothers constituted 18.7 percent each of all mothers. The census did not break down single motherhood by district or racial group, but it and wage labor undoubtedly played a role in politicizing Creole and Garifuna women.

34. *Billboard*, 25 April 1948. These were Annie Barber, Vicenta Gonzalez, and Margaret Catthouse.

35. Interview with George Flowers, November 1993. In 1948 there were seventy-five GWU members in the Orange Walk District and in 1952 the branch was one of those

described as "neglected" (*Billboard*, 28 April 1952). Flowers remembered most growth occurring from 1952 to 1954.

36. Shoman, "The Birth of the Nationalist Movement in Belize, 1950–1954," 201–203, and *Party Politics*, 21; Grant, *The Making of Modern Belize*, 126. Interviews with May Davis, 25 and 26 October 1994. Interview with Gladys Stuart and Diane Haylock, 25 July 1991, and *Billboard*, 12 and 16 February 1950.

37. *Billboard*, 9 February 1950 (on Orange Walk), 16 February and 2 and 5 March 1950 (on Cayo). Miss Laura Smith of the Garbutt Creek GWU spoke in Spanish. On the GWU's women's sections see *Billboard*, 2 and 5 March and 30 April 1950. On Harriet Durante see *Billboard*, 30 April 1950.

38. *Billboard*, 4 May and 14 September 1952.

39. *Billboard*, 16 July and 20 August 1950.

40. Interview with Tharine Rudon, 28 July 1991; *Billboard*, 7 January 1951.

41. Shoman, "The Birth of the Nationalist Movement in Belize, 1950–1954," 223.

42. Interview with Philip Goldson, 3 July 1991. Tharine Rudon and Mrs. Juanita Joseph also emphasized that women did most fund-raising. *Clarion*, 18 November 1950.

43. *Billboard*, 15 October (on women pickets), and 3 and 7 December (on domestics) 1950.

44. British Honduras, *Annual Report of the Labour Department*, 1951, 9.

45. *Billboard*, 1 May 1951.

46. Interview with Gladys Stuart and Diane Haylock, 25 July 1991; *Billboard*, 7 August 1951.

47. *Billboard*, 15 August and 10 September 1951; Shoman, "The Birth of the Nationalist Movement in Belize, 1950–1954," 210.

48. On women raising money see *Billboard*, 30 October 1951 and 3 January 1952. On women celebrating Richardson's and Goldson's release see *Billboard*, 8 and 30 July 1952. On Rudon see *Billboard*, 2 April 1952. On the Maypole festival see *Billboard*, 2 May 1952 and interview with Elfreda Reyes, 10 July 1991.

49. Grant, *The Making of Modern Belize*, 157; *Billboard*, 11 and 30 September 1950.

50. *Billboard*, 3 October 1950. Interview with Andrea Nunez, 8 April 1994. Medina, *Negotiating Economic Development*, 84, finds that the mostly Garifuna female workforce would stage wildcat strikes in this period to get the attention of both management and the GWU leadership.

51. On the beginning of the general strike see *Billboard*, 20 and 24 October 1952. On the GWU waitresses see *Billboard*, 18, 20, and 25 November 1952. They were working fifty hours per week for $4–$6, without meal breaks.

52. On women's aid to the male strikers see interview with Idolly Erskine, 8 October 1994; Shoman, "The Birth of the Nationalist Movement in Belize, 1950–1954," 229; and *Billboard*, 27 October and 7 November 1952. On women in marches and pickets see *Billboard*, 21, 26, and 31 October 1952.

53. Interview with Elfreda Reyes, 10 July 1991. *Billboard*, 25 November 1952, lists the women charged with following as Elsa Vasquez, Hazel Gentle, Merlene Middleton, Violet Hughes, Mavis Sealey, Leolin Hewitt, Clarine Gentle, Irma Middleton, and Liza Gray. When I read this list to May Davis, she identified most of these women as *bembes*. Those charged with watching were Stella Soberanis, Hortense Terry, Muriel Bevans, Mavis Hall, Inez Webster, Lexie Neal, Manuela Rivero, Dorothy Andrews, Mildred Bevans, Hazel Frazer, and Sarita Bood (*Billboard*, 5 December 1952). On the women's sections in the GWU see *Billboard*, 17 November 1952.

54. *Billboard*, 14 November 1952, and interview with Elfreda Reyes, 10 July 1991.

55. *Billboard*, 15 December 1952.

56. *Billboard*, 15 February and 3 March 1952.

57. *Billboard*, 15 February 1953, and interview with Elfreda Reyes, 11 July 1991.

58. *Billboard*, 3 March and 12 April 1953.

59. *Billboard*, 30 April 1953.

60. *Billboard*, 1 October 1953, and Grant, *The Making of Modern Belize*, 153, on constitutional change.

61. *Billboard*, 5 April 1954. Elsa Vasquez, Jane Hall, and Mrs. Enid Panting signed for Price, Virginia and Ianthe Stanford signed for Goldson, as well as his mother, and Maude King signed for Richardson. Reyes's speech was noted in *Billboard*, 26 February 1954.

62. *Clarion*, 28 April 1954.

63. Grant, *The Making of Modern Belize*, 198; D. A. G. Waddell, *British Honduras*, 295.

64. Interviews with Alan Arthurs, 18 May 1994, and Dolores Mejia, 24 April 1994. *Billboard*, 14 September 1952 and 22 March 1954.

65. Interviews with Eduardo Espat, 1 July 1994, Melida Samos (Maria Samos's daughter), 7 July 1994, and Aurelia Humes, 7 July 1994.

66. Interview with Adolfa Garcia, 27 September 1993.

67. Grant, *The Making of Modern Belize*, 169–72.

68. *Billboard*, 22 November 1954 and 9 February 1956.

69. *Clarion*, 6 July, 11 August, and 28 September 1956. Interview with Elfreda Reyes, 11 July 1991, and Grant, *The Making of Modern Belize*, 177. Shoman, *Party Politics*, 23.

70. Shoman, *Party Politics*, 6 and 13 July, 10 and 18 August, and 6 and 20 October

1946; 11 and 28 January 1948; 12 and 16 January 1949; 27 March and 9 October 1949; and 14 January 1951.

71. Annette B. Ramírez de Arellano and Conrad Seipp, *Colonialism, Catholicism, and Contraception*.

72. *Billboard*, 22 February, 21 March, and 25 April 1948.

73. *Billboard*, 18 August and 4 September 1949.

74. *Billboard*, 20 July 1951.

75. *Billboard*, 9, 16, and 23 February 1950. On the memorial see Shoman, "The Birth of the Nationalist Movement in Belize, 1950–1954," 202.

76. *Billboard*, 5 and 12 March and 23 April 1950.

77. *Billboard*, 21 May and 6, 17, and 28 August 1950.

78. *Billboard*, 30 November 1950.

79. *Billboard*, 4, 9, 16, and 17 January, 11, 18, and 28 February, 5 March, 5, 8, 9, 19, 20, and 27 July, 3, 16, and 18 August, and 16 November 1951.

80. *Billboard*, 11 and 28 February and 20 July 1951. On the cannery wages see *Billboard*, 30 November 1951, and British Honduras, *Annual Report of the Labour Department*, 1952, 16.

81. *Billboard*, 24 April 1952.

82. BA, Minute Paper Collection 1312-1952, 2 December 1952.

83. BA, Minute Paper Collection 1312-1952, 15 December 1952, and 15 February and 3 March 1953. Interview with Elfreda Reyes, 11 July 1991.

84. BA, Minute Paper Collection 1312-1952, 23 July 1952.

85. BA, Minute Paper Collection 1312-1952, 5 April 1954. *Clarion*, 16 September 1953 (emphasis added).

86. *Billboard*, 9 May 1954.

87. *Billboard*, 8 May and 20 January 1955, 8 March 1956, and 9 September 1954. BA, Miscellaneous Collection 62, *Speeches by Philip Goldson as Member of Social Services*, "Statement by M. S. S. in Legislative Assembly Friday, 12th August, 1955," 22, "Extract from Radio Broadcast by M. S. S. Launching the Survey of Unemployed Persons in Belize, Thursday September 8th to Thursday September 15th," 25, and speech to the YWCA, 31.

88. *Billboard*, 24 May 1956. *Billboard* and *Clarion*, 26 October to 4 November 1953.

89. Grant, *The Making of Modern Belize*, 170–71.

90. *Billboard*, February 26, 1956.

91. Interview with Tharine Rudon, 28 July 1991, and interview with Elfreda Reyes, 11 July 1991.

92. *Clarion*, 12 March 1948, and *Billboard*, 25 July 1948. Woods, *Mothers of Modern Belize*, 14–18.

93. British Honduras, *Annual Report of the Social Development Department*, 1953, 1, and BA, Social Development Department file 3842/6, Prison Officer's Report for 1957.

94. On Mrs. Grant's prodivorce stance see *Independent*, 7 February 1934. She was still soliciting donations for the Orange Walk Infant Welfare League in late 1937 from the family's home in Belize City (*Independent*, 17 November 1937). On the Jamaican Federation of Women see Shepherd, *Women in Caribbean History*, 163. Ezekiel Grant's speech appeared in the *Clarion*, 14 January 1948. Mina Grant did give talks on topics like "Women's Worth," but their substance was not reported.

95. *Clarion*, 23 January 1948, 18 July and 19 October 1950. Grant's letter about domestics also appeared in *Billboard*, 20 July 1950.

96. Assad Shoman, *Party Politics*, 22. *Billboard*, 22 February 1952. Seay's and the BCNS' antipathy toward the PUP and Price were no secret. They viewed Price as an upstart and the PUP's mass politics as an anathema (Interviews with C.L.B. Rogers, 1 May 1994 and Miss Adelia Dixon, 1992).

97. *Clarion*, 14 September 1953.

98. On the founding of the BHFW see BA, Social Development Department File 148-1952, Social Development Officer McNair to colonial secretary, 6 March 1952. Both newspapers printed accounts of the meeting on 22 February 1952. From March to July the government gave the BHFW access to its film collection, and the BHFW sold tickets to schoolchildren for screenings at the Palace Theatre, which merchant Santiago Castillo allowed it to use for free. In July a fire destroyed the collection. For Lizarraga's speech see *Clarion*, 19 February 1952.

99. *Clarion*, 16 May 1952.

100. *Billboard*, 27 and 29 May 1952, and *Clarion*, 29, 30, and 31 May 1952.

101. *Billboard*, 4 July 1952. At this time the nationalists printed a letter dated May 24 from Sharpe to Grant, which alluded to previous contacts between Grant and Sharpe's female supervisor.

102. *Billboard*, 17 June 1952.

103. Great Britain, *British Honduras Colonial Report*, 1952, 9.

104. *Clarion*, 24 June 1952.

105. *Billboard*, 26 September 1952.

106. BA, Social Development Department File 148-1952, 22 September, Mina Grant to acting colonial secretary, conveying resolutions of 8 August 1952 BHFW meeting.

107. BA, Minute Paper Collection 1152-1952, supt. of police to colonial secretary, 10 October 1952; BA, Minute Paper Collection 1153-1952, attorney general to colonial secretary, 4 November 1952, and colonial secretary to attorney general, 20 January

1953; BA, Minute Paper Collection 1154-1952, Social Development Officer McNair to colonial secretary, 27 October 1952, and acting magistrate to colonial secretary, 5 November 1952.

108. *Clarion*, 27 June, 1 July, and 3 September 1952.

109. On efforts to secure support for the daycare see BA, Social Development Department File #11, 3813/2, "Child Care, Establishment of a Day Nursery in Belize, 1961–65," *Clarion*, 19 February 1954 and 4 January 1955, and BA, Minute Paper Collection 148-1952. Mina Grant even went to Washington to ask UNESCO to contribute funds (*Clarion*, 6 January 1953). On Renison and Thornley see *Billboard*, 23 July 1954, and BA, Minute Paper Collection 148-1952. On Reyes see *Billboard*, 13 March 1959.

110. On the founding of the UWGS see the *Times*, 7 February 1959. On the founding of the Pioneers see *Billboard*, 11 April 1959. On the NIP see *Billboard*, 5 July 1958. Its assistant secretary was Jeannette Buller, the two representatives for women were Mrs. Gertrude Card and Mrs. Claire Gill, and one of the two representatives for labor was Mrs. Reginald Bevins. *Billboard*, 12 April 1959, denounced Price's treatment of PUP women. The NIP was an amalgamation of the NP and the short-lived Honduras Independence Party, formed by Richardson and Goldson after they left the PUP; the HIP was trounced in the 1957 elections.

111. For coverage of the elections and their results, see the *Clarion*, 1, 10, and 16 December 1958; the *Times*, 17 December 1958; and the *Goverment Gazette*, 3 January 1959, 4. The *Billboard* of 29 June 1957 listed Lizarraga as a committee chair within the BHFW.

112. Woods, *Mothers of Modern Belize*, 15–16.

113. *Billboard*, 5 October 1954 and 23 June 1956.

114. Miller, *Latin American Women*, 101–103; Stoner, *From the House to the Streets*, 67–77, 104–26, 160–65; Reddock, *Women, Labour and Politics*, 167–68, 181.

115. *Times*, 2 February 1959.

116. On the growth of the UWGS see the *Times*, 22 March, 22 April, 12 May and 27 May, 4 June, 28 July, 9 and 12 August, 9 October, and 3 November 1959.

117. On Stann Creek, see the *Times*, 12 May and 28 July 1959. On Punta Gorda, interview with Modesta Norales, 13 May 1994. On Orange Walk, see *Billboard*, 6 May 1960 and interview with Rita Orellana, October 1993.

118. Interview with Winifred Flowers, 20 May 1994.

119. On Queen's Square see the *Times*, February 1963. Mrs. Flora Ellis, founding member of Housing Group #9, said that few women in her group ever got a house (interview, October 1994). Pressure on government from UWG groups is discussed in BA, Social Development Department File 3814/4, 6 October 1959, S. D. O. Smith to M. S. S. Catthouse.

120. Grant, *The Making of Modern Belize*, 195.

121. *Times*, 29 November 1959.

122. Grant, *The Making of Modern Belize*, 190, 195.

123. *Times*, 11 August 1959.

124. Interviews with Philip Goldson, 16 July 1991, and C. L. B. Rogers, 1 May 1994.

125. Grant, *The Making of Modern Belize*, 217–24. This committee was a short-lived cooperative venture of the PUP and NIP against the recommendations of Hilary Blood, *Report of the Constitutional Commissioner, 1959*, which advised against rapid constitutional decolonization.

126. *Times*, 12 January, 7 and 9 February, and 9 March 1960.

127. BA, Miscellaneous Collection 694, *Manifesto of the People's United Party 1960*, 5. *Times*, 19 July 1960, 12 January and 4 November 1961.

128. *Times*, 25 December 1960.

129. BA, Ordinance no. 14 of 1960.

130. Shoman, *Party Politics*, 88.

131. Edgell, *Beka Lamb*, 105–109.

6. Negotiating Nationalist Patriarchy

1. *Times*, 1 May and 2–6 June 1963.

2. *Times*, 3 June 1963.

3. Grant, *The Making of Modern Belize*, 248.

4. *Amandala*, 9 September 1977, mentioned Nora Parham in reporting on a young mother's murder of her common-law husband. Unlike Parham, this woman was acquitted (*Amandala*, 27 January 1978).

5. *Times*, 21 February and 8 March 1963, and *Billboard*, 28 January 1964. The woman, a mestiza, began her sentence in 1964 after giving birth. A man who brutally murdered his wife in 1966 received a five-year manslaughter sentence (*Times*, 1 June and 5 November 1966).

6. Landes, "The Performance of Citizenship," 306.

7. Cynthia Ellis, "Reflections on Women's Problems, Issues and Prospects for Change, with Special Reference to Belize and the International Women's Movement, Part 2," 9.

8. Carmen Middleton, editorial, 2.

9. Rhoda Reddock, "Feminism, Nationalism, and the Early Women's Movement in the English-speaking Caribbean," 62, argues that the blossoming of Caribbean feminism in the 1970s was provoked by nationalist and radical orders to reject the ideology as foreign to the region.

10. Young and Young, "The Impact of the Anglo-Guatemalan Dispute on the Internal Politics of Belize." For election statistics see Shoman, *Party Politics*, 38.

11. Shoman, *13 Chapters*, ch. 10, gives the most thorough analysis to date of this movement.

12. John Watler, "The Story of Belize City."

13. Assad Shoman, "The Making of Belize's Foreign Policy," 20. Central American support for Guatemala broke only in 1977, when Panama's Omar Torrijos allied with Belize, and in 1979, when the victorious Sandinistas reversed Somoza's solidarity with the Guatemalan generals.

14. Assad Shoman, "The Making and Breaking of the United General Workers' Union."

15. On Grenada see Rhoda Reddock, "Popular Movement to 'Mass Organization.'" On Jamaica see Lynn Bolles, "Michael Manley in the Vanguard Towards Gender Equality". On the WICP see Senior, *Working Miracles*, 1.

16. Grant, *The Making of Modern Belize*, 227 and 262.

17. Grant, *The Making of Modern Belize*, 262–65, and Shoman, *Party Politics*, 29–32.

18. Shoman, *Party Politics*, 29, and the *Times*, 7 February 1965, quoted in Grant, *The Making of Modern Belize*, 286.

19. See Shoman, *13 Chapters*, 217, on government efforts to control civil society and 231–41 for an original account of Ken's *cañeros* movement.

20. Grant, *The Making of Modern Belize*, 255.

21. Grant, *The Making of Modern Belize*, 264.

22. Cedric Grant, "The Civil Service Strike in British Honduras; Grant, *The Making of Modern Belize*, 285–86.

23. Grant, *The Making of Modern Belize*, 269.

24. Ernest E. Cain, *Cyclone "Hattie"*, 67.

25. The results of the 1963 PUP Convention illustrate the limits of women's strength within the party. All four executive seats were won by men, while the Central Party Council comprised the regional male power brokers as well as eleven women, including Gwendolyn Lizarraga, Hazel Gentle, Jane Hall, Ianthe Stanford, and Inez Webster.

26. Bolland, "Race, Ethnicity and National Integration in Belize," 201.

27. *Times*, 19 July 1961, and *Billboard*, 23 February and 13 March 1961.

28. *Billboard*, 29 June 1962.

29. *Billboard*, 24 January 1961.

30. *Billboard*, 29 September 1962.

31. *Billboard*, 3 October and 13 December 1962.

32. *Billboard*, 14 March 1962.

33. *Times*, 17 March 1962. About one thousand UWG members gathered to elect Lizarraga as president, Hazle Gentle as vice president, Lois Encalada as secretary, Mrs. Elvina Torres as treasurer, and Iris Staine as assistant treasurer. The councilors were Virginia Stanford, Jane Robateau, Enid Panting, Hazel Stuart, Harriet Coe, Idolly Simpson, and Maud Hamilton.

34. *Billboard*, 21 March 1962.

35. *Billboard*, 31 June 1962.

36. *Billboard*, 1 June 1962.

37. *Billboard*, 13 June 1962.

38. *Billboard*, 9 September 1962.

39. *Times*, 10 February 1963.

40. *Times*, 29 May 1962.

41. *Times*, 24 August 1962.

42. *Times*, 11 and 19 October 1962.

43. *Times*, 13 February 1963.

44. *Times*, 9 February 1963. The other executive officers of the CWU women's branch were Mrs. Lucille Carter, who was treasurer, and Mrs. Louise Menzies, who was assistant treasurer. The trustees were Miss Olive Dawson and Lydia Yorke, the committee was Mrs. Amy Bernard and Florence Swift, and the organizers were Mrs. Lily McClaren and Mrs. Jaqueline Usher.

45. British Honduras, *Annual Report of the Labour Department*, 1962, 23. Four other women on the committee were Mrs. Sadie Castillo, Florence Myvett, C. P. Cacho, and Gladys Reneau. There were also three men (two civil servants and the minister of labour). The *Annual Report of the Labour Department*, 1961, 32, maintained that because men and women did not perform the same jobs, women "do not . . . suffer any disadvantage in regard to wages as compared to males."

46. *Billboard*, 24 May 1962.

47. "Labour Ordinance (Application to Domestic Servants) Regulations," in British Honduras, *Subsidiary Laws of British Honduras in Force the 31st Day of December* 1963.

48. *Times*, 6 June 1963.

49. *Times*, 26 November, 4 and 19 December 1963.

50. *Billboard*, 1 November 1964.

51. BA, Miscellaneous Collection 2137, *The National Manifesto of the N.I.P.*, 6 and 14.

52. *Billboard*, 10 and 12 January 1965.

53. *Billboard*, 27 January 1965.

54. *Times*, 18 June 1968.

55. *Billboard*, 9 February 1964.

56. *Times*, 19 March 1965.

57. *Billboard*, 16 December 1966.

58. *Billboard*, 18 November and 12 December 1965.

59. *Times*, 15 October 1965.

60. *Times*, 18 and 29 January 1966.

61. *Times*, 26 and 27 June 1966, and Assad Shoman, "The Making of Belize's Foreign Policy," 14.

62. Grant, "The Civil Service Strike in British Honduras," 47.

63. Webster, as an agent of the U.S. government, may have designed his proposals in order to reward Guatemala for allowing the Bay of Pigs force to train in the Petén (Grant, *The Making of Modern Belize*, 239). On the NIP delegation, see *Billboard*, 26 March 1968. The delegation included three women from southern Belize, Mrs. Paula Foreman of Monkey River, Mrs. Victoria Martinez of Punta Gorda, and Mrs. Lydia Blanco of Stann Creek. The others were Miss Theola Pinks of the Albert division, Mrs. Rosita Hynds of the Fort George division, Mrs. Thelma Goodin of the Collet division, Mrs. Leonie Adolphus, Miss Esme Diaz, Mrs. Lucille Heusner, Mrs. Francisca Arnold, Miss Rosita Maldonado, and Mrs. Rosita Williams.

64. *Billboard*, 2 April 1968.

65. BA, Miscellaneous Collection 767, "Premier's UN Day Address," 24 October 1969.

66. V.S. Naipaul, "The Ultimate Colony," in *The Overcrowded Barracoon*, 236, originally published in the *Daily Telegraph Magazine*, 4 July 1969.

67. *Billboard*, 6 and 30 July 1969.

68. BA, *Amandala with Fire*, 25 October 1969.

69. *Billboard*, 27 March 1968.

70. Naipaul, "The Ultimate Colony," 236.

71. *Amandala*, Christmas issue 1981. From the story "Blackout" by UBAD leader Evan X Hye, first published in 1975.

72. Evan X Hyde, *North Amerikkkan Blues* , 18.

73. BA, *Vanguard*, August and November 1969.

74. Interview with Bert Tucker, September 1993. Tucker was briefly active in UBAD in the early 1970s in Belize and also served as its "Caribbean liason" in Jamaica. Tucker's involvement in Michael Manley's administration of 1972–76 brought him into contact with fellow Belizean Cynthia Ellis, and they both helped to coordinate the 1979 workshop where the Belize Committee for Women and Development originated.

75. *Amandala*, 22 November 1969.

76. *Amandala*, 8 October 1969.

77. *Amandala*, 10 August 1973, from an article headlined "Woman—Man's Best Friend."

78. *Amandala, 10 August 1973*.

79. Interview with Cynthia Ellis, 5 July 1994.

80. Evan X Hyde, *The Crowd Called* UBAD, 12.

81. Interview with Lillette Barkeley Waite, September 1994.

82. For coverage of the ward maids' strike see *Amandala*, 18 September to 23 October 1970.

83. *Billboard*, 6 August 1969, carried a notice from UBAD calling "sisters" to a meeting.

84. Hyde, *The Crowd Called* UBAD, 39, and *Amandala*, 14 August 1970.

85. *Amandala*, 20 August 1969, 30 April and 5 June 1970.

86. *Amandala*, 18 September 1970.

87. Interview with Bert Tucker, 1993.

88. *Amandala*, 18 September 1970.

89. *Amandala*, 16 May 1972.

90. *Amandala*, 10 August 1973.

91. Dylan Vernon, "International Migration and Development in Belize," 37–46, establishes that almost 12,000 Belizeans left for the United States in the 1960s, twice that number in the 1970s. Women represented on average 55 percent of the yearly outflow.

92. *Amandala*, 18 August 1981.

93. Hyde, *North Amerikkkan Blues*, 32, 38–39, 46. He had a memorable one-night stand in Madison, Wisconsin, for example, on a road trip to visit Belizean students in La Crosse.

94. *Amandala*, 1 October 1969.

95. *Amandala*, 26 March 1971.

96. *Amandala*, 10 April 1970.

97. *Amandala*, 12 February 1971.

98. *Amandala*, 7 September 1979.

99. *Amandala*, 14 September 1979.

100. *Times*, 7 October 1973.

101. *Amandala*, 12 October 1973.

102. *Amandala*, 25 April 1975, "Women's Liberation—A Belizean Version."

103. *Amandala*, 17 and 31 October 1975.

104. *Amandala*, 5 March 1976.

105. *Amandala*, 4 February 1977.

106. *Amandala*, 17 November 1978. Belizean newspapers regularly reported cases of dead fetuses or newborns found in the Belize City canals, the Belize River, or in the sea, and sometimes of mothers held, charged, and convicted of infanticide. See for example *Independent*, 6 December 1933, and 30 March 1938; *Billboard*, 18 September 1951; and *Times*, May and October 1964, February and April 1965.

107. *Times*, 21 November, 5 December, and Christmas issue, 1980.

108. *Times*, 21 August 1981.

109. The Legal Aid Centre was funded by the Belize Bar Association, Inter-American Legal Services, and the Canadian International Development Agency, so Zoila Ellis was not a civil servant who could be fired.

110. On the Fairweather family connections see Judd, "Elite Reproduction and Ethnic Identity in Belize," 281. *Amandala*, 3 April 1981, reported that Mrs. Bette Lindo, Dean Lindo's wife, had been arrested for picketing during the Heads of Agreement crisis.

111. *Brukdown* 3 (1977). Cynthia Pitts was thus a second cousin of NIP leader Leotine Gillette, their grandfathers being the brothers Calvert and Morrel Staine who had led the Garveyite PP in the 1920s and who had maintained their political activism into the late 1940s and early 1950s.

112. Cynthia Ellis, for example, went on to found the Belize Rural Women's Association in the 1980s, which became a strong multiethnic network.

113. *Times*, 12 and 19 January, 2 and 23 February, 13 April, 1 and 29 June, 27 July, 15 October, 2 and 30 November 1975.

114. *The New Belize*, August 1977.

115. *The New Belize*, June 1978.

116. BA, Miscellaneous Collection 105, Roland E. Price, "Underprivileged Families in Belize City, British Honduras, C.A.," 1, 29–30.

117. BA, Social Development Department File 959, 213/2 "Maintenance," letter from Middleton to the attorney general, 8 September 1971.

118. Senior, *Working Miracles*, 155 n. 1.

119. Interview with Cynthia Ellis, 5 July 1994.

120. BOWAND File, "History of BOWAND," n.d. but probably 1982.

121. *The New Belize*, August 1981.

122. Edgell, *In Times Like These*, 58, 159, 195, and 214–17.

123. Interview with Cynthia Pitts, August 1994.

124. *The New Belize*, August 1981.

125. BOWAND File, letter from Bette Lindo, March 1980.

126. BOWAND Files, letter from Elaine Middleton, 1 February 1980, and undated list

of members of the Committee to Review the Law Affecting the Situation of Women and Children. This committee reported by mid-1980.

127. *The New Belize*, July 1980, "Negotiating the Consequences of Illegitimacy."

128. Zoila Ellis, "A Brief Review of Recent Social Legislation—The Status of Children Ordinance 1980," 22.

129. Bette Lindo, "Preface," 6.

130. *Network* 1:2 (1981): 19.

131. BOWAND File, report of evaluation held in mid-1983.

132. As a volunteer for Canadian Crossroads International (a Third World development education organization) I was posted by CCI local coordinator Sadie Vernon to the Council of Voluntary Social Services when I first arrived in Belize in May 1988. I remained there for about two months. I was assigned to speak to a women's group in San Antonio, Cayo, about how to cook food that tourists would buy, heard derogatory remarks from senior staff about the Garinagu, and grew frustrated with the lethargic atmosphere.

133. Cynthia Ellis, "Reflections on Women's Problems, Issues and Prospects for Change, with Special Reference to Belize and the International Women's Movement."

134. Cynthia Ellis, "Reflections on Women's Problems, Issues and Prospects for Change, with Special Reference to Belize and the International Women's Movement Part 2," 7.

135. Interview by Nan Peacocke with Cythia Ellis, Margaret McCann, and Diane Haylock in *Womanspeak!*, journal of the Women and Development Unit of the University of the West Indies in Barbados, 10.

136. Interview with Zoila Ellis, 16 July 1994.

137. Interview with Rita Garcia, 23 October 1994.

138. Interviews with Cynthia Pitts, August 1994, and Lynda Moguel, 24 October 1994.

139. Interview with Cynthia Pitts, August 1994.

140. BOWAND Files, minutes of 26 May 1983 meeting and letter from Lynda Moguel, BOWAND treasurer, 26 May 1986.

141. BOWAND File, report on the 6 December 1981 Sand Hill workshop.

142. BOWAND File, review of BOWAND activities in 1982.

143. BOWAND File, letter from Zoila Ellis to Assad Shoman, 15 February 1982.

144. BOWAND File, description of various projects, n.d. but probably 1982, and "Urban Food Project," *Network* 1:3 (1982): 5.

145. BOWAND File, minutes of meetings on 29 March 1982 and 13 April 1982.

146. BOWAND Files, minutes of Market Day planning meetings, 12 and 14 January 1983.

147. BOWAND file, *Pataki: Rural Women's Newsletter* (1983), sponsored by BOWAND.

148. *The New Belize*, January 1983.

149. Ellis, McCann, and Haycock, *Womanspeak!*, 6.

Conclusion

1. Adele Catzim, "The Women Workers' Union"; Elizabeth Margaret Waight, *A Woman's Turn* (BOWAND's magazine) 7:2 (August 1995–January 1996), 12.

2. Camille Moreno and Robert Johnson, compilers, *Belize Report for the Fourth World Conference on Women (Beijing 1995)*, 16.

3. *A Woman's Turn*, 4:3 (October 1992–January 1993), 1–2; *A Woman's Turn*, 5:1 (February–May 1993), 14.

4. Irma McClaurin, *Women of Belize*, 189–90; *Equality* (quarterly report of the DWA) 3:2 (November 1992), 1; *A Woman's Turn* 4:3 (October 1992–January 1993), 8–9; Moreno and Johnson, compilers, *Belize Report for the Fourth World Conference on Women (Beijing 1995)*, 2.

5. On more recent times see McClaurin, *Women of Belize*.

6. Grant Jones, *Maya Resistance to Spanish Rule*.

7. See Rosemblatt, *Gendered Compromises*, and Klubock, *Contested Communities*.

8. Grant, *The Making of Modern Belize*, 325.

Bibliography

Archival Sources

BA=Belize Archives
BOWAND=Belize Organization for Women and Development
CO=Colonial Office

BA. Judges Notes. 1913–1929.

BA. Legislative Council Minutes. 1919 and 1948.

BA. Minute Paper Collection. 1909–1953.

BA. Miscellaneous Collection 27. Soberanis, Antonio. "This is my life history and background." Letter to Vernon Leslie, 10 July 1973.

BA. Miscellaneous Collection 105. Roland E. Price, *Underprivileged Families in Belize City, British Honduras C.A.* Belize: British Honduras Christian Social Council, 1968.

BA. Miscellaneous Collection 164. Black Cross Nurses. *Compendium of Living Conditions and Dietary Statistics of the Labouring Classes of Belize* (Belize, 1938).

BA. Miscellaneous Collection 191. "A Town Planning Scheme for Belize." 1946.

BA. Miscellaneous Collection 694. *Peoples United Party Manifesto 1960.*

BA. Miscellaneous Collection 744. *The Manifesto for the New and Progressive Revolution, 1979–84.* People's United Party, 1975.

BA. Miscellaneous Collection 767. *Premier's UN Day Address, 24 October 1969.* Government Information Service, 1969.

BA. Miscellaneous Collection 1677. *Report of the Committee on Nutrition in the Colony of British Honduras.* Belize, 1937.

BA. Miscellaneous Collection 62. "Speeches by Philip Goldson as Member for Social Services." 1954–56.

BA. Miscellaneous Collection 2137. *The National Manifesto of the N.I.P.* Belize: National Independence Party, 1963.

BA. Miscellaneous Collection 4901. *Programme of the September 10, 1948 Celebrations.*

BA. Miscellaneous Collection. People's United Party. "Memorial for a Democratic Constitution for British Honduras." 1951.

BA. Miscellaneous Collection. People's United Party. *25 Years of Struggle and Achievement 1950–1975.* 1975.

BA. Miscellaneous Collection. Sologaistoa Brothers, compilers. *Guide to British Honduras.* Belize: The Trumpet Press, 1919.

BA. Miscellaneous Collection. *Targets for Progress—Manifesto of the PUP Government, March 1st 1961.*

BA. Miscellaneous Collection. *Your Government of 1961–1965 at Work.* Belize, 1965.

BA. Orange Walk District Court Records. 1910–1925.

BA. Ordinance No. 14 of 1960. "The Development Incentives Ordinance." 17 August 1960.

BA. Probates. 1912–1913.

BA. Records 128. Despatches Out. 1913–1915.

BA. Social Development Department Files 213/2 "Maintenance;" 3813/2 "Child Care, Establishment of a Day Nursery in Belize, 1961–65; 3814/4; 3842/6 "Prison Officer's Report for 1957."

BA. Supreme Court Actions. 1912–1925.

BOWAND. Files. 1979–1983.

Great Britain. British Honduras Colonial Report. 1946.

Great Britain. CO. 123/295/48749. Hutson, "Causes and Handling of Outbreak." 30 July 1919.

———. CO. 123/296/65699. "Riot at Belize. Report of the Riot Commission, Appendix P: List of Persons alleged to have committed offenses. Annie Flowers: inciting to crime, testimony of William Hoar[,] . . . September 22, 1919."

———. CO. 123/353/66568. "On the disturbances in Stann Creek Town, May 1935."

———. CO. 123/380/10. "Memorandum on the Constitution of British Honduras, (secret)" Governor Hutson to the Secretary of State for the Colonies. 8 February 1943.

———. CO. 123/3767/66824. Governor Burns to the Secretary of State for the Colonies, 28 December 1938.

Published Primary and Secondary Sources

Note: All government publications changed from British Honduras to Belize as the corporate author starting in 1973. Precise titles of departmental annual reports varied slightly in different periods.

Acosta-Belén, Edna. *Opening New Paths: Research on Women in Latin America and the Caribbean*. Washington, DC: Woodrow Wilson International Center for Scholars, 1994.

Aguilera Peralta, Gabriel. "Dependencia Politica y Colonialismo: Ideologia Independentista y Lucha de Clases en Belice." *Anuario de Estudios Centroamericanos* 3 (1977): 81–95.

Alarcón, Norma. "The Theoretical Subject(s) of *This Bridge Called My Back* and *Anglo-American Feminism*." In *Making Face, Making Soul/Haciendo Caras: Creative and Critical Perspectives by Feminists of Color*, edited by Gloria Anzaldúa, 356–69. San Francisco: Aunt Lute Books, 1990.

Alonso, Ana Maria. *Thread of Blood: Colonialism, Revolution, and Gender on Mexico's Northern Frontier*. Tucson: Arizona University Press, 1995.

Alvarez, Sonia. *Engendering Democracy in Brazil: Women's Movements in Transition Politics*. Princeton: Princeton University Press, 1990.

Alvarez Icasa, Pablo. *Belice: La Crisis, el Neocolonialismo y las Relaciones con México 1978–1986*. México: Centro de Investigaciones y Docencia Económicas, 1987.

Ashcraft, Norman. *Colonialism and Underdevelopment: Processes of Political Economic Change in British Honduras*. New York: Teachers College Press, 1973.

Ashdown, Peter D. "Antonio Soberanis and the Disturbances in Belize, 1934–1937." *Caribbean Quarterly* 24 (1978): 61–74.

———. "Race, Class and the Unofficial Majority in British Honduras, 1890–1949." PhD diss., Sussex University, 1979.

———. "The Belize Elite and Its Power Base: Land, Labour and Commerce circa 1890." *Belizean Studies* 9:5/6 (1981): 30–43.

———. "Marcus Garvey, the U.N.I.A. and the Black Cause in British Honduras, 1914–1949." *Journal of Caribbean History* 15 (1981): 41–55.

———. "The Growth of Black Consciousness in Belize, 1914–1919: The Background to the Ex-Servicemen's Riot of 1919." *Belcast Journal of Belizean Affairs* 2:2 (December 1985): 1–5.

———. "Race Riot, Class Warfare and Coup d'Etat: The Ex-Servicemen's Riot of July 1919." *Belcast Journal of Belizean Affairs* 3:1 and 2 (1986): 8–14.

———. "The Colonial Administrator as Historian: Burdon, Burns and the Battle of St. George's Caye." *Belizean Studies* 15:1 (1987): 3–11.

———. "A Democracy Too Soon: The Constitutional Proposals 1923–1925." *Belizean Studies* 17:2 (1989): 23–33.

Badran, Margot. *Feminists, Islam and Nation: Gender and the Making of Modern Egypt*. Princeton: Princeton University Press, 1995.

Bair, Barbara. "True Women, Real Men: Gender, Ideology and Social Roles in the Garvey Movement." In *Gendered Domains: Rethinking Public and Private in Women's History*, edited by Dorothy O. Helly and Susan M. Reverby, 154–66. Ithaca: Cornell University Press, 1992.

———. "Universal Negro Improvement Association." In *Black Women in America: A Historical Encyclopaedia*, edited by Darlene Clark Hine, 1188. Brooklyn: Carlson Publishing, 1993.

———. "Pan-Africanism as Process: Adelaide Casely Hayford, Garveyism, and the Cultural Roots of Nationalism." In *Imagining Home: Class, Culture and Nationalism in the African Diaspora*, edited by Sidney Lemelle and Robin Kelley, 121–44. London: Verso, 1994.

Baker Fox, Annette. *Freedom and Welfare in the Caribbean: A Colonial Dilemma*. New York: Harcourt, Brace, and Company, 1949.

Banton, Michael. *Racial Theories*. Cambridge: Cambridge University Press, 1987.

Barceló-Miller, María de F. *La lucha por el sufragio femenino en Puerto Rico, 1896–1935*. Río Piedras, Puerto Rico: Ediciones Huracán y Centro de Investigaciones Sociales, 1997.

Basu, Aparnu. "Feminism and Nationalism in India, 1917–1947." *Journal of Women's History* 7:4 (Winter 1995): 95–107.

Beasley-Murray, Jon. "Peronism and the Secret History of Cultural Studies: Populism and the Substitution of Culture for State." *Cultural Critique* 39 (1998): 189–217.

Becker, Marjorie. *Setting the Virgin on Fire: Lázaro Cárdenas, Michoácan Peasants, and the Redemption of the Mexican Revolution*. Berkeley: University of California Press, 1996.

Beckles, Hilary McD. *Natural Rebels: A Social History of Enslaved Black Women in Barbados*. New Brunswick: Rutgers University Press, 1989.

Belize. *The Manifesto for an Independent Belize, 1974–1979*. Belmopan: Government Printer, 1974.

———. Camille Moreno, and Robert Johnson, compilers. *Belize Report for the Fourth World Conference on Women (Beijing 1995): Action for Equality, Development, and Peace*. Belmopan: Department of Women's Affairs, 1994.

Bennett, Joseph A. "Goals, Priorities and the Decolonization of Education in Belize." *Belizean Studies* 7:5 (1979): 18–23.

Besse, Susan K. *Restructuring Patriarchy: The Modernization of Gender Inequality in Brazil, 1914–1940*. Chapel Hill: University of North Carolina Press, 1996.

Bhabha, Homi. *The Location of Culture*. London: Routledge, 1994.

"The Black Cross Nurses' Activities in Social Work and Otherwise." *British Honduras Agricultural Journal* (1942).

Blood, Hilary. *Report of the Constitutional Commissioner, 1959*. Belize, 1959.

Bohning, Don. "Bargain Price." *The New Belize* (July 1979): 3–8.

Bolland, O. Nigel. *The Formation of a Colonial Society: Belize, From Conquest to Crown Colony*. Baltimore: Johns Hopkins University Press, 1977.

———. *Belize: A New Nation in Central America*. Boulder: Westview, 1986.

———. *Colonialism and Resistance in Belize: Essays in Historical Sociology*. Belize: Cubola/Society for the Promotion of Education and Research/Institute for Social and Economic Research, 1988.

———. "The Extraction of Timber in the Slave Society of Belize." Unpublished paper. 1991.

———. *The Politics of Labour in the British Caribbean: The Social Origins of Authoritarianism and Democracy in the Labour Movement*. Princeton: Markus Wiener, 2001.

———, and Assad Shoman. *Land in Belize, 1765–1871*. Mona, Jamaica: ISER, 1977.

Bolles, A. Lynn. "Doing It for Themselves: Women's Research and Action in the Commonwealth Caribbean." In *Researching Women in Latin America and the Caribbean*, edited by Edna Acosta-Belén and Christine Bose,. Boulder: Westview Press, 1993.

———. "Michael Manley in the Vanguard Towards Gender Equality." *Caribbean Quarterly* 48:1 (2002): 45–56.

Bowman, H. T. A. *Emerald Valley and Twinkling Town: My Autobiography*. Stone Haven, Belize: H. T. A. Bowman, 1979.

Brereton, Bridget. "The Development of an Identity: The Black Middle Class of Trinidad in the Later Nineteenth Century." In *Caribbean Freedom: Economy and Society from Emancipation to the Present*, edited by Hilary Beckles and Verene Shepherd, 274–83. Princeton: Markus Weiner, 1996.

British Honduras. Annual Reports of the Education Department. 1909, 1911, 1919, 1922, 1935–36, 1947, 1956, 1963–66.

———. Annual Reports of the Labour Department. 1939–71, 1974–76, 1983.

———. Annual Reports of the Medical Department. 1897, 1899, 1907–08, 1910, 1913, 1916, 1923, 1925–27, 1929–30, 1935, 1938, 1941, 1944–46, 1951, 1954–55, 1957, 1959, 1960–63, 1965–68, 1973.

———. Annual Reports of the Prison Department. 1914, 1918, 1922, 1923, 1939, 1947, 1981.

———. Annual Reports of the Social Development Department. 1950–54, 1956, 1964–66, 1968, 1971–77.

———. *Annual Reports on the Vital Statistics of British Honduras*. 1915, 1916.

————. *Blue Books*. Belize: Government Printer, 1911–15, 1917, 1922.

————. *Census of British Honduras, 1931*. Belize: Government Printer, 1933.

————. *Government Gazette*. Belize: Government Printer, 1915, 1918, 1921, 1924, 1927, 1930.

————. *Report of the Development Planning Committee*. Belize, 1946.

————. *Report on the Result of the Census of British Honduras taken on the 31st March 1901*. Belize: Government Printer, 1901.

————. *Report on the Result of the Census of the Colony of British Honduras taken on the 2nd April, 1911*. Belize, 1912.

————. *Report on the Result of the Census of 1921, taken on the 24th April, 1921*. Belize: Government Printer, 1922.

————. *Subsidiary Laws of British Honduras in Force the 31st Day of December 1963*. Rev. ed. Vol. 3. London: R. Madley, 1968.

Bryan, Patrick. *The Jamaican People 1880–1920: Race, Class and Social Control*. London: Macmillan, 1991.

————. "The Black Middle Class in Nineteenth Century Jamaica." In *Caribbean Freedom: Economy and Society from Emancipation to the Present*, edited by Hilary Beckles and Verene Shepherd, 284–95. Princeton: Markus Weiner, 1996.

Burdon, Lady Katherine. "Hurricane Housekeeping." *The Listener* 22 January 1936: 164–65.

Burdon, Sir John A. *A Brief Sketch of British Honduras Past, Present, and Future*. London: The West India Committee, 1927.

Burton, Antoinette. "The Feminist Quest for Identity: British Imperial Suffragism and 'Global Sisterhood,' 1900–1915." *Journal of Women's History* 3:2 (Fall 1991): 46–81.

————. "The White Woman's Burden: British Feminists and 'The Indian Woman,' 1865–1915." In *Western Women and Imperialism: Complicity and Resistance*, edited by Nupur Chaudhuri and Margaret Strobel, 137–57. Bloomington: University of Indiana Press, 1992.

————. *Gender, Sexuality and Colonial Modernities*. New York: Routledge, 1999.

Bush, Barbara. *Slave Women in Caribbean Society, 1650–1838*. Bloomington: Indiana University Press, 1990.

Cain, Ernest E. *Cyclone!* Belize, 1932. Reprinted as *Cyclone: Being an Illustrated Official Record of the Hurricane and Tidal Wave Which Destroyed the City of Belize (British Honduras) on the Colony's Birthday, 10th September 1931*. London: A. H. Stockwell, 1933.

————. *Cyclone "Hattie": Being an Illustrated Record of the Hurricane and Tidal Wave*

Which Destroyed the City of Belize in British Honduras on the 31st day of October, *1961* . . . Devon, England: Arthur H. Stockwell, 1963.

Cal, Angel E. "Anglo-Maya Contact in Northern Belize: A Study of British Policy toward the Maya During the Caste War of Yucatán, 1847–1872." Master's thesis, University of Calgary, 1983.

——. "Capital-Labor Relations on a Colonial Frontier: Nineteenth-Century Northern Belize." In *Land, Labor, and Capital in Modern Yucatán: Essays in Regional History and Political Economy,* edited by Jeffrey T. Brannon and Gilbert M. Joseph, 83–106. Tuscaloosa: University of Alabama Press, 1991.

Carlson, Marifran. *Feminismo! The Women's Movement in Argentina from Its Beginnings to Eva Perón.* Chicago: Academy Publishers, 1988.

Catzim, Adele. "The Women Workers' Union." Belize: Society for the Promotion of Education and Research, 1991.

——. "Sewing the Threads of Dependency: Women in the Garment Industry Ten Years after Independence." *Independence Ten Years After: Fifth Annual Studies on Belize Conference.* Belize: Society for the Promotion of Education and Research, 1992.

Chatterjee, Partha. *Nationalist Thought and the Colonial World: A Derivative Discourse?* London: Zed Books, 1986.

——. "Colonialism, Nationalism and Colonialized Women: The Contest in India." *American Ethnologist* 16:4 (1989): 622–33.

——. *The Nation and Its Fragments: Colonial and Postcolonial Histories.* Princeton: Princeton University Press, 1993.

——. "Was There a Hegemonic Project of the Colonial State?" In *Contesting Colonial Hegemony: State and Society in Africa and India,* edited by Dagmar Engels and Shula Marks, 79–84. London: British Academic Press, 1995.

Chinchilla, Norma Stoltz. "Marxism, Feminism and the Struggle for Democracy in Latin America." *Gender and Society* 5:3 (1991): 291–310.

——. "Gender and National Politics: Issues and Trends in Women's Participation in Latin American Movements." In *Researching Women in Latin America and the Caribbean,* edited by Edna Acosta Belén and Christine Bose, 37–54. Boulder: Westview Press, 1993.

Chrisman, Laura. "'Journeying to Death': Gilroy's Black Atlantic." *Race and Class* 39:2 (1997): 51–53.

Clegern, Wayne M. *British Honduras: Colonial Dead End, 1859–1900.* Baton Rouge: Louisiana State University Press, 1967.

Comaroff, Jean, and John. "Home-Made Hegemony: Modernity, Domesticity and

Colonialism in South Africa" In *African Encounters with Domesticity*, edited by Karen Tranberg Hansen, 37–74. New Brunswick: Rutgers University Press, 1992.

Connell, R. W. *Gender and Power: Society, the Person and Sexual Politics*. Stanford: Stanford University Press, 1987.

Cooper, Frederick. "From Free Labor to Family Allowances: Labor and African Society in Colonial Discourse," *American Ethnologist* 16:4 (1989): 745–65.

———. *Decolonization and African Society: The Labor Question in French and British Africa*. Cambridge: Cambridge University Press, 1996.

———, Thomas Holt, and Rebecca Scott. *Beyond Slavery: Explorations of Race, Labor, and Citizenship in Postemancipation Societies*. Chapel Hill: University of North Carolina Press, 2000.

Cornell, Drucilla. *At the Heart of Freedom: Feminism, Sex, and Equality*. Princeton: Princeton University Press, 1998.

Coronil, Fernando. "Listening to the Subaltern: The Poetics of Necolonial States." *Poetics Today* 15:4 (Winter 1994): 643–58.

Corrigan, Philip, and Derek Sayer. *The Great Arch: English State Formation as Cultural Revolution*. Oxford: Basil Blackwell, 1985.

Dale, Jennifer and Peggy Foster. *Feminists and State Welfare*. London: Routledge and Kegan Paul, 1986.

De Barros, Juanita. *Order and Place in a Colonial City: Patterns of Struggle and Resistance in Georgetown, British Guiana, 1889–1924*. Montreal: McGill-Queen's University Press, 2002.

De la Fuente, Alejandro. *A Nation for All: Race, Inequality and Politics in Twentieth-Century Cuba*. Chapel Hill: University of North Carolina Press, 2001.

De Lauretis, Teresa. "Eccentric Subjects: Feminist Theory and Historical Consciousness." *Feminist Studies* 16:1 (Spring 1990): 115–50.

Denzer, LaRay. "Toward a Study of the History of West African Women's Participation in Nationalist Politics: The Early Phase, 1935–1950." *Africana Research Bulletin* 6 (1976): 65–85.

———. "Domestic Science Training in Colonial Yorubaland, Nigeria." In *African Encounters with Domesticity*, edited by Karen Tranberg Hansen, 116–42. New Brunswick: Rutgers University Press, 1992.

Dobson, Narda. *A History of Belize*. London: Longman Caribbean, 1973.

Duara, Prasenjit. *Rescuing History from the Nation: Questioning Narratives of Modern China*. Chicago: Chicago University Press, 1995.

Duncan, Neville, and Kenneth O'Brien. *Women and Politics in Barbados, 1948–1981*. Vol. 3 of Women in the Caribbean Project. Cave Hill, Barbados: Institute for Social and Economic Research, 1983.

Dunkerley, James. *Power in the Isthmus: A Political History of Modern Central America*. London: Verso, 1988.

Eagleton, Terry. *Ideology—an Introduction*. London: Verso, 1981.

Easter, B. H. *Report of an Enquiry into the Educational System of British Honduras, 1933–34*. Belize: Government Printing Office, 1935.

Edgell, Zee. *Beka Lamb*. Oxford: Heinemann, 1982.

Edgell, Zee. *In Times Like These*. Portsmouth, NH: Heinemann, 1991.

Ellis, Cynthia. "Reflections on Women's Problems, Issues and Prospects for Change, with Special Reference to Belize and the International Women's Movement." *Network: Journal of Belizean Women's Affairs* 1:1 (December 1980): 8–13.

———. "Reflections on Women's Problems, Issues and Prospects for Change, with Special Reference to Belize and the International Women's Movement, Part 2." *Network: Journal of Belizean Women's Affairs* 1:2 (1981): 6–9.

———, Margaret McCann, and Diane Haylock. Interview with Nan Peacocke. Womanspeak! c. 1986: 9–16

Ellis, Zoila. "A Brief Review of Recent Social Legislation—The Status of Children Ordinance 1980." *Network: Journal of Belizean Women's Affairs* 1:1 (December 1980): 22–33.

Engels, Dagmar. "The Limits of Gender Ideology: Bengali Women, the Colonial State and the Private Sphere, 1890–1930." *Women's Studies International Forum* 12:4(1989): 425–37.

Everitt, John. "The Growth and Development of Belize City." *Journal of Latin American Studies* 18:1 (May 1986): 75–111.

Fairweather, D. N. A. *A Short History of the Volunteer Forces of British Honduras (now Belize)*. Belize, 1977.

Ferrer, Ada. *Insurgent Cuba: Race, Nation, and Revolution, 1868–1898*. Chapel Hill: University of North Carolina Press, 1999.

Fieldhouse, D. K. "The Labour Governments and the Empire-Commonwealth." In *The Foreign Policy of the British Labour Governments, 1945–51*, edited by Ritchie Ovendale, 83–120. Leicester: Leicester University Press, 1984.

Findlay, Eileen J. "Free Love and Domesticity: Sexuality and the Shaping of Working Class Feminism in Puerto Rico, 1900–1917." In *Identity and Struggle at the Margins of the Nation-State: The Laboring Peoples of Central America and the Hispanic Caribbean*, edited by Aviva Chomsky and Aldo Lauria-Santiago, 229–59. Durham: Duke University Press, 1998.

Findlay, Eileen J. Suárez. *Imposing Decency: The Politics of Sexuality and Race in Puerto Rico, 1870–1920*. Durham: Duke University Press, 1999.

Ford-Smith, Honor. "Making White Ladies: Race, Gender and the Production of Identities in Late Colonial Jamaica." *Resources for Feminist Research/Documentation sur la Recherche Feministe* 23:4 (Winter 1994/95): 55–67.

———. "Women and the Garvey Movement in Jamaica." In *Garvey: His Work and Impact*, edited by Rupert Lewis and Patrick Bryan, 73–83. Trenton, NJ: Africa World Press, 1991.

Foucault, Michel. *Power/Knowledge: Selected Interviews and Other Writings 1972–1977.* Edited by Colin Gordon. New York: Pantheon, 1980.

Fraser, Nancy. *Unruly Practices: Power, Discourse, and Gender in Contemporary Social Theory.* Minneapolis: University of Minnesota Press, 1989.

———. "False Antitheses: A Response to Seyla Benhabib and Judith Butler." In *Feminist Contentions: A Philosophical Exchange*, Seyla Benhabib et al., 59–74. New York: Routledge, 1995.

———. "Beyond the Master/Subject Model: On Carole Pateman's *The Sexual Contract.*" In *Justice Interruptus: Critical Reflections on the "Postsocialist" Condition*, 225–35. New York: Routledge, 1997.

Fraser, Nicholas, and Marysa Navarro. *Evita.* New York: Norton, 1996.

French, John D., and Daniel James. "Squaring the Circle: Women's Factory Labor, Gender Ideology and Necessity." In *The Gendered Worlds of Latin American Women Workers: From Household and Factory to the Union Hall and the Ballot Box*, edited by John D. French and Daniel James, 1–30. Durham: Duke University Press, 1997.

Gann, Thomas. *The Maya of Southern Yucatan and Northern British Honduras.* Bureau of American Ethnology Bulletin 64. Washington, DC: Smithsonian Institution, 1918.

Geiger, Susan. "Women and African Nationalism." *Journal of Women's History* 2:1 (Spring 1990): 227–44.

———. *TANU Women: Gender and Culture in the Making of Takanyikan Nationalism, 1955–1965.* Portsmouth: Heinemann, 1997.

Gilroy, Paul. *The Black Atlantic: Modernity and Double Consciousness.* Cambridge: Harvard University Press, 1993.

Goldberg, David Theo. *Racist Culture: Philosophy and the Politics of Meaning.* Oxford: Blackwell, 1993.

Goldsworthy, D. J. *Colonial Issues in British Politics, 1945–61.* Oxford: Clarendon, 1971.

Gramsci, Antonio. *Selections from the Prison Notebooks.* Edited by Quentin Hoare and Geoffrey Nowell Smith. New York: International Publishers, 1971.

Grant, Cedric H. "The Civil Service Strike in British Honduras: A Case Study of

Politics and the Civil Service." *Caribbean Quarterly* 12:13 (September 1966): 37–49.

———. *The Making of Modern Belize: Politics, Society, and British Colonialism in Central America*. Cambridge: Cambridge University Press, 1976.

Great Britain. *Annual Report on the Social and Economic Progress of the People of British Honduras* (titled changed to *British Honduras Colonial Report* after 1938). London: HMSO, 1898, 1910, 1916–24, 1926–38, 1946, 1950–65.

———. *The Peace Handbooks*. Vol. 21, *North, Central, and South America: Atlantic Islands*. London: Historical Section of the Foreign Office, 1920.

———. *West India Royal Commission Report 1938–1939*. Cmd. 6607. London: HMSO, 1945.

———. *West India Royal Commission 1938–1939: Statement of Action Taken on the Recommendations*. Cmd 6656 (June 1945).

Grossberg, Lawrence. "On Postmodernism and Articulation: An Interview with Stuart Hall." In *Stuart Hall: Critical Dialogues in Cultural Studies*, edited by David Morley and Kuan-Hsing Chen, 131–50. London: Routledge, 1996.

Gudmundson, Lowell, and Francisco Scarano. "Conclusion: Imagining the Future of the Subaltern Past—Fragments of Race, Class, and Gender in Central America and the Hispanic Caribbean, 1850–1950." In *Identity and Struggle at the Margins of the Nation-State: The Laboring Peoples of Central America and the Hispanic Caribbean*, edited by Aviva Chomsky and Aldo Lauria-Santiago, 336–45. Durham: Duke University Press, 1998.

Guerra, Lillian. *Popular Expression and National Identity in Puerto Rico: The Struggle for Self, Community and Nation*. Gainesville: University Press of Florida, 1998.

Guha, Ranajit. "On Some Aspects of the Historiography of Colonial India." In *Subaltern Studies 1: Writings on South Asian History and Society*, edited by Ranajit Guha, 1–8. Delhi: Oxford University Press, 1982.

———. "Chandra's Death." In *Subaltern Studies 5: Writings on South Asian History and Society*, edited by Ranajit Guha, 135–65. Delhi: Oxford University Press, 1986.

———. *Dominance without Hegemony: History and Power in Colonial India*. Cambridge: Harvard University Press, 1997.

Gupta, P. S. *Imperialism and the British Labour Movement, 1914–1964*. London: Macmillan, 1975.

Hahner, June. *Emancipating the Female Sex: The Struggle for Women's Rights in Brazil*. Durham: Duke University Press, 1990.

Hall, Catherine. "Gender Politics and Imperial Politics: Rethinking the Histories of Empire." In *Engendering History: Caribbean Women in Historical Perspective,* edited by Verene Shepherd, Bridget Brereton, and Barbara Bailey, 48–59. New York: St. Martin's Press, 1995.

Hall, Stuart. "Negotiating Caribbean Identities." *New Left Review* 209 (January–February 1995): 3–14.

Hannaford, Ivan. Race: *The History of an Idea in the West.* Washington, DC: Woodrow Wilson Center Press and Baltimore: Johns Hopkins University Press, 1996.

Hasian, Marouf Arif, Jr. *The Rhetoric of Eugenics in Anglo-American Thought.* Athens: University of Georgia Press, 1996.

Helg, Aline. *Our Rightful Share: The Afro-Cuban Struggle for Equality, 1886–1912.* Chapel Hill: University of North Carolina Press, 1995.

Henderson, Peta, and Anne Bryn Haughton, eds. *Rising Up: Life Histories of Belizean Women by Women of the Orange Walk District.* Toronto: Sister Vision Press, 1993.

Henry-Wilson, Maxine. "The Status of the Jamaican Woman, 1962 to the Present." In *Jamaica in Independence: Essays on the Early Years,* edited by Rex Nettleford, 229–53. Kingston: Heinemann, 1989.

Hernandez, Felicia. *Those Ridiculous Years and Other Garifuna Stories.* San Diego: Windsor Associates, 1988.

Herrmann, Eleanor Krohn. "Black Cross Nursing in Belize: A Labour of Love." *Belizean Studies* 8:2 (March 1980): 1–7.

———. *Origins of Tomorrow: A History of Belizean Nursing Education.* Belize: Ministry of Health, 1985.

Higginbotham, Evelyn Brooks. "African-American Women's History and the Metalanguage of Race." In *Feminism and History,* edited by Joan Wallach Scott, 183–208. Oxford: Oxford University Press, 1996. Originally published in *Signs* 17:2 (1992): 251–74.

Hill, Robert A., ed. *The Marcus Garvey and Universal Negro Improvement Association Papers.* Vols. 1, 2, 3, 7. Berkeley: University of California Press, 1983–90.

Hobsbawm, Eric. *Age of Extremes: The Short Twentieth Century, 1914–1991.* London: Michael Joseph, 1994.

Holt, Thomas C. *The Problem of Freedom: Race, labor, and Politics in Jamaica and Britain, 1832–1938.* Baltimore: Johns Hopkins University Press, 1992.

Howe, Stephen. *Anticolonialism in British Politics: The Left and the End of Empire.* Oxford: Clarendon Press, 1993.

Humphries, Francis. "The Implementation of Belizean Studies Programmes in Secondary Schools, 1964–1987." *Belizean Studies* 17:2 (1989): 3–15.

Hunt, Nancy Rose. "Domesticity and Colonialism in Belgian Africa: Usumbura's *Foyer Social,* 1946–1960." *Signs* 15:3 (1990): 447–74.

Hunter Krohn, Lita, Fr. M. Murray S.J., and Lena Ysaguirre, eds. and compilers. *Readings in Belizean History*. 2nd ed. Belize: Belizean Studies, 1987.

Hurford, Graham. "The Moyne Commission in British Honduras Public Opinion and the Policies of the Burns Administration, 1934–1940." Master's thesis, University of London, 1987.

Hutchison, Elizabeth Quay. *"Labors Appropriate to their Sex': Gender, Labor, and Politics in Urban Chile, 1900–1930.*" Durham: Duke University Press, 2001.

Hyde, Evan X. *The Crowd Called* UBAD: *The Story of a People's Movement*. Belize: 1970.

———. *North Amerikkkan Blues*. Belize: 1971.

Jamaica Central Bureau of Statistics. *West India Census 1946, Part E: Census of Population of British Honduras*. Kingston: Department of Statistics, 1948.

James, C. L. R. "The West Indian Middle Classes." In *Spheres of Existence: Selected Writings*, 131–140. Westport, CT: Lawrence Hill and Co., 1980.

James, Winston. *Holding Aloft the Banner of Ethiopia: Caribbean Radicalism in Early Twentieth-Century America*. London: Verso, 1998.

Jayawardena, Kumari. *Feminism and Nationalism in the Third World*. London: Zed Books, 1986.

Johnson, Cheryl. "Class and Gender: A Consideration of Yoruba Women during the Colonial Period." In *Women and Class in Africa*, edited by Claire Robertson and Iris Berger, 237–54. New York: Africana, 1986.

Jolly, Margaret, and Kaplana Ram, eds. *Maternities and Modernities: Colonial and Postcolonial Experiences in Asia and the Pacific*. Cambridge: Cambridge University Press, 1998.

Jones, Grant D. *Maya Resistance to Spanish Rule: Time and History on a Colonial Frontier*. Albuquerque: University of New Mexico Press, 1989.

Joseph, Gilbert M., and Daniel Nugent, eds. *Everyday Forms of State Formation: Revolution and the Negotiation of Rule in Modern Mexico*. Durham: Duke University Press, 1994.

Judd, Karen. "Elite Reproduction and Ethnic Identity in Belize." PhD diss., City University of New York, 1992.

Kandyoti, Deniz. "Bargaining with Patriarchy." *Gender and Society* 2:3 (1988): 274–89.

———. "Identity and its Discontents: Women and the Nation." In *Colonial Discourse and Colonial Theory: A Reader*, edited by Patrick Williams and Laura Chrisman, 376–91. New York: Columbia University Press, 1994.

Kanogo, Tabitha. "Kikuyu Women and the Politics of Protest: Mau Mau." In *Images of*

Women in Peace and War: Cross-Cultural Perspectives, edited by Sharon Macdonald, Pat Holden and Shirley Ardener, 78–99. Madison: University of Wisconsin Press, 1987.

Kaplan, Temma. "Female Consciousness and Collective Action: The Case of Barcelona, 1910–1918." *Signs* 7:3 (1982): 545–66.

Kerns, Virginia. *Women and the Ancestors: Black Carib Kinship and Ritual.* Urbana: University of Illinois Press, 1983.

Klubock, Thomas Miller. *Contested Communities: Class, Gender, and Politics in Chile's El Teniente Copper Mine, 1904–1951.* Durham: Duke University Press, 1998.

Knight, Alan. "Populism and Neo-populism in Latin America, Especially Mexico." *Journal of Latin American Studies* 30:2 (May 1988): 223–48.

Knight, Franklin. *The Caribbean: The Genesis of a Fragmented Nationalism.* 2nd ed. Oxford: Oxford University Press, 1990.

Laclau, Ernesto. "Towards a Theory of Populism." In *Politics and Ideology in Marxist Theory: Capitalism, Fascism, Populism*, 143–98. London: NLB, 1977.

———, and Chantal Mouffe. *Hegemony and Socialist Strategy: Towards a Radical Democratic Politics.* London: Verso, 1985.

Ladd-Taylor, Molly. *Mother-Work: Women, Child Welfare, and the State, 1890–1930.* Urbana: University of Illinois Press, 1995.

Landes, Joan. "The Performance of Citizenship: Democracy, Gender, and Difference in the French Revolution." In *Democracy and Difference: Contesting the Boundaries of the Political*, edited by Seyla Benhabib, 295–313. Princeton: Princeton University Press, 1996.

Lavrin, Asunción. *Women, Feminism, and Social Change in Argentina, Chile, and Uruguay, 1890–1940.* Lincoln: University of Nebraska Press, 1995.

Lindo, Bette. Preface. *Network: Journal of Belizean Women's Affairs* 1:1 (December 1980): 6.

López Springfield, Consuelo. *Daughters of Caliban.* Bloomington: University of Indiana Press, 1997.

Macías, Anna. *Against All Odds: The Feminist Movement in Mexico to 1940.* Westport, CT: Greenwood Press, 1982.

Macpherson, Anne. "Women's Activism in the Nationalist Movement and the Gendered Creation of State Hegemony in Belize, 1950–1960." Master's thesis, University of Wisconsin-Madison, 1992.

———. "Viragoes, Victims, and Volunteers: Female Political Cultures and Gendered State Policy in 19th Century Belize." In *Belize: Proceedings from the Second Interdisciplinary Conference*, edited by Michael D. Phillips, 73–44. New York: University Press of America, 1996.

———. "Citizens vs. Clients: Working Women and Colonial Reform in Puerto Rico and Belize, 1932–1945." *Journal of Latin American Studies* 35:2 (May 2003): 279–310.

———. "Colonial Matriarchs: Garveyism, Maternalism, and Belize's Black Cross Nurses, 1920–1952." *Gender and History* 15:3 (November 2003): 507–27.

———. "Imagining the Colonial Nation: Race, Gender, and Middle-Class Politics in Belize, 1888–1898." In *Race and Nation in Modern Latin America*, edited by Nancy Appelbaum, Anne S. Macpherson, and Karin Alejandra Rosemblatt, 108–31. Chapel Hill: University of North Carolina Press, 2003.

Mallon, Florencia. *Peasant and Nation: State Formation in Postcolonial Peru and Mexico*. Berkeley: University of California Press, 1994.

———. "The Promise and Dilemma of Subaltern Studies: Perspectives from Latin American History." *American Historical Review* 99:5 (December 1994): 1491–1515.

Mani, Lata. "Contentious Traditions: The Debate on Sati in Colonial India." In *Recasting Women: Essays in Colonial History*, edited by Kumkum Sangari and Sudesh Vaid, 88–126. Delhi: Kali for Women, 1986.

Martin, Tony. *Race First: The Ideological and Organizational Struggles of Marcus Garvey and the Universal Negro Improvement Association*. Westport, CT: Greenwood, 1976.

Martínez-Echazábal, Lourdes. "*Mestizaje* and the Discourse of National/Cultural Identity in Latin America, 1845–1959." *Latin American Perspectives* 25:3 (1998): 21–42.

Mathurin, Lucille. *The Rebel Woman in the West Indies during Slavery*. Kingston: Institute of Jamaica, 1975.

———. "Reluctant Matriarchs." *Savacou* 13 (1977): 1–6.

Mba, Nina Emma. *Nigerian Women Mobilized: Women's Political Activity in Southern Nigeria, 1900–1965*. Berkeley, CA: Institute of International Studies, 1982.

McClaurin, Irma. *Women of Belize: Gender and Change in Central America*. New Brunswick: Rutgers University Press, 1996.

McClintock, Anne. *Imperial Leather: Race, Gender, and Sexuality in the Colonial Contest*. New York: Routledge, 1995.

———. "'No Longer in a Future Heaven': Nationalism, Gender, and Race." In *Becoming National: A Reader*, edited by Geoff Eley and Ronald Grigor Suny, 260–85. New York: Oxford University Press, 1996.

McNairn, Rosemarie. "Crime and Punishment in British Honduras: A Gender Analysis." Paper delivered at the Annual Conference of the Rocky Mountain Council on Latin American Studies, Ft. Worth, Texas, 1994.

Medina, Laurie Kroshus. *Negotiating Economic Development: Identity Formation and Collective Action in Belize*. Tucson: University of Arizona Press, 2004.

Metzgen, Monrad. *Shoulder to Shoulder: The Battle of St. George's Caye, 1798*. Belize: Goodrich, 1928.

———— and, H. E. C. Cain. *The Handbook of British Honduras*. London: The West India Committee, 1925.

Middleton, Carmen. Editorial. *Network: Journal of Belizean Women's Affairs* 1:3 (1982): 2.

Midgely, Clare. *Women Against Slavery: The British Campaigns, 1780–1870*. New York: Routledge, 1992.

————. "Anti-slavery and the Roots of 'Imperial Feminism.'" In *Gender and Imperialism*, edited by Clare Midgely, 161–79. Manchester: Manchester University Press, 1998.

Mies, Maria. *Indian Women and Patriarchy: Conflicts and Dilemmas of Students and Working Women*. New Delhi: Concept, 1980.

Miller, Francesca. *Latin American Women and the Search for Social Justice*. Hanover: University Press of New England, 1991.

Mintz, Sidney. "The Caribbean Region." In *Slavery, Colonialism, and Racism*, edited by Sidney Mintz, 45–48. New York: Norton, 1974.

Moberg, Mark. *Citrus, Strategy and Class: The Politics of Development in Southern Belize*. Iowa City: University of Iowa Press, 1992.

————. "Crown Colony as Banana Republic: The United Fruit Company in British Honduras, 1900–1920." *Journal of Latin American Studies* 28 (1996): 357–81.

————. *Myths of Ethnicity and Nation: Immigration, Work, and Identity in the Belize Banana Industry*. Knoxville: University of Tennessee Press, 1997.

Mohammed, Patricia. "Writing Gender into History: The Negotiation of Gender Relations among Indian Men and Women in Post-indenture Trinidad Society, 1917–47." In *Engendering History: Caribbean Women in Historical Perspective*, edited by Verene Shepherd, Bridget Brereton, and Barbara Bailey, 20–47. New York: St. Martin's Press, 1995.

Mohanty, Chandra. "Under Western Eyes: Feminist Scholarship and Colonial Discourses." *Feminist Review* 30 (August 1988): 61–88.

Molyneux, Maxine. "Mobilization without Emancipation? Women's Interests, the State and Revolution in Nicaragua." *Feminist Studies* 11:2 (1985): 227–54.

————. "The Politics of Abortion in Nicaragua: Revolutionary Pragmatism—or Feminism in the Realm of Necessity?" *Feminist Review* 29 (1988): 114–131.

Mosse, George. *Toward the Final Solution: A History of European Racism*. New York: Howard Fertig, 1978.

————. *Nationalism and Sexuality: Middle-Class Morality and Sexual Norms in Modern Europe.* Madison: University of Wisconsin Press, 1985.

Mouffe, Chantal. "Feminism, Citizenship and Radical Democratic Politics." In *Feminists Theorize the Political*, edited by Judith Butler and Joan Wallach Scott, 369–84. New York: Routledge, 1992.

Naipaul, V. S. *The Overcrowded Barracoon.* Harmondsworth: Penguin, 1972.

Nair, Janaki. "On the Question of Agency in Indian Feminist Historiography." *Gender and Society* 6:1 (April 1994): 82–100.

Nazzari, Muriel. "The 'Woman Question' in Cuba: An Analysis of Material Constraints on its Solution." *Signs* 9:2 (1983): 246–265.

New Edition of the Consolidated Laws of British Honduras. Rev. ed. London: Waterman and Sons, 1924.

Newton, Melanie. "Dirty Trollops and Matron Ladies: Gender and Public Life in Barbados, c. 1790–1850." Paper presented at the Berkshire Conference of Women's Historians in Storrs, CT, June 2002.

O'Callaghan, Evelyn. *Woman Version: Theoretical Approaches to West Indian Fiction by Women.* New York: St. Martin's Press, 1993.

O'Hanlon, Rosalind. "Recovering the Subject: *Subaltern Studies* and Histories of Resistance in Colonial South Asia." *Modern Asian Studies* 22:1 (1988): 189–224.

Orde-Browne, Major St. G. *Labour Conditions in the West Indies.* Cmd. 607. London: Colonial Office, 1939.

Palacio, Myrtle. "Elections in Belize City: Who is Participating? A Critique of our Voting System." In *Fourth Annual Studies on Belize Conference*, 48–60. Belize: Society for the Promotion of Education and Research, 1991.

Pateman, Carole. *The Disorder of Women: Democracy, Feminism and Political Theory.* Stanford: Stanford University Press, 1989.

————. "'God Hath Ordained to Man a Helper': Hobbes, Patriarchy and Conjugal Right." In *Feminist Interpretations and Political Theory*, edited by Carole Pateman and Mary Lydon Shanley, 53–73. Cambridge: Polity Press, 1991.

Petch, Trevor. "Dependency, land, and oranges in Belize." *Third World Quarterly* 8:3 (July 1986): 1002–17.

Phillip-Lewis, Kathleen. "European Stereotypes and the Position of Women in the Caribbean: A Historical Overview." In *Crossroad of Empire: The Europe-Caribbean Connection 1492–1992*, edited by Alan Cobley. Mona, Jamaica: UWI Department of History, 1994.

Pim, Sir Alan. *Report of the Commissioner on the Financial and Economic Postition of British Honduras.* Cmd 4586. House of Commons 1933–34, vol. 10, Report of Commissioners.

Prakash, Gyan. *After Colonialism: Imperial Histories and Postcolonial Displacements*. Princeton: Princeton University Press, 1995.

Proudfoot, Mary. *Britain and the United States in the Caribbean: a Comparative Study in Methods of Development*. London: Faber and Faber, 1954.

Quiñones, María I. "Gender, Power and Politics among the Rural Working Class in Barbados, West Indies." PhD diss., Columbia University, 1990.

Ramírez de Arellano, Annette, and Conrad Seipp. *Colonialism, Catholicism and Contraception: A History of Birth Control in Puerto Rico*. Chapel Hill: University of North Carolina Press, 1983.

Randall, Margaret. *Sandino's Daughters Revisited*. New Brunswick: Rutgers University Press, 1994.

———. "The Creation of a Regional Woman: Debbie Ewens of Belize." In *Our Voices/ Our Lives: Stories of Women from Central America and the Caribbean*, edited by Margaret Randall, 65–82. Monroe, ME: Common Courage Press, 1995.

Reddock, Rhoda. "Popular Movement to 'Mass Organization': The Case of the National Women's Organization of Grenada (NOW), 1979–1983." In *New Social Movements and the State in Latin America*, edited by David Slater, 261–94. Amsterdam: CEDLA, 1985.

———. "Feminism, Nationalism and the Early Women's Movement in the English Speaking Caribbean." In *Caribbean Women Writers: Essays from the First International Conference*, edited by Selwyn Cudjoe, 61–81. Wellesley, MA: Callaloux Publications, 1990.

———. *Women, Labour and Politics in Trinidad and Tobago: A History*. London: Zed Books, 1994.

Restall, Matthew. "'He Wished It in Vain': Subordination and Resistance among Maya Women in Post-Conquest Yucatan." *Ethnohistory* 42:4 (Fall 1995): 577–90.

Rich, Paul. "Sydney Olivier, Jamaica and the debate on British colonial policy in the West Indies." In *Labour in the Caribbean*, edited by Malcolm Cross and Gad Heuman, 208–33. London: Macmillan Caribbean, 1988.

Riley, Denise. *Am I That Name? Feminism and the Category of Women in History*. Minneapolis: University of Minnesota Press, 1988.

Romney, D. H. *Land in British Honduras—A Report of the British Honduras Land Use Survey Team*. London: Colonial Office, 1959.

Rosemblatt, Karin Alejandra. *Gendered Compromises: Political Cultures and the State in Chile, 1920–1950*. Chapel Hill: University of North Carolina Press, 2000.

Rutheiser, Charles C. "Culture, Schooling and Necolonialism in Belize." PhD diss., Johns Hopkins, 1991.

Salas, Elizabeth. *Soldaderas in the Mexican Military: Myth and History*. Austin: University of Texas Press, 1990.

Sanchez, Inez. *The Easter and Dixon Reports: An Analysis and Discussion of their Impact on our Educational Development*. BISRA Occasional Publications, no. 7. Belize, 1977.

Sangari, Kumkum, and Sudesh Vaid, eds. *Recasting Women: Essays in Colonial History*. Delhi: Kali for Women, 1986.

Schwartz, Norman B. *Forest Society: A Social History of the Petén*. Philadelphia: University of Pennsylvania Press, 1990.

Scott, Joan Wallach. *Gender and the Politics of History*. New York: Columbia University Press, 1988.

———. *Feminism and History*. Oxford: Oxford University Press, 1996.

Sen, Samita. "Motherhood and Mothercraft: Gender and Nationalism in Bengal." *Gender and History* 5:2 (1993): 231–43.

Senior, Olive. *Working Miracles Women's Lives in the English-Speaking Caribbean*. London: James Currey, 1991.

Sharpe, Frank. "Activities of the Citrus Company of British Honduras." In *Citrus Culture in British Honduras: The Development of the Citrus Industry in the Stann Creek Valley*, edited by W. A. J. Bowman, 20. N.p.: 1955.

Sheller, Mimi. "Quasheba, Mother, Queen: Black Women's Public Leadership and Political Protest in Post-emancipation Jamaica, 1834–65." *Slavery and Abolition* 19:3 (1998): 90–117.

———. *Black Publics and Peasant Radicalism in Haiti and Jamaica*. Gainesville: University Press of Florida, 2000.

Shepherd, Verene, Bridget Brereton, and Barbara Bailey, eds. *Engendering History: Caribbean Women in Historical Perspective*. New York: St. Martin's Press, 1995.

Shepherd, Verene, compiler and editor. *Women in Caribbean History*. Princeton: Markus Weiner, 1999.

Shoman, Assad. "The Birth of the Nationalist Movement in Belize, 1950–1954." In *Readings in Belizean History*, edited by Lita Hunter Krohn, Fr. M. Murray S.J., Lena Ysaguirre, 194–238. 2nd ed. Belize: Belizean Studies and St. John's College, 1987. Originally published in *Journal of Belizean Affairs* 2 (1973): 3–40.

———. "The Making and Breaking of the United General Workers' Union." In *Belize: Ethnicity and Development*, 1–32. Belize: Society for the Promotion of Education and Research, 1987.

———. *Party Politics in Belize, 1950–1986*. Belize: Cubola, 1987.

———. "Belize: An Authoritarian Democratic State in Central America." *Second*

Annual Studies on Belize Conference, 42–63. Belize: Society for the Promotion of Education and Research, 1990.

———. "The Making of Belize's Foreign Policy: From Colony to Independent State." In *Independence Ten Years After: Fifth Annual Studies on Belize Conference*, 13–31. Belize: Society for the Promotion of Education and Research, 1992.

———. *13 Chapters of a History of Belize*. Belize: Angelus Press, 1994.

———. *Backtalking Belize: Selected Writings*. Edited by Anne S. Macpherson. Belize: Angelus Press, 1995.

Silverblatt, Irene. "Women in States." *Annual Review of Anthropology* 17 (1988): 427–60.

Silvestrini, Blanca. "Women as Workers: The Experience of the Puerto Rican Woman in the 1930s." In *The Puerto Rican Woman: Perspectives on Culture, History, and Society*, edited by Edna Acosta-Belen, 59–74. 2nd ed. New York: Praeger, 1986.

Sinha, Mrinalini. "Gender in the Critiques of Colonialism and Nationalism: Locating the 'Indian Woman.'" In *Feminism and History*, edited by Joan Wallach Scott, 477–503. Oxford: Oxford University Press, 1996.

———. "Gender and Imperialism: Colonial Policy and the Ideology of Moral Imperialism in Late Nineteenth-Century Bengal." In *Changing Men: New Directions in Research on Men and Masculinity*, edited by Michael S. Kimmel, 217–31. Beverley Hills, CA: Sage, 1987.

Sistren with Honor Ford-Smith. *Lionheart Gal: Life Stories of Jamaican Women*. London: Women's Press, 1986.

Slater, David, ed. *New Social Movements and the State in Latin America*. Amsterdam: CEDLA, 1985.

Soberanis Gomez, Antonio, and Luke D. Kemp. *The Third Side of the Anglo-Guatemalan Dispute over Belize or British Honduras*. Belize: The Open Forum, 1949.

Spivak, Gayatri. "Deconstructing Historiography." In *The Spivak Reader: Selected Works of Gayatri Chakravorty Spivak*, edited by Donna Landry and Gerald MacLean, 203–36. New York: Routledge, 1996.

Stein, Judith. *The World of Marcus Garvey: Race and Class in Modern Society* Baton Rouge: Louisiana State University Press, 1986.

Stepan, Nancy Leys. *"The Hour of Eugenics": Race, Gender and Nation in Latin America*. Ithaca: Cornell University Press, 1991.

Stephens, Julie. "Feminist Fictions." In *Subaltern Studies VI: Writings on South Asian History and Society*, edited by Ranajit Guha, 92–125. Delhi: Oxford University Press, 1987.

Stern, Steve J. *The Secret History of Gender: Women, Men and Power in Late Colonial Mexico.* Chapel Hill: University of North Carolina Press, 1995.

Stockdale, Sir Frank. *Development and Welfare in the West Indies, 1943–44.* London: Colonial Office, 1945.

Stocking, George. *Race, Culture, and Evolution: Essays in the History of Anthropology.* New York: The Free Press, 1968.

Stoler, Ann Laura. "Making Empire Respectable: The Politics of Race and Sexual Morality in 20th-Century Colonial Cultures." In *Imperial Monkey Business: Racial Supremacy in Social Darwinist Theory and Colonial Practice*, edited by Jan Breman, Piet de Rooy, Ann Stoler, and Wim F. Wertheim, 35–70. Amsterdam: VU University Press, 1990.

———. *Race and the Education of Desire: Foucault's History of Sexuality and the Colonial Order of Things.* Durham: Duke University Press, 1995.

Stoner, K. Lynn. "Directions in Latin American Women's History, 1977–1985." *Latin American Research Review* 22:2 (1987): 101–34.

———. *From the House to the Streets: The Cuban Women's Movement for Legal Reform, 1898–1940.* Durham: Duke University Press, 1991.

Stubbs, Jean. "Social and Political Motherhood in Cuba: Mariana Grajales Cuello." In *Engendering History: Caribbean Women in Historical Perspective*, edited by Verene Shepherd, Bridget Brereton, and Barbara Bailey, 296–315. New York: St. Martin's Press, 1995.

Summers, Carol. "Intimate Colonialism: The Imperial Production of Reproduction in Uganda, 1907–1925." *Signs* 16:4 (1991): 787–807.

Taylor, Douglas MacRae. *The Black Carib of British Honduras.* Viking Publications in Anthropology 17. N.p.: Wenner-Gren Foundation for Anthropological Research, 1951.

Thane, Pat. "Visions of Gender in the Making of the British Welfare State: the case of women in the British Labour Party and social policy, 1906–1945." In *Maternity and Gender Policies: Women and the Rise of the European Welfare States, 1880s–1950s*, edited by Gisela Bock and Pat Thane, 343–77. New York: Routledge, 1991.

Tharu, Susie. "Response to Julie Stephens." *Subaltern Studies VI: Writings on South Asian History and Society*, edited by Ranajit Guha, 126–31. Delhi: Oxford University Press, 1987.

Thomas, Clive Y. *The Rise of the Authoritarian State in Peripheral Societies.* New York: Monthly Review Press, 1984.

Thorndike, Tony. "The Conundrum of Belize: An Anatomy of a Dispute." *Social and Economic Studies* 32:2 (1983): 65–101.

———. "Belizean Political Parties: The Independence Crisis and After." *Journal of Commmonwealth and Comparative Politics* 21: 2 (July 1983): 195–211.

Travers, Ann. "Radical Democracy's Feminist Potential." *Praxis International* 12:3(October 1992): 269–83.

Tzul, Alfonso A. *After 100 Years: The Oral History and Traditions of San Antonio, Cayo District, Belize.* U Kuxtal Masewal Maya Institute of Belize, 1993.

Vernon, Dylan. "International Migration and Development in Belize: An Overview of Determinants and Effects of Recent Movements." Master's thesis, Carleton University, Ottawa, 1988.

———. "Ten Years of Independence in Belize: An Analysis of the Socio-Economic Crisis." *Independence Ten Years After: Fifth Annual Studies on Belize Conference,* 38–50. Belize: Society for the Promotion of Education and Research, 1992.

Vincent, Theodore G. *Black Power and the Garvey Movement.* San Francisco: The Ramparts Press, 1976.

Waddell, D. A. G. *British Honduras: A Historical and Contemporary Survey.* London: Oxford University Press, 1961.

Watler, John. "The Story of Belize City." *Brukdown* 5 (1980): 9–10.

White, Luise. "Separating the Men from the Boys: Constructions of Gender, Sexuality and Terrorism in Central Kenya, 1939–1959." *International Journal of African Historical Studies* 23:1 (1990): 1–25.

———. *The Comforts of Home: Prostitution in Colonial Nairobi.* Chicago: University of Chicago Press, 1990.

Wilk, Richard. *Household Ecology: Economic Change and Domestic Life among the Kekchi Maya in Belize.* Tucson: University of Arizona Press, 1991.

———. "Connections and Contradictions: From the Crooked Tree Cashew Queen to Miss World Belize." In *Beauty Queens on the Global Stage: Gender, Contests and Power,* edited by Colleen Ballerino Cohen, Richard Wilk, and Beverly Stoeltje, 217–33. London: Routledge, 1996.

Williams, Raymond. *Marxism and Literature.* Oxford: Oxford University Press, 1977.

Wilmot, Swithin. "Females of Abandoned Character? Women and Protest in Jamaica, 1838–65." In *Engendering History: Caribbean Women in Historical Perspective,* edited by Verene Shepherd, Bridget Brereton, and Barbara Bailey, 279–95. New York: St. Martin's Press, 1995.

Wolfe, Joel. "'Father of the Poor or Mother of the Rich?': Getúlio Vargas, Industrial Workers, and Constructions of Class, Gender, and Populism in São Paulo, 1930–1954." *Radical History Review* 59 (Spring 1994): 81–103.

Woods, Silvana. *Mothers of Modern Belize.* Belize: National Women's Commission, 1991.

Young, Alma H., and Dennis H. Young, "The Impact of the Anglo-Guatemalan Dispute on the Internal Politics of Belize." *Latin American Perspectives* 15:2 (1988): 6–30.

Young, Robert J. C. *Colonial Desire: Hybridity in Theory, Culture, and Race.* London: Routledge, 1995.

Yuval-Davis, Nira, and Floya Anthias, eds. *Woman-Nation-State.* London: Macmillan, 1989.

Index

CPSIA information can be obtained
at www.ICGtesting.com
Printed in the USA
LVHW040157150723
752404LV00001B/89